—— 🏆 🏆 🏆 ——

538 Home-Style Recipes Right at Your Fingertips

WHEN we published the first volume of our *Taste of Home Annual Recipes* in late 1996, we shouldn't have been surprised when it became our best-selling book ever. After all, many of our magazine readers had been asking for just that kind of thoroughly indexed book that gathered an entire year's worth of *Taste of Home* recipes into one convenient source.

So when we began receiving letters asking us to compile every single recipe from 1995 into the same kind of practical cookbook, we knew we had to respond with this all-new edition.

Like the other previously published volumes, this *1996 Taste of Home Annual Recipes* book will become a treasured time-saver in your kitchen for a number of reasons:

1. Its 308 pages are organized into 16 handy chapters for easy reference. Between its covers, you have at hand every single *Taste of Home* recipe we published in 1995.

2. Finding all of the 538 recipes is a snap with this book's *three different indexes*— one indexes dishes by food category, one tells you which issue of *Taste of Home* it originally appeared in, and one designates every recipe that includes Nutritional Analysis and Diabetic Exchanges. These handy indexes can be found on pages 290-302.

3. The full-color pictures in this cookbook are *bigger* than ever so you can plainly see what many of these dishes will look like before you begin preparing them.

4. We've used larger print for easy reading while cooking. And each recipe is presented "all-on-a-page", so you never have to turn back and forth while cooking.

5. This volume is printed on the highest quality coated paper to make the foods more attractive and appealing. More importantly, it lets you wipe away spatters easily.

6. The book lies open and *stays open* as you cook. Its durable hard cover will give you *years* of use (you'll never have to worry about dog-earring your magazine collection again).

But the real proof of this volume's value is in the tasting. Your family will *rave* at the results of these recipes, all of which are favorites of other families.

Tight on time? Rely on the fast-to-fix recipes in our "Meals in Minutes" chapter. Each complete meal goes from stovetop to tabletop in 30 minutes or less.

On a budget? You need just *80¢ a plate* to serve your family "Hearty Minestrone", "Pop-Up Rolls" and "Apple Nut Crunch". (You'll find this flavorful feast on page 274.)

Family picnic? The 42 "Potluck Pleasers" recipes fill the bill when you need to feed 10, 100 or any number in between!

Planning a special supper? For 12 delectable menus that come straight from the kitchens of fellow country cooks, turn to the "My Mom's Best Meal" and "Editors' Meals" chapters.

With 538 down-home dishes, this taste treasury sets the table for delicious dining in your home year after year!

—— 🏆 🏆 🏆 ——

1996 Taste of Home Annual Recipes

Editor: Julie Schnittka
Art Director: Claudia Wardius
Food Editor: Coleen Martin
Associate Editor: Jean Steiner
Assistant Art Director: Linda Dzik
Cover Photography: Scott Anderson

Taste of Home®

Executive Editor: Kathy Pohl
Food Editor: Coleen Martin
Associate Food Editor: Corinne Willkomm
Senior Recipe Editor: Sue A. Jurack
Senior Editor: Bob Ottum
Managing Editor: Ann Kaiser
Assistant Managing Editor: Faithann Stoner
Associate Editors: Kristine Krueger, Sharon Selz
Test Kitchen Home Economist: Sue Draheim
Test Kitchen Assistants: Sherry Smalley,
Sue Hampton
Editorial Assistants: Barb Czysz,
Mary Ann Koebernik
Design Director: Jim Sibilski
Art Director: Vicky Marie Moseley
Food Photography: Scott Anderson,
Glenn Thiesenhusen
Food Photography Artist: Stephanie Marchese
Photo Studio Manager: Anne Schimmel
Production: Ellen Lloyd, Claudia Wardius
Publisher: Roy Reiman

Taste of Home Books
©1999 Reiman Publications, LLC
5400 S. 60th St., Greendale WI 53129

International Standard Book Number:
0-89821-263-4
International Standard Serial Number:
1094-3463

PICTURED AT RIGHT. Clockwise from upper left:
Pork with Mustard Sauce (p. 76), Raspberry Linzer
Cookies (p. 235), Marinated Thanksgiving Turkey,
Unstuffing, Ken's Sweet Potatoes and Fall Pear Pie
(pp. 246 and 247), Turtle Cheesecake (p. 150) and
Layered Chicken Salad (p. 24).

Taste of Home 1996
Annual Recipes

PICTURED ON FRONT COVER. Clockwise from upper left: Spaghetti and Meatballs (p. 74), Caesar Salad (p. 235), Soft Breadsticks (p. 264) and Luscious Almond Cheesecake (p. 154).

PICTURED ON BACK COVER. Clockwise from upper left: Almond Biscotti (p. 122), Pineapple Bundt Cake (p. 158) and Chocolate Date Squares (p. 158).

FOR ADDITIONAL COPIES of this book or information on other books, write: *Taste of Home* Books, P.O. Box 990, Greendale WI 53129. **Credit card orders call toll-free 1-800/558-1013.**

Snacks & Beverages

For special treats anytime of day, turn to these hearty appetizers, satisfying snacks and refreshing beverages.

MEMORABLE MUNCHING. Clockwise from upper left: Savory Rye Snacks (p. 9), Rhubarb Slush (p. 21), Spinach Dip in a Bread Bowl (p. 13), Sugar-Free Holiday Nog (p. 15) and Creamy Caramel Dip (p. 8).

Creamy Caramel Dip

(Pictured above and on page 6)

Because I feed three hungry "men" (my husband, a member of the Royal Canadian Mounted Police, and our two little boys), I love satisfying snacks that are easy to make like this dip. I modified a friend's recipe. We sure appreciate this cool light treat in the summertime.   —Karen Laubman, Spruce Grove, Alberta

> 1 package (8 ounces) cream cheese, softened
> 3/4 cup packed brown sugar
> 1 cup (8 ounces) sour cream
> 2 teaspoons vanilla extract
> 2 teaspoons lemon juice
> 1 cup cold milk
> 1 package (3.4 ounces) instant vanilla pudding mix

Assorted fresh fruit

In a mixing bowl, beat cream cheese and brown sugar until smooth. Add the sour cream, vanilla, lemon juice, milk and pudding mix, beating well after each addition. Cover and chill for at least 1 hour. Serve as a dip for fruit. **Yield:** 3-1/2 cups.

— 🎺 🎺 🎺 —

Soft Pretzels

Our kids enjoy every step of making soft homemade pretzels. Each one has a chance to add ingredients, mix and shape the dough, brush on the egg and sprinkle on salt.   —Lori Hoogland, Catawba, Wisconsin

> 1 package (1/4 ounce) active dry yeast
> 1-1/2 cups warm water (110° to 115°)
> 1 tablespoon sugar
> 1 teaspoon salt
> 4 cups all-purpose flour
> 1 egg, beaten

Coarse salt

In a large bowl, dissolve yeast in water. Add the sugar, salt and enough flour to make a soft dough. Turn onto a floured surface; knead until smooth and elastic, about 6-8 minutes. Pinch off about 2 tablespoons of dough for each pretzel. Shape into traditional pretzel twists or letters or animals as desired. Place on greased baking sheets. Brush with egg; sprinkle with salt. Bake at 425° for 15 minutes or until golden brown. Cool on a wire rack. **Yield:** 18-20 servings.

— 🎺 🎺 🎺 —

Angel Frost

I've served this refreshing beverage for holiday breakfasts and brunches for more than 20 years. No one can stop with one sip of this sweet frothy drink.
—Susan O'Brien, Scottsbluff, Nebraska

> 3/4 cup pink lemonade concentrate
> 1 cup milk

1 package (10 ounces) frozen strawberries
   in syrup, partially thawed
1 pint vanilla ice cream
Fresh strawberries, optional

In a blender, combine the lemonade concentrate, milk, strawberries and ice cream; cover and process until smooth. Pour into glasses. Garnish with fresh strawberries if desired. **Yield:** 4-6 servings (about 1 quart).

━━━ 🥄 🥄 🥄 ━━━

Savory Rye Snacks

(Pictured on page 6)

I make the flavorful spread ahead of time and refrigerate it. Then all I have to do to have a quick snack is put it on the rye bread and bake. —Connie Simon
Reed City, Michigan

1 cup sliced green onions
1 cup mayonnaise
1 cup (4 ounces) shredded Monterey Jack
   cheese
1 cup (4 ounces) shredded cheddar cheese
1 can (4 ounces) mushroom stems and
   pieces, drained
1/2 cup chopped ripe olives
1/2 cup chopped stuffed olives
1 loaf (1 pound) cocktail rye bread

In a bowl, combine the green onions, mayonnaise, cheeses, mushrooms and olives. Spread on bread slices and place on ungreased baking sheets. Bake at 350° for 8-10 minutes or until bubbly. **Yield:** about 4 dozen.

━━━ 🥄 🥄 🥄 ━━━

Crispy Coconut Balls

For satisfying a sweet tooth, these light, bite-size snacks are our favorite on-the-road treats. I like the fact that they're quick and easy to make.
—Elaine Wilkins, Jasper, Alabama

1/4 cup butter *or* margarine
40 large marshmallows *or* 4 cups miniature
   marshmallows
5 cups crisp rice cereal
1 cup flaked coconut

Melt butter in a saucepan over low heat. Add marshmallows and cook, stirring constantly, until marshmallows are melted. Remove from heat; stir in cereal until well coated. With buttered hands, shape into 1-in. balls. Roll in coconut, pressing gently to coat. **Yield:** about 3 dozen.

Mexican Deviled Eggs

(Pictured below)

With two young children, my husband and I live on a beautiful lake and host lots of summer picnics and cookouts. I adapted this recipe to suit our tastes. Folks who are expecting the same old deviled eggs are surprised when they try this delightful tangy variation. —Susan Klemm, Rhinelander, Wisconsin

8 hard-cooked eggs
1/2 cup shredded cheddar cheese
1/4 cup mayonnaise
1/4 cup salsa
2 tablespoons sliced green onions
1 tablespoon sour cream
Salt to taste

Slice the eggs in half lengthwise; remove yolks and set whites aside. In a small bowl, mash yolks with cheese, mayonnaise, salsa, onions, sour cream and salt. Stuff or pipe into egg whites. Refrigerate until serving. **Yield:** 16 servings.

Making Mashing Easy

When making deviled eggs, it can be slow and cumbersome to mash the yolks using a fork. A potato masher works really well to do this job quickly.

Iced Strawberry Tea

Strawberry season here coincides with the herald of the first day of summer and the conclusion of our school year. So it's no wonder that popular fruit is treasured in favorite recipes like this colorful and refreshing quencher. —Laurie Andrews, Milton, Ontario

    1 pint fresh strawberries
    4 cups cold tea
    1/3 to 1/2 cup sugar
    1/4 cup fresh lemon juice

Set aside five whole strawberries. Cover and puree the rest in a blender; strain into a pitcher. Stir in tea, sugar and lemon juice until sugar dissolves. Chill. Serve over ice; garnish with berries. **Yield:** 5 cups.

— ☕ ☕ ☕ —

⋏ Favorite Snack Mix

(Pictured below)

This snack mix is a nice change of pace from the usual mix. It's almost impossible to stop eating this sweet and salty snack. —Carol Allen, McLeansboro, Illinois

    6 cups Crispix cereal
    1 can (10 ounces) mixed nuts
    1 package (10 ounces) pretzel sticks
    3/4 cup butter *or* margarine
    3/4 cup packed brown sugar

In a large bowl, combine the cereal, nuts and pretzels. In a small saucepan over low heat, melt butter. Add brown sugar; cook and stir until dissolved. Pour over cereal mixture; stir to coat. Place

a third of the mixture on a greased 15-in. x 10-in. x 1-in. baking pan. Bake at 325° for 8 minutes; stir and bake for 6 minutes more. Spread on waxed paper to cool. Repeat with remaining mixture. Store in airtight containers. **Yield:** about 14 cups.

— ☕ ☕ ☕ —

Hot Beef Dip

This meaty appetizer really reflects the Lone Star State. As a busy science teacher, I find ground beef fits nicely into my schedule. —Sonja Hanks, Snyder, Texas

    1 pound ground beef
    2/3 cup chopped onion
    1/2 cup chopped green pepper
    3 to 4 garlic cloves, minced
    1 can (8 ounces) tomato sauce
    1/4 cup ketchup
    1 teaspoon sugar
    3/4 teaspoon dried oregano
    1/4 teaspoon pepper
    1 package (8 ounces) cream cheese,
      softened
    1/4 cup grated Parmesan cheese
Tortilla chips

In a large skillet, cook beef, onion, green pepper and garlic until meat is browned. Add the tomato sauce, ketchup, sugar, oregano and pepper; simmer for 10 minutes. Remove from the heat and stir in cheeses until melted. Serve warm with tortilla chips. **Yield:** 16-20 servings.

— ☕ ☕ ☕ —

Caramel Marshmallow Delights

(Pictured above right)

Our children like to take these sweet and chewy treats to school to share on their birthday. Caramels make them a little extra special. —Susan Kerr Crown Point, Indiana

    1 can (14 ounces) sweetened condensed
      milk
    1/2 cup butter *or* margarine
    1 package (14 ounces) caramels
    1 package (16 ounces) large marshmallows
    1 package (10 ounces) crisp rice cereal

In the top of a double boiler, combine milk, butter and caramels. Heat over boiling water, stirring until smooth. Remove from the heat. With a fork, dip marshmallows quickly into hot mixture, then roll in cereal. Place on a foil-lined pan; chill for 30 minutes. Remove from the pan and store in an airtight container in the refrigerator. **Yield:** 5-6 dozen.

FLAVORFUL FINGER FOODS. Around-the-clock snacking calls for terrific tastes like Caramel Marshmallow Delights, Linda's BLT Spread and Cheese Squares (shown above, clockwise from upper left).

Linda's BLT Spread

(Pictured above)

This spread is a different way to enjoy the winning combination of bacon, lettuce and tomato. It's especially flavorful using garden tomatoes.
—*Linda Nilsen, Anoka, Minnesota*

- 1/2 cup sour cream
- 1/2 cup mayonnaise *or* salad dressing
- 1/2 pound bacon, cooked and crumbled
- 1 small tomato, diced
- Small lettuce leaves
- Toasted snack bread *or* crackers
- Assorted fresh vegetables

In a bowl, combine sour cream, mayonnaise and bacon; mix well. Stir in tomato. Serve with lettuce, bread, crackers and fresh vegetables. **Yield:** 1-1/2 cups.

— 🥄 🥄 🥄 —

Cheese Squares

(Pictured above)

If you're looking for a great make-ahead snack, try these. They're nice to have in the freezer for lunch with

soup or a salad. *My family loves to nibble on them any-time.* —*Anita Curtis, Camarillo, California*

- 1 cup butter *or* margarine, softened
- 2 jars (5 ounces *each*) Old English Cheese Spread, softened
- 1 egg
- 1 can (4 ounces) chopped green chilies, drained
- 1/4 cup salsa
- 2 cups (8 ounces) shredded cheddar cheese
- 2 loaves (1-1/2 pounds *each*) thinly sliced sandwich bread, crusts removed

In a mixing bowl, cream butter, cheese spread and egg until smooth. Stir in chilies, salsa and cheddar cheese. Spread about 1 tablespoon of cheese mixture on each slice of one loaf of bread. Top with remaining bread; spread with more cheese mixture. Cut each sandwich into four squares; place on a greased baking sheet. Bake at 350° for 10-15 minutes. To freeze, place in a single layer on a baking sheet. Freeze for 1 hour. Remove from the baking sheet and store in an airtight container in the freezer until needed. To bake frozen, place squares on a greased baking sheet. Bake at 350° for 15-20 minutes or until bubbly and browned. **Yield:** 8 dozen.

TASTY TEMPTERS like Buttermilk Shakes and Ham and Cheese Bread (shown above) are a treat to eat.

Ham and Cheese Bread

(Pictured above)

Ham and cheese baked inside bread dough makes a hearty snack. I keep these ingredients on hand so I can make this treat whenever my family requests it.
—Marian Christensen, Sumner, Michigan

- 1 **package (16 ounces) frozen chopped broccoli**
- 2 **loaves (1 pound *each*) frozen bread dough, thawed**
- 3 **cups (12 ounces) shredded cheese (cheddar, Swiss *and/or* Monterey Jack)**
- 2 **cups finely chopped fully cooked ham**
- 2 **tablespoons butter *or* margarine, melted**
- 1 **teaspoon poppy seeds**

Cook broccoli according to package directions. Drain and cool. Roll each loaf of dough into a 15-in. x 10-in. rectangle. Place one in a greased 15-in. x 10-in. x 1-in. baking pan. Sprinkle with broccoli, cheese and ham to within 1/2 in. of edges. Place second rectangle on top, sealing edges. Brush the top with butter; sprinkle with poppy seeds. Bake at 350° for 35-45 minutes or until golden brown. Serve warm. **Yield:** 10-12 servings.

Buttermilk Shakes

(Pictured at left)

These rich shakes taste like liquid cheesecake! With just five ingredients, they're a snap to prepare at a moment's notice. *—Gloria Jarrett, Loveland, Ohio*

- 1 **pint vanilla ice cream**
- 1 **cup buttermilk**
- 1 **teaspoon grated lemon peel**
- 1/2 **teaspoon vanilla extract**
- 1 **drop lemon extract**

Combine all ingredients in a blender; cover and process until smooth. Pour into glasses. Refrigerate any leftovers. **Yield:** 2 servings.

Cheese Crisps

The surprising crunch of these fun snacks makes them great for parties or anytime of day. It's a simple recipe I rely on often when entertaining. *—Janelle Lee Sulphur, Louisiana*

- 1 **cup butter *or* margarine, softened**
- 2 **cups all-purpose flour**
- 1/2 **teaspoon salt**
- 1/4 **teaspoon cayenne pepper**
- 2 **cups (8 ounces) shredded sharp cheddar cheese**
- 3 **cups crisp rice cereal**

In a mixing bowl, cream the butter until fluffy. Slowly mix in the flour, salt and cayenne pepper. Stir in cheese and cereal. Shape into 1-1/2-in. balls and place on ungreased baking sheets. Bake at 350° for 15-17 minutes or until lightly browned. Serve warm or cold. **Yield:** 3 dozen.

Frozen Fruit Pops

Making these frozen pops has been a favorite summer activity in our family for years. The hardest part for the kids is letting the pops freeze before eating! *—Jeannette Mack, Rushville, New York*

1 package (3 ounces) fruit-flavored gelatin
1/2 cup sugar
2 cups boiling water
1-1/2 cups cold water
10 to 12 Popsicle molds *or* paper cups
    (3 ounces)
10 to 12 Popsicle sticks *or* plastic spoons

In a bowl, dissolve gelatin and sugar in boiling water. Stir in cold water. Pour into molds or paper cups. Freeze for 2 hours or until almost firm. Insert sticks or spoons. Freeze 8 hours. To serve, unmold or tear away paper cup from pop. **Yield:** 10-12 servings.

——— 🍴 🍴 🍴 ———

Cheesy Olive Snacks

When guests stop by unexpectedly, this is an ideal recipe to whip up. The olives and onion provide a unique flavor. Many people have complimented on it.
—Alma Hardy, Tulsa, Oklahoma

1 cup grated process American cheese
1 can (4-1/4 ounces) chopped ripe olives,
    drained
1/2 cup chopped onion
5 to 6 English muffins, split

Combine the cheese, olives and onion. Spread over muffin halves. Broil 4 in. from the heat for 5 minutes or until the cheese is melted. Serve immediately. **Yield:** 10-12 servings.

——— 🍴 🍴 🍴 ———

Crunchy Granola

This crisp, lightly sweet mixture is great just eaten out of hand or as an ice cream topping. My husband and I grow wheat, barley and canola.
—Lorna Jacobsen, Arrowwood, Alberta

2/3 cup honey
1/2 cup vegetable oil
1/3 cup packed brown sugar
2 teaspoons vanilla extract
4 cups old-fashioned oats
1 cup sliced almonds
1 cup flaked coconut
1/2 cup sesame seeds
1/2 cup salted sunflower kernels
2 cups raisins

In a small saucepan, combine honey, oil and brown sugar; cook and stir over medium heat until the sugar dissolves. Remove from the heat; add vanilla. In a large bowl, combine the next five ingredients. Add honey mixture, stirring until evenly coated.

Spread onto two ungreased 15-in. x 10-in. x 1-in. baking pans. Bake at 300° for 20 minutes, stirring frequently. Stir in raisins. Bake for 10 minutes longer. Cool, stirring occasionally. Store in an airtight container. **Yield:** 10 cups.

——— 🍴 🍴 🍴 ———

Spinach Dip in a Bread Bowl

(Pictured below and on page 6)

We often get together with friends and family. I like to prepare this creamy dip. It's a crowd-pleaser.
—Janelle Lee, Sulphur, Louisiana

2 cups (16 ounces) sour cream
1 envelope ranch salad dressing mix
1 package (10 ounces) frozen chopped
    spinach, thawed and well drained
1/4 cup chopped onion
3/4 teaspoon dried basil
1/2 teaspoon dried oregano
1 round loaf (1 pound) bread
Assorted fresh vegetables

In a bowl, combine the first six ingredients. Chill for at least 1 hour. Cut a 1-1/2-in. slice off the top of the loaf; set aside. Hollow out the bottom part, leaving a thick shell. Cut or tear the slice from the top of the loaf and the bread from inside into bite-size pieces. Fill the shell with dip; set on a large platter. Arrange the bread pieces and vegetables around it and serve immediately. **Yield:** 10-15 servings.

Hot Pizza Dip

(Pictured below)

I'm a busy stay-at-home mom with an active son. I love this recipe because it's easy to prepare in advance and keep refrigerated. Put it in the oven when guests arrive, and by the time you've poured beverages, the dip is ready. It gets gobbled up quickly! —Karen Riordan Fern Creek, Kentucky

 1 package (8 ounces) cream cheese, softened
 1 teaspoon Italian seasoning
 1/4 teaspoon garlic powder
 2 cups (8 ounces) shredded mozzarella cheese
 1 cup (4 ounces) shredded cheddar cheese
 1/2 cup pizza sauce
 1/2 cup finely chopped green pepper
 1/2 cup finely chopped sweet red pepper
Tortilla chips *or* breadsticks

In a bowl, combine cream cheese, Italian seasoning and garlic powder; spread on the bottom of a greased 9-in. pie plate. Combine cheeses; sprinkle half over the cream cheese layer. Top with the pizza sauce and peppers. Sprinkle with the remaining cheeses. Bake at 350° for 20 minutes. Serve warm with tortilla chips or breadsticks. **Yield:** about 3-1/2 cups.

Trail Mix

My husband has been taking this snack mix in lunch for more than 10 years. I've given the recipe to many people. —Chris Kohler, Nelson, Wisconsin

 1 jar (12 ounces) dry roasted peanuts
 2 cups (12 ounces) semisweet chocolate chips
 1 package (9 ounces) raisins
1-3/4 cups salted sunflower kernels

Combine ingredients in a large bowl; mix gently. Store in an airtight container. **Yield:** about 8 cups.

— 🎺 🎺 🎺 —

Chocolate-Dipped Fruit

This recipe combines two of my family's favorite foods—fruit and chocolate. Pretty pieces of dipped fruit add something special to any table. —Dorothy Anderson, Ottawa, Kansas

 1 cup (6 ounces) semisweet chocolate chips
 1 to 2 teaspoons shortening
 1 package (6 ounces) dried apricots
 1 pint fresh strawberries

In a saucepan over low heat, melt chocolate chips and shortening, stirring constantly until smooth. Spear fruit with toothpicks; dip into chocolate. Place

on waxed paper or stick toothpicks into a block of Styrofoam to harden. **Yield:** 10-12 servings.

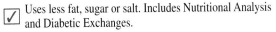

Sugar-Free Holiday Nog
(Pictured on page 6)

Coming up with holiday beverages that everyone is able to enjoy can be a real challenge. I created the recipe for this refreshing nog for my diabetic mother.
—Nancy Shickling, Bedford, Virginia

☑ Uses less fat, sugar or salt. Includes Nutritional Analysis and Diabetic Exchanges.

- 7 **cups skim milk, *divided***
- 1 **package (.9 ounce) sugar-free instant vanilla pudding mix**
- 1 **to 2 teaspoons vanilla extract *or* rum flavoring**
- 2 **to 4 packets sugar substitute**
- 1 **cup evaporated skim milk**

Combine 2 cups of milk, pudding mix, vanilla and sugar substitute in a bowl; mix according to pudding directions. Pour into a half-gallon container with a tight-fitting lid. Add 3 cups milk; shake well. Add evaporated milk and shake. Add remaining milk; shake well. Chill. **Yield:** 8 servings. **Nutritional Analysis:** One serving equals 107 calories, 187 mg sodium, 1 mg cholesterol, 15 gm carbohydrate, 10 gm protein, 1 gm fat. **Diabetic Exchanges:** 1 skim milk, 1/4 starch.

Sesame Chicken Strips
(Pictured above right)

These tasty chicken strips dipped in the lightly sweet sauce are a wonderful finger food. They go over really well at outdoor summer gatherings. —*Teri Rasey Cadillac, Michigan*

- 1 **cup mayonnaise**
- 2 **teaspoons dried minced onion**
- 2 **teaspoons ground mustard**
- 1 **cup crushed butter-flavored crackers (about 25 crackers)**
- 1/2 **cup sesame seeds**
- 8 **boneless skinless chicken breast halves (2 pounds)**

SAUCE:
- 1 **cup mayonnaise**
- 2 **tablespoons honey**

In a bowl, combine mayonnaise, onion and mustard. In another bowl, combine the cracker crumbs and sesame seeds. Cut chicken lengthwise into 1/4-

in. strips. Dip strips into mayonnaise mixture, then into the sesame seed mixture. Place in a single layer on a large greased baking sheet. Bake at 425° for 15-18 minutes or until juices run clear. Combine sauce ingredients and serve with chicken strips. **Yield:** 10-12 servings.

"Broccomole" Dip

For a snack that's very much like guacamole—but without the avocados which are high in fat—try this recipe. —*Sue Gronholz, Columbus, Wisconsin*

☑ Uses less fat, sugar or salt. Includes Nutritional Analysis and Diabetic Exchanges.

- 2 **cups chopped fresh broccoli, cooked and chilled**
- 1/4 **cup light sour cream**
- 2 **to 3 tablespoons lemon juice**
- 1 **to 2 tablespoons minced onion**
- 1 **tablespoon fat-free mayonnaise**
- 1/4 **to 1/2 teaspoon chili powder**

Fresh vegetables *or* baked tortilla chips

In a food processor or blender, combine the first six ingredients; cover and process until smooth. Refrigerate for several hours. Serve with vegetables or tortilla chips. **Yield:** 6 servings. **Nutritional Analysis:** One serving (3 tablespoons) equals 27 calories, 33 mg sodium, 5 mg cholesterol, 3 gm carbohydrate, 2 gm protein, 2 gm fat. **Diabetic Exchanges:** 1 vegetable.

Cinnamon Candy Popcorn

(Pictured above)

This crisp, bright-colored snack is more festive than traditional caramel corn. My family just loves it! A friend shared the recipe, and I've given it to several people myself. Set out in pretty bowls, it makes a tasty table decoration. I also put it in sandwich bags for a children's party snack.
—Kaye Kemper
Windfall, Indiana

- 8 quarts popped popcorn
- 1 cup butter *or* margarine
- 1/2 cup light corn syrup
- 1 package (9 ounces) red-hot candies

Place popcorn in a large bowl and set aside. In a saucepan, combine butter, corn syrup and candies; bring to a boil over medium heat, stirring constantly. Boil for 5 minutes, stirring occasionally. Pour over popcorn and mix thoroughly. Turn into two greased 15-in. x 10-in. x 1-in. baking pans. Bake at 250° for 1 hour, stirring every 15 minutes. Remove from pans and place on waxed paper to cool. Break apart; store in airtight containers. **Yield:** 8 quarts.

Coconut Snacks

These tasty treats are so easy that even the kids can make them. Surprise school-age children by tucking some of these snacks into their brown bag lunches.
—Stacie Yarbrough, Huntsville, Alabama

- 1 cup creamy peanut butter
- 1 cup confectioners' sugar
- 1/2 cup instant nonfat dry milk powder
- 4 tablespoons water
- 1 cup (6 ounces) semisweet chocolate chips
- 1-1/2 cups flaked coconut

In a mixing bowl, beat peanut butter, sugar, milk and water until smooth. Fold in chocolate chips. Form into 1-in. balls; roll in coconut. Chill until firm. **Yield:** 4 dozen.

Nacho Cheese Dip

(Pictured below right)

With jobs, schools and sports activities, evening is our time for family fun. We munch on this zippy dip while visiting or watching a movie.
—Dawn Taylor
Milton, Kentucky

- 1/4 pound bulk spicy pork *or* Mexican-style sausage
- 2 tablespoons chopped green pepper
- 2 tablespoons chopped onion
- 1 pound process American cheese, cubed
- 3/4 cup salsa
- Tortilla chips *or* fresh vegetables

In a 1-1/2-qt. microwave-safe bowl, cook sausage, green pepper and onion on high for 2-3 minutes or until sausage is fully cooked; drain. Add the cheese and salsa. Cover and microwave on high for 2-3 minutes longer, stirring frequently until cheese is melted and mixture is smooth. Serve with tortilla chips or vegetables. **Yield:** about 3 cups. **Editor's Note:** This recipe was tested in a 700-watt microwave.

Icebox Sandwiches

(Pictured at right)

My mother liked making these cool creamy treats when I was growing up in the States because they're so quick to fix. Now my three kids enjoy them. —Sandy Armijo
Naples, Italy

- 2 cups cold milk
- 1 package (3.4 ounces) instant vanilla pudding mix
- 2 cups whipped topping
- 1 cup (6 ounces) miniature semisweet chocolate chips
- 48 graham cracker squares

Mix milk and pudding according to package directions and refrigerate until set. Fold in whipped topping and chocolate chips. Place 24 graham crackers on a baking sheet; top each with about 3 tablespoons filling. Place another graham cracker on top. Freeze for 1 hour or until firm. Wrap individually in plastic wrap; freeze. Serve sandwiches frozen. **Yield:** 2 dozen.

—— ⛏ ⛏ ⛏ ——

✕ Southwest Appetizer Pizza
(Pictured below)

My husband and I created the recipe for this hearty snack that bulks up ordinary vegetable pizza. Our whole family enjoys it. —Sandra McKenzie
Braham, Minnesota

- 2 tubes (8 ounces *each*) refrigerated crescent rolls
- 1 package (8 ounces) cream cheese, softened
- 1 cup (8 ounces) sour cream
- 1 pound ground beef
- 1 envelope taco seasoning mix
- 1 can (2-1/4 ounces) sliced ripe olives, drained
- 1 medium tomato, chopped
- 3/4 cup shredded cheddar cheese
- 3/4 cup shredded mozzarella cheese
- 1 cup shredded lettuce

Unroll crescent roll dough and place in an ungreased 15-in. x 10-in. x 1-in. baking pan. Flatten dough to fit the pan, sealing seams and perforations. Bake at 375° for 8-10 minutes or until light golden brown; cool. In a small bowl, blend cream cheese and sour cream with a wire whisk; spread over crust. Chill 30 minutes. Meanwhile, in a skillet, brown beef; drain. Stir in taco seasoning. Add water according to package directions and simmer for 5 minutes, stirring occasionally. Spread over cream cheese layer. Top with olives, tomato, cheeses and lettuce. Cut into serving-size pieces. Serve immediately or refrigerate. **Yield:** 12-16 servings.

SATISFYING SNACKS like Nacho Cheese Dip, Southwest Appetizer Pizza and Icebox Sandwiches (shown above, clockwise from upper right) are sure to tackle the late-night "munchies".

Savory Potato Skins

For a simple hot snack that really hits the spot on a cool evening, put together a plate of these crisp potato skins. —Andrea Holcomb, Torrington, Connecticut

- **4 large baking potatoes, baked**
- **3 tablespoons butter *or* margarine, melted**
- **1 to 2 teaspoons salt**
- **1 teaspoon garlic powder**
- **1 teaspoon paprika**
- **Sour cream and chives, optional**

Cut potatoes in half lengthwise; scoop out pulp, leaving a 1/4-in.-thick shell. (Save pulp for another use.) Cut shells lengthwise into quarters and place on a greased baking sheet. Brush insides with butter. Combine salt, garlic powder and paprika; sprinkle over the skins. Broil until golden brown, about 5-8 minutes. If desired, combine sour cream and chives and serve with potato skins. **Yield:** 32 appetizers.

Beef and Olive Spread

Whenever I'm invited to a get-together, I'm asked to bring this special spread. No one can resist the combination of ingredients. —Shirley Harrison, Portland, Oregon

- **1 teaspoon dried minced onion**
- **1 tablespoon milk**
- **1 package (8 ounces) cream cheese, softened**
- **1 tablespoon mayonnaise *or* salad dressing**
- **1 package (2-1/2 ounces) sliced dried beef, chopped**
- **1/4 cup chopped stuffed olives**
- **Assorted crackers**

In a small bowl, soften onion in milk. Stir in cream cheese and mayonnaise. Add beef and olives; mix well. Chill. Serve on crackers. **Yield:** 1-1/2 cups.

Layered Veggie Dip

My sister shared this recipe with me years ago. It will serve quite a hungry bunch. But at my house, a few kids have been known to eat a whole plateful by themselves. —Katie Koziolek, Hartland, Minnesota

- **2 cans (10-1/2 ounces *each*) jalapeno bean dip**
- **2 cups mashed ripe avocado**
- **1 tablespoon lemon juice**
- **1/2 teaspoon seasoned salt**
- **1-1/2 cups (12 ounces) sour cream, *divided***

'I Wish I Had That Recipe...'

"MY HUSBAND and I have been to many Mexican restaurants, but none has an appetizer as good as the Super Nachos served at Loma-Linda's just outside my hometown of Toledo," reports Ohio cook Pat Garcia.

Owner Adela Mundt happily shares the tasty recipe. "Like most of our recipes, the Super Nachos were inspired by my mother, Ventura Cavazos, who started this restaurant over 40 years ago," says Adela. "My husband and I carry on the tasty family tradition."

Loma-Linda Mexican Cuisine, at 10400 Airport Highway in Swanton, Ohio, is open Monday-Saturday 11 a.m. until midnight; 1-419/865-5455.

Super Nachos

- **1 large ripe avocado, peeled**
- **1 teaspoon lemon juice**
- **1/2 cup finely chopped onion**
- **1/2 cup chopped tomato**
- **1/4 teaspoon salt**
- **1/8 teaspoon pepper**
- **1 can (15 ounces) pinto beans, rinsed and drained**
- **2/3 cup water, *divided***
- **2 tablespoons vegetable oil**
- **1/2 pound ground beef**
- **1 tablespoon chili powder**
- **7 ounces tortilla chips**
- **2 cups (8 ounces) shredded cheddar cheese**
- **1 cup (8 ounces) sour cream**

In a small bowl, mash the avocado with lemon juice. Stir in the onion, tomato, salt and pepper; set aside. Mash beans with 1/3 cup water; place in a skillet and cook over medium heat until hot. Stir in oil; remove from the heat and set aside. In another skillet, brown beef; drain. Stir in chili powder and remaining water; cook until liquid evaporates. Line a baking sheet with foil. Arrange chips in a single layer. Top with teaspoonfuls of bean and meat mixtures. Sprinkle with cheese. Bake at 400° until cheese is melted, about 4 minutes. Top with avocado mixture and sour cream. Serve immediately. **Yield:** 6-8 servings.

1/2 cup mayonnaise *or* salad dressing
1 envelope taco seasoning mix
1 cup (4 ounces) shredded cheddar cheese
1 medium tomato, chopped
1/2 cup sliced ripe olives
1/4 cup chopped green onions
Assorted fresh vegetables

Spread bean dip over the bottom of a 10-in. pie plate. Combine the avocado, lemon juice and seasoned salt; spread over the bean dip. Combine 1 cup sour cream, mayonnaise and taco seasoning; spread over the avocado layer. Beat remaining sour cream; carefully spread on top. Sprinkle with cheese, tomato, olives and onions. Chill for 1 hour. Serve with vegetables. **Yield:** 10-12 servings.

— 🍴 🍴 🍴 —

Matt's Mexican Pizza

My brother and I have fond childhood memories of Saturday morning breakfasts on our Minnesota farm. It was a big production, with everyone involved. That's where we developed our love of cooking.
— *Matt Walter, Grand Rapids, Michigan*

2 flour tortillas (10 inches)
3 ounces sliced pepperoni
2 medium tomatoes, chopped
1/2 cup salsa
1 can (2-1/4 ounces) sliced ripe olives, drained
1 cup (4 ounces) shredded Monterey Jack cheese
1 cup shredded lettuce

Place one tortilla on a microwave-safe plate. Layer with half of the pepperoni, tomatoes, salsa, olives and cheese. Microwave on high for 1-1/2 to 2 minutes or until cheese is melted. Top with half of the lettuce. Make a second pizza with remaining ingredients. **Yield:** 2 servings. **Editor's Note:** This recipe was tested in a 700-watt microwave.

— 🍴 🍴 🍴 —

Aunt Frances' Lemonade

(Pictured above right)

My sister and I spent a week each summer with Aunt Frances, who always had this thirst-quenching lemonade in a stoneware crock in the refrigerator. It tastes so much like fresh citrus. — *Debbie Blackburn, Camp Hill, Pennsylvania*

5 lemons
5 limes
5 oranges
3 quarts water
1-1/2 to 2 cups sugar

Squeeze the juice from four of the lemons, limes and oranges; pour into a gallon container. Thinly slice the remaining fruit and set aside for garnish. Add water and sugar to juices; mix well. Store in the refrigerator. Serve on ice with fruit slices. **Yield:** 12-16 servings (about 1 gallon).

Mini Apple Pies

My kids set up an assembly line when making these snacks—one chops the apples and mixes the filling, one rolls out the biscuits and one puts the pies together.
— *Marsha Dingbaum, Aurora, Colorado*

1 tube (7-1/2 ounces) refrigerated biscuits
1 tart apple, peeled and finely chopped
1/4 cup raisins
3 tablespoons sugar
1 teaspoon ground cinnamon
2 tablespoons butter *or* margarine

Using a rolling pin, flatten each biscuit to a 3-in. to 4-in. circle. Combine the apple, raisins, sugar and cinnamon; place a tablespoonful on each biscuit. Dot with butter. Bring up sides of biscuit to enclose filling and pinch to seal. Place in ungreased muffin cups. Bake at 375° for 11-13 minutes or until golden brown. **Yield:** 10 servings.

sauce for dipping. **Yield:** 4-6 servings. **Editor's Note:** Regular mozzarella cheese, cut into 4-in. x 1/2-in. sticks, can be substituted for the string cheese.

— 🍵 🍵 🍵 —

Perky Ham Spread

This hearty spread is convenient to have chilling in the refrigerator on busy days on our farm. Serve with crackers for a snack or spread on bread for a light lunch. —Rochelle Marquette, Rutland, North Dakota

- 1 can (4-1/4 ounces) deviled ham spread
- 1/2 cup shredded cheddar cheese
- 1/2 cup *each* finely chopped celery and green onions
- 1/4 cup shredded carrot
- 1/4 cup mayonnaise *or* salad dressing
- 2 hard-cooked eggs, chopped
- 2 tablespoons chopped stuffed olives
- 1/2 teaspoon garlic powder
- 1/4 teaspoon pepper
Assorted crackers

In a medium bowl, combine the first nine ingredients; mix well. Chill thoroughly. Serve with crackers. **Yield:** 2 cups.

— 🍵 🍵 🍵 —

Cinnamon Popcorn

My family can't get enough of this crisp, lightly sweet snack. It's a great finger food for traveling since it's not sticky. —Caroline Roberts, Findlay, Ohio

- 2 quarts popped popcorn
- 1 egg white, lightly beaten
- 1/2 cup sugar
- 1 teaspoon ground cinnamon
- 1/4 teaspoon salt

Place popcorn in a 15-in. x 10-in. x 1-in. baking pan. In a small bowl, mix egg white, sugar, cinnamon and salt. Pour over popcorn and mix thoroughly. Bake at 300° for 20 minutes. Cool. Store in an airtight container. **Yield:** 2 quarts.

— 🍵 🍵 🍵 —

Party Pizzas

A batch of these snacks gets cleared away fast with the irresistible combination of creamy cheese and lightly seasoned meat on crispy toast. —Carolyn Snow, Sedalia, Missouri

- 1 pound ground beef

Mozzarella Sticks

(Pictured above)

I'm particularly fond of these tasty snacks because they're baked, not fried. Cheese is one of my family's favorite foods. Being of Italian descent, I cook often with ricotta and mozzarella cheeses.
—Mary Merchant, Barre, Vermont

- 2 eggs
- 1 tablespoon water
- 1 cup dry bread crumbs
- 2-1/2 teaspoons Italian seasoning
- 1/2 teaspoon garlic powder
- 1/8 teaspoon pepper
- 12 sticks string cheese
- 3 tablespoons all-purpose flour
- 1 tablespoon butter *or* margarine, melted
- 1 cup marinara *or* spaghetti sauce, heated

In a small bowl, beat eggs and water. In a plastic bag, combine bread crumbs, Italian seasoning, garlic powder and pepper. Coat cheese sticks in flour, then dip in egg mixture and bread crumb mixture. Repeat egg and bread crumb coatings. Cover and chill for at least 4 hours or overnight. Place on an ungreased baking sheet; drizzle with butter. Bake, uncovered, at 400° for 6-8 minutes or until heated through. Allow to stand for 3-5 minutes before serving. Use marinara or spaghetti

1 pound bulk Italian sausage
1 pound process American cheese, cubed
3 tablespoons Worcestershire sauce
3 tablespoons ketchup
1 teaspoon dried oregano
1 teaspoon garlic salt
1/4 teaspoon salt
1/4 teaspoon pepper
1 loaf (1 pound) sliced party rye bread

In a large skillet, brown the beef and sausage; drain. Add cheese, Worcestershire sauce, ketchup and seasonings; stir until cheese is melted. Spread 1-2 tablespoons hot mixture on each slice of bread. Place on an ungreased baking sheet. Bake at 350° for 10-15 minutes or until heated through. Pizzas may be frozen and baked 15-20 minutes without thawing. **Yield:** about 3 dozen.

— 🍶 🍶 🍶 —

Warm Olive Dip

My husband, Mike, and I grow olives, so they often appear on our menus. In this recipe, olives add a little extra spark to ordinary artichoke dip.
—*Cindy Armstrong, Portersville, California*

1-1/4 cups mayonnaise
1 cup shredded *or* grated Parmesan cheese
1 can (14 ounces) water-packed artichoke hearts, drained and chopped
1 cup chopped stuffed olives
Assorted crackers

In a bowl, combine the mayonnaise and Parmesan cheese. Add artichokes and olives; mix well. Transfer to an ungreased 1-qt. baking dish. Bake, uncovered, at 350° for 30 minutes or until bubbly. Serve with crackers. **Yield:** 3 cups.

— 🍶 🍶 🍶 —

Rhubarb Slush

(Pictured at right and on page 6)

This thirst-quenching slush is a fun way to use rhubarb. I love to serve it for special get-togethers like a ladies' brunch or holiday meal. The rosy color and tangy flavor of this favorite spring crop come through in every sip. —*Theresa Pearson, Ogilvie, Minnesota*

3 cups chopped fresh *or* frozen rhubarb
1 cup water
1/3 cup sugar
1 cup apple juice
3/4 cup pink lemonade concentrate
1 bottle (2 liters) lemon-lime soda

In a saucepan, combine rhubarb, water and sug-

ar; bring to a boil. Reduce heat; cover and simmer for 5 minutes or until rhubarb is tender. Cool for about 30 minutes. In a food processor or blender, puree mixture, half at a time. Stir in apple juice and lemonade concentrate. Pour into a freezer container; cover and freeze until firm. Let stand at room temperature for 45 minutes before serving. For individual servings, scoop 1/3 cup into a glass and fill with soda. To serve a group, place all of the mixture in a large pitcher or punch bowl; add soda and stir. Serve immediately. **Yield:** about 10 servings.

Pieplant Pointers

When buying rhubarb, look for crisp, bright stalks. The leaves should look fresh and be blemish free. One pound equals about 3 cups chopped. Tightly wrap rhubarb in a plastic bag and store in the refrigerator for up to 3 days. Wash and discard the leaves just before using the stalks. To freeze for up to 9 months, simply cut the stalks into 1-inch pieces and place in a heavy-duty resealable plastic bag.

Garden-Fresh Salads

Toss together these refreshing side or main-dish salads for a nice accompaniment to any dinner or as a hearty meal in itself.

TOSSED-TOGETHER TREATS. Clockwise from upper left: Minted Melon Salad (p. 28), German Cucumber Salad (p. 35), Spectacular Overnight Slaw (p. 30), Asparagus Vinaigrette (p. 29) and Southwestern Bean Salad (p. 37).

Layered Chicken Salad

(Pictured below)

I prepare this satisfying salad Saturday evening and serve it to my husband and sons on Sunday after a round of golf. It's a winner on warm days—with a unique mix of vegetables like bean sprouts, green onions, water chestnuts and pea pods. And it's lovely in a glass bowl.
—Joanne Trentadue
Racine, Wisconsin

      4 to 5 cups shredded iceberg lettuce
      1 medium cucumber, thinly sliced
      1 cup fresh bean sprouts
      1 can (8 ounces) sliced water chestnuts, drained
   1/2 cup thinly sliced green onions
      1 pound fresh pea pods, halved
      4 cups cubed cooked chicken
      2 cups mayonnaise
      1 tablespoon sugar
      2 teaspoons curry powder
   1/2 teaspoon ground ginger
Cherry tomatoes and fresh parsley sprigs, optional

Place lettuce in the bottom of a 4-qt. glass salad bowl. Layer with cucumber, bean sprouts, water chestnuts, onions, pea pods and chicken. In a small bowl, combine mayonnaise, sugar, curry and ginger. Spread over top of salad. Garnish with cherry tomatoes and parsley if desired. Cover and chill several hours or overnight. **Yield:** 8-10 servings.

Strawberries and Romaine with Poppy Seed Dressing

I often include this recipe in our strawberry farm newsletter. I get so many compliments on this pretty mix of strawberries, lettuce and onion. The mayonnaise-based poppy seed dressing is actually nice and light. —Laurie Andrews, Milton, Ontario

      1 bunch romaine, torn
      1 quart fresh strawberries, sliced
      1 small sweet onion, sliced
   1/2 cup mayonnaise *or* salad dressing
   1/3 cup sugar
      2 tablespoons vinegar
   1/4 cup milk
      1 tablespoon poppy seeds

Combine lettuce, berries and onion in a large bowl. In a jar with tight-fitting lid, combine remaining ingredients; shake well. Just before serving, pour over salad; toss lightly. **Yield:** 6-8 servings.

Light Potato Salad

My husband and I are both from big families, so we're always getting together. The first time I served this nutritious salad, everyone loved it.
—Sharon Thom, Lavina, Montana

Uses less fat, sugar or salt. Includes Nutritional Analysis and Diabetic Exchanges.

      2 pounds unpeeled red potatoes, cooked and cubed (5 cups)
   1/2 cup chopped celery
   1/4 cup chopped dill pickle
      2 tablespoons chopped sweet red pepper
      2 tablespoons chopped onion
      2 tablespoons snipped fresh parsley
1-1/2 teaspoons snipped fresh mint *or* 1/2 teaspoon dried mint
      2 tablespoons plain light yogurt
      2 tablespoons lemon juice
   1/2 teaspoon honey
   1/4 teaspoon ground mustard
   3/4 teaspoon snipped fresh basil *or* 1/4 teaspoon dried basil
   1/4 teaspoon pepper

In bowl, combine potatoes, celery, pickle, red pepper, onion, parsley and mint. Combine all remaining ingredients; pour over salad and mix gently. Cover and chill for several hours. **Yield:** 10 servings. **Nutritional Analysis:** One 1/2-cup serving equals 63 calories, 74 mg sodium, 0 cholesterol, 14 gm carbohydrate, 2 gm protein, trace fat. **Diabetic Exchanges:** 1 starch.

Pineapple Gelatin Salad

(Pictured above)

My family enjoys this lovely layered salad in the summer with grilled hamburgers. Although I haven't used the recipe long, it's quickly become a favorite. A good friend shared it with me, and every time I make it, I think of her. —Susan Kirby, Tipton, Indiana

- 1 **can (20 ounces) crushed pineapple**
- 1 **package (6 ounces) lemon gelatin**
- 3 **cups boiling water**
- 1 **package (8 ounces) cream cheese, softened**
- 1 **carton (16 ounces) frozen whipped topping, thawed**
- 3/4 **cup sugar**
- 3 **tablespoons lemon juice**
- 3 **tablespoons water**
- 2 **tablespoons all-purpose flour**
- 2 **egg yolks, lightly beaten**

Drain pineapple, reserving juice. Dissolve gelatin in water; add pineapple. Pour into a 13-in. x 9-in. x 2-in. dish; chill until almost set, about 45 minutes. In a mixing bowl, beat cream cheese and whipped topping until smooth. Carefully spread over gelatin; chill for 30 minutes. Meanwhile, in a saucepan over medium heat, combine sugar, lemon juice, water, flour, egg yolks and reserved pineapple juice; bring to a boil, stirring constantly. Cook 1 minute or until thickened. Cool. Carefully spread over cream cheese layer. Chill for at least 1 hour. **Yield:** 12-16 servings.

Turkey Curry Salad

My sister picked up this winning recipe at our state fair several years ago. Cucumbers, apples and a touch of curry make this salad distinctive. —June Mullins Livonia, Missouri

- 3/4 **cup mayonnaise**
- 3/4 **cup sour cream *or* plain yogurt**
- 1 **to 2 teaspoons curry powder**
- 4 **cups diced cooked turkey**
- 2 **cups chopped apples**
- 1 **cup chopped celery**
- 1 **cup chopped peeled cucumber**
- 2 **tablespoons chopped onion**

In a large bowl, combine mayonnaise and sour cream; stir in curry powder. Fold in remaining ingredients. Chill at least 2 hours before serving. **Yield:** 4-6 servings.

Southwestern Pork Salad

(Pictured above)

As pork producers, we're proud to cook and serve the delicious product we raise. This tempting salad is refreshing and colorful. It's a succulent showcase for pork. I know your family will enjoy it as much as we do. —Sue Cunningham, Prospect, Ohio

>   2 **cups cooked pork strips**
>   1 **can (16 ounces) kidney beans, rinsed and drained**
>   1/2 **cup sliced ripe olives**
>   1 **medium onion, chopped**
>   1 **large green pepper, chopped**
>   1 **large tomato, chopped**
>   1/4 **cup cider vinegar**
>   1/4 **cup vegetable oil**
>   2 **tablespoons sugar**
>   2 **tablespoons minced fresh parsley**
>   1 **teaspoon ground mustard**
>   1 **teaspoon ground cumin**
>   1 **teaspoon dried oregano**
>   1/2 **teaspoon salt**

In a large bowl, toss pork, beans, olives, onion, green pepper and tomato. Combine remaining ingredients in a jar with tight-fitting lid; shake well. Pour over pork mixture; toss gently. Cover and refrigerate for 4-6 hours, stirring occasionally. **Yield:** 4 servings.

Dilly Broccoli Salad

Since we're retired, we travel out of state in summer to visit our children and grandchildren. But we're here all winter long while plenty of broccoli is in the fields. This is one of our favorite recipes. —Jean Gaines
Bullhead City, Arizona

>   2 **pounds fresh broccoli, cut into florets**
> 1-1/2 **pounds fresh cauliflower, cut into florets**
>   1 **cup mayonnaise**
>   1/2 **cup sour cream**
>   1 **small onion, chopped**
>   1 **tablespoon snipped fresh dill *or* 1-1/2 teaspoons dill weed**
>   1/2 **teaspoon salt**

In a large bowl, combine the broccoli and cauliflower; set aside. Combine mayonnaise, sour cream, onion, dill and salt; mix well. Pour over vegetables; toss to coat. Cover and chill 4 hours or overnight. **Yield:** 6-8 servings.

Baked Potato Salad

(Pictured below)

I was tired of the ordinary potato salads served so often in summer, so I came up with this hearty flavorful variation. My family has enjoyed it now for several years, and I'm asked to make it whenever there's a get-together or cookout. I'm sure you'll like it as much as we do.
—Barbara O'Kane
Greenwood Lake, New York

4-1/2 pounds potatoes, peeled and cut into
     3/4-inch chunks
  1/4 cup olive *or* vegetable oil
    2 envelopes Italian salad dressing mix
    1 medium green pepper, chopped
    1 medium sweet red pepper, chopped
    1 bunch green onions, chopped
    2 large tomatoes, chopped
    4 hard-cooked eggs, chopped
    5 bacon strips, cooked and crumbled
1-1/2 cups mayonnaise
    1 tablespoon vinegar
    1 tablespoon lemon juice
    2 teaspoons dried basil
    1 teaspoon salt
  1/2 teaspoon pepper
  1/4 teaspoon garlic powder

In a large bowl, toss the potatoes with oil and dressing mixes. Place in two greased 13-in. x 9-in. x 2-in. baking pans. Bake, uncovered, at 400° for 45 minutes or until tender. Cool. Transfer to a large bowl; add peppers, onions, tomatoes, eggs and bacon. Toss gently. Combine remaining ingredients in a small bowl; mix well. Pour over salad and stir gently. Cover and refrigerate for at least 1 hour. **Yield:** 16-20 servings.

'I Wish I Had That Recipe...'

"WHILE visiting in Knoxville, Tennessee, I lunched at the Apple Cake Tea Room. I was served the best chicken salad I've ever eaten," states Martha Yant from Waco, Texas. "I'd love to make it at home if the owners would be willing to share the recipe."

Tea Room owner Mary Henry is happy to oblige, saying, "It's wonderful to know that we have satisfied a customer well enough that she would want to 'share us'.

"The secret to our chicken salad is just plain fresh (not frozen) chicken, cooked in water with a little salt," Mary maintains. "We usually make 20 pounds at a time, but our cook, Dorothy, and I have cut down the recipe quantity."

Tea Room Medley, the house specialty, is chicken salad served with glazed fruit and a banana nut bread sandwich with cream cheese filling. Apple cake, brownie pie, and a crisp waffle filled with ice cream and sauteed bananas are just some of the noteworthy desserts.

Housed in a cozy log cabin, the Apple Cake Tea Room is on Campbell Station Rd. at Farragut, just outside Knoxville, Tennessee. It's open Monday-Saturday 11 a.m. to 2:30 p.m.; 1-423/966-7848.

Tea Room Chicken Salad

    2 cups mayonnaise
  3/4 cup chopped celery
    1 tablespoon prepared mustard
1-1/4 teaspoons poppy seeds
  1/2 teaspoon salt
  10 cups cubed cooked chicken
Chopped pecans

In a large bowl, combine mayonnaise, celery, mustard, poppy seeds and salt. Fold in chicken. Cover and chill for 3-4 hours. Top with pecans before serving. **Yield:** about 12 servings.

Spiced Peach Salad

(Pictured below)

This refreshing salad is my most requested recipe. A touch of cinnamon makes it taste like fresh peach pie. My father-in-law is an especially big fan of this fruity salad, and I know you'll love it, too.
—Karen Hamilton, Ludington, Michigan

1/2 cup sugar
3 tablespoons vinegar
2 cups water
1 tablespoon whole cloves
4 cinnamon sticks
1 package (6 ounces) peach gelatin
1 can (29 ounces) peach halves, undrained

In a medium saucepan, combine sugar, vinegar and water. Tie cloves and cinnamon in a cheesecloth bag; place in the saucepan. Bring to a boil. Reduce heat; simmer, uncovered, for 10 minutes. Remove from the heat and discard spice bag. Add gelatin; stir until dissolved. Drain peaches, reserving syrup; set peaches aside. Add water to syrup to equal 2 cups. Add to gelatin mixture; stir well. Chill until slightly thickened. Thinly slice peaches; add to gelatin. Pour into a 2-qt. glass bowl; chill until firm. **Yield:** 8-10 servings. **Editor's Note:** If desired, 1/2 teaspoon ground cinnamon and 1/4 teaspoon ground cloves may be substituted for the whole spices; combine with the gelatin before adding to sugar mixture.

French Potato Salad

Here's an easy-to-make potato salad that features a fresh, zippy tarragon dressing instead of the traditional mayonnaise. This is one of my husband's favorite recipes. I like to bring along a large bowlful for picnics, potlucks and backyard barbecues.
—Cheryl Ruhr, Brookfield, Missouri

2 pounds potatoes, peeled, cooked and sliced
1/4 cup chopped onion
1/3 cup olive *or* vegetable oil
4 teaspoons cider vinegar
1 to 2 tablespoons minced fresh tarragon *or* 1 to 2 teaspoons dried tarragon
2 tablespoons minced fresh *or* dried chives
1/2 teaspoon salt
1/2 teaspoon pepper

In a large bowl, toss potatoes and onion. In a small bowl or jar with tight-fitting lid, combine oil and vinegar. Add tarragon, chives, salt and pepper; mix or shake well. Pour over potatoes and mix gently. Let stand 1 hour; serve at room temperature. **Yield:** 4-6 servings.

Making a Spice Bag

To make a cheesecloth spice bag, place spices on several thicknesses of cheesecloth that has been cut into 3-in. squares. Tie with kitchen string.

If you don't have cheesecloth, tuck the spices into a metal tea ball instead and hook the chain over the side of the saucepan.

Minted Melon Salad

(Pictured on page 22)

People can't resist digging into a salad made with colorful summer fruits. The unique dressing is what makes this salad a crowd-pleaser. I get compliments whenever I serve it, especially when I put it on the table in a melon boat. It's a warm-weather treat.
—Terry Saylor, Vermillion, South Dakota

1 cup water

3/4 cup sugar
3 tablespoons lime juice
1-1/2 teaspoons chopped fresh mint
3/4 teaspoon aniseed
Pinch salt
5 cups cubed watermelon
1 medium cantaloupe, cut into cubes
1 medium honeydew, cut into cubes
2 medium peaches, sliced
1 cup fresh blueberries

In a small saucepan, combine the water, sugar, lime juice, mint, aniseed and salt; bring to a boil. Boil for 2 minutes; remove from the heat. Cover and cool syrup completely. In a large bowl, combine watermelon, cantaloupe, honeydew, peaches and blueberries; add syrup and stir to coat. Cover and refrigerate for at least 2 hours, stirring occasionally. Drain before serving. **Yield:** 12-14 servings.

Asparagus Vinaigrette

(Pictured on page 22)

I love to cook and especially enjoy trying new recipes. I took a cooking class and discovered this delightful salad. It's nice for a spring luncheon with the fresh taste of the asparagus, parsley and chives drizzled with a zesty dressing. —Marcy Fechtig
Burnt Prairie, Illinois

1-1/2 cups olive *or* vegetable oil
1/2 cup cider *or* white wine vinegar
2 teaspoons Dijon mustard
1/2 teaspoon salt
1/8 teaspoon pepper
3 to 4 radishes, sliced
1/4 cup chopped green pepper
3 tablespoons dill pickle relish
1 tablespoon chopped fresh parsley
1 tablespoon snipped fresh chives
2 pounds fresh asparagus spears, cooked and drained
Lettuce leaves
3 hard-cooked eggs, sliced
2 medium tomatoes, cut into wedges

In a bowl, whisk together the oil, vinegar, mustard, salt and pepper. Add radishes, green pepper, relish, parsley and chives. Place asparagus in a glass baking dish; pour dressing over asparagus. Cover and chill at least 4 hours or overnight. To serve, arrange the lettuce on a serving platter; remove asparagus from dressing with a slotted spoon and arrange over lettuce. Garnish with eggs and tomatoes. Drizzle with some of the dressing. **Yield:** 6-8 servings.

Calico Corn Salad

(Pictured above)

With a full-time job and my own catering business, I appreciate delicious food that can be prepared ahead, like this colorful zippy salad. My family and friends are glad to sample the new dishes I prepare, especially when they turn out as good as this one.
—Henry Tindal, Red Bank, New Jersey

2 packages (16 ounces *each*) frozen corn, thawed
4 small zucchini, diced
1 large sweet red pepper, diced
2 cans (4 ounces *each*) chopped green chilies, drained
1 medium onion, chopped
2/3 cup olive *or* vegetable oil
1/4 cup fresh lime juice
2 tablespoons cider vinegar
2 to 2-1/2 teaspoons ground cumin
1-1/2 teaspoons salt
1 teaspoon pepper
1/2 teaspoon garlic salt

In a bowl, toss corn, zucchini, red pepper, chilies and onion. In a jar with tight-fitting lid, combine remaining ingredients; shake well. Pour over the salad and stir gently. Chill for several hours or overnight. **Yield:** 8-10 servings.

Tomato Asparagus Salad

Instead of reaching for the old reliable head of iceberg lettuce to make a plain salad, whip up this refreshing variation instead. With just six ingredients, it's a cinch to prepare and makes an attractive presentation. The fresh flavor of the asparagus and tomato complement each other well. —Ruby Williams
Bogalusa, Louisiana

☑ Uses less fat, sugar or salt. Includes Nutritional Analysis and Diabetic Exchanges.

> 1 pound fresh asparagus, trimmed
> 4 romaine leaves
> 4 cups torn romaine
> 1/3 cup fat-free Italian salad dressing
> 10 cherry tomatoes, halved
> 2 tablespoons grated Parmesan cheese

In a large saucepan, cook asparagus in boiling water for 5-6 minutes or until crisp-tender. Place in ice water to stop cooking. Line an 11-in. x 7-in. x 2-in. pan with romaine leaves. Top with torn romaine. Arrange asparagus over the romaine; top with tomatoes. Pour dressing over all. Sprinkle with cheese. Chill for 1 hour. **Yield:** 6 servings. **Nutritional Analysis:** One serving equals 62 calories, 174 mg sodium, 1 mg cholesterol, 11 gm carbohydrate, 4 gm protein, 2 gm fat. **Diabetic Exchanges:** 2 vegetable.

Kansas Cucumber Salad

(Pictured above)

Cucumbers are my very favorite garden vegetable, so I use this recipe often. I got it from a friend years ago. I've heard this refreshing dish keeps very well in the refrigerator, but it goes so fast around our house, I've never found out for myself. —Karen Ann Bland
Gove, Kansas

☑ Uses less fat, sugar or salt. Includes Nutritional Analysis and Diabetic Exchanges.

> 1 cup mayonnaise *or* salad dressing
> 1/4 cup sugar
> 4 teaspoons vinegar
> 1/2 teaspoon dill weed
> 1/2 teaspoon salt, optional
> 4 medium cucumbers, peeled and thinly sliced
> 3 green onions, chopped

In a large bowl, combine mayonnaise, sugar, vinegar, dill and salt if desired; mix well. Add cucumbers and onions; toss. Cover and chill for at least 1 hour. **Yield:** 8 servings. **Nutritional Analysis:** One 2/3 cup serving (prepared with low-fat mayonnaise and without added salt) equals 126 calories, 197 mg sodium, 6 mg cholesterol, 14 gm carbohydrate, 1 gm protein, 8 gm fat. **Diabetic Exchanges:** 2 vegetable, 1-1/2 fat.

Spectacular Overnight Slaw

(Pictured on page 22)

To come up with this dish, I used a number of different recipes plus some ideas of my own. It's great for potlucks because it's made the night before and the flavor keeps getting better. Whenever I serve it, I'm inundated with recipe requests. —Ruth Lovett
Bay City, Texas

> 1 medium head cabbage, shredded
> 1 medium red onion, thinly sliced
> 1/2 cup chopped green pepper
> 1/2 cup chopped sweet red pepper
> 1/2 cup sliced stuffed olives
> 1/2 cup cider *or* white wine vinegar
> 1/2 cup vegetable oil
> 1/2 cup sugar
> 2 teaspoons Dijon mustard
> 1 teaspoon *each* salt, celery seed and mustard seed

In a 4-qt. bowl, combine the cabbage, onion, peppers and olives. In a saucepan, combine remaining ingredients; bring to a boil. Cook and stir for 1 minute. Pour over vegetables and stir gently.

Cover and refrigerate overnight. Mix well before serving. **Yield:** 12-16 servings.

Fruit Salad Supreme

(Pictured below)

For a delightful fruit salad that's a snap to prepare, give this recipe a try. The sweet combination, topped with onion and a tangy dressing, is one family and friends ask for often. It's also one of my favorites to serve.   *—Lois Rutherford, St. Augustine, Florida*

☑ Uses less fat, sugar or salt. Includes Nutritional Analysis and Diabetic Exchanges.

    2 cups watercress, stems removed
    8 fresh *or* canned pineapple rings, halved
    2 oranges, peeled and sliced crosswise
1-1/2 cups cantaloupe chunks
  1/4 cup sliced green onions *or* 1 small sweet
      onion, chopped
LIME DRESSING:
  1/4 cup vegetable oil
    2 tablespoons lime juice
    1 tablespoon sugar
  1/4 teaspoon hot pepper sauce

    1 tablespoon sour cream

On individual plates, arrange watercress, pineapple and oranges. Top with cantaloupe and onions. In a small bowl, whisk oil, lime juice, sugar and hot pepper sauce until sugar is dissolved. Stir in sour cream. Serve with salads. **Yield:** 4 servings. **Nutritional Analysis:** One serving with 2 tablespoons of dressing (prepared with fresh pineapple and light sour cream) equals 216 calories, 15 mg sodium, 0 cholesterol, 27 gm carbohydrate, 2 gm protein, 15 gm fat. **Diabetic Exchanges:** 3 fat, 1-1/2 fruit.

Perfect Pineapple

When selecting a fresh pineapple, choose one that has a piney aroma, is golden in color (not green) and slightly soft to the touch. Allow unripe pineapples to ripen at room temperature.

Tightly wrap whole, ripe pineapple in the refrigerator for up to 3 days. Seal cut pineapple in an airtight container for an additional 3 days.

One medium pineapple yields about 3 cups of pineapple chunks.

Sour Cream Cucumbers

This is a tasty way to make a plentiful vegetable acceptable to my three children. Not only is this the only way they'll eat cucumbers, but they actually request it! —Karen Holt, Redding, California

  2 large cucumbers, peeled and sliced
  1 large onion, sliced into rings
3/4 cup sour cream
  3 tablespoons cider vinegar
  2 tablespoons sugar
Salt and pepper to taste

In a bowl, combine the cucumbers and onion. Combine remaining ingredients and pour over cucumbers. Mix well. Chill. **Yield:** 6-8 servings.

—— 🥣 🥣 🥣 ——

Almond Chicken Salad

(Pictured below)

My mother used to prepare this salad for an evening meal during the hot summer months. It also serves well as a delicious but quick luncheon or potluck dish. You can't beat the tasty combination of chicken, grapes and almonds. —Kathy Kittell, Lenexa, Kansas

    4 cups cubed cooked chicken
1-1/2 cups halved green grapes
    1 cup chopped celery
  3/4 cup sliced green onions

    3 hard-cooked eggs, chopped
1/2 cup mayonnaise *or* salad dressing
1/4 cup sour cream
    1 tablespoon prepared mustard
    1 teaspoon salt
1/2 teaspoon pepper
1/4 teaspoon onion powder
1/4 teaspoon celery salt
1/8 teaspoon ground mustard
1/8 teaspoon paprika
1/2 cup slivered almonds, toasted
    1 kiwifruit, peeled and sliced, optional

In a large bowl, combine chicken, grapes, celery, onions and eggs. In another bowl, combine the next nine ingredients; stir until smooth. Pour over the chicken mixture and toss gently. Stir in almonds and serve immediately, or refrigerate and add the almonds just before serving. Garnish with kiwi if desired. **Yield:** 6-8 servings.

—— 🥣 🥣 🥣 ——

Cajun Potato Salad

(Pictured at right)

I have been making this mouth-watering potato salad for more than 10 years. My family likes spicy foods, and thanks to a son living in New Orleans, we have a constant supply of Cajun sausage for this recipe. Made with extra sausage, it's a filling one-dish meal. —Margaret Scott, Murfreesboro, Tennessee

    2 pounds small red potatoes
1/2 cup chopped red onion
1/2 cup sliced green onions
1/4 cup minced fresh parsley
    6 tablespoons cider vinegar, *divided*
1/2 pound precooked smoked kielbasa *or*
     Cajun sausage, sliced
    6 tablespoons olive *or* vegetable oil
    1 tablespoon Dijon mustard
    2 garlic cloves, minced
1/2 teaspoon pepper
1/4 to 1/2 teaspoon cayenne pepper

Cook the potatoes in boiling salted water for 20-30 minutes or until tender; drain. Rinse with cold water; cool completely. Cut into 1/4-in. slices; place in a large bowl. Add onions, parsley and 3 tablespoons vinegar; toss. In a medium skillet, cook sausage in oil for 5-10 minutes or until it begins to brown. Remove with slotted spoon and add to potato mixture. To drippings in skillet, add mustard, garlic, pepper, cayenne pepper and remaining vinegar; bring to a boil, whisking constantly. Pour over salad; toss gently. Serve immediately. **Yield:** 6 servings.

LIGHTER FARE. Garden-fresh mixtures like Orange Avocado Salad and Cajun Potato Salad (shown above, top to bottom) look inviting on the table.

Orange Avocado Salad

(Pictured above)

For a beautiful salad with an unbeatable combination of flavors, you can't miss with this recipe. We love the mellow avocado together with sweet mandarin oranges and crisp cucumber. The tangy dressing makes this dish special. —Latressa Allen, Fort Worth, Texas

DRESSING:
- 1/2 cup orange juice
- 1/4 cup vegetable oil
- 2 tablespoons cider *or* red wine vinegar
- 1 tablespoon sugar
- 1 teaspoon grated orange peel
- 1/4 teaspoon salt

SALAD:
- 1 medium head iceberg lettuce, torn
- 2 cups torn red leaf lettuce
- 1 medium ripe avocado, peeled and sliced
- 1/4 cup orange juice
- 1 medium cucumber, sliced
- 1/2 medium red onion, thinly sliced into rings
- 1 can (11 ounces) mandarin oranges, drained

In a jar with tight-fitting lid, combine dressing ingredients; shake well. Chill. Just before serving, toss greens in a large salad bowl. Dip the avocado slices into orange juice; arrange over greens (discard remaining juice). Add cucumber, onion and oranges. Serve with dressing. **Yield:** 6-8 servings.

duce heat and simmer for 20 minutes; cool. In a 3- or 4-qt. glass bowl, layer vegetables in order given. Top with chilies, beef mixture and cheese. Combine sour cream and remaining salsa; serve with salad and tortilla chips if desired. **Yield:** 6-8 servings.

Tomato Basil Salad

Tomatoes team up with red onion and fresh basil in this pleasant salad. The combination of ingredients just says "Summer!" It's easy to adjust the ingredients when you need to serve a bigger crowd.
—Joyce Brown, Genesee, Idaho

- **6 tomato slices (1/4 inch thick)**
- **6 red onion slices**
- **2 tablespoons olive *or* vegetable oil**
- **4 teaspoons cider *or* red wine vinegar**
- **2 tablespoons chopped fresh basil**
- **1 teaspoon sugar**

Place tomatoes in a shallow dish; top each slice with an onion. In a small jar with tight-fitting lid, combine remaining ingredients; shake well. Pour over tomatoes and onions. Cover and refrigerate for at least 1 hour. **Yield:** 2 servings.

Mexican Garden Salad

(Pictured above)

I'm always watching for delicious new recipes to try, and when I found this salad, I knew it would taste as good as it looks. Although similar to a traditional taco salad, this recipe adds tasty extras like broccoli and carrot. It's stunning on the table.
—Dianne Esposite, New Middletown, Ohio

- **1 pound ground beef**
- **1 jar (16 ounces) thick and chunky salsa, *divided***
- **1/4 cup water**
- **1 envelope taco seasoning mix**
- **1-1/2 heads iceberg lettuce, torn**
- **3 cups broccoli florets**
- **1 small red onion, thinly sliced into rings**
- **1 medium carrot, shredded**
- **1 large tomato, chopped**
- **1 can (4 ounces) chopped green chilies, drained**
- **1/2 to 1 cup shredded cheddar cheese**
- **1 cup (8 ounces) sour cream**
Tortilla chips, optional

In a skillet, brown ground beef; drain. Add 1 cup salsa, water and taco seasoning; bring to a boil. Re-

Strawberry-Orange Chicken Salad

I first started cooking when I was 4 years old! This fruity chicken salad is light and tasty. I often serve it to guests for a special lunch. —Jerry Minerich
Westminster, Colorado

- **2 cups torn spinach**
- **2 cups torn leaf lettuce**
- **3/4 cup cubed cooked chicken**
- **2/3 cup sliced fresh strawberries**
- **1 medium orange, peeled and sectioned**
- **1/4 cup strawberry-flavored pancake syrup**
- **2 tablespoons cider *or* red wine vinegar**
- **1/4 cup cashews *or* pecans, optional**

Divide spinach and lettuce among two salad plates. Arrange chicken, strawberries and oranges on lettuce. Combine syrup and vinegar; drizzle over salads. Top with cashews or pecans if desired. **Yield:** 2 servings.

Snappy Potato Salad

Folks who like their food with some zip will love this unique potato salad. Horseradish and mustard com-

bine for a zesty flavor, while celery, carrots and onion add some crunch. —*Madeleine Haney
San Carlos, California*

8 medium potatoes, peeled, cubed and cooked
8 bacon strips, cooked and crumbled
1 cup chopped onion
3/4 teaspoon salt
2 cups mayonnaise
1/4 cup prepared mustard
1/4 cup prepared horseradish
1 cup sliced celery
1/4 cup shredded carrot

In a large bowl, combine potatoes, bacon, onion and salt; set aside. In a small saucepan, combine mayonnaise, mustard and horseradish; cook until heated through, stirring constantly. Add celery and carrot; mix well. Pour over potato mixture and toss lightly to coat. Serve warm. **Yield:** 8-10 servings.

— 🥄 🥄 🥄 —

German Cucumber Salad

(Pictured on page 22)

This recipe came from a friend who ran his own inn in Germany. It's a very cool, light salad with an exhilarating taste that's delicious anytime of the year—especially when made with fresh-from-the-garden cucumbers and tomatoes. —*Julie Koren
Kennesaw, Georgia*

2 medium cucumbers, thinly sliced
4 green onions, thinly sliced
3 small tomatoes, sliced
2 tablespoons snipped fresh parsley
DRESSING:
1/4 cup sour cream
1/4 teaspoon prepared mustard
2 tablespoons minced fresh dill
1 tablespoon vinegar
1 tablespoon milk
1/2 teaspoon salt
1/8 teaspoon pepper

In a bowl, combine cucumbers, onions, tomatoes and parsley. Combine dressing ingredients; pour over cucumber mixture and toss gently. Cover and chill for at least 1 hour. **Yield:** 4-6 servings.

— 🥄 🥄 🥄 —

Fruited Wild Rice Salad

(Pictured at right)

I created this salad recipe to feature wild rice, a deli-

cious state crop, plus other harvest ingredients like apples and pecans. I make bushels of it each August when the small nearby village of Dorset hosts several thousand visitors at the Taste of Dorset festival.* —*Larren Wood, Nevis, Minnesota*

DRESSING:
1/4 cup olive *or* vegetable oil
1/3 cup orange juice
2 tablespoons honey
SALAD:
1 cup uncooked wild rice
2 Golden Delicious apples, chopped
Juice of 1 lemon
1 cup golden raisins
1 cup seedless red grapes, halved
2 tablespoons *each* minced fresh mint, parsley and chives
Salt and pepper to taste
1 cup pecan halves

Combine dressing ingredients; set aside. Cook rice according to package directions; drain if needed and allow to cool. In a large bowl, toss apples with lemon juice. Add raisins, grapes, mint, parsley, chives and rice. Add dressing and toss. Season with salt and pepper. Cover and chill several hours or overnight. Just before serving, add pecans and toss lightly. **Yield:** 8-10 servings.

Parmesan Vegetable Toss

(Pictured below)

The first time I made this salad it was with two others for a Fourth of July party years ago. This one disappeared long before the other two! It's great for feeding a hungry crowd. At our house, there's never any left over. I hope you enjoy it as much as we do.
—Judy Barbato, North Easton, Massachusetts

    2 cups mayonnaise *or* salad dressing
  1/2 cup grated Parmesan cheese
  1/4 cup sugar
  1/2 teaspoon dried basil
  1/2 teaspoon salt
    4 cups fresh broccoli florets
    4 cups fresh cauliflowerets
    1 medium red onion, sliced
    1 can (8 ounces) sliced water chestnuts, drained
    1 large head iceberg lettuce, torn
    1 pound sliced bacon, cooked and crumbled
    2 cups salad croutons, optional

In a large bowl, combine mayonnaise, Parmesan cheese, sugar, basil and salt. Add broccoli, cauliflower, onion and water chestnuts; toss. Cover and refrigerate for several hours or overnight. Just before serving, place lettuce in a salad bowl and top with vegetable mixture. Sprinkle with bacon. Top with croutons if desired. **Yield:** 16-18 servings.

Portable Salad

For a picnic or potluck tossed salad, mix all the salad fixings and the dressing in a clean plastic bag (as large as you need). The salad will then be easy to pack in a cooler, since it's not in a big bowl.

To serve, simply set the bagful of salad inside of an empty box and pull the edges of the bag over the edges of the box. There won't be any serving dishes to wash!

Tomato Spinach Salad

When I serve this fresh spinach salad tossed with a creamy dill dressing, I receive plenty of compliments and recipe requests. This is a longtime favorite. I appreciate that the dressing can be made ahead of time and chilled.   —Ruth Seitz, Columbus Junction, Iowa

  1/2 cup mayonnaise *or* salad dressing
  1/2 cup grated Parmesan cheese
  1/4 cup milk
1-1/2 teaspoons dill weed
1-1/2 teaspoons dried minced onion
1-1/2 teaspoons lemon-pepper seasoning
    1 package (10 ounces) fresh spinach, torn
    2 cups cherry tomatoes

In a small bowl or a jar with tight-fitting lid, combine the mayonnaise, cheese, milk, dill weed, onion and lemon pepper; mix or shake well. Chill for at least 1 hour. Just before serving, combine spinach and tomatoes in a large salad bowl. Whisk or shake dressing; pour over salad and toss. **Yield:** 6-8 servings. **Editor's Note:** If dressing thickens, thin with additional milk if desired.

Cherry Cranberry Salad

Not a Christmas goes by that I don't fix this bright molded salad. I've taken it to many holiday dinners, and everyone loves it—even people who don't usually enjoy cranberries.
—Deb Amrine
Grand Haven, Michigan

    1 package (6 ounces) cherry gelatin
    1 cup sugar
    2 cups boiling water

1 can (20 ounces) crushed pineapple, undrained
3 cups fresh *or* frozen cranberries, chopped
1-1/2 cups diced apples
1 cup chopped celery
1 cup chopped walnuts

In a large bowl, combine gelatin and sugar. Add water; stir until gelatin and sugar are dissolved. Stir in pineapple, cranberries, apples, celery and walnuts. Pour into a 2-qt. serving bowl; chill until firm, about 3-4 hours. **Yield:** 12-16 servings.

— 🍷 🍷 🍷 —

Tarragon Pasta Salad

The refreshing tuna salad with pasta and a savory tarragon dressing makes a colorful and flavorful addition to any summer lunch or picnic menu. The recipe can be easily doubled if you need to feed a hungry crowd.　　—Toni Churchin, Irvine, California

8 ounces bow tie pasta, cooked and drained
1 can (9 ounces) tuna, drained and flaked
1/3 cup chopped sweet red pepper
1/4 cup sliced green onions
3/4 cup mayonnaise *or* salad dressing
4 teaspoons minced fresh tarragon *or*
1 teaspoon dried tarragon
2 teaspoons lemon juice
1/2 teaspoon salt
1/4 teaspoon pepper

In a large bowl, combine pasta, tuna, red pepper and onions. In a small bowl or jar with tight-fitting lid, combine mayonnaise, tarragon, lemon juice, salt and pepper; mix or shake well. Pour over salad and toss gently. Chill for 1 hour. **Yield:** 4-6 servings.

— 🍷 🍷 🍷 —

Southwestern Bean Salad

(Pictured above right and on page 22)

I've used this zippy salad many times and received compliments. When it comes to bean salad, most people think of the sweet, three-bean variety, so this is a nice surprise.　　—Lila Jean Allen, Portland, Oregon

☑ Uses less fat, sugar or salt. Includes Nutritional Analysis and Diabetic Exchanges.

1 can (16 ounces) kidney beans, rinsed and drained
1 can (15 ounces) black beans, rinsed and drained
1 can (15 ounces) garbanzo beans, rinsed and drained

2 celery ribs, sliced
1 medium red onion, diced
1 medium tomato, diced
1 cup frozen corn, thawed
DRESSING:
3/4 cup thick and chunky salsa
1/4 cup vegetable oil
1/4 cup lime juice
1-1/2 teaspoons chili powder
1 teaspoon salt, optional
1/2 teaspoon ground cumin

In a bowl, combine beans, celery, onion, tomato and corn. In a small bowl, combine salsa, oil, lime juice, chili powder, salt if desired and cumin; mix well. Pour over the bean mixture and toss to coat. Cover and chill for at least 2 hours. **Yield:** 10 servings. **Nutritional Analysis:** One 3/4-cup serving (prepared without added salt) equals 210 calories, 382 mg sodium, 0 cholesterol, 32 gm carbohydrate, 8 gm protein, 7 gm fat. **Diabetic Exchanges:** 2 starch, 1 vegetable, 1 fat.

Soups & Sandwiches

Whether you team them up or serve them individually, these kettle creations and piled-high sandwiches are sure to please.

——— 🍵 🍵 🍵 ———

DELICIOUS DUOS. Clockwise from upper left: Zesty Steak Chili (p. 52), Savory Cheese Soup (p. 43), Zesty Sloppy Joes (p. 51), Panfish Chowder (p. 44) and Corn Dogs (p. 54).

Pork Spiedis

(Pictured above)

Spiedis (pronounced "speed-eez") are a type of grilled meat sandwich considered a local specialty. This recipe is my own, but there are many variations in our area. In nearby Binghamton, Spiedi-Fest is held in August, featuring this delicious dish made of all different kinds of meat. Thousands of people attend.
—Beatrice Riddell, Chenango Bridge, New York

✓ Uses less fat, sugar or salt. Includes Nutritional Analysis and Diabetic Exchanges.

- **4 pounds pork tenderloin, cut into 1-inch cubes**
- **2 cups tomato juice**
- **2 large onions, finely chopped**
- **4 to 5 garlic cloves, minced**
- **2 tablespoons Worcestershire sauce**
- **2 teaspoons chopped fresh basil *or* 1 teaspoon dried basil**
- **Pepper to taste**
- **12 slices Italian bread, optional**

In a large bowl, combine the first seven ingredients. Cover and refrigerate overnight. Drain, discarding marinade. Thread pork on small skewers; grill or broil for 15-20 minutes, turning occasionally, until the meat is no longer pink and pulls away easily from the skewers. To serve, wrap a slice of bread around about five pork cubes and pull off skewer. **Yield:** 12 servings. **Nutritional Analysis:** One serving (served without bread) equals 214 calories, 152 mg sodium, 77 mg cholesterol, 1 gm carbohydrate, 24 gm protein, 12 gm fat. **Diabetic Exchanges:** 4 lean meat.

Microwave Clam Chowder

This tastes as good as chowder served at many restaurants on Fisherman's Wharf in San Francisco. In my opinion, nothing beats homemade cooking.
—_Mary Jane Cantrell, Turlock, California_

 4 bacon strips, cut into 1/2-inch pieces
 2 cans (6-1/2 ounces _each_) chopped clams
1-1/2 cups diced peeled raw potatoes
 1/3 cup chopped onion
 2 tablespoons all-purpose flour
1-1/2 cups milk, _divided_
 1/2 teaspoon salt
Pinch pepper
 1 teaspoon butter _or_ margarine
Minced fresh parsley

In a covered 2-qt. microwave-safe dish, cook bacon on high for 4-5 minutes or until crisp. Remove with a slotted spoon to drain; set aside. Drain clam juice into the drippings. Stir in potatoes and onion. Cover and cook on high for 8-10 minutes or until potatoes are tender, stirring once or twice. Stir flour into 1/4 cup of milk; add to potato mixture. Stir in salt, pepper and remaining milk. Cover and cook on medium for 6 minutes, stirring once or twice. Let stand for 3-5 minutes. Stir in clams and butter. Garnish with bacon and parsley. **Yield:** 4 servings (1 quart). **Editor's Note:** This recipe was tested in a 700-watt microwave.

Broccoli Soup

This thick, creamy soup has wonderful broccoli flavor with just a hint of nutmeg. When it comes to broccoli recipes, this is one of my favorites.
—_Marion Tipton, Phoenix, Arizona_

 4 cups chicken broth
 2 to 2-1/2 pounds broccoli, cut into florets
 1/2 cup chopped green onions
 1 tablespoon olive _or_ vegetable oil
 1/4 cup all-purpose flour
 1 teaspoon salt
 1/4 teaspoon ground nutmeg
 1/8 teaspoon pepper
 1 cup half-and-half cream

In a large saucepan, bring the broth to a boil; add broccoli. Reduce heat; cover and simmer until tender, about 10 minutes. Meanwhile, in a small skillet, saute onions in oil until tender; stir into broth. Remove from the heat; cool 10-15 minutes. Puree in small batches in a blender or food processor until smooth. Return all to the saucepan; set aside. In a bowl, combine flour, salt, nutmeg and pepper. Slowly add cream, stirring constantly. Gradu-

ally stir into broccoli mixture. Return to the heat; cook over medium until heated through, stirring occasionally. **Yield:** 4 servings.

Egg Salad/Cucumber Sandwiches

This is a tasty variation of the traditional egg salad sandwich. The cucumbers and onion add a refreshing crunch. —_Lucy Meyring, Walden, Colorado_

 3 hard-cooked eggs, chopped
 1/2 cup chopped green pepper
 1/4 cup mayonnaise _or_ salad dressing
 2 tablespoons chopped red onion
 1/2 teaspoon lemon juice
 1/8 teaspoon salt
 1/8 teaspoon pepper
 8 slices whole wheat bread
 1 small cucumber, thinly sliced
Lettuce leaves

In a bowl, combine the eggs, green pepper, mayonnaise, onion, lemon juice, salt and pepper. Spread on four slices of bread. Top with cucumber and lettuce. Top with remaining bread slices. **Yield:** 4 servings.

Potato-Leek Soup

This savory soup is a dish we especially enjoy for dinner on a cold night. Served with hot homemade bread or rolls, it's delicious. —_Patricia Wells, Riverhead, New York_

1-1/2 cups sliced leeks _or_ green onions
 1/2 cup butter _or_ margarine, _divided_
 5 cups cubed peeled potatoes
 3/4 cup chopped celery
1-1/3 cups cubed carrots
 2 teaspoons salt, _divided_
 2 cups water
 4 tablespoons all-purpose flour
 1/4 teaspoon pepper
 4 cups milk
 2 chicken bouillon cubes

In a large Dutch oven, saute leeks in 1/4 cup butter until tender. Add potatoes, celery, carrots, 1 teaspoon salt and water; cover and simmer for 20-25 minutes or until vegetables are tender. Meanwhile, in a medium saucepan, melt remaining butter. Add flour, pepper and remaining salt; cook until smooth and bubbly. Gradually add milk and bouillon; cook and stir until mixture thickens. Stir into vegetables. Simmer, stirring occasionally, until heated through. **Yield:** 6-8 servings (about 2 quarts).

— 🥄 🥄 🥄 —

'I Wish I Had That Recipe...'

OFTEN a dish that sounds quite unusual turns out to be delicious. Such is the case with the specialty soup from S'ghetti's Inn at Orchard Heights!

"Dill pickles are one of my favorite foods, and we have a restaurant here in Salem, Oregon that makes a great creamy Dill Pickle Soup," says Nancy Ross. "I'd love to make this soup in my own kitchen."

"Dill Pickle Soup is made from a century-old Swiss recipe," relates restaurant owner Lois Mason. "Traditionally a winter soup, we serve it year-round because of customer demand."

Overlooking the Cascade Mountains at 695 Orchard Heights Rd. NW is where you'll find S'ghetti's Inn at Orchard Heights in Salem. Lunch and dinner are served Monday through Sunday. Phone 1-503/378-1780.

Dill Pickle Soup

    1 cup butter *or* margarine
  1/2 cup all-purpose flour
1-1/2 quarts chicken broth
   12 ounces dill pickles, shredded *or* finely
        chopped (about 1-1/2 cups)
    1 cup white wine *or* additional chicken
        broth
  1/2 medium onion, finely chopped
    3 tablespoons sugar
    2 tablespoons vinegar
    1 tablespoon Worcestershire sauce
    3 to 4 garlic cloves, minced
    2 teaspoons salt
    1 teaspoon dill weed
    1 teaspoon curry powder
  1/2 teaspoon white pepper
    2 bay leaves
    2 cups warm milk
Dash green food coloring, optional
Croutons, optional

In a large kettle, melt butter. Add flour; cook and stir until bubbly. Gradually add broth. Add the next 12 ingredients; bring to a boil over medium heat. Reduce the heat; add milk. Remove bay leaves. Add food coloring and garnish with croutons if desired. **Yield:** 8-10 servings (2 quarts).

— 🥄 🥄 🥄 —

Cream Soup Mix

This easy-to-make soup mix is great to keep on hand for those nights you need to whip up a satisfying supper in a hurry. It's a great substitute for canned cream soup in a recipe. Or, add leftover chicken, asparagus or mushrooms, for example, and you'll have a steaming bowl of delicious soup in minutes.
—Kay Beard, Vass, North Carolina

☑ Uses less fat, sugar or salt. Includes Nutritional Analysis and Diabetic Exchanges.

    2 cups instant nonfat dry milk powder
  3/4 cup cornstarch
  1/4 cup low-sodium chicken bouillon granules
    1 teaspoon onion powder
  1/2 teaspoon dried thyme
  1/2 teaspoon dried basil
  1/4 teaspoon pepper

Combine all ingredients; mix well. Store in an airtight container. **Yield:** 3 cups dry mix. **Nutritional Analysis:** 1/3 cup of mix equals 149 calories, 168 mg sodium, 5 mg cholesterol, 25 gm carbohydrate, 10 gm protein, 1 gm fat. **Diabetic Exchanges:** 1 skim milk, 1 starch. **For a condensed cream soup substitute:** Blend 1/3 cup mix and 1-1/4 cups water in a 1-qt. saucepan or microwave-safe dish until smooth. Bring to boil or microwave for 2-1/2 to 3 minutes. Stir occasionally; cool. Use as a substitute for one 10-3/4-ounce can condensed cream of chicken, celery or mushroom soup. **For 1-1/2 cups soup:** Blend 1/3 cup mix and 1-1/2 cups water in 1-1/2-qt. saucepan or microwave-safe dish until smooth. Boil or microwave for 3 to 3-1/2 minutes. Stir occasionally.

— 🥄 🥄 🥄 —

Sausage Lentil Soup

I like to serve this hearty soup with slices of oven-fresh sourdough bread for a complete meal. The addition of lentils makes this soup a little different from others. They pair perfectly with the Italian sausage.
—Kathy Anderson, Casper, Wyoming

  1/2 pound bulk Italian sausage
    1 large onion, chopped
    1 medium green pepper, chopped
    1 large carrot, chopped
    2 cans (10-1/2 ounces *each*) chicken broth
    1 can (14-1/2 ounces) diced tomatoes,
        undrained
    1 cup water
    1 garlic clove, minced
    1 teaspoon salt
  1/2 teaspoon pepper
  3/4 cup dry lentils, rinsed

In a Dutch oven or soup kettle, brown and crumble sausage; drain. Add next nine ingredients; bring to a boil. Add lentils. Reduce heat; cover and simmer for 60-70 minutes or until the lentils are tender. **Yield:** 6-8 servings (2 quarts).

A Lesson in Lentils

Store dry lentils in an airtight container for up to 1 year. They stay fresh in the freezer indefinitely.

Unlike dry beans, lentils don't need to be soaked before cooking. But before using, you should put them in a colander, rinse and pick out any broken lentils or any debris.

Nutty Tuna Sandwiches

Here's a fresh-tasting sandwich that'll spark up a lunch. Chopped salted peanuts and ranch dressing add an unexpected twist to traditional tuna salad.
—*Cheryl Miller, Fort Collins, Colorado*

    1 can (6-1/8 ounces) tuna, drained and
       flaked
    1 hard-cooked egg, chopped
    1 green onion, sliced
1/4 cup chopped salted peanuts
1/4 cup ranch salad dressing
    2 teaspoons lemon juice
    2 whole wheat pita breads, halved
    4 lettuce leaves

In a bowl, combine the tuna, egg, onion, peanuts, dressing and lemon juice. Line each pita half with a lettuce leaf; stuff with tuna mixture. **Yield:** 2-4 servings.

Savory Cheese Soup

(Pictured at right and on page 38)

This delicious soup recipe was shared by a friend and instantly became a hit with my husband. Its big cheese flavor blends wonderfully with the flavor of the vegetables. I first served this creamy soup as part of a holiday meal, but now we enjoy it throughout the year.
—*Dee Falk, Stromsburg, Nebraska*

1/4 cup chopped onion
    3 tablespoons butter *or* margarine
1/4 cup all-purpose flour
1/4 teaspoon salt
1/8 teaspoon pepper

1/8 teaspoon garlic powder
    2 cups milk
    1 can (14-1/2 ounces) chicken broth
1/2 cup shredded carrots
1/2 cup finely chopped celery
1-1/2 cups (6 ounces) shredded cheddar cheese
  3/4 cup shredded mozzarella cheese
Fresh *or* dried chives, optional

In a large saucepan, saute onion in butter until tender. Add flour, salt, pepper and garlic powder; stir until smooth. Gradually add milk; cook and stir over medium heat until thickened and bubbly. Meanwhile, bring chicken broth to a boil in a small saucepan. Add carrots and celery; simmer for 5 minutes or until vegetables are tender. Add to milk mixture and stir until blended. Add cheeses. Cook and stir until melted (do not boil). Garnish with chives if desired. **Yield:** about 4 servings.

1 cup half-and-half cream

In a 3-qt. saucepan, cook the bacon until crisp. Remove bacon and set aside; discard all but 2 tablespoons of drippings. Saute onion and celery in drippings until tender. Add the next eight ingredients. Simmer until vegetables are tender, about 30 minutes. Add fish and bacon; simmer for 5 minutes or just until fish flakes with a fork. Add cream and heat through. **Yield:** 4-6 servings.

— ☕ ☕ ☕ —

Scrumptious Turkey Sandwich

Here's a great way to use leftovers from a holiday turkey dinner. Cranberry sauce and cream cheese make each bite flavorful. And alfalfa sprouts add a little crunch. —Linda Nilsen, Anoka, Minnesota

2 tablespoons jellied cranberry sauce
2 slices whole wheat bread
2 thin slices cooked turkey
1/3 cup alfalfa sprouts
2 tablespoons softened cream cheese

Spread cranberry sauce on one slice of bread; top with turkey and alfalfa sprouts. Spread cream cheese on the other slice of bread and place over sprouts. **Yield:** 1 serving.

— ☕ ☕ ☕ —

Creamy Vegetable Soup

I like to experiment with new low-fat recipes. This creamy, good-for-you soup is loaded with vegetables and never fails to satisfy. —Rita Zagrzebski
Eagle River, Wisconsin

✓ Uses less fat, sugar or salt. Includes Nutritional Analysis and Diabetic Exchanges.

3 cans (16 ounces *each*) low-sodium chicken broth
4 carrots, chopped
2 medium unpeeled potatoes, chopped
2 medium onions, chopped
1/2 cup uncooked brown rice
8 cups coarsely chopped fresh broccoli
8 cups coarsely chopped fresh cauliflower
4 cups skim milk
1/4 teaspoon pepper

In a large kettle, combine broth, carrots, potatoes, onions and rice; cover and bring to a boil. Reduce heat; simmer for 20 minutes. Add broccoli and cauliflower; simmer for 20 minutes or until the vegetables are tender. Cool slightly. Puree half of the mixture in a blender or food processor; return to kettle. Add milk and pepper; mix well. Heat

Panfish Chowder

(Pictured above and on page 38)

With my husband being an avid hunter and fisherman, I can never have enough new fish and wild game recipes. We especially enjoy this rich chowder. It's a hearty dish with big chunks of fish, potatoes and bacon in a tempting creamy broth. —Cyndi Fliss
Bevent, Wisconsin

6 bacon strips, cut into 1-inch pieces
2/3 cup chopped onion
1/2 cup chopped celery
3 medium potatoes, peeled and cubed
2 cups water
1/2 cup chopped carrots
2 tablespoons minced fresh parsley
1 tablespoon lemon juice
1/2 teaspoon dill weed
1/4 teaspoon garlic salt
1/8 teaspoon pepper
1 pound panfish fillets (perch, sunfish *or* crappie), cut into 1-inch chunks

through (do not boil). **Yield:** 16 servings (4-1/2 quarts). **Nutritional Analysis:** One serving equals 105 calories, 83 mg sodium, 1 mg cholesterol, 17 gm carbohydrate, 6 gm protein, 1 gm fat. **Diabetic Exchanges:** 1 vegetable, 1/2 starch, 1/2 skim milk.

Dandelion Soup

I like to use dandelion greens in many recipes. With hearty meatballs in a wonderful chicken broth, this dish is dandy for the entire family.
—Dorothy Collins, Decatur, Illinois

    2 quarts chicken broth
    1 teaspoon dried oregano
    1 teaspoon dried basil
    1 teaspoon garlic powder
    8 cups loosely packed dandelion greens *or* fresh spinach
    1 egg
    3 tablespoons grated Parmesan cheese
    2 tablespoons sour cream
    2 tablespoons bread crumbs
    2 tablespoons finely chopped fresh parsley
    1 tablespoon finely chopped onion
  1/4 teaspoon salt
  1/8 teaspoon pepper
  1/8 teaspoon ground nutmeg
    1 pound mixed ground meat (beef, veal and pork)

In a large saucepan, combine broth, oregano, basil and garlic powder; bring to a boil. Add the dandelion greens and cook until tender, about 5-10 minutes. Meanwhile, combine next nine ingredients; add ground meat. Mix well; shape into 1/2-in. meatballs. Add to soup. Cook over medium-low for 10 minutes or until the meatballs are done. Serve immediately. **Yield:** 6-8 servings (2-1/2 quarts). **Editor's Note:** When harvesting leaves from dandelions, be sure the dandelions have not been treated with chemicals.

Just Dandy

Dandelion leaves are most tender and flavorful in early spring, before the first flower buds appear. Wash dandelion greens carefully to remove insects and soil from the undersides of the leaves.

Lemon can help mellow the hint of bitterness common in dandelion greens, which may be used as a substitute in recipes calling for chicory, arugula, escarole or curly endive.

French Onion Soup

(Pictured below)

Our daughter, Heather, and I enjoy spending time together cooking, but our days are busy, so we appreciate quick and tasty recipes like this one. Hot and delicious, this soup hits the spot for lunch or dinner.
—Sandra Chambers, Carthage, Mississippi

    4 cups thinly sliced onions
    1 garlic clove, minced
  1/4 cup butter *or* margarine
    6 cups water
    8 beef bouillon cubes
    1 teaspoon Worcestershire sauce
    6 slices French bread (3/4 inch thick), buttered and toasted
    6 slices Swiss cheese

In a large covered saucepan, cook onions and garlic in butter over medium-low heat for 8-10 minutes or until tender and golden, stirring occasionally. Add water, bouillon and Worcestershire sauce; bring to a boil. Reduce heat; cover and simmer for 30 minutes. Ladle hot soup into six ovenproof bowls. Top each with a piece of French bread. Cut each slice of cheese in half and place over the bread. Broil until cheese is melted. Serve immediately. **Yield:** 6 servings.

Simmer a Hearty Soup With Homemade Flavor

SATISFYING SOUPS from these family-approved recipes can provide new tastes for your tureen, set mugs a-steaming or spark a lunch to go.

— 🥄 🥄 🥄 —

Vegetable Beef Soup

(Pictured below)

When we come in from playing in the snow, I serve this hearty soup. I don't spend time slicing and dicing because the recipe calls for a bag of frozen mixed vegetables.   —Nancy Soderstrom, Roseville, Minnesota

1 beef chuck roast (2-1/2 to 3 pounds)

4 quarts water
1 cup medium pearl barley
1-1/2 cups chopped onion
1-1/2 cups chopped celery
1 tablespoon salt
1 teaspoon pepper
1 can (28 ounces) diced tomatoes, undrained
1-1/2 cups chopped carrots
1 package (16 ounces) frozen mixed vegetables
1/4 cup minced fresh parsley
1/2 teaspoon dried basil
1/4 teaspoon dried thyme
1/4 teaspoon garlic salt

SOUP'S ON! For a great start to a meal or as a simple supper by itself, ladle up Best Broccoli, Golden Vegetable and Vegetable Beef Soups (shown above, clockwise from upper right).

Place roast in a large Dutch oven or soup kettle. Add water, barley, onion, celery, salt and pepper; bring to a boil. Reduce heat; cover and simmer for 1 hour and 15 minutes or until meat is tender. Remove meat; cool. Cut into bite-size pieces. Skim fat from broth. Add beef and remaining ingredients; bring to a boil. Reduce heat; cover and simmer for 45 minutes or until vegetables are tender. **Yield:** 15-20 servings (6 quarts).

— 🍲 🍲 🍲 —

Golden Vegetable Soup

(Pictured below left)

This blended soup makes a great first course for a special meal. The vegetables are pureed, so finicky eaters will never know how nutritious this dish is!
—*Valerie Jones, Portland, Maine*

☑ Uses less fat, sugar or salt. Includes Nutritional Analysis and Diabetic Exchanges.

    3 cups thinly sliced carrots
    1 cup chopped onion
  2/3 cup chopped celery
1-1/2 cups diced peeled potatoes
    1 garlic clove, minced
  1/2 teaspoon sugar
    2 teaspoons vegetable oil
    4 cups chicken broth
Dash ground nutmeg
Pepper to taste

In a Dutch oven or soup kettle over medium-low heat, saute carrots, onion, celery, potatoes, garlic and sugar in oil for 5 minutes. Add broth, nutmeg and pepper; bring to a boil. Reduce heat; cover and simmer for 30-40 minutes or until vegetables are tender. Remove from the heat and cool to room temperature. Puree in batches in a blender or food processor. Return to the kettle and heat through. **Yield:** 4 servings (1-1/2 quarts). **Nutritional Analysis:** One serving (prepared with low-sodium chicken broth) equals 136 calories, 116 mg sodium, 0 cholesterol, 23 gm carbohydrate, 5 gm protein, 3 gm fat. **Diabetic Exchanges:** 2 vegetable, 1 starch, 1/2 fat.

— 🍲 🍲 🍲 —

Best Broccoli Soup

(Pictured at left)

I'm always looking for ways to work broccoli into my family's diet. Here's a creamy combination that showcases that versatile vegetable. —*Carolyn Weinberg Custer, Montana*

    2 cups water
    4 cups chopped fresh broccoli
    1 cup chopped celery
    1 cup chopped carrots
  1/2 cup chopped onion
    6 tablespoons butter *or* margarine
    6 tablespoons all-purpose flour
    3 cups chicken broth
    2 cups milk
    1 tablespoon minced fresh parsley
    1 teaspoon onion salt
  1/2 teaspoon garlic powder
  1/2 teaspoon salt

In a Dutch oven or soup kettle, bring water to a boil. Add the broccoli, celery and carrots; boil 2-3 minutes. Drain; set vegetables aside. In the same kettle, saute onion in butter until tender. Stir in flour to form a smooth paste. Gradually add the broth and milk, stirring constantly. Bring to a boil; boil and stir for 1 minute. Add the vegetables, parsley, onion salt, garlic powder and salt. Reduce heat; cover and simmer for 30-40 minutes or until vegetables are tender. **Yield:** 6-8 servings (2 quarts).

— 🍲 🍲 🍲 —

Spinach Garlic Soup

During the years I owned and operated a deli, this was one of the most popular soups I served. It's an unusual cream soup using splendid spinach.
—*Marilyn Paradis, Woodburn, Oregon*

    1 package (10 ounces) fresh spinach,
      trimmed and coarsely chopped
    4 cups chicken broth
  1/2 cup shredded carrots
  1/2 cup chopped onion
    8 garlic cloves, minced
  1/3 cup butter *or* margarine
  1/4 cup all-purpose flour
  3/4 cup whipping cream
  1/4 cup milk
  1/2 teaspoon pepper
  1/8 teaspoon ground nutmeg

In a 5-qt. Dutch oven, bring spinach, broth and carrots to a boil. Reduce heat; simmer 5 minutes, stirring occasionally. Remove from the heat; cool to lukewarm. Meanwhile, in a skillet, saute onion and garlic in butter until onion is tender, about 5-10 minutes. Add flour; cook and stir over low heat for 3-5 minutes. Add to spinach mixture. Puree in small batches in a blender or food processor until finely chopped. Place in a large saucepan. Add cream, milk, pepper and nutmeg; heat through but do not boil. **Yield:** 4-6 servings.

Creamy Corn Chowder

(Pictured above)

Corn really stars in this delectable recipe—it hits the spot whenever you crave a rich, hearty soup. I make it each year for a luncheon at our church's flea market, where it's always a big seller. —Carol Sundquist
Rochester, New York

    2 chicken bouillon cubes
    1 cup hot water
    5 bacon strips
    1 cup chopped green pepper
1/2 cup chopped onion
1/4 cup all-purpose flour
    3 cups milk
1-1/2 cups fresh *or* frozen whole kernel corn
    1 can (14-3/4 ounces) cream-style corn
1-1/2 teaspoons seasoned salt
1/4 teaspoon salt
1/8 teaspoon white pepper
1/8 teaspoon dried basil

Dissolve bouillon in water; set aside. In a 5-qt. Dutch oven, cook bacon until crisp. Remove bacon; crumble and set aside. In the drippings, saute green pepper and onion until tender. Add flour; cook and stir until bubbly. Cook 1 minute longer. Gradually stir in milk and dissolved bouillon; bring to a boil. Reduce heat; cook and stir until thickened. Add corn and seasonings. Cook for 10 minutes or until heated through. Sprinkle with bacon. **Yield:** 6-8 servings (2 quarts).

Beef Noodle Soup

Folks will think you had this soup simmering all day. But quick-cooking ground beef and convenient canned broth and vegetables make it a meal in minutes.
—Margery Bryan, Royal City, Washington

    1 pound ground beef
1/2 cup chopped onion
    2 cans (14-1/2 ounces *each*) Italian stewed tomatoes
    2 cans (10-1/2 ounces *each*) beef broth
    1 can (16 ounces) mixed vegetables, drained
    1 teaspoon dried oregano
1/2 teaspoon salt
1/4 teaspoon pepper
    1 cup uncooked medium egg noodles

In a Dutch oven or soup kettle, brown beef and onion; drain. Add tomatoes, broth, vegetables and seasonings. Bring to a boil; add noodles. Reduce heat to medium-low; cover and cook for 10-15 minutes or until the noodles are done. **Yield:** 6-8 servings (2 quarts).

Cajun Chili

Cajun cooking is one of my specialties. For a meaty meal with a little zip, this is the recipe I reach for. I think you'll enjoy every bite. —James Harris
Columbus, Georgia

    2 pounds ground beef
    1 cup chopped onion
    1 cup chopped green pepper
    1 garlic clove, minced
    1 can (15 ounces) pinto beans, undrained
    1 can (14-1/2 ounces) diced tomatoes, undrained
    1 can (8 ounces) tomato sauce
    1 to 2 tablespoons chili powder
    1 tablespoon honey
    1 teaspoon dried parsley flakes
    1 teaspoon dried oregano
    1 teaspoon ground cumin
    1 teaspoon Cajun seasoning

In a Dutch oven, brown beef with onion, green pepper and garlic. Meanwhile, in a blender or food processor, process beans with liquid until smooth. Drain fat from Dutch oven; add the beans and remaining ingredients. Simmer, uncovered, for 35-45 minutes. **Yield:** 6 servings.

Toasted Turkey Sandwiches

(Pictured at right)

With a special cranberry sauce, these sandwiches

make a yummy supper. I often add a slice of American or cheddar cheese to the sandwiches for another flavor.   —Patricia Kile, Greentown, Pennsylvania

12 slices buttered French bread (1/2 inch thick)
 6 thin slices cooked turkey
 6 thin slices fully cooked ham
 2 eggs, lightly beaten
1/2 cup milk
 2 tablespoons butter *or* margarine
1/2 cup mayonnaise *or* salad dressing
1/3 cup whole-berry cranberry sauce

Make six sandwiches, dividing turkey and ham evenly between bread. In a shallow bowl, beat eggs and milk. Dip sandwiches, turning to coat both sides. In a large skillet over medium heat, melt butter. Brown sandwiches on both sides. Combine the mayonnaise and cranberry sauce; mix well. Serve with sandwiches. **Yield:** 6 servings.

Basic Turkey Soup

(Pictured below)

I simmer a rich broth using the turkey carcass, than add favorite vegetables and sometimes noodles. This soup really warms you up on a cold winter day.
—Katie Koziolek, Hartland, Minnesota

TURKEY BROTH:
 1 leftover turkey carcass
 2 quarts water
 1 chicken bouillon cube
 1 celery rib with leaves
 1 small onion, halved
 1 carrot
 3 whole peppercorns
 1 garlic clove
 1 teaspoon seasoned salt
1/4 teaspoon dried thyme
TURKEY VEGETABLE SOUP:
 8 cups turkey broth
 2 chicken bouillon cubes
1/2 to 3/4 teaspoon pepper
 4 cups sliced carrots, celery *and/or* other vegetables
3/4 cup chopped onion
 4 cups diced cooked turkey

Place all broth ingredients in a large soup kettle; cover and bring to a boil. Reduce heat; simmer for 25 minutes. Strain broth; discard bones and vegetables. Cool; skim fat. Use immediately for turkey vegetable soup or refrigerate and use within 24 hours. For soup, combine broth, bouillon, pepper, vegetables and onion in a large soup kettle. Cover and simmer for 15-20 minutes or until the vegetables are tender. Add turkey and heat through. **Yield:** 8-10 servings.

GIVE TURKEY LEFTOVERS more meal appeal with Toasted Turkey Sandwiches and Basic Turkey Soup (shown above).

Turtle Soup

(Pictured below)

This hearty soup has a real "snappy" flavor from the cayenne pepper and lemon juice. It's a treat and good use of turtle meat. With a salad and fresh bread, a steaming bowlful makes a nice meal. —Dave Wood
Elmwood Park, New Jersey

```
1-1/3  pounds turtle meat
4-1/2  cups water
    2  medium onions
    1  bay leaf
  1/4  teaspoon cayenne pepper
1-1/4  teaspoons salt
    5  tablespoons butter or margarine
  1/3  cup all-purpose flour
    3  tablespoons tomato puree
    3  tablespoons Worcestershire sauce
  1/3  cup chicken broth
    2  hard-cooked eggs, chopped
  1/4  cup lemon juice
```
Chopped fresh parsley, optional

In a heavy 4-qt. saucepan, bring turtle meat and water to a boil. Skim off foam. Chop 1 onion and set aside. Quarter the other onion; add to saucepan along with bay leaf, cayenne pepper and salt. Cover and simmer for 2 hours or until the meat is tender. Remove meat with a slotted spoon and cut into 1/2-in. cubes; set aside. Strain broth and set aside. Rinse and dry saucepan; melt butter over medium-high heat. Cook chopped onion until tender. Add flour; cook and stir until bubbly and light-

ly browned. Whisk in reserved broth; cook and stir until thickened. Reduce heat; stir in tomato puree and Worcestershire sauce. Simmer, uncovered, for 10 minutes. Add chicken broth, eggs, lemon juice and meat. Simmer for 5 minutes or until heated through. Garnish with parsley if desired. **Yield:** 4-6 servings.

Lunch Box Special

Dates, oranges and apples bring a refreshing zest and crunch to a plain old peanut butter sandwich. Kids of all ages enjoy this. —Bernice Morris
Marshfield, Missouri

```
1/2  cup peanut butter
1/4  cup orange juice
1/2  cup finely chopped apples
1/2  cup finely chopped dates
1/2  cup chopped walnuts, optional
  8  slices bread
```

In a bowl, mix the peanut butter and orange juice until smooth. Add apples, dates and walnuts if desired. Spread on four slices of bread; top with remaining bread. **Yield:** 4 servings.

Harvest Chicken Soup

I like reading cookbooks and finding new twists to traditional recipes. This hearty soup is made with a colorful and tasty mix of vegetables and avocados. Spending time in the kitchen has kept me busy after retiring some years ago. —Bob Crabb, Scio, Oregon

```
  3  medium onions
  3  bone-in chicken breast halves, skinned
  4  cups water
  3  celery ribs, halved
  1  teaspoon salt
1/8  teaspoon pepper
  1  can (14-1/2 ounces) diced tomatoes,
       undrained
  3  medium carrots, thinly sliced
  4  teaspoons chicken bouillon granules
  1  small zucchini, halved and thinly sliced
  1  cup frozen peas
  1  avocado, peeled and sliced
```

Chop one onion; set aside. Quarter the other two; place in a Dutch oven with chicken, water, celery, salt and pepper. Cover and simmer for 2 hours or until chicken is tender. Remove chicken; set aside. Discard celery and onion. To broth, add the tomatoes, carrots, bouillon and chopped onion. Cover

and simmer for 30 minutes or until the carrots are tender. Debone and cube chicken; add to soup with zucchini and peas. Cover and simmer for 10 minutes or until zucchini is tender. Spoon into bowls. Garnish with avocado. **Yield:** 8-10 servings (2-1/4 quarts).

—— 🍵 🍵 🍵 ——

Zesty Sloppy Joes

(Pictured above and on page 38)

For a big family gathering, these sandwiches are a hit. I have never served them without getting recipe requests. A fantastic blend of seasonings in a hearty sandwich means no one can eat just one.
> —Sandy Abrams, Greenville, New York

    4 pounds ground beef
    1 cup chopped onion
    1 cup finely chopped green pepper
    2 cans (10-3/4 ounces *each*) condensed
      tomato soup, undiluted
    1 can (15 ounces) thick and zesty tomato
      sauce
    1 can (8 ounces) tomato sauce
  3/4 cup packed brown sugar
  1/4 cup ketchup
    3 tablespoons Worcestershire sauce
    1 tablespoon prepared mustard
    1 tablespoon ground mustard
    1 teaspoon chili powder
    1 teaspoon garlic salt
   20 to 25 hamburger buns

In a large saucepan or Dutch oven over medium heat, brown beef and onion. Add green pepper. Cook and stir for 5 minutes; drain. Add the next 10 ingredients; bring to a boil. Reduce heat; cover and simmer for 1 hour, stirring occasionally. Serve on buns. **Yield:** 20-25 servings.

Fast Sandwich Filling

The next time you have leftovers after serving barbecue sandwiches or sloppy joes, try this handy trick. Line a muffin tin with paper cupcake liners, fill each with leftover meat and freeze in the pan. When solid, place the individual servings in a freezer bag and store them in the freezer. For a quick sandwich, heat one filled cupcake liner in the microwave and spread filling on bread or a bun.

Chase Away Chills with Chili

A POT of hearty chili is always welcome during winter weather. Next time you're thinking of simmering some, sample these savory suggestions. As an added bonus, all of these sure-to-satisfy dishes contain less fat, sugar or salt.

— 🍷 🍷 🍷 —

Zesty Steak Chili

(Pictured below and on page 38)

This full-flavored, medium-hot, Texas-style chili tastes even better the second day. That's a real plus when you have a hectic day ahead of you. This is a nice change from typical chili made with ordinary ground beef.
—*Michelle Smith, Running Springs, California*

☑ Uses less fat, sugar or salt. Includes Nutritional Analysis and Diabetic Exchanges.

4 **pounds round steak, cut into 1-inch cubes**
4 **garlic cloves, minced**
1/4 **cup vegetable oil**
3 **cups chopped onion**
2-3/4 **cups water,** *divided*
2 **cups sliced celery**
3 **cans (14-1/2 ounces** *each***) diced tomatoes, undrained**
2 **cans (15 ounces** *each***) tomato sauce**
1 **jar (16 ounces) salsa**
3 **tablespoons chili powder**
2 **teaspoons ground cumin**
2 **teaspoons dried oregano**
1 **teaspoon salt, optional**

CHEERS FOR CHILI. Ladle up friends and family steaming bowls of Zesty Steak Chili, White Chili and Confetti Bean Chili (shown above, top to bottom).

1 teaspoon pepper
1/4 cup all-purpose flour
1/4 cup yellow cornmeal
**Shredded cheddar cheese, sour cream, sliced
    green onions and sliced ripe olives, optional**

In a Dutch oven over medium-high heat, saute steak and garlic in oil until browned. Add onion; cook and stir for 5 minutes. Stir in 2 cups water and next nine ingredients; bring to a boil. Reduce heat; cover and simmer 2 hours or until tender. Combine flour, cornmeal and remaining water; stir until smooth. Bring chili to a boil. Add flour mixture; cook and stir 2 minutes or until thickened. Garnish with cheese, sour cream, onions and olives. **Yield:** 20 servings. **Nutritional Analysis:** One 1-cup serving (prepared with no-salt-added tomato sauce and without additional salt; served without cheese, sour cream, onions and olives) equals 187 calories, 155 mg sodium, 44 mg cholesterol, 13 gm carbohydrate, 19 gm protein, 7 gm fat. **Diabetic Exchanges:** 2 meat, 2 vegetable.

— ▽ ▽ ▽ —

White Chili

(Pictured at left)

This recipe was given to me by a friend who got it from another friend. The day after I served it to company, someone called for the recipe, too! —*Karen Gardiner Eutaw, Alabama*

☑ Uses less fat, sugar or salt. Includes Nutritional Analysis and Diabetic Exchanges.

  2 pounds dried great northern beans
1-1/2 cups diced onion
  1 tablespoon vegetable oil
  1 tablespoon dried oregano
  2 teaspoons ground cumin
1-1/2 teaspoons seasoned salt
  1/2 teaspoon cayenne pepper
4-1/2 quarts chicken broth
  2 garlic cloves, minced
  8 boneless skinless chicken breast halves,
    cubed
  2 cans (4 ounces *each*) chopped green
    chilies

Place beans in a saucepan; cover with water and bring to a boil. Boil 2 minutes. Remove from heat. Soak 1 hour; drain and rinse. In a 5-qt. Dutch oven, saute onion in oil until tender. Combine seasonings; add half to Dutch oven. Saute 1 minute. Add beans, broth and garlic; bring to a boil. Reduce heat; simmer 2 hours. Coat chicken with remaining seasoning mixture; place in a 15-in. x 10-in. x 1-in. baking pan. Bake at 350° for 15 minutes or

until juices run clear; add to beans. Stir in chilies. Simmer 1-1/2 to 2 hours. **Yield:** 20 servings. **Nutritional Analysis:** One 1-cup serving (prepared with low-sodium broth) equals 169 calories, 365 mg sodium, 29 mg cholesterol, 17 gm carbohydrate, 18 gm protein, 3 gm fat. **Diabetic Exchanges:** 2 lean meat, 1 starch.

— ▽ ▽ ▽ —

Confetti Bean Chili

(Pictured below far left)

A medley of vegetables and beans adds color and appeal to the recipe. It's a tasty way to get more vegetables into your diet. —*Kathleen Drott Pineville, Louisiana*

☑ Uses less fat, sugar or salt. Includes Nutritional Analysis and Diabetic Exchanges.

  1 large onion, chopped
  2 cans (14-1/2 ounces *each*) chicken broth
  2 garlic cloves, minced
  3 tablespoons chili powder
1-1/2 teaspoons ground cumin
  1/2 teaspoon dried oregano
  1 pound carrots, sliced
  1 pound red potatoes, cubed
  2 cans (14-1/2 ounces *each*) diced
    tomatoes, undrained *or* 3 cups diced fresh
    tomatoes
  1 can (15 ounces) black beans, rinsed and
    drained
  1 can (16 ounces) kidney beans, rinsed and
    drained
  1 can (15 ounces) garbanzo beans, rinsed
    and drained
2-1/2 cups water

In a Dutch oven, simmer onion in broth for 5 minutes. Add garlic, chili poder, cumin, oregano, carrots and potatoes; bring to a boil. Reduce heat. Cover; simmer 10 minutes. Add remaining ingredients. Cover; simmer 20 minutes. **Yield:** 12 servings. **Nutritional Analysis:** One 1-cup serving (prepared with low-sodium broth and fresh tomatoes) equals 178 calories, 456 mg sodium, 0 cholesterol, 34 gm carbohydrate, 9 gm protein, 1 gm fat. **Diabetic Exchanges:** 2 starch, 1 vegetable.

Leftover Chili?

When you have leftover chili, don't fret! Chili freezes well. So pop some in the freezer for a fast meal later. Chili also tastes great over cooked pasta, hamburgers, hot dogs or baked potatoes.

Vegetable Beef Chili

This chili is big on tomato taste. When I know I have a busy day ahead of me, I brown and drain the ground beef and then combine all the ingredients in a slow cooker. —Marlene Muckenhirn, Delano, Minnesota

   1 pound ground beef
   6 medium tomatoes, cubed
   2 medium green peppers, chopped
   2 medium onions, chopped
   3 garlic cloves, minced
   1 can (16 ounces) kidney beans, rinsed and drained
   1 can (15-1/2 ounces) chili beans, undrained
   3 tablespoons chili powder
1-1/2 teaspoons salt
 1/2 teaspoon ground turmeric
 1/2 teaspoon Italian seasoning
 1/2 teaspoon ground cumin

In a 5-qt. Dutch oven or saucepan, brown beef; drain. Add tomatoes, green peppers, onions and garlic. Cook over medium-low heat, stirring occasionally, for 20-30 minutes or until vegetables are tender. Add beans and seasonings; mix well. Simmer, uncovered, for 45-50 minutes or until thickened, stirring occasionally. **Yield:** 8-10 servings.

— 🥄 🥄 🥄 —

Corn Dogs

(Pictured below and on page 38)

This recipe makes it easy to prepare corn dogs at home just like those at the fair. Both kids and grown-ups will like this hearty snack. —Ruby Williams
Bogalusa, Louisiana

 3/4 cup yellow cornmeal
 3/4 cup self-rising flour*
   1 egg, beaten
 2/3 cup milk
 10 small wooden sticks
 10 hot dogs
Oil for deep-fat frying

In a bowl, combine cornmeal, flour and egg; mix well. Stir in milk to make a thick batter; let stand 4 minutes. Insert sticks into hot dogs; dip in batter. Heat oil to 375°. Fry corn dogs until golden brown, about 5-6 minutes. Drain on paper towel. **Yield:** 10 servings. ***Editor's Note:** As a substitute for self-rising flour, place 1 teaspoon baking powder and 1/4 teaspoon salt in a measuring cup. Add enough all-purpose flour to equal 3/4 cup.

— 🥄 🥄 🥄 —

Creamy Squash Soup

This smooth, full-flavored soup uses whatever winter squash is available. Serve steaming bowls with rolls, fruit and cheese for a complete meal. —Gayle Lewis
Yucaipa, California

 3 bacon strips
 1 cup finely chopped onion
 2 garlic cloves, minced
 2 cups mashed cooked winter squash
 2 tablespoons all-purpose flour
 1 can (12 ounces) evaporated milk, *divided*
 3 cups chicken broth
1/2 teaspoon curry powder
1/2 teaspoon salt
1/4 teaspoon pepper
1/8 teaspoon ground nutmeg
Sour cream, optional

In a saucepan or Dutch oven, cook bacon until crisp; crumble and set aside. Drain all but 1 tablespoon drippings; saute onion and garlic in drippings until tender. In a blender or food processor, puree squash, flour, 1/3 cup milk and onion mixture; add to pan. Add broth, curry powder, salt, pepper, nutmeg and remaining milk; bring to a boil over medium heat. Boil for 2 minutes. Top servings with a dollop of sour cream if desired. Sprinkle with bacon. **Yield:** 6-8 servings.

Cool Cucumber Sandwich

This is one of my favorite summertime sandwiches. It's refreshing and a great way to use crisp garden cucumbers sliced very thin. The recipe can be easily doubled. —Denise Baumert, Dalhart, Texas

  1 tablespoon ranch salad dressing
  2 slices bread, toasted
12 to 15 thin cucumber slices
  2 bacon strips, cooked
  1 tomato slice

Spread salad dressing on one side of each slice of toast. Layer cucumber, bacon and tomato on one slice; top with second slice. **Yield:** 1 serving.

Dandy Ham Sandwiches

These open-faced sandwiches make good use of leftover ham. I serve them for lunch and as an afternoon snack. —Mrs. Wallace Carlson
Two Harbors, Minnesota

    2 cups (8 ounces) shredded cheddar cheese
1-1/2 cups ground fully cooked ham
  1/2 cup finely chopped onion
  1/3 cup French salad dressing
    2 tablespoons prepared mustard
    4 teaspoons caraway seed
    5 hamburger buns, split

Combine the first six ingredients; mix well. Spread over cut side of buns. Place on a greased baking sheet. Bake at 350° for 15-20 minutes or until the cheese is melted. **Yield:** 10 sandwiches.

Spicy Pork Chili

(Pictured above right)

This zippy chili is a pleasant change from the traditional beef chili recipes I've tried. It tastes so good served with your garden-fresh steamed green beans,

sliced cucumbers and hot crusty bread. It's especially satisfying on a cold day. —Christine Hartry
Emo, Ontario

  1 pound ground pork
  2 large onions, chopped
  4 garlic cloves, minced
  1 medium sweet red pepper, chopped
  1 medium green pepper, chopped
  1 cup chopped celery
  2 cans (14-1/2 ounces *each*) diced
    tomatoes, undrained
  1 can (16 ounces) kidney beans, rinsed and
    drained
  1 can (6 ounces) tomato paste
3/4 cup water
  2 teaspoons brown sugar
  1 teaspoon dried oregano
  1 teaspoon chili powder
1/4 teaspoon crushed red pepper flakes
1/4 teaspoon cayenne pepper
Dash hot pepper sauce

In a Dutch oven, brown pork and onions until pork is no longer pink; drain. Stir in the garlic, peppers and celery; cook for 5 minutes. Add remaining ingredients; bring to a boil. Reduce heat; cover and simmer for 45 minutes. **Yield:** 6-8 servings (2-1/2 quarts).

Side Dishes

These country-style side dishes will add a little something special to everyday dinners and memorable meals.

COUNTRY COMPLEMENTS. Clockwise from upper left: Broccoli-Pasta Side Dish (p. 60), Vegetable Noodle Casserole (p. 64), Delicious Corn Pudding (p. 61), Garden Vegetable Medley (p. 63) and Herb-Buttered Corn (p. 58).

Herb-Buttered Corn

(Pictured above and on page 56)

New York is one of the nation's biggest sweet corn producers. So it's no wonder that husband Walt and I love fresh corn on the cob and also corn I've frozen. For a flavorful, different way to serve sweet corn, try this recipe. —Donna Smith, Victor, New York

    1/2 cup butter *or* margarine, softened
      1 tablespoon minced fresh chives
      1 tablespoon minced fresh dill
      1 tablespoon minced fresh parsley
    1/2 teaspoon dried thyme
    1/4 teaspoon salt
Dash garlic powder
Dash cayenne pepper
     10 ears fresh corn, husked and cooked

In a bowl, combine first eight ingredients; mix well. Spread over each ear of corn. **Yield:** 10 servings.

Far North Wild Rice Casserole

I find wild rice a very versatile ingredient to cook with. In this side dish, the rich flavor of this hearty grain combines beautifully with vegetables and bacon.
—Mina Dyck, Boissevain, Manitoba

      1 medium onion, chopped
      1 medium green pepper, chopped

    3/4 cup chopped celery
    1/2 pound sliced bacon, diced
    1/2 pound fresh mushrooms, sliced
      6 cups cooked wild rice
      1 cup frozen peas, optional
      1 to 2 tablespoons soy sauce
    1/4 teaspoon pepper

In a large skillet, cook onion, green pepper, celery and bacon until the vegetables are tender, about 3 minutes. Add mushrooms. Cook for 2 minutes; drain. Add the rice, peas if desired, soy sauce and pepper. Cook and stir gently over medium heat for 5 minutes. **Yield:** 10-12 servings.

Sweet Potato Balls

Before my husband quickly gobbled up two big help-ings of these balls after trying them at a holiday din-ner years ago, he never really cared for sweet potatoes. Now this festive side dish is a yearly tradition for us and many of our friends as well. —Tammy Neubauer
Ida Grove, Iowa

      2 cups mashed sweet potatoes
     12 large marshmallows
    3/4 cup finely crushed cornflakes
    1/2 cup packed brown sugar
      2 tablespoons milk
    1/4 cup butter *or* margarine

Mold a spoonful of the sweet potatoes around each marshmallow; roll in cornflake crumbs. Place in a shallow 1-1/2-qt. baking dish. In a saucepan, bring brown sugar, milk and butter to a boil; pour over the balls. Bake, uncovered, at 350° for 15 minutes. **Yield:** 1 dozen.

Four-Bean Casserole

This sweet, tangy side dish reminds me of the many zesty dishes I enjoyed while growing up in the South. Everyone loves the different blend of beans.
—*Bob Crabb, Scio, Oregon*

    1 **can (16 ounces) pork and beans, undrained**
    1 **can (15 ounces) pinto beans, rinsed and drained**
    1 **can (16 ounces) kidney beans, rinsed and drained**
    1 **can (14-1/2 ounces) French-style green beans, drained**
    1 **bunch green onions, sliced**
    1 **medium green pepper, chopped**
    1 **cup chili sauce**
1/4 **cup packed brown sugar**

Combine all ingredients in an ungreased 2-qt. casserole. Bake, uncovered, at 350° for 1 hour or until heated through and bubbly. **Yield:** 8-10 servings.

Kernels of Wisdom

On ripe ears of corn, the silks are brown and dried on the ends. To determine freshness, see how crisp the husk is. Avoid flimsy husks.

Peel down the husk and poke your thumb into a kernel. Look for clear juice to squirt out. The more milky the juice, the older and more starchy the corn.

To preserve freshness, refrigerate your corn as soon as possible.

Husk the ears by peeling back the leaves of the husk like you're peeling a banana. Once they're all pulled down, grasp them firmly with your hand and snap off that end. Remove the silks by rubbing dry ears with dry hands—using water will only make them stick more.

If you find the corn you've selected doesn't taste sweet enough, give it a boost by adding a bit of sugar or honey to the water you're cooking it in.

Green Bean Medley

Onion, celery and carrots add additional color and crunch to this basic green bean side dish. I use savory grown in my garden in this recipe.
—*Janice Cox, Smithfield, Kentucky*

✓ Uses less fat, sugar or salt. Includes Nutritional Analysis and Diabetic Exchanges.

1-1/2 **pounds fresh green beans, halved**
    1 **medium onion, cut into rings**
    1 **celery rib, sliced**
    2 **to 3 carrots, cut into 2-inch strips**
    1 **teaspoon salt, optional**
    2 **to 3 tablespoons minced fresh savory *or* 2 to 3 teaspoons dried savory**
1/8 **teaspoon pepper**
    1 **cup water**

In a large saucepan, combine all ingredients; bring to a boil. Reduce heat; cover and simmer for 5-10 minutes or until vegetables are tender, stirring occasionally. Remove with a slotted spoon to a serving bowl. **Yield:** 6 servings. **Nutritional Analysis:** One serving (prepared without added salt) equals 41 calories, 20 mg sodium, 0 cholesterol, 9 gm carbohydrate, 2 gm protein, trace fat. **Diabetic Exchanges:** 1-1/2 vegetable.

Secret Brussels Sprouts

My husband and I have always loved brussels sprouts, but our kids wouldn't touch them until I discovered this recipe. Tomato sauce and cheese give this vegetable a place on the family table.
—*Diane Hixon*
Niceville, Florida

    1 **small onion, sliced**
    2 **tablespoons butter *or* margarine**
    2 **tablespoons all-purpose flour**
    1 **cup tomato juice**
    1 **teaspoon sugar**
1/2 **teaspoon salt**
1/8 **teaspoon pepper**
    2 **packages (10 ounces *each*) frozen brussels sprouts *or* 1-1/4 pounds fresh brussels sprouts, cooked and drained**
1/4 **cup shredded cheddar cheese**

In a skillet, saute onion in butter until tender. Remove onion and set aside. Blend flour into the drippings. Add tomato juice; cook and stir over low heat until thickened and smooth. Stir in the sugar, salt, pepper and onion. Arrange the brussels sprouts in a greased 1-qt. baking dish; top with the tomato juice mixture. Sprinkle with cheese. Bake, uncovered, at 350° for 15 minutes. **Yield:** 6 servings.

Broccoli-Pasta Side Dish

(Pictured below and on page 56)

I love to fix new recipes for my husband, Robert, and our children. With garlic and cheese, this is a tasty way to get kids to eat broccoli. —Judi Lacourse
Mesa, Arizona

```
2-1/2 pounds fresh broccoli
    2 garlic cloves, minced
  1/3 cup olive or vegetable oil
    1 tablespoon butter or margarine
    1 teaspoon salt
  1/4 teaspoon pepper
Pinch cayenne pepper
    8 ounces linguine or thin spaghetti, cooked
      and drained
Grated Romano or Parmesan cheese
```

Cut florets and tender parts of broccoli stems into bite-size pieces. In a large skillet, saute broccoli with garlic, oil, butter, salt, pepper and cayenne over medium heat for about 10 minutes or until just tender, stirring frequently. Place hot pasta in a serving dish; top with the broccoli mixture. Sprinkle with cheese. **Yield:** 4-6 servings.

Mashed Potatoes with Horseradish

Instead of the ever-popular garlic mashed potatoes, this unusual recipe calls for prepared horseradish. This zippy side dish would be great with roast beef.
—Cynthia Gobeli, Norton, Ohio

```
    6 medium potatoes, peeled and cubed
  1/4 cup butter or margarine, melted
  3/4 teaspoon salt
  1/8 teaspoon pepper
  1/2 cup sour cream
    2 tablespoons prepared horseradish
```

Cook the potatoes in boiling salted water until tender, about 8-10 minutes; drain. Add butter, salt and pepper. Whip with an electric mixer on low speed or mash with a potato masher. Add sour cream and horseradish; mix well. Serve immediately. **Yield:** 6-8 servings.

Italian Zucchini

I enjoy planning and preparing daily meals. Cooking is a great way to relax at the end of the day. This Italian-style side dish is one I make often. Made with fresh zucchini, tomatoes and onion, it's as good for you as it is good to eat! —Christopher Gordon
Springfield, Missouri

✓ Uses less fat, sugar or salt. Includes Nutritional Analysis and Diabetic Exchanges.

```
    4 cups sliced zucchini
    1 medium onion, sliced into rings
    2 medium tomatoes, sliced
    1 lemon, quartered
1-1/2 teaspoons Italian seasoning
  3/4 teaspoon red pepper flakes
    1 tablespoon butter or margarine
```

In a greased 2-1/2-qt. casserole, layer one-third of the zucchini, onion and tomatoes. Squeeze one lemon quarter over all. Sprinkle with 1/2 teaspoon Italian seasoning and 1/4 teaspoon red pepper flakes. Repeat layers. Dot with butter. Squeeze remaining lemon over all. Cover and bake at 350° for 1 hour or until vegetables are tender. Serve immediately. **Yield:** 4 servings. **Nutritional Analysis:** One serving (prepared with margarine) equals 64 calories, 35 mg sodium, 0 cholesterol, 9 gm carbohydrate, 2 gm protein, 3 gm fat. **Diabetic Exchanges:** 1-1/2 vegetable, 1/2 fat.

Grilled Mushrooms

Once reserved for Oriental royalty and guarded by warriors, shiitake mushrooms are prized for their rich flavor and meaty texture. Seasoned with oil and herbs, they taste great hot off the grill.
—*Steven Stumpf, Shiocton, Wisconsin*

  1/2 **pound fresh shiitake mushooms**
  1/4 **cup olive *or* vegetable oil**
    1 **tablespoon minced fresh thyme, sage,
      oregano *and/or* basil**
Salt and pepper to taste

In a mixing bowl, beat sweet potatoes, 6 tablespoons brown sugar, vanilla, salt, nutmeg and cardamom. Add milk; mix well. Spoon into a greased 1-qt. casserole. Drizzle with butter; sprinkle with remaining brown sugar. Bake at 350° for 40 minutes or until top is lightly browned. **Yield:** 6 servings.

Remove and discard stems from mushroom caps or cut flush with caps. Score caps lightly with a sharp knife. Brush both sides with oil. Rub with herbs and sprinkle with salt and pepper. Place on hot grill, inside down. Cook for 2-3 minutes; turn and cook 2 minutes more or until juices form in the caps. Serve hot or at room temperature. **Yield:** 8-10 servings. **Editor's Note:** Medium fresh white mushrooms can be substituted for the shiitakes, but do not score them. Thread on skewers to grill.

Cardamom Sweet Potatoes

If you're looking for a tasty change of pace from traditional mashed potatoes, give this recipe a try. You can use either canned or fresh sweet potatoes with wonderful results. —*Sandy Waters
Mt. Lebanon, Pennsylvania*

    1 **can (40 ounces) sweet potatoes, drained
      or 1-1/2 pounds fresh sweet potatoes,
      cooked**
    9 **tablespoons brown sugar, *divided***
    1 **tablespoon vanilla extract**
  1/2 **teaspoon salt**
  1/2 **teaspoon ground nutmeg**
  1/2 **teaspoon ground cardamom**
  2/3 **cup milk**
    2 **tablespoons butter *or* margarine, melted**

Delicious Corn Pudding

(Pictured above and on page 57)

Corn has been a staple for generations in my family. This comforting dish from my grandma was a part of our meals for years and shared at gatherings. I hope to one day pass this recipe onto my granddaughter.
—*Paula Marchesi, Rocky Point, New York*

    4 **eggs, *separated***
    2 **tablespoons butter *or* margarine, melted
      and cooled**
    1 **tablespoon sugar**
    1 **tablespoon brown sugar**
    1 **teaspoon salt**
  1/2 **teaspoon vanilla extract**
Pinch ground cinnamon and nutmeg
    2 **cups fresh whole kernel corn (4 medium
      ears)**
    1 **cup half-and-half cream**
    1 **cup milk**

In a mixing bowl, beat egg yolks until thick and lemon-colored, about 5-8 minutes. Add butter, sugars, salt, vanilla, cinnamon and nutmeg; mix well. Add corn. Stir in cream and milk. Beat egg whites until stiff; fold into yolk mixture. Pour into a greased 1-1/2-qt. baking dish. Bake, uncovered, at 350° for 35 minutes or until a knife inserted near the center comes out clean. Cover loosely during last 10 minutes of baking if necessary to prevent over-browning. **Yield:** 8 servings.

25 minutes or until heated through. Sprinkle with chives. **Yield:** 6-8 servings.

Ginger-Orange Squash

You can prepare this side dish quickly in your microwave. It has a festive holiday flavor.
—Vonna Wendt, Ephrata, Washington

    1 butternut squash (about 2 pounds)
    2 tablespoons frozen orange juice
      concentrate
    2 tablespoons brown sugar
    1 tablespoon butter *or* margarine
  1/4 teaspoon ground ginger

Puncture squash several times with a knife or fork; place on a microwave-safe plate. Cook on high for 5 minutes. Cut into quarters; remove seeds and pulp. Return to plate, cut side down, and cover with waxed paper; microwave on high for 7 minutes. Turn over; microwave on high for 6-8 minutes or until soft. Scoop out squash and place in bowl; add remaining ingredients and mix well. **Yield:** 4 servings. **Editor's Note:** Recipe was tested in a 700-watt microwave oven.

Corn and Bacon Casserole

(Pictured above)

Corn is my three boys' favorite vegetable, so we eat a lot of it. This recipe has been a favorite for years. My husband, Bob, and the boys really enjoy it.
—Marcia Hostetter, Canton, New York

    6 bacon strips
  1/2 cup chopped onion
    2 tablespoons all-purpose flour
    2 garlic cloves, minced
  1/2 teaspoon salt
  1/2 teaspoon pepper
    1 cup (8 ounces) sour cream
3-1/2 cups fresh *or* frozen whole kernel corn
    1 tablespoon chopped fresh parsley
    1 tablespoon chopped fresh chives

In a large skillet, cook bacon until crisp. Drain, reserving 2 tablespoons of drippings. Crumble bacon; set aside. Saute onion in drippings until tender. Add flour, garlic, salt and pepper. Cook and stir until bubbly; cook and stir 1 minute more. Remove from the heat and stir in sour cream until smooth. Add corn, parsley and half of the bacon; mix well. Pour into a 1-qt. baking dish. Sprinkle with remaining bacon. Bake, uncovered, at 350° for 20-

Potato Pie

I've collected a large variety of recipes using our farm's crop of potatoes. This is a favorite. It has a wonderful pastry crust and is chock-full of sliced potatoes with onion, parsley and seasoning. —Patricia Wells
Riverhead, New York

2-1/4 cups all-purpose flour
    1 tablespoon sugar
1-1/4 teaspoons salt
  1/2 cup shortening
  1/4 cup cold butter *or* margarine
3-1/2 to 4 tablespoons cold water
FILLING:
    7 cups sliced peeled potatoes
    1 medium onion, sliced
    1 tablespoon minced fresh parsley
1-1/2 teaspoons salt
  1/2 teaspoon pepper
    2 tablespoons butter *or* margarine
  1/2 cup half-and-half cream

Combine flour, sugar and salt in a bowl; cut in the shortening and butter until crumbly. Add water and mix lightly with a fork. Shape dough into a ball; divide in half. On a lightly floured surface, roll out one half to fit a 9-in. pie plate. For filling, combine potatoes, onion, parsley, salt and pepper.

Spoon into crust; dot with butter. Roll out remaining dough to fit top of pie; place over filling. Seal and flute edges; make several slits in the top crust. Bake at 375° for 1 hour. Pour cream into slits in crust; return to the oven for 25 minutes or until potatoes are tender. Let stand 5 minutes before cutting. **Yield:** 6 servings.

Zesty Buttered Peas

Whenever I share this recipe with some, I include a small jar of my homegrown savory. This is my favorite recipe using that lively herb. —Claire Talone
Morrisville, Pennsylvania

✓ Uses less fat, sugar or salt. Includes Nutritional Analysis and Diabetic Exchanges.

- 2 tablespoons butter *or* margarine
- 1 package (10 ounces) frozen peas, thawed
- 1 cup sliced celery
- 1/2 cup chopped onion
- 1 tablespoon minced fresh savory *or* 1-1/2 teaspoons dried savory
- 1/2 teaspoon salt, optional
- 2 tablespoons diced pimientos

Melt butter in a heavy saucepan; add the next five ingredients. Cover and cook over medium heat for 6-8 minutes or until vegetables are tender. Stir in pimientos. **Yield:** 6 servings. **Nutritional Analysis:** One serving (prepared with margarine and without added salt) equals 74 calories, 93 mg sodium, 0 cholesterol, 8 gm carbohydrate, 2 gm protein, 4 gm fat. **Diabetic Exchanges:** 1 fat, 1/2 starch.

Spinach Noodles

Imagine homemade noodles that are green! This easy recipe gives "from scratch" satisfaction even if you've never made noodles before. —Bernice Smith
Sturgeon Lake, Minnesota

- 1 package (10 ounces) frozen chopped spinach, thawed and well drained
- 2 eggs
- 1 teaspoon salt
- 2 cups all-purpose flour

In a blender or food processor, combine spinach, eggs and salt; process until smooth. Pour into a bowl. Gradually add enough flour to make a firm, but not sticky, dough. On a floured surface, knead about 20 times. Wrap in plastic wrap and let rest 30 minutes. Divide dough in half. On a floured surface, roll each half to 1/16-in. thickness. Roll up jel-ly-roll style and cut into 1/4-in. slices. Separate the slices and let rest on a clean towel for at least 1 hour. Cook noodles in boiling salted water until tender, about 15-20 minutes; drain. **Yield:** 4-6 servings.

Garden Vegetable Medley
(Pictured below and on page 57)

I'm a vegetarian and enjoy experimenting with vegetable combinations. This relatively fat-free dish with squash, onion, green pepper, tomatoes and seasonings goes well with any meal. —Suzanne Pelgrin
Ocala, Florida

✓ Uses less fat, sugar or salt. Includes Nutritional Analysis and Diabetic Exchanges.

- 1 medium yellow summer squash
- 1 medium zucchini
- 1 medium onion, halved
- 1 medium green pepper
- 3 garlic cloves, minced
- 1-1/2 teaspoons minced fresh oregano *or* 1/2 teaspoon dried oregano
- 1-1/2 teaspoons minced fresh basil *or* 1/2 teaspoon dried basil
- 1/2 cup low-sodium chicken broth
- 2 cups cherry tomatoes, halved

Cut vegetables into 2-in. x 1/2-in. strips. In a skillet or wok, simmer vegetables, garlic and seasonings in broth over medium heat. Stir constantly until crisp-tender, about 7 minutes. Add tomatoes; heat through. Serve immediately. **Yield:** 8 servings. **Nutritional Analysis:** One serving equals 36 calories, 11 mg sodium, 0 cholesterol, 8 gm carbohydrate, 2 gm protein, trace fat. **Diabetic Exchanges:** 1-1/2 vegetable.

Vegetable Noodle Casserole

(Pictured below and on page 57)

If you're looking for a filling side dish, this recipe fits the bill. It combines nutritious vegetables and hearty noodles in a delectable cream sauce. Whenever I serve this dish at potlucks and family gatherings, it gets passed around until the pan is scraped clean.
—*Jeanette Hios, Brooklyn, New York*

  1 can (10-3/4 ounces) condensed cream of chicken soup, undiluted
  1 can (10-3/4 ounces) condensed cream of broccoli soup, undiluted
1-1/2 cups milk
  1 cup grated Parmesan cheese, *divided*
  3 garlic cloves, minced
  2 tablespoons dried parsley flakes
1/2 teaspoon pepper
1/4 teaspoon salt
  1 package (16 ounces) wide egg noodles, cooked and drained
  1 package (16 ounces) frozen broccoli, cauliflower and carrot blend, thawed
  2 cups frozen corn, thawed

In a bowl, combine soups, milk, 3/4 cup Parmesan cheese, garlic, parsley, pepper and salt; mix well. Add noodles and vegetables; mix well. Pour into a greased 13-in. x 9-in. x 2-in. baking dish. Sprinkle with the remaining Parmesan. Cover and bake at 350° for 45-50 minutes or until heated through. **Yield:** 12-14 servings.

———— 🥄 🥄 🥄 ————

Savory Dressing

This unusual dressing has a surprising blend of bread and mashed potatoes so that it appeals to all people. Savory adds just the right amount of flavor without being overpowering. —*Marlene Jastura*
Prince George, British Columbia

  2 medium onions, finely chopped
1/2 cup butter *or* margarine
  2 tablespoons water
  1 loaf (1 pound) day-old bread, crusts removed
1-1/2 cups mashed potatoes (without added butter or milk)

1/4 cup chicken broth
   2 tablespoons minced fresh savory *or* 2
      teaspoons dried savory
   1 teaspoon salt
1/2 teaspoon pepper

In a skillet, saute onions in butter and water until tender, stirring occasionally. Break bread into small pieces; place in a large bowl. Add potatoes, broth, savory, salt, pepper and onion mixture; mix well. Place in a greased 2-qt. baking dish. Cover and bake at 325° for 1 hour or until lightly browned. **Yield:** 8-10 servings.

Dressed-Up Dressing

For an attractive change of pace, bake your dressing in a fluted tube pan coated with nonstick cooking spray. To serve, turn the ring of dressing onto a pretty serving plate for a nice look.

Spinach Souffle

I've coaxed our grandchildren to eat spinach by "disguising" it in this fluffy egg dish. It's so good, we've been known to eat it as a main course. This is a tasty way to get more nutritious spinach into your diet.
—Ruth Andrewson, Leavenworth, Washington

   1 package (10 ounces) fresh spinach
1/4 cup butter *or* margarine
1/4 cup all-purpose flour
1/4 teaspoon pepper
   1 cup milk
   1 teaspoon dried minced onion
   1 teaspoon salt
1/8 teaspoon ground nutmeg
   3 eggs, *separated*
1/4 teaspoon cream of tartar

Wash and trim spinach, leaving the water that clings to the leaves. Place in a large skillet and steam just until wilted, about 3-5 minutes. Drain and chop; set aside. Melt butter in a small saucepan over medium heat. Blend in flour and pepper; cook and stir until bubbly. Slowly add milk; bring to a boil, stirring constantly. Cook and stir 1 minute. Remove from the heat. Stir in onion, salt and nutmeg. In a large mixing bowl, beat egg whites until soft peaks form. Add cream of tartar, continuing to beat until stiff peaks form. In another bowl, beat egg yolks until thick and lemon-colored; stir into white sauce. Gently fold into egg whites along with spinach. Pour into a greased 1-1/2-qt. casserole or souffle dish. Place casserole in a larger pan; fill larger pan with 1 in. of water. Bake, uncovered, at

350° for 50-60 minutes or until a knife inserted halfway near the center comes out clean. Serve immediately. **Yield:** 6 servings.

Stuffed Acorn Squash

One of my husband's favorite foods is acorn squash. I had an abundance of zucchini and acorn squash, so I put together this concoction. It has a hearty flavor that pairs nicely with any meat. Or serve it as a main dish.
—Susan Reynolds, Livermore, Colorado

   1 cup shredded zucchini
1/2 cup crushed saltine *or* butter-flavored
      crackers (about 15 crackers)
1/3 cup ketchup
   1 egg
1-1/2 teaspoons dried minced onion
1/2 teaspoon garlic salt
1/2 teaspoon dried oregano
1/2 teaspoon salt
1/4 teaspoon pepper
3/4 pound ground beef
   2 large acorn squash

In a medium bowl, combine the first nine ingredients. Add beef; mix well. Cut squash in half; remove and discard the seeds. Fill with meat mixture. Place in a greased 13-in. x 9-in. x 2-in. baking dish. Cover and bake at 400° for 1 hour or until squash is tender. Uncover and bake for 10 minutes more. **Yield:** 4 servings.

Caraway Sauerkraut

Over the years, I've found that learning to cook with herbs and spices is fun and rewarding. With sauerkraut, bacon and caraway, this side dish really reflects my German heritage.
—Trudy Johnson
Hixson, Tennessee

   6 bacon strips, chopped
   1 medium onion, chopped
   2 packages *or* jars (32 ounces *each*)
      sauerkraut, rinsed and drained
   1 tablespoon caraway seed
   2 cups water
   1 large potato, peeled and shredded

In a 5-qt. Dutch oven, cook bacon and onion until onion is golden brown, about 8-10 minutes. Add sauerkraut and caraway; mix well. Add water; bring to a boil. Reduce heat; cover and simmer for 1-1/2 hours, stirring occasionally. Add potato. Cook for 20 minutes or until potato is tender. **Yield:** 18-20 servings.

Main Dishes

From beef, poultry and pork to seafood, game and more, these comforting casseroles, oven meals, skillet suppers and grilled favorites will take top billing on your menus.

ENJOYABLE ENTREES. Clockwise from upper left: Grilled Salmon (p. 73), Cider Beef Stew (p. 84), Quail in Mushroom Gravy (p. 92), Roast Pork with Apple Topping (p. 78) and Chicken Broccoli Casserole (p. 89).

er loosely with foil. Bake at 350° for 20-25 minutes. Uncover; sprinkle with remaining cheddar and mozzarella. Return to the oven for 2-3 minutes or until the cheese is melted. **Yield:** 8 servings.

Pepper Steak

The marinade for this recipe is also excellent for steak or chicken on the grill. Everyone enjoys this full-flavored, hearty main dish. —James Harris
Columbus, Georgia

    1 boneless sirloin steak (1-1/2 to 2 pounds)
1/2 cup soy sauce
    1 teaspoon sugar
    2 garlic cloves, minced
    1 tablespoon vegetable oil
    1 to 2 medium green peppers, julienned
    1 medium onion, halved and thinly sliced
1/2 cup water
    2 tablespoons cornstarch
Hot cooked rice

Cut steak into 2-1/2-in. x 1/2-in. x 1/4-in. strips. In a medium bowl, combine soy sauce, sugar and garlic. Add meat; toss lightly to coat. Cover and refrigerate 3-4 hours. Drain, discarding marinade. In a skillet or wok, stir-fry meat in oil for 5-6 minutes or until no longer pink. Add peppers and onion; stir-fry for 3-4 minutes. Combine water and cornstarch; mix well. Add to meat and vegetables; stir-fry for 2-3 minutes or until thickened. Serve over rice. **Yield:** 4 servings.

Ham 'n' Cheese Pie

There's no need to make a crust for this eye-opening quiche. My family and friends love it for brunch or anytime. —Iris Posey, Albany, Georgia

    1 cup diced fully cooked ham
3/4 cup shredded Swiss cheese
    5 bacon strips, cooked and crumbled
3/4 cup shredded sharp cheddar cheese
    3 tablespoons chopped onion
    3 tablespoons chopped green pepper
    1 cup milk
1/4 cup biscuit/baking mix
    2 eggs
1/4 teaspoon salt
1/8 teaspoon pepper

In a greased 10-in. quiche dish or pie plate, layer ham, Swiss cheese, bacon, cheddar cheese, onion and green pepper. Place the remaining ingredients in a blender in the order given; blend for 30-

Lasagna in a Bun

(Pictured above)

Here's an interesting and delicious way to serve a great main dish and enjoy several different cheeses. My family loves the meat sauce and cheese tucked into the hollowed-out buns. Add a crisp green salad for a complete meal. —Cindy Morelock, Afton, Tennessee

    8 sub *or* hoagie buns (8 inches)
    1 pound ground beef
    1 cup spaghetti sauce
    1 tablespoon garlic powder
    1 tablespoon Italian seasoning
    1 cup ricotta cheese
1/4 cup grated Parmesan cheese
    1 cup (4 ounces) shredded cheddar cheese, *divided*
    1 cup (4 ounces) shredded mozzarella cheese, *divided*

Cut thin slices off tops of buns. Hollow out centers, leaving 1/4-in.-thick shells; discard tops and center or save for another use. In a skillet, brown ground beef; drain. Add spaghetti sauce, garlic powder and Italian seasoning. Cook 4-5 minutes or until heated through. Meanwhile, combine ricotta, Parmesan and half of cheddar and mozzarella cheeses; mix well. Spoon meat sauce into buns; top with cheese mixture. Place on a baking sheet. Cov-

40 seconds. Pour over meat, cheese and vegetables; do not stir. Bake, uncovered, at 350° for 30-35 minutes or until a knife inserted near the center comes out clean. Let stand 5 minutes before cutting. **Yield:** 6-8 servings.

—— 🏆 🏆 🏆 ——

Country Meat Loaf

This meat loaf has a comforting combination of three meats and is held together uniquely with corn bread stuffing. —*Jim Hopkins, Whittier, California*

    2 eggs
    1 can (10-3/4 ounces) condensed cream of
      celery soup, undiluted
    1/2 teaspoon pepper
    1 box (6 ounces) corn bread stuffing mix
    1-1/2 pounds ground beef
    1/2 pound ground veal
    1/4 pound ground pork

In a large bowl, beat eggs. Add soup, pepper and stuffing mix. Combine beef, veal and pork; add to egg mixture and mix well. Press into a 9-in. x 5-in. x 3-in. loaf pan. Bake at 350° for 1-1/2 hours or until no pink remains and a meat thermometer reads 160°. Drain. **Yield:** 6-8 servings.

Pork Chops Olé

(Pictured below)

This recipe is a fun and simple way to give pork chops south-of-the-border flair. The flavorful seasoning, rice and melted cheddar cheese make this dish a crowd-pleaser. —*Laura Turner, Channelview, Texas*

    6 loin pork chops (1/2 inch thick)
    2 tablespoons vegetable oil
Seasoned salt and pepper to taste
    3/4 cup uncooked long grain rice
    1-1/2 cups water
    1 can (8 ounces) tomato sauce
    1/2 envelope taco seasoning mix
      (2 tablespoons)
    1 medium green pepper, chopped
    1/2 cup shredded cheddar cheese

In a large skillet, brown pork chops in oil; sprinkle with seasoned salt and pepper. Meanwhile, in a greased 13-in. x 9-in. x 2-in. baking dish, combine rice, water, tomato sauce and taco seasoning; mix well. Arrange chops over rice; top with green pepper. Cover and bake at 350° for 1-1/2 hours or until chops are browned and juices run clear. Uncover and sprinkle with cheese; bake until cheese is melted. **Yield:** 4-6 servings.

Marinated Pork Kabobs

(Pictured below)

This recipe was originally for lamb, but I adapted it to pork and adjusted the spices. After tasting these flavorful kabobs, my husband became an instant fan of this recipe. It's always requested when the grill comes out for the season. —Bobbie Jo Devany
Fernly, Nevada

✓ Uses less fat, sugar or salt. Includes Nutritional Analysis and Diabetic Exchanges.

  2 cups plain yogurt
  2 tablespoons lemon juice
  4 garlic cloves, minced
1/2 teaspoon ground cumin
1/4 teaspoon ground coriander
  **2 pounds pork tenderloin, cut into
    1-1/2-inch cubes**
  8 small white onions, halved
  8 cherry tomatoes
  **1 medium sweet red pepper, cut into
    1-1/2-inch pieces**
  **1 medium green pepper, cut into
    1-1/2-inch pieces**

In a medium glass bowl, combine yogurt, lemon juice, garlic, cumin and coriander; mix well. Add pork; cover and refrigerate for 6 hours or overnight. Alternate pork, onions, tomatoes and peppers on eight skewers. Grill over medium heat for 30-35 minutes or until meat reaches desired doneness.

Yield: 8 servings. **Nutritional Analysis:** One serving (prepared with nonfat yogurt) equals 299 calories, 87 mg sodium, 94 mg cholesterol, 8 gm carbohydrate, 31 gm protein, 7 gm fat. **Diabetic Exchanges:** 4 lean meat, 2 vegetable, 1/2 fat.

———— 🥄 🥄 🥄 ————

Baked Stuffed Tomatoes

My family loves these tasty garden "containers" filled with rice and ground beef. It's a nice variation on traditional stuffed green peppers.
—Bertille Cooper, St. Inigoes, Maryland

  6 medium tomatoes
1/2 pound ground beef
  1 teaspoon chili powder
  1 teaspoon sugar
1/2 teaspoon salt
1/2 teaspoon pepper
1/4 teaspoon dried oregano
  2 cups uncooked instant rice
1/2 cup dry bread crumbs
  2 tablespoons butter *or* margarine, melted
  2 tablespoons water

Cut a thin slice off the top of each tomato. Leaving a 1/2-in.-thick shell, scoop out and reserve pulp. Invert tomatoes onto paper towels to drain. Meanwhile, in a skillet, brown beef; drain. Add tomato pulp, chili powder, sugar, salt, pepper and oregano; bring to a boil. Reduce heat; simmer 45-50 minutes or until slightly thickened, stirring occasionally. Add rice; mix well. Simmer 5-6 minutes longer or until rice is tender. Stuff tomatoes and place in a greased 13-in. x 9-in. x 2-in. baking dish. Combine bread crumbs and butter; sprinkle over tomatoes. Add water to baking dish. Bake, uncovered, at 375° for 20-25 minutes or until crumbs are lightly browned. **Yield:** 6 servings.

———— 🥄 🥄 🥄 ————

Beef Barley Stew

I like barley, so I knew I had to try this recipe when I ran across it in a newspaper some years ago. It's nice to have a tasty, filling dish that's lower in fat.
—June Formanek, Belle Plaine, Iowa

✓ Uses less fat, sugar or salt. Includes Nutritional Analysis and Diabetic Exchanges.

**1-1/2 pounds lean beef stew meat, cut into
    1/2-inch cubes**
    1 medium onion, chopped
    1 tablespoon vegetable oil
    3 cans (14-1/2 ounces *each*) beef broth
    1 cup medium pearl barley

1 teaspoon dried thyme
1/2 teaspoon dried marjoram
1/4 teaspoon dried rosemary, crushed
1/4 teaspoon pepper
4 medium carrots, sliced
2 tablespoons chopped fresh parsley

In a large saucepan or Dutch oven over medium heat, brown meat and onion in oil. Add broth, barley, thyme, marjoram, rosemary and pepper; bring to a boil. Reduce heat; cover and simmer for 1 hour. Add carrots; bring to a boil. Reduce heat; cover and simmer 30-40 minutes or until meat and carrots are tender. Add parsley just before serving. **Yield:** 8 servings. **Nutritional Analysis:** One 1-cup serving equals 266 calories, 618 mg sodium, 40 mg cholesterol, 24 gm carbohydrate, 23 gm protein, 8 gm fat. **Diabetic Exchanges:** 3 lean meat, 1 starch, 1 vegetable.

Mexi-Italian Spaghetti

This spaghetti sauce has some "kick" that's lacking in other recipes. It makes for memorable meals whenever it appears on the table.
—*Scott Walter, Little Rock, Arkansas*
Matt Walter, Grand Rapids, Michigan

SAUCE:
2 cans (10-3/4 ounces *each*) condensed tomato soup, undiluted
2-2/3 cups water
1 can (12 ounces) tomato paste
1 jar (4-1/2 ounces) sliced mushrooms, undrained
1 medium onion, chopped
3 tablespoons Worcestershire sauce
3 tablespoons chili powder
1 teaspoon salt
1/2 teaspoon cayenne pepper
2 garlic cloves, minced
Pinch pepper
MEATBALLS:
2 eggs, beaten
1/4 cup chopped onion
1 teaspoon garlic salt
1/2 teaspoon pepper
2 pounds ground beef
Hot cooked spaghetti

In a large Dutch oven or kettle, combine all sauce ingredients. Simmer, uncovered, for 2 hours. In a bowl, combine the eggs, onion, garlic salt and pepper. Add beef; mix well. Shape into 1-in. meatballs; brown in a skillet, a few at a time. Add meatballs to sauce and simmer for 1 hour. Serve over spaghetti. **Yield:** 8-10 servings.

'I Wish I Had That Recipe...'

"THE Cajun Chicken Pasta at the Monroe Street Grille in Tallahassee, Florida is so good that I'd love to be able to make it myself if you can get the recipe," informs Tracy Price of South Hadley, Massachusetts.

Chef Tyler Lamm at the Monroe Street Grille, located in Tallahassee's Ramada Inn North, generously shares the recipe.

"Our Cajun Chicken Pasta began as a special, but due to its overwhelming popularity, we made it a permanent part of our menu," he informs.

"In the 9 years we've been open, we have become a favorite restaurant with locals and travelers alike because our food is not typical hotel fare," Tyler adds.

You'll find the Monroe Street Grille at 2900 N. Monroe St. in Tallahassee, serving breakfast, lunch and dinner; 1-850/386-1027.

Cajun Chicken Pasta

2 boneless skinless chicken breast halves, cut into thin strips
2 teaspoons Cajun seasoning
2 tablespoons butter *or* margarine
8 slices *each* green and sweet red pepper
4 large fresh mushrooms, sliced
1 green onion, sliced
1 to 2 cups whipping cream
1/4 teaspoon dried basil
1/4 teaspoon lemon-pepper seasoning
1/4 teaspoon salt
1/8 teaspoon garlic powder
1/8 teaspoon pepper
4 ounces linguine, cooked and drained
Grated Parmesan cheese, optional

Place chicken and Cajun seasoning in a bowl or resealable plastic bag; toss or shake to coat. In a large skillet over medium heat, saute chicken in butter until almost tender, about 5-7 minutes. Add peppers, mushrooms and onion; cook and stir for 2-3 minutes. Reduce heat. Add cream and seasonings; heat through. Add linguine and toss; heat through. Sprinkle with Parmesan cheese if desired. **Yield:** 2 servings.

Maple-Glazed Ribs

(Pictured above)

I love maple syrup and so does my family, so I gave this recipe a try. It's well worth the effort! I make these ribs often, and I never have leftovers. With two teenage boys who like to eat, this main dish is a real winner.
—Linda Kobeluck, Ardrossan, Alberta

    3 **pounds pork spareribs, cut into serving-size pieces**
    1 **cup maple syrup**
    3 **tablespoons orange juice concentrate**
    3 **tablespoons ketchup**
    2 **tablespoons soy sauce**
    1 **tablespoon Dijon mustard**
    1 **tablespoon Worcestershire sauce**
    1 **teaspoon curry powder**
    1 **garlic clove, minced**
    2 **green onions, minced**
    1 **tablespoon sesame seeds, toasted**

Place ribs, meaty side up, on a rack in a greased 13-in. x 9-in. x 2-in. baking pan. Cover pan tightly with foil. Bake at 350° for 1-1/4 hours. Meanwhile, combine the next nine ingredients in a saucepan. Bring to a boil over medium heat. Reduce heat; simmer for 15 minutes, stirring occasionally. Drain ribs; remove rack and return ribs to pan. Cover with sauce. Bake, uncovered, for 35 minutes, basting occasionally. Sprinkle with sesame seeds just before serving. **Yield:** 6 servings.

Turkey Curry

You can make this zesty entree as spicy as you like by varying the amount of curry powder used.
—Martha Balser, Cincinnati, Ohio

☑ Uses less fat, sugar or salt. Includes Nutritional Analysis and Diabetic Exchanges.

    1 **cup sliced celery**
  1/2 **cup sliced carrots**
    1 **cup skim milk,** *divided*
    2 **tablespoons cornstarch**
  3/4 **cup low-sodium chicken broth**
    2 **tablespoons dried minced onion**
  1/2 **teaspoon garlic powder**
    1 **to 4 teaspoons curry powder**
    2 **cups diced cooked turkey** *or* **chicken**
Hot cooked rice, optional

In a skillet lightly coated with nonstick cooking spray, saute celery and carrots until tender. In a bowl, mix 1/4 cup milk and cornstarch until smooth. Add broth and remaining milk; mix until smooth. Pour over vegetables in skillet. Add onion, garlic and curry powder. Cook and stir over medium heat for 4-5 minutes or until mixture thickens and bubbles. Add turkey; cook and stir until heated through. Serve over rice if desired. **Yield:** 4 servings. **Nutritional Analysis:** One serving (served without rice) equals 232 calories, 206 mg sodium, 37 mg cholesterol, 15 gm carbohydrate, 29 gm protein, 6 gm fat. **Diabetic Exchanges:** 2-1/2 lean meat, 1 vegetable, 1/2 starch, 1/2 skim milk.

Spaghetti Pie

Here's a nice change of pace from traditional spaghetti. The spaghetti noodle crust makes a pretty presentation. —Ruth Andrewson, Leavenworth, Washington

    6 **ounces spaghetti**
    2 **tablespoons butter** *or* **margarine**
    2 **eggs, beaten**
  1/2 **cup grated Parmesan cheese**
    1 **cup cottage cheese**
    1 **pound ground beef**
  1/2 **cup chopped onion**
  1/4 **cup chopped sweet red pepper**
    1 **cup canned diced tomatoes with liquid**
    1 **can (6 ounces) tomato paste**
    1 **teaspoon sugar**
    1 **teaspoon dried oregano**
  1/2 **teaspoon garlic salt**
  1/2 **cup shredded mozzarella cheese**

Cook spaghetti according to package directions; drain and place in a bowl. Add butter, eggs and Parmesan cheese; mix well. Spread over the bottom and up the sides of a greased 10-in. deep-dish pie plate. Spoon cottage cheese into crust; set aside. In a skillet, brown beef, onion and red pepper until beef is no longer pink; drain. Stir in tomatoes, tomato paste, sugar, oregano and garlic salt. Spoon over cottage cheese. Bake, uncovered, at 350° for 20 minutes. Sprinkle with mozzarella cheese; return to the oven for 5 minutes or until cheese is melted. Cut into wedges. **Yield:** 6 servings.

Purchasing Pork

Buy pork that's pale pink with a small amount of marbling. The darker pink the flesh is, the older the meat is.

Pork Chow Mein

I credit my love of cooking to my mother, grandmother and mother-in-law. That trio inspired dishes like this skillet dinner.—Helen Carpenter, Marble Falls, Texas

✓ Uses less fat, sugar or salt. Includes Nutritional Analysis and Diabetic Exchanges.

- **1 pound boneless pork loin**
- **2 garlic cloves, minced**
- **4 tablespoons soy sauce, *divided***
- **1 cup chicken broth**
- **2 tablespoons cornstarch**
- **1/2 to 1 teaspoon ground ginger**
- **1 tablespoon vegetable oil**
- **1 cup thinly sliced carrots**
- **1 cup thinly sliced celery**
- **1 cup chopped onion**
- **1 cup coarsely chopped cabbage**
- **1 cup coarsely chopped fresh spinach**
- **Hot cooked rice, optional**

Cut pork into 4-in. x 1/2-in. x 1/4-in. strips; place in a bowl. Add garlic and 2 tablespoons soy sauce. Cover and refrigerate 2-4 hours. Meanwhile, combine broth, cornstarch, ginger and remaining soy sauce; mix well and set aside. Heat oil in a large skillet or wok on high; stir-fry pork until no longer pink. Remove and keep warm. Add carrots and celery; stir-fry 3-4 minutes. Add onion, cabbage and spinach; stir-fry 2-3 minutes. Stir broth mixture and add to skillet along with pork. Cook and stir until broth thickens, about 3-4 minutes. Serve immediately over rice if desired. **Yield:** 6 servings. **Nutritional Analysis:** One serving (prepared with low-sodium broth and light soy sauce and served without rice) equals 173 calories, 419 mg sodium, 40 mg cholesterol, 11 gm carbohydrate, 14 gm protein, 8 gm fat. **Diabetic Exchanges:** 2 meat, 1 vegetable.

Grilled Salmon

(Pictured below and on page 66)

We love to cook on the grill at our house. I've used this flavorful salmon recipe several times and we always enjoy it. The parsley, rosemary and green onions help make the tender fillets a tempting main dish that looks impressive. —Monell Nuckols
Carpinteria, California

- **2 salmon fillets (about 1 pound *each*)**
- **1/2 cup vegetable oil**
- **1/2 cup lemon juice**
- **4 green onions, thinly sliced**
- **3 tablespoons minced fresh parsley**
- **1-1/2 teaspoons minced fresh rosemary *or* 1/2 teaspoon dried rosemary, crushed**
- **1/2 teaspoon salt**
- **1/8 teaspoon pepper**

Place salmon in a shallow dish. Combine remaining ingredients and mix well. Set aside 1/4 cup for basting; pour the rest over the salmon. Cover and refrigerate for 30 minutes. Drain, discarding marinade. Grill salmon over medium heat, skin side down, for 15-20 minutes or until fish flakes easily with a fork. Baste occasionally with reserved marinade. **Yield:** 4 servings.

Ground Beef's a Sure Bet For Robust Family Fare

ARE you looking for some fresh ideas for preparing ground beef? These recipes from fellow cooks reinforce how versatile this "staple" can be.

— 🏳 🏳 🏳 —

Spaghetti and Meatballs

(Pictured below and on front cover)

When you have time, simmer some of this hearty sauce with home-style meatballs. It makes a memorable main course you'll rely on for years to come.
— *Dawnetta McGhee, Lewiston, Idaho*

- 1 large onion, finely chopped
- 2 garlic cloves, minced
- 2 tablespoons vegetable *or* olive oil
- 3 cans (10-3/4 ounces *each*) tomato puree
- 1 can (12 ounces) tomato paste
- 1-1/2 cups water
- 1/4 cup grated Parmesan cheese
- 1 tablespoon dried oregano

GRAB THE GROUND BEEF. Hearty helpings of Spaghetti and Meatballs, Calico Burgers and Stuffed Zucchini (shown above, clockwise from upper left) are sure cures for "the hungries".

1 tablespoon salt
1 tablespoon sugar
MEATBALLS:
  4 eggs, beaten
  2 garlic cloves, minced
  3 tablespoons grated Parmesan cheese
  1 teaspoon dried oregano
  1 pound ground beef
  1/4 pound ground pork
  3/4 cup finely crushed saltines
Hot cooked spaghetti

In a Dutch oven, saute onion and garlic in oil until tender. Add the next seven ingredients; mix well. Simmer, uncovered, for 1-1/2 hours. Meanwhile, combine the eggs, garlic, Parmesan cheese and oregano in a large bowl. Add beef, pork and cracker crumbs; mix well. Shape into 1-1/2-in. balls; brown in a skillet, turning once. Add to sauce; simmer, uncovered, 1-1/2 hours longer. Serve over spaghetti. **Yield:** 6-8 servings.

Stuffed Zucchini

(Pictured at left)

An abundance of squash from my garden inspired me to make up this recipe. It's now a family favorite.
—*Marjorie Roberts, West Chazy, New York*

1-1/2 pounds lean ground beef
  1 large onion, chopped
  1 large green pepper, chopped
  1 jalapeno pepper, minced
1-1/4 cups soft bread crumbs
  1 egg, beaten
  1 tablespoon dried parsley flakes
  1 teaspoon dried basil
  1 teaspoon Italian seasoning
  1 teaspoon salt
  1/8 teaspoon pepper
  2 cans (8 ounces *each*) tomato sauce, *divided*
  2 medium tomatoes, coarsely chopped
  4 to 5 medium zucchini
  2 cups (8 ounces) shredded mozzarella cheese

In a large bowl, combine the first 11 ingredients and one can of tomato sauce; mix well. Stir in tomatoes. Halve zucchini lengthwise; scoop out seeds. Fill with meat mixture; place in two 13-in. x 9-in. x 2-in. baking dishes. Spoon remaining tomato sauce over each. Bake, uncovered, at 375° for 45 minutes or until the zucchini is tender. Sprinkle with cheese during the last few minutes of baking. **Yield:** 8-10 servings.

Calico Burgers

(Pictured below far left)

On summer Sundays when our children were young, we'd often invite guests for cookouts. These unique burgers featuring rice and special seasonings were always a hit. Instead of ketchup, top the burgers with homemade barbecue sauce. —*Maryann Bondonese Nazareth, Pennsylvania*

1/2 cup cooked rice
1/4 cup chopped onion
1/4 cup chopped green pepper
  1 tablespoon dried parsley flakes
  1 teaspoon salt
1/4 teaspoon garlic powder
Dash pepper
1-1/2 pounds ground beef
BARBECUE SAUCE:
  2/3 cup water
  1/4 cup ketchup
  3 tablespoons chili sauce
  1 teaspoon Worcestershire sauce
  1/4 teaspoon dried basil

In bowl, combine the first seven ingredients. Add beef; mix well. Shape into four to six oval patties. Grill, uncovered, over medium-hot heat until no longer pink, about 15-20 minutes. Combine all sauce ingredients in a saucepan; simmer for 15 minutes. Serve with burgers. **Yield:** 4-6 servings.

Inside-Out Stuffed Peppers

Our daughters Kimberly and Kristina don't like the way the meat and rice mixture is usually stuffed inside big green peppers. So Kristina added a chopped pepper to the other ingredients in a casserole.
—*Darlene Markel, Sublimity, Oregon*

  1 pound ground beef
1/2 cup chopped onion
  1 can (16 ounces) stewed tomatoes, cut up
  1 large green pepper, chopped
1/2 cup uncooked long grain rice
1/2 cup water
  2 teaspoons Worcestershire sauce
1/2 teaspoon salt
1/4 teaspoon pepper
  1 cup (4 ounces) shredded cheddar cheese

In a skillet, brown beef; drain. Transfer to a greased 2-qt. casserole. Add the next eight ingredients. Cover and bake at 350° for 1 hour or until rice is tender. Uncover and sprinkle with the cheese; return to the oven until cheese is melted, about 5 minutes. **Yield:** 4-6 servings.

Pork with Mustard Sauce

(Pictured above)

Back when I was a girl, I couldn't wait until I was grown up and could start cooking for my own family! Now that I am, I really enjoy using pork. The tender meat and the rich mustard sauce in this recipe are delectable together. —Irma Pomeroy
Enfield, Connecticut

   1 **pound pork tenderloin**
   2 **tablespoons butter** *or* **margarine**
1/2 **cup beef broth**
3/4 **teaspoon dried tarragon**
1/2 **cup whipping cream**
   1 **tablespoon Dijon mustard**
Salt and pepper to taste
Hot cooked noodles, optional

Cut tenderloin into eight pieces. Slice each piece again, but do not cut all of the way through; open and flatten each piece, pounding slightly with meat mallet. In a large skillet over medium-high heat, cook the pork in butter until no longer pink, 5-6 minutes per side. Remove to a serving dish and keep warm; discard drippings. In the same skillet, cook broth and tarragon over high heat until reduced by half. Reduce heat; stir in cream and mustard. Season with salt and pepper. Spoon over pork. Serve with noodles if desired. **Yield:** 4 servings.

— 🏺 🏺 🏺 —

Turkey Biscuit Stew

Served over biscuits, this chunky stew makes a hearty

supper. Plus, it's a great way to use extra turkey during the holidays.* —Lori Schlecht
Wimbledon, North Dakota

1/3 **cup chopped onion**
1/4 **cup butter** *or* **margarine**
1/3 **cup all-purpose flour**
1/2 **teaspoon salt**
1/8 **teaspoon pepper**
   1 **can (10-1/2 ounces) condensed chicken** *or* **turkey broth, undiluted**
3/4 **cup milk**
   2 **cups cubed cooked turkey**
   1 **cup cooked peas**
   1 **cup cooked whole baby carrots**
   1 **tube (10 ounces) refrigerated buttermilk biscuits**

In a 10-in. ovenproof skillet, saute onion in butter until tender. Stir in flour, salt and pepper until smooth. Gradually add broth and milk; cook, stirring constantly, until thickened and bubbly. Add the turkey, peas and carrots; heat through. Separate biscuits and arrange over the stew. Bake at 375° for 20-25 minutes or until biscuits are golden brown. **Yield:** 6-8 servings.

— 🏺 🏺 🏺 —

Fish Fillets with Stuffing

This fish is so tender and the stuffing moist and nicely seasoned, folks are surprised to learn it's made in the microwave. —Donna Smith, Victor, New York

1/2 **cup finely chopped onion**
1/2 **cup finely grated carrots**
1/2 **cup chopped fresh mushrooms**
1/2 **cup dry bread crumbs**
1/3 **cup chicken broth**
1/4 **cup minced fresh parsley**
   1 **egg, beaten**
   2 **tablespoons butter** *or* **margarine, melted**
   1 **tablespoon lemon juice**
   1 **teaspoon salt**
1/8 **teaspoon pepper**
2-1/2 **to 3 pounds fish fillets (cod, whitefish, haddock, etc.)**
Paprika

In a large bowl, combine the first 11 ingredients and mix well. In a greased 13-in. x 9-in. x 2-in. microwave-safe dish, arrange the fillets with stuffing between them. Moisten paper towels with water; place over fish. Cook on high for 15-16 minutes or until fish flakes easily with a fork, rotating dish occasionally. Sprinkle with paprika. **Yield:** 6-8 servings. **Editor's Note:** This recipe was tested in a 700-watt microwave.

Savory Roast Chicken

Brushing the bird with a savory-seasoned butter makes the meat nice and moist. This roasted chicken is so easy to make. —Connie Moore, Medway, Ohio

- 1 broiler-fryer chicken (2-1/2 to 3 pounds)
- 2 tablespoons butter *or* margarine, melted
- 3 tablespoons lemon juice
- 1 tablespoon minced fresh savory *or* 1 teaspoon dried savory

Place chicken, breast side up, on a rack in a shallow roasting pan. Combine butter, lemon juice and savory; brush over chicken. Bake, uncovered, at 375° for 1-1/2 hours or until juices run clear, basting occasionally with the pan drippings. **Yield:** 4 servings.

Favorite Meat Loaf

Meat loaf is my all-time favorite dish to cook. One year, an aunt and I put together a cookbook that included over 50 variations of that hearty, old-fashioned main course. —Jim Hopkins, Whittier, California

- 2 eggs
- 1/4 cup milk
- 1 tablespoon Worcestershire sauce
- 1 teaspoon seasoned salt
- 1 teaspoon onion powder
- 1 cup quick-cooking oats
- 1 carrot, shredded
- 2 tablespoons chopped fresh parsley
- 1-1/2 pounds ground beef
- 1 pound ground pork
- 1/2 cup ketchup

In a large bowl, beat eggs. Add milk, Worcestershire sauce, seasoned salt and onion powder; mix well. Stir in oats, carrot and parsley. Combine beef and pork; add to egg mixture and mix well. Press into a 9-in. x 5-in. x 3-in. loaf pan. Top with ketchup. Bake at 350° for 1-1/2 hours or until no pink remains and a meat thermometer reads 160°. Drain. **Yield:** 6-8 servings.

Four-Cheese Lasagna

(Pictured at right)

This cheese-packed lasagna can be prepared ahead of time and baked later. I sometimes make up a couple batches and freeze them in case company drops by. —Janet Myers, Napanee, Ontario

- 1 pound ground beef
- 1 medium onion, chopped
- 2 garlic cloves, minced
- 1 can (28 ounces) diced tomatoes, undrained
- 1 can (8 ounces) sliced mushrooms, drained
- 1 can (6 ounces) tomato paste
- 1 teaspoon salt
- 1 teaspoon dried oregano
- 1 teaspoon dried basil
- 1/2 teaspoon pepper
- 1/2 teaspoon fennel seed
- 1 carton (16 ounces) cottage cheese
- 2/3 cup grated Parmesan cheese
- 1/4 cup shredded mild cheddar cheese
- 1-1/2 cups (6 ounces) shredded mozzarella cheese, *divided*
- 2 eggs
- 1 pound lasagna noodles, cooked and drained

In a skillet, cook beef, onion and garlic until beef is browned and onion is tender; drain. In a blender, process the tomatoes until smooth. Stir into beef mixture along with mushrooms, tomato paste and seasonings; simmer 15 minutes. In a bowl, combine cottage cheese, Parmesan, cheddar, 1/2 cup mozzarella and eggs. Spread 2 cups meat sauce in the bottom of an ungreased 13-in. x 9-in. x 2-in. baking dish. Arrange half the noodles over sauce. Spread cottage cheese mixture over noodles. Top with remaining noodles and meat sauce. Cover and bake at 350° for 45 minutes. Uncover; sprinkle with remaining mozzarella. Return to the oven for 15 minutes or until cheese is melted. **Yield:** 12 servings.

Pheasant Potpie

(Pictured below)

A hearty meal in itself, this savory pie features delicious pheasant. Here in central Pennsylvania, that game bird isn't as plentiful as in times past, and so this dish is a real treat. I make it for special occasions.
—Tawnya Coyne, Harrisburg, Pennsylvania

   2 pheasants (2-1/2 pounds *each*)
   4 cups water
   1 medium onion, quartered
   1 celery rib, quartered
   1 garlic clove, minced
   2 tablespoons lemon juice
1-1/4 teaspoons salt
 1/2 teaspoon pepper
 1/4 teaspoon Worcestershire sauce
 1/8 teaspoon ground nutmeg
 3/4 cup all-purpose flour
   1 jar (16 ounces) whole onions, drained
   1 package (10 ounces) frozen peas
1-1/2 cups sliced carrots
   1 jar (2 ounces) sliced pimientos, drained
 1/4 cup minced fresh parsley
Pastry for single-crust pie

In a large saucepan or Dutch oven, place pheasants, water, quartered onion, celery and garlic; bring to a boil. Reduce heat; cover and simmer for 1 hour or until tender. Remove pheasants; cool. Remove meat from bones and set aside. Strain broth, discarding vegetables. Measure 3-1/2 cups broth and place in a saucepan. Add lemon juice, salt, pepper, Worcestershire sauce and nutmeg. Remove 1/2 cup and stir in flour. Bring broth in saucepan to a boil. Add flour mixture; boil 1 minute or until thickened and bubbly. Add the whole onions, peas, carrots, pimientos, parsley and pheasant; mix well. Spoon into a 2-1/2-qt. baking dish. Roll pastry to fit dish; place over meat mixture and seal edges to dish. Cut small steam vents in crust. Bake at 425° for 35-40 minutes or until bubbly and golden. **Yield:** 6 servings.

— 🥄 🥄 🥄 —

Roast Pork with Apple Topping

(Pictured on page 66)

I enjoy cooking and am constantly on the lookout for new recipes to try. I feel very fortunate when I find a dish like this that becomes a family favorite. Ever since I found this recipe several years ago, it's the main way I fix pork loin.
—Virginia Barrett
Rochester, New York

   2 tablespoons all-purpose flour
1-3/4 teaspoons salt, *divided*
   1 teaspoon ground mustard
   1 teaspoon caraway seed
 1/2 teaspoon sugar
 1/4 teaspoon pepper
 1/4 teaspoon rubbed sage
   1 pork loin roast (4 to 5 pounds)
1-1/2 cups applesauce
 1/2 cup packed brown sugar
 1/4 teaspoon ground mace

In a small bowl, combine flour, 1-1/2 teaspoons salt, mustard, caraway, sugar, pepper and sage; rub over roast. Cover and let stand for 30 minutes. Place on a greased baking rack, fat side up, in a roasting pan. Bake, uncovered, at 325° for 1 hour. Combine applesauce, brown sugar, mace and remaining salt; mix well. Spread over roast. Roast 1 hour longer or until the internal temperature reaches 160°-170°. Let stand 15 minutes before slicing. **Yield:** 8-10 servings.

— 🥄 🥄 🥄 —

Low-Fat Chicken Divan

No one will ever guess this creamy, hearty casserole is actually low in fat. My daughter requests this dish often, and I happily oblige. It's a good-for-you meal with broccoli and chicken.
—Debbie Wheeler
Nampa, Idaho

☑ Uses less fat, sugar or salt. Includes Nutritional Analysis and Diabetic Exchanges.

1-1/4 pounds chopped fresh broccoli, cooked

3 cups cubed cooked chicken
1 can (10-3/4 ounces) low-fat condensed cream of chicken soup, undiluted
1 cup low-sodium chicken broth
1 cup fat-free mayonnaise
2 tablespoons fresh lemon juice
1/2 teaspoon pepper
1/4 teaspoon garlic powder
3/4 cup fat-free shredded cheddar cheese

Arrange the broccoli in a 13-in. x 9-in. x 2-in. baking pan coated with nonstick cooking spray; cover with chicken. Combine the soup, broth, mayonnaise, lemon juice, pepper and garlic powder; pour over chicken. Sprinkle with cheese. Cover and bake at 350° for 30 minutes. Uncover; bake 5-10 minutes or until bubbly. **Yield:** 6 servings. **Nutritional Analysis:** One serving equals 201 calories, 501 mg sodium, 63 mg cholesterol, 17 gm carbohydrate, 20 gm protein, 5 gm fat. **Diabetic Exchanges:** 2 lean meat, 1 starch, 1 vegetable.

Easy Oven Stew

I like to serve this satisfying stew to guests because it can be made ahead. When guests arrive, I just pop it in the oven. With some fresh bread and a garden salad, it's a complete meal. —Rita Zagrzebski
Eagle River, Wisconsin

✓ Uses less fat, sugar or salt. Includes Nutritional Analysis and Diabetic Exchanges.

3/4 pound boneless beef round steak, trimmed and cubed
1 tablespoon vegetable oil
4 medium unpeeled potatoes, cut into 1-inch cubes
5 medium carrots, cut into 1-1/2-inch chunks
1 celery rib, cut into 1-inch chunks
1 large onion, cut into 1-inch chunks
1 can (14-1/2 ounces) chunky stewed tomatoes
3 tablespoons quick-cooking tapioca
1 teaspoon browning sauce
1/8 to 1/4 teaspoon pepper
1 cup frozen peas

In a Dutch oven, brown the steak in oil. Add the next eight ingredients; cover and bake at 300° for 4-5 hours, stirring twice. Add the peas during the last 30 minutes of baking. **Yield:** 6 servings. **Nutritional Analysis:** One serving equals 263 calories, 257 mg sodium, 33 mg cholesterol, 38 gm carbohydrate, 17 gm protein, 5 gm fat. **Diabetic Exchanges:** 2 starch, 2 vegetable, 1 meat.

Kielbasa Skillet Stew

(Pictured above)

I grew up on a Montana ranch, and this dish reminds me of the kind we used to prepare for the hay and harvest crews. The bacon and sausage provide rich flavor to this comforting stew. When I make this dish, I share a taste of my country memories with my family. —Machelle Lewis, Henderson, Nevada

5 bacon strips
1 medium onion, chopped
1 to 1-1/2 pounds smoked fully cooked kielbasa, thinly sliced
2 cans (15-1/2 ounces *each*) great northern beans, undrained
2 cans (8 ounces *each*) tomato sauce
1 can (4 ounces) chopped green chilies
2 medium carrots, thinly sliced
1/2 medium green pepper, chopped
1/2 teaspoon Italian seasoning
1/2 teaspoon dried thyme
1/8 teaspoon pepper

In a 12-in. skillet, cook bacon until crisp; remove to paper towel to drain. In drippings, cook onion and sausage until the onion is tender; drain. Stir in remaining ingredients; bring to a boil. Reduce heat; cover and simmer for 45 minutes or until vegetables are tender, stirring occasionally. Crumble bacon and sprinkle on top. **Yield:** 6-8 servings.

Tuscan Pork Roast

(Pictured above)

Everyone's eager to eat after the wonderful aroma of this roast tempts us all afternoon. This is a great Sunday dinner with little fuss. Since I found this recipe a few years ago, it's become a favorite with our seven grown children and their families. —Elinor Stabile Canmore, Alberta

    5 **to 8 garlic cloves, peeled**
    1 **tablespoon dried rosemary**
    1 **tablespoon olive oil**
1/2 **teaspoon salt**
    1 **boneless pork loin roast (3 to 4 pounds)**

In a blender or food processor, combine garlic, rosemary, olive oil and salt; blend until mixture turns to paste. Rub over the roast; cover and let stand for 30 minutes. Place on a greased baking rack, fat side up, in a roasting pan. Bake, uncovered, at 325° for 2 to 2-1/2 hours or until the internal temperature reaches 160°-170°. Let stand for 15 minutes before slicing. **Yield:** 10-12 servings.

🛒 🛒 🛒

Mushroom Beef Skillet

This good-for-you recipe proves you can still enjoy the flavor of beef stroganoff even when you're watching your diet. —Vicki Raatz, Waterloo, Wisconsin

✓ Uses less fat, sugar or salt. Includes Nutritional Analysis and Diabetic Exchanges.

    1 **pound beef flank steak**
    2 **cups low-sodium beef broth**
    1 **cup chopped onion**
    1 **pound fresh mushrooms, sliced**
1/4 **cup cold water**
    2 **tablespoons all-purpose flour**
    2 **tablespoons cornstarch**
1/2 **cup plain nonfat yogurt**
    1 **teaspoon paprika**
    1 **teaspoon prepared mustard**
1/2 **teaspoon garlic powder**
Hot cooked noodles, optional

Broil steak 6 in. from the heat until rare, about 5 minutes on each side. Cut diagonally into thin strips; set aside and keep warm. In a large skillet, bring broth to a boil. Add onion and mushrooms; cover and simmer until tender, about 5 minutes. In a small bowl, mix cold water, flour and cornstarch until smooth. Whisk into broth; cook and stir over low heat until thickened and bubbly. Remove from heat. In a bowl, combine yogurt, paprika, mustard and garlic powder; add to broth and stir until smooth. Add the beef; cook over low heat, stirring constantly, until heated through, about 5 minutes. Serve over noodles if desired. **Yield:** 6 servings. **Nutritional Analysis:** One serving (served without noodles) equals 239 calories, 103 mg sodium, 47 mg cholesterol, 13 gm carbohydrate, 21 gm protein, 11 gm fat. **Diabetic Exchanges:** 2 meat, 1 vegetable, 1/2 starch.

Stuffed Trout

Fish is perfect for a busy cook like me, since it's so quick and easy to prepare. This recipe enhances trout's naturally pleasant taste. —Shirley Coleman
Monkton, Vermont

     2 bacon strips, cooked and crumbled
 1/2 cup fresh coarse bread crumbs
 1/4 cup chopped onion
     2 tablespoons chopped fresh parsley
 1/8 teaspoon salt
 1/8 teaspoon pepper
     4 dressed trout (1/2 pound *each*)

In a medium bowl, combine the first six ingredients; mix well. Stuff 1/4 cup into cavity of each trout. Place on a lightly greased rack in a shallow roasting pan. Bake at 350° for 35-40 minutes or until fish flakes easily with a fork. **Yield:** 4 servings.

Turkey Stroganoff

This main dish cooks up in a jiffy and is a great way to team up leftover turkey (or chicken) with broccoli. It's good enough to serve company.
—Karen Ann Bland, Gove, Kansas

     2 cups frozen cut broccoli
     1 tablespoon butter *or* margarine
 1/4 cup chopped onion
     3 tablespoons all-purpose flour
     1 can (10-3/4 ounces) condensed chicken broth, undiluted
     2 cups cubed cooked turkey
     1 cup (8 ounces) sour cream
     1 can (4 ounces) sliced mushrooms, drained
 1/2 teaspoon dried rosemary
 1/4 teaspoon salt
 1/4 teaspoon pepper
Hot cooked noodles

Cook broccoli according to package directions. Drain and set aside. In a 2-qt. microwave-safe dish, melt butter. Add onion; cover and cook on high until tender. Add flour and blend well. Whisk in broth; cook on high for 4-6 minutes or until thickened and bubbly, stirring every 2 minutes. Add turkey, sour cream, mushrooms, rosemary, salt and pepper. Cook on high for 2-3 minutes or until heated through, stirring once. Serve over noodles. **Yield:** 4 servings. **Editor's Note:** This recipe was tested in a 700-watt microwave.

Swedish Meatballs

(Pictured below)

I can still remember how happy it made my mom to cook something special for a family gathering. My parents were ranchers all their lives, so almost every main dish featured beef. This is Mom's recipe for tender Swedish meatballs with a thick savory gravy.
—Donna Hanson, Lusk, Wyoming

     4 eggs
     1 cup milk
     8 slices white bread, torn
     2 pounds ground beef
 1/4 cup finely chopped onion
     4 teaspoons baking powder
     1 to 2 teaspoons salt
     1 teaspoon pepper
     2 tablespoons shortening
     2 cans (10-3/4 ounces *each*) condensed cream of chicken soup, undiluted
     2 cans (10-3/4 ounces *each*) condensed cream of mushroom soup, undiluted
     1 can (12 ounces) evaporated milk
Minced fresh parsley

In a large bowl, beat eggs and milk. Add bread; mix gently and let stand for 5 minutes. Add beef, onion, baking powder, salt and pepper; mix well (mixture will be soft). Shape into 1-in. balls. In a large skillet, brown meatballs, a few at a time, in shortening. Place in an ungreased 3-qt. baking dish. In a bowl, stir soups and milk until smooth; pour over meatballs. Bake, uncovered, at 350° for 1 hour. Sprinkle with parsley. **Yield:** 8-10 servings.

▼ ▼ ▼

'I Wish I Had That Recipe...'

CHICKEN and potatoes have long been a popular mealtime pairing. But Myrtle Carrington found these dishes particularly memorable as served at the Grecian Steak House in Sikeston, Missouri.

"I'd love to have the recipes for the wonderfully seasoned chicken and sliced potatoes," says Myrtle of Morehouse, Missouri.

Restaurant owners Tom and Athena Zorbas share, "Our chicken and potatoes have been favorites with customers since we started serving them over a decade ago."

Located at 531 Greer Ave. in Sikeston, the restaurant is open Sunday-Thursday 10:30 a.m. to 9:30 p.m. and Friday and Saturday from 10:30 a.m. to 10:30 p.m. Phone 1-573/471-6877.

Grecian Chicken and Potatoes

    2 broiler-fryer chickens (2-1/2 to 3 pounds *each*), cut up
    1 cup fresh lemon juice
    1 teaspoon garlic salt
    1 teaspoon pepper
    1 teaspoon dried oregano
    4 teaspoons seasoned salt
POTATOES:
  1/2 cup diced onion
    5 cups sliced unpeeled red potatoes (about 3 pounds)
    4 cups water
  1/2 cup butter *or* margarine, melted
  1/4 cup fresh lemon juice
    1 teaspoon chicken bouillon granules
  1/2 teaspoon *each* paprika, salt, pepper and dried oregano

Place the chicken in a large shallow baking pan. Combine the lemon juice, garlic salt, pepper and oregano; pour over chicken. Sprinkle with seasoned salt. Bake, uncovered, at 350° for 1-1/4 hours or until chicken is tender and juices run clear. For potatoes, place the onion in an ungreased 13-in. x 9-in. x 2-in. baking pan. Arrange potatoes in rows over the onion, with slices slightly overlapping. Combine remaining ingredients; pour over potatoes. Bake, uncovered, at 350° for 1 hour and 20 minutes or until tender. **Yield:** 6-8 servings.

▼ ▼ ▼

Sunday Sausage Breakfast

This filling, delicious dish looks as appealing as it is tasty. Servings of this rich casserole go a long way.
—Bill Schultz, Walden, New York

    1 pound bulk pork sausage
    1 package (6 ounces) onion and garlic croutons
    2 cups cubed mild cheddar cheese
    2 cups cubed Monterey Jack cheese
    1 dozen eggs, beaten
  1/2 cup milk
  1/2 teaspoon dried basil
  1/4 teaspoon salt
  1/4 teaspoon pepper

In a skillet, brown sausage; drain. In a greased 13-in. x 9-in. x 2-in. baking dish, layer the croutons, sausage and cheese. Combine eggs and milk; mix well. Pour over cheese; sprinkle with basil, salt and pepper. Bake, uncovered, at 350° for 40-45 minutes or until the top is lightly browned and a knife inserted near the center comes out clean. Serve immediately. **Yield:** 6-8 servings.

▼ ▼ ▼

Light Tuna Noodle Casserole

This recipe updates an old classic by using low-fat products. It's a rich, creamy casserole that will satisfy the whole family.
—Sharen Oglesby
Anderson, California

✓ Uses less fat, sugar or salt. Includes Nutritional Analysis and Diabetic Exchanges.

  1/3 cup Cream Soup Mix (see page 42)
  1/2 cup chopped celery
  1/4 cup chopped green onions
    2 tablespoons olive *or* vegetable oil
    2 cans (6-1/2 ounces *each*) chunk light tuna in water, drained
    1 container (8 ounces) egg substitute
    1 cup cooked noodles
  1/2 cup skim milk
  1/4 teaspoon ground mustard
  1/8 teaspoon pepper
  1/2 cup shredded light cheddar cheese

Prepare Cream Soup Mix as directed for a condensed cream soup substitute. Saute celery and onions in oil until celery is tender. Place in a large bowl; add tuna, egg substitute, noodles, skim milk, mustard and pepper. Mix well. Pour into 2-qt. baking dish coated with nonstick cooking spray. Sprinkle with cheese. Bake at 375° for 50-60 minutes or until a knife inserted in the center comes out clean. **Yield:** 6 servings. **Nutritional Analysis:**

One serving equals 246 calories, 684 mg sodium, 34 mg cholesterol, 12 gm carbohydrate, 29 gm protein, 9 gm fat. **Diabetic Exchanges:** 3 lean meat, 1 starch. **Editor's Note:** One can low-fat condensed cream of mushroom soup diluted with 2/3 cup water may be used in place of the homemade Cream Soup Mix.

— 🝙 🝙 🝙 —

Farmhouse Pork and Apple Pie

(Pictured above)

I've always loved pork and apples together, and this recipe combines them nicely to create a comforting main dish. It calls for a bit of preparation, but my family and I agree that its wonderful flavor makes it well worth the extra effort. —Suzanne Strocsher
Bothell, Washington

    1 **pound sliced bacon, cut into 2-inch pieces**
    3 **medium onions, chopped**
    3 **pounds boneless pork, cubed**
3/4 **cup all-purpose flour**
Vegetable oil, optional
    3 **medium tart apples, peeled and chopped**
    1 **teaspoon rubbed sage**
1/2 **teaspoon ground nutmeg**
    1 **teaspoon salt**
1/4 **teaspoon pepper**
    1 **cup apple cider**
1/2 **cup water**
    4 **medium potatoes, peeled and cubed**
1/2 **cup milk**
    5 **tablespoons butter *or* margarine, *divided***
Additional salt and pepper
Snipped fresh parsley, optional

Cook bacon in an ovenproof 12-in. skillet until crisp. Remove with a slotted spoon to paper towels to drain. In drippings, saute onions until tender; remove with a slotted spoon and set aside. Dust pork lightly with flour. Brown a third at a time in drippings, adding oil if needed. Remove from the heat and drain. To pork, add bacon, onions, apples, sage, nutmeg, salt and pepper. Stir in cider and water. Cover and bake at 325° for 2 hours or until pork is tender. In a saucepan, cook potatoes in boiling water until tender. Drain and mash with milk and 3 tablespoons butter. Add salt and pepper to taste. Remove skillet from the oven and spread potatoes over pork mixture. Melt remaining butter; brush over potatoes. Broil 6 in. from the heat for 5 minutes or until topping is browned. Sprinkle with parsley if desired. **Yield:** 10 servings.

cover and simmer for 1-1/2 hours or until tender; drain. Combine all sauce ingredients in a saucepan. Simmer, uncovered, for 1 hour or until slightly thickened, stirring occasionally. Arrange ribs on a rack in a broiler pan. Brush with sauce. Broil 5 in. from the heat for 5 minutes on each side, brushing frequently with sauce. **Yield:** 4 servings.

———— 🥄 🥄 🥄 ————

Cider Beef Stew

(Pictured on page 66)

When I was a new bride, this recipe was inside a serving dish I received as a gift. It's great on winter evenings served with a loaf of fresh bread.
—Carol Hendrickson, Laguna Beach, California

        3 tablespoons all-purpose flour
        1 teaspoon salt
    1/2 teaspoon pepper
        1 pound beef stew meat, cut into 1-inch
            pieces
        2 tablespoons vegetable oil
        1 cup apple cider
    1/2 cup water
        1 tablespoon vinegar
    1/2 teaspoon dried thyme
        2 large carrots, cut into 1-inch pieces
        1 celery rib, cut into 1-inch pieces
        1 large potato, peeled and cubed
        1 medium onion, sliced

In a bowl or bag, combine flour, salt and pepper; add beef and toss to coat. In a saucepan, brown beef in oil. Add cider, water, vinegar and thyme; bring to a boil. Reduce heat; cover and simmer for 1 hour and 45 minutes or until meat is tender. Add carrots, celery, potato and onion; return to a boil. Reduce heat; cover and simmer for 45 minutes or until vegetables are tender. **Yield:** 4 servings.

———— 🥄 🥄 🥄 ————

Pork Chops with Caraway Cabbage

Pork and cabbage naturally bring out the best flavors in each other. Each fall, my family requests this hearty skillet supper. —David Frame, Waxahachie, Texas

        4 pork loin chops (3/4 inch thick)
        2 tablespoons vegetable oil
    1/2 teaspoon pepper
1-1/2 cups finely chopped onion
        3 tablespoons butter *or* margarine
        6 cups shredded cabbage
        2 garlic cloves, minced
        3 tablespoons cider *or* red wine vinegar
        1 teaspoon caraway seed

Barbecued Spareribs

(Pictured above)

My husband is a meat cutter at a supermarket and likes to find new ways to smoke or barbecue meat. Several years ago, he discovered this recipe for pork ribs covered in a rich tangy sauce. It was an instant success with our family and friends. —Bette Brotzel
Billings, Montana

        4 pounds pork spareribs, cut into
            serving-size pieces
        1 medium onion, quartered
        2 teaspoons salt
    1/4 teaspoon pepper
SAUCE:
    1/2 cup cider vinegar
    1/2 cup packed brown sugar
    1/2 cup ketchup
    1/4 cup chili sauce
    1/4 cup Worcestershire sauce
        2 tablespoons chopped onion
        1 tablespoon lemon juice
    1/2 teaspoon ground mustard
        1 garlic clove, minced
Dash cayenne pepper

Place ribs and onion in a large kettle or Dutch oven; sprinkle with salt and pepper. Add enough water to cover ribs; bring to a boil. Reduce heat;

1/2 teaspoon salt

In a skillet over high heat, brown the pork chops in oil; drain. Sprinkle with pepper; remove from skillet. Set aside. In same skillet, saute onion in butter for 1-2 minutes or until tender. Add cabbage, garlic, vinegar, caraway and salt; cook, stirring occasionally, until cabbage wilts. Place chops on top of cabbage. Cover and simmer for 15-17 minutes or until meat is tender. Serve immediately. **Yield:** 4 servings.

🍃 🍃 🍃

Apricot Chicken Stir-Fry

Ever since my husband and I began growing apricots more than 30 years ago, collecting recipes featuring that elegant fruit has been a favorite hobby.
—Jo Martin, Patterson, California

1/2 cup dried apricot halves, cut in half
1/4 cup hot water
  1 tablespoon all-purpose flour
  1 tablespoon chopped fresh cilantro *or* parsley
1/2 teaspoon salt
1/8 teaspoon pepper
3/4 pound boneless skinless chicken breasts, cut into 1/2-inch pieces
  3 tablespoons vegetable oil, *divided*
  1 medium onion, halved and sliced
  1 cup chopped celery
1/2 cup halved snow peas
1/2 teaspoon ground ginger
  1 garlic clove, minced
  1 to 2 tablespoons lemon juice
Hot cooked rice

In a small bowl, soak apricots in water; set aside (do not drain). Combine flour, cilantro, salt and pepper; sprinkle over the chicken and set aside. Heat 1 tablespoon oil in a large skillet or wok over medium heat; stir-fry onion and celery for 2-3 minutes or until tender. Add peas, ginger, garlic and apricots; stir-fry for 2 minutes. Remove and keep warm. Add remaining oil to skillet; stir-fry chicken for 6-7 minutes or until no longer pink. Sprinkle with lemon juice. Return apricot mixture to skillet and heat through. Serve over rice. **Yield:** 4 servings.

> ### *Sharp Tip*
> It's easier to cut dried fruit with a kitchen shears instead of a knife. To keep the fruit from sticking, occasionally dip the shears in hot water or sugar.

Chicken and Barley Boiled Dinner
(Pictured below)

I was looking for a recipe that was nutritious and would adequately feed my two teenage sons and husband. I'm a busy teacher, and time is of the essence.
—Susan Greeley, Morrill, Maine

  2 broiler-fryer chickens (about 3 pounds *each*), cut up and skinned
  3 tablespoons vegetable oil
  2 quarts chicken broth
  1 cup uncooked brown rice
1/2 cup medium pearl barley
  1 medium onion, chopped
  2 bay leaves
1/2 teaspoon dried basil
  2 teaspoons salt
1/4 teaspoon pepper
  8 carrots, cut into 1-inch pieces
2-1/2 cups frozen cut green beans
  2 celery ribs, cut into 1-inch pieces

In an 8-qt. kettle or Dutch oven, brown chicken in oil. Remove chicken and set aside. Drain. In the same kettle, combine the broth, rice, barley, onion, bay leaves, basil, salt and pepper; bring to a boil. Reduce heat. Return chicken to pan; cover and simmer for 45 minutes. Stir in the carrots, beans and celery. Cook over medium heat for 30 minutes or until the chicken and grains are tender. Remove bay leaves before serving. **Yield:** 6-8 servings.

Cheese-Stuffed Shells

(Pictured below)

When I was living in California, I tasted this rich cheesy pasta dish at a neighborhood Italian restaurant. I got the recipe and made a few changes to it in my own kitchen. —Lori Mecca, Grants Pass, Oregon

- 1 pound bulk Italian sausage
- 1 large onion, chopped
- 1 package (10 ounces) frozen chopped spinach, thawed and well drained
- 1 package (8 ounces) cream cheese, softened
- 1 egg, beaten
- 2 cups (8 ounces) shredded mozzarella cheese, *divided*
- 2 cups (8 ounces) shredded cheddar cheese
- 1 cup cottage cheese
- 1/4 cup grated Parmesan cheese
- 1/4 teaspoon *each* salt and pepper
- 1/8 teaspoon ground cinnamon, optional
- 20 jumbo shell noodles, cooked and drained

SAUCE:
- 1 can (29 ounces) tomato sauce
- 1 tablespoon dried minced onion
- 1-1/2 teaspoons *each* dried basil and parsley flakes
- 2 garlic cloves, minced
- 1 teaspoon *each* sugar and dried oregano
- 1/2 teaspoon salt
- 1/4 teaspoon pepper

In a skillet, brown sausage and onion; drain. Transfer to a large bowl. Stir in the spinach, cream cheese and egg. Add 1 cup mozzarella, cheddar, cottage cheese, Parmesan, salt, pepper and cinnamon if desired; mix well. Stuff shells and arrange in a greased 13-in. x 9-in. x 2-in. baking dish. Combine sauce ingredients; mix well. Spoon over shells. Cover and bake at 350° for 40 minutes. Uncover; sprinkle with remaining mozzarella. Return to the oven for 5 minutes or until cheese is melted. **Yield:** 8-10 servings.

Spinach Bacon Quiche

This versatile dish fits nicely into a menu for brunch or supper. It slices easily for pretty presentation. —Lois Sundheim, Fairview, Montana

- 4 eggs
- 2 cups milk
- 1-1/4 cups shredded cheddar cheese, *divided*
- 1/4 cup finely chopped onion
- 4 bacon strips, cooked and crumbled
- 1/2 teaspoon salt
- 1/2 teaspoon ground mustard
- 1/4 teaspoon paprika
- 1 package (10 ounces) frozen chopped spinach, thawed and well drained
- 1 unbaked pastry shell (9 inches)

In a large bowl, beat eggs; whisk in milk, 1 cup cheese, onion, bacon, salt, mustard and paprika. Add spinach. Pour into pie shell. Sprinkle with the remaining cheese. Bake at 400° for 40 minutes or until a knife inserted near the center comes out clean. **Yield:** 6 servings.

Mushroom-Chicken Stir-Fry

Hearty flavor distinguishes shiitake mushrooms from white mushrooms. Here they're paired with chicken and other vegetables for an irresistible meal in one. —Steven Stumpf, Shiocton, Wisconsin

- 1 ounce dried shiitake mushrooms
- 1 cup warm water
- 1 egg white, lightly beaten
- 2 tablespoons plus 1 teaspoon cornstarch, *divided*
- 1 tablespoon plus 1 teaspoon soy sauce, *divided*

Pinch pepper
- 4 boneless skinless chicken breast halves, cut into 1-inch cubes
- 4 tablespoons vegetable oil, *divided*
- 1 garlic clove, minced
- 1 cup frozen peas
- 1/2 cup sliced celery
- 1 can (8 ounces) water chestnuts, drained and diced

3/4 cup chicken broth, *divided*
1 teaspoon sugar
1/4 teaspoon ground ginger
1 jar (2 ounces) diced pimientos, drained
1/4 cup whole almonds, toasted
1 green onion, chopped

Combine the mushrooms and water; let stand 15 minutes. Drain, reserving liquid; set liquid and mushrooms aside. In another bowl, combine egg white, 1 teaspoon cornstarch, 1 teaspoon soy sauce and pepper; add chicken and stir to coat. Heat 2 tablespoons oil in a large skillet or wok; stir-fry chicken until no longer pink. Remove and set aside. In the same skillet, stir-fry garlic in remaining oil until browned. Add peas, celery, water chestnuts and mushrooms; stir-fry for 2 minutes. Add 1/2 cup broth and the chicken; cover and simmer for 3 minutes. Combine sugar, ginger, reserved mushroom liquid and remaining cornstarch, soy sauce and broth; stir into skillet and cook until thickened, about 4 minutes. Add pimientos. Garnish with almonds and onion. **Yield:** 6 servings. **Editor's Note:** Small fresh white mushrooms can be substituted for the dried shiitakes. Eliminate the warm water and the soaking step.

Pan-Fried Trout

Having fresh trout on hand for supper is a great benefit of owning a trout farm! I depend on this simple recipe often.   —Shirley Coleman, Monkton, Vermont

2 eggs
8 trout fillets
2/3 cup grated Parmesan cheese
2 tablespoons vegetable oil

In a shallow bowl, beat the eggs. Dip fillets in eggs, then dredge in the Parmesan cheese. Shake off excess. Heat oil in a large skillet over high heat; brown fillets lightly on both sides until the fish flakes easily with a fork, about 5-7 minutes. **Yield:** 4 servings.

Venison Pot Roast
(Pictured above right)

My husband enjoyed deer hunting for many years, so I was challenged to find ways to put that meat to good use. This nicely seasoned roast is a real treat.   —Helen Featherly, Hamburg, Michigan

1 boneless shoulder venison roast (3 to 4 pounds)
3 tablespoons vegetable oil

1 can (14-1/2 ounces) chicken broth
1/3 cup soy sauce
1 large onion, sliced
4 garlic cloves, minced
1/2 teaspoon ground ginger
SPAETZLE:
2 eggs
1/2 teaspoon salt
2-1/4 cups all-purpose flour
2/3 cup milk
2 quarts beef broth
1/4 cup butter *or* margarine, melted
1/8 teaspoon pepper
GRAVY:
1/3 cup water
1/3 cup all-purpose flour

In a Dutch oven, brown roast in oil; add the next five ingredients. Cover and simmer for 4 hours or until meat is tender. For spaetzle, beat eggs and salt in a medium bowl. With a wooden spoon, gradually stir in flour and milk. In a large saucepan, bring broth to a boil. Place dough in a colander or spaetzle maker; place over boiling broth. Press dough with a wooden spoon until bits drop into broth. Cook for 5 minutes or until tender. Drain; toss spaetzle with butter. Sprinkle with pepper and keep warm. Remove roast to a serving platter and keep warm. Measure 3 cups pan juices; return to pan. Combine water and flour; stir into pan juices. Cook and stir until thickened and bubbly. Cook and stir 1 minute more. Slice roast; serve with spaetzle and gravy. **Yield:** 6-8 servings.

Southwestern Omelet

Flavors of another region spark the eggs in this recipe. Hearty home-style food is popular in our small farming and timber community. —Patricia Collins
Imbler, Oregon

  1/2 cup chopped onion
    1 jalapeno pepper, minced
    1 tablespoon vegetable oil
    6 eggs, beaten
    6 bacon strips, cooked and crumbled
    1 small tomato, chopped
    1 ripe avocado, cut into 1-inch slices
    1 cup (4 ounces) shredded Monterey Jack
      cheese, *divided*
Salt and pepper to taste
Salsa, optional

In a skillet, saute onion and jalapeno in oil until tender; remove with a slotted spoon and set aside. Pour eggs into the same skillet; cover and cook over low heat for 3-4 minutes. Sprinkle with onion, jalapeno, bacon, tomato, avocado and 1/2 cup cheese. Season with salt and pepper. Fold omelet in half over filling. Cover and cook for 3-4 minutes or until eggs are set. Sprinkle with remaining cheese. Serve with salsa if desired. **Yield:** 4 servings.

Barbecued Chicken

(Pictured above)

If you're like me, you can never have enough delicious ways to grill chicken. The savory sauce in this recipe gives the chicken a wonderful herb flavor. It's easy to put together a great meal when you start with these juicy golden pieces. —Joanne Shew Chuk
St. Benedict, Saskatchewan

✓ Uses less fat, sugar or salt. Includes Nutritional Analysis and Diabetic Exchanges.

    1 broiler-fryer chicken (3-1/2 to 4 pounds),
      quartered
  1/4 cup vinegar
  1/4 cup butter *or* margarine
  1/4 cup water
  1/4 teaspoon *each* dried thyme, oregano,
      rosemary and garlic powder
  1/8 teaspoon salt
  1/8 teaspoon pepper

Place chicken in a shallow glass dish. In a small saucepan, combine all remaining ingredients; bring to a gentle boil. Remove from the heat. Pour over chicken. Cover and refrigerate for 4 hours, turning once. Drain and discard marinade. Grill chicken, covered, over medium heat for 30-40 minutes or until juices run clear. **Yield:** 4 servings. **Nutritional Analysis:** One serving (prepared with margarine and served without the skin) equals 224 calories, 225 mg sodium, 58 mg cholesterol, 1 gm carbohydrate, 21 gm protein, 14 gm fat. **Diabetic Exchanges:** 3 meat.

Meatless Spaghetti Sauce

When the tomatoes in my garden ripen, the first things I make are BLT's and this homemade spaghetti sauce. I like that it's deliciously different from some heavy meat sauces. —Sondra Bergy, Lowell, Michigan

    4 medium onions, chopped
1-1/4 teaspoons pepper
  1/2 cup vegetable oil
    4 garlic cloves, minced
  12 cups chopped peeled fresh tomatoes
    3 bay leaves
    4 teaspoons salt
    2 teaspoons dried oregano
  1/2 teaspoon dried basil
    2 cans (6 ounces *each*) tomato paste
  1/3 cup packed brown sugar
Hot cooked pasta

In a large Dutch oven, saute the onions and pepper in oil until onions are tender. Add garlic, tomatoes, bay leaves, salt, oregano and basil. Simmer for 2 hours, stirring occasionally, Add tomato paste and brown sugar; simmer 1 hour longer. Remove bay leaves. Serve over pasta. **Yield:** 2 quarts. **Editor's Note:** Browned ground beef or Italian sausage can be added to the cooked sauce if desired. The sauce also freezes well.

— 🥄 🥄 🥄 —

Chicken Broccoli Casserole

(Pictured on page 66)

Broccoli is a favorite vegetable in our home. This is one dish that always gets rave reviews. Serve it for a brunch or dinner. —Colleen Lewis
Cottonwood, Arizona

3 cups broccoli florets
2 cups cubed cooked chicken *or* turkey
1 can (10-3/4 ounces) condensed cream of chicken soup, undiluted
1/2 cup mayonnaise *or* salad dressing
1/2 cup grated Parmesan cheese
1/2 teaspoon curry powder
1 cup cubed fresh bread
2 tablespoons butter *or* margarine, melted

In a covered saucepan, cook broccoli in water until crisp-tender; drain. Place in a greased 11-in. x 7-in. x 2-in. baking dish; set aside. Combine chicken, soup, mayonnaise, Parmesan cheese and curry powder; spoon over broccoli. Top with bread cubes and butter. Bake, uncovered, at 350° for 25-30 minutes or until heated through. **Yield:** 6 servings.

— 🥄 🥄 🥄 —

Cabbage with Meat Sauce

A flavorful meat sauce is served over thinly sliced cabbage—instead of hot cooked noodles—for a deliciously different dish. —Janet Carter
Tullahoma, Tennessee

1 pound bulk pork sausage
1 green pepper, chopped
1 cup chopped onion
1 cup tomato juice
1 can (14-1/2 ounces) diced tomatoes, undrained
2 tablespoons minced fresh oregano *or* 2 teaspoons dried oregano
1/4 teaspoon salt
Dash pepper
1/4 cup butter *or* margarine
1 medium head cabbage, thinly sliced

In a skillet, cook sausage, green pepper and onion until the sausage is browned; drain. Stir in the tomato juice, tomatoes, oregano, salt and pepper; simmer for 1 hour. Melt butter in a Dutch oven;

saute cabbage over medium heat until tender, about 15 minutes. Transfer to a serving platter; top with the meat sauce. **Yield:** 4-6 servings.

— 🥄 🥄 🥄 —

Old-World Stuffed Pork Chops

(Pictured below)

Years ago, a relative ran a restaurant in downtown Milwaukee, where several well-known German restaurants still operate. This is one of the recipes she developed. The savory stuffing and juicy pork chops are always a hit. —Jeanne Schuyler
Wauwatosa, Wisconsin

4 pork chops (1/2 inch thick)
1 to 2 tablespoons vegetable oil
Salt and pepper to taste
3 cups dry unseasoned bread cubes
1 can (16 ounces) cream-style corn
1 egg, lightly beaten
1 teaspoon grated onion
1/2 teaspoon rubbed sage
1/2 teaspoon dried basil
1/2 teaspoon salt
1/4 teaspoon pepper

In a skillet, brown pork chops in oil on both sides; sprinkle with salt and pepper. Meanwhile, in a bowl, combine remaining ingredients and mix well. Alternate the pork chops and stuffing lengthwise in a greased 3-qt. or 11-in. x 7-in. x 2-in. baking dish. Bake, uncovered, at 350° for 1 hour or until juices run clear. **Yield:** 4 servings.

Lone Star Pot Roast

(Pictured below)

The addition of chopped green chilies and taco seasoning mix make this pot roast especially flavorful.
— *Helen Carpenter, Marble Falls, Texas*

1 boneless beef chuck roast (3 to 3-1/2 pounds)
2 tablespoons vegetable oil
1 can (14-1/2 ounces) diced tomatoes, undrained
1 can (4 ounces) chopped green chilies
1/2 envelope taco seasoning mix (2 tablespoons)
2 teaspoons beef bouillon granules
1 teaspoon sugar
1/4 cup cold water
3 tablespoons all-purpose flour

In a Dutch oven, brown roast in oil. Combine tomatoes, chilies, taco seasoning, bouillon and sugar; pour over the roast. Cover and simmer 2 to 2-1/2 hours or until meat is tender. Remove roast to a platter and keep warm. For gravy, pour 2 cups pan juices into a saucepan. Combine the cold water and flour; stir until smooth. Add to juices; cook and stir over high heat until thickened and bubbly, about 3 minutes. Slice roast. Serve with gravy. **Yield:** 6-8 servings.

MEATY MEALS. Beef up your menu monotony by offering hearty dishes. Barbecued Beef Short Ribs, Best Meat Loaf, Lone Star Pot Roast and Texas Taco Platter (shown above, clockwise from top) are some of the very best beef recipes.

Texas Taco Platter

(Pictured below left)

I take full advantage of versatile ground beef when entertaining by serving up this fun-filled dish. I've used this recipe many times, and everyone enjoys it. No one can resist this beefy entree topped with cheese, lettuce, tomatoes and olives. —*Kathy Young, Weatherford, Texas*

        2 pounds ground beef
        1 large onion, chopped
        1 can (14-1/2 ounces) diced tomatoes, undrained
        1 can (12 ounces) tomato paste
        1 can (15 ounces) tomato puree
        2 tablespoons chili powder
        1 teaspoon ground cumin
    1/2 teaspoon garlic powder
        2 teaspoons salt
        1 can (28 ounces) ranch-style beans, undrained
        1 package (10-1/2 ounces) corn chips
        2 cups hot cooked rice
TOPPINGS:
        2 cups (8 ounces) shredded cheddar cheese
        1 medium onion, chopped
        1 head iceberg lettuce, shredded
        3 medium tomatoes, chopped
        1 can (2-1/4 ounces) sliced ripe olives, drained
        1 cup picante sauce, optional

In a large skillet or Dutch oven, brown beef and onion; drain. Add next seven ingredients; simmer for 1-1/2 hours. Add beans and heat through. On a platter, layer the corn chips, rice, meat mixture, cheese, onion, lettuce, tomatoes and olives. Serve with picante sauce if desired. **Yield:** 10-12 servings.

Best Meat Loaf

(Pictured at left)

If you're like my husband, you enjoy a hearty meat loaf. Everyone who's ever tried it agrees it lives up to its name. This delicious dish doesn't last long! —*Dorothy Pritchett, Wills Point, Texas*

    1/3 cup chopped onion
    1/3 cup chopped sweet red pepper
    1/3 cup chopped green pepper
        3 tablespoons minced fresh parsley
        3 garlic cloves, minced
    1-1/4 teaspoons chili powder
    1-1/4 teaspoons dried sage
    1-1/4 teaspoons salt
        1 teaspoon pepper
        2 pounds ground beef

    3/4 cup milk
        2 eggs, beaten
    1/4 cup Worcestershire sauce
    2/3 cup dry bread crumbs
        4 bacon strips
SAUCE:
    1/4 cup chopped canned tomatoes
    1/4 cup ketchup
        2 tablespoons brown sugar
        1 teaspoon salt
        1 teaspoon ground mustard
    1/2 teaspoon pepper

In a large bowl, combine the first 9 ingredients. Add beef; mix well. Combine the milk, eggs and Worcestershire sauce; mix into the beef mixture. Add crumbs. Grease a large sheet of foil. Place bacon on foil. Mold meat mixture into a loaf and place over bacon. Seal foil tightly around loaf. Refrigerate for 2 hours or overnight. Place wrapped loaf on a baking sheet. Bake at 350° for 1 hour. Open foil; drain juices. Combine sauce ingredients and spoon over loaf. Bake, uncovered, 30 minutes longer or until no pink remains and a meat thermometer reads 160°. **Yield:** 8 servings.

Barbecued Beef Short Ribs

(Pictured at far left)

For a real straight-from-the-chuckwagon beef meal, you can't rope a better recipe than this! This is the recipe I rely on when feeding a hungry group. The wonderfully tangy sauce is lip-smacking good. —*Mildred Sherrer, Bay City, Texas*

        3 to 4 pounds bone-in beef short ribs
        1 tablespoon vegetable oil
    2-1/2 cups water, *divided*
        1 can (6 ounces) tomato paste
        1 cup ketchup
        1 garlic clove, minced
    3/4 cup packed brown sugar
    1/2 cup chopped onion
    1/2 cup vinegar
        2 tablespoons prepared mustard
    1-1/2 teaspoons salt
Hot cooked noodles, optional

In a Dutch oven, brown ribs in oil. Add 2 cups water; bring to a boil. Reduce heat; cover and simmer for 1-1/2 hours. Drain. Combine the tomato paste, ketchup, garlic, brown sugar, onion, vinegar, mustard, salt and remaining water; mix well. Pour over ribs; bring to a boil. Reduce heat; cover and simmer for 1 hour or until meat is tender. Serve over noodles if desired. **Yield:** 4-6 servings.

Sweet-and-Sour Pork

(Pictured above)

After my sister moved away to the university, I used to visit her on weekends. She often made this wonderful and tangy pork dish. Now, every time I make it for my family, it reminds me of those special visits.
—*Cherry Williams, St. Albert, Alberta*

  1 **pound pork tenderloin**
  2 **cans (8 ounces *each*) pineapple tidbits, undrained**
1/3 **cup ketchup**
1/3 **cup water**
  2 **tablespoons *each* soy sauce, vinegar, brown sugar and cornstarch**
3/4 **teaspoon salt**
1/4 **teaspoon pepper**
1/4 **teaspoon ground ginger**
  2 **tablespoons vegetable oil**
  1 **medium onion, chopped**
  1 **green pepper, cut into thin strips**
Hot cooked rice

Cut the tenderloin into 1-1/2-in. x 1/4-in. strips; set aside. Drain pineapple, reserving juice in a small bowl. Set pineapple aside. To juice, add ketchup, water, soy sauce, vinegar, brown sugar, cornstarch, salt, pepper and ginger; stir until smooth. Heat oil in a large skillet or wok on high; stir-fry pork and onion for 5-7 minutes or until pork is no longer pink. Stir pineapple juice mixture; add to skillet. Cook and stir until thickened and bubbly. Add pineapple and green pepper. Reduce heat; cover and cook for 5 minutes. Serve immediately over rice. **Yield:** 4 servings.

Yankee Pot Roast

Rubbing garlic onto the roast before browning adds lots of flavor. With this recipe, the meat and vegetables turn out moist and tender. —*Bill Schultz Walden, New York*

  2 **garlic cloves, minced**
  1 **beef chuck roast (3 to 3-1/2 pounds)**
1/4 **cup all-purpose flour**
1/4 **cup vegetable oil**
  1 **cup tomato juice**
  4 **medium carrots, sliced**
  2 **medium onions, chopped**
  1 **cup thinly sliced celery**
  2 **bay leaves**
  1 **teaspoon salt**
1/2 **teaspoon dried thyme**
1/4 **teaspoon pepper**
  4 **medium potatoes, peeled and quartered**

Rub garlic onto roast, then coat with flour. In a large Dutch oven, brown roast in oil. Add tomato juice, carrots, onions, celery, bay leaves, salt, thyme and pepper; bring to a boil. Reduce heat; cover and simmer for 3-1/2 hours, turning meat occasionally. Add potatoes; simmer for 30 minutes or until tender. Remove bay leaf. Remove roast and slice; serve with vegetables and gravy. **Yield:** 4-6 servings.

Quail in Mushroom Gravy

(Pictured on page 66)

We live in an area with many Southern plantations, and quail are abundant. I cook this tasty dish with rich mushroom gravy often when my two boys are home.
—*Jean Williams, Hurtsboro, Alabama*

3/4 **cup all-purpose flour, *divided***
  1 **teaspoon salt**
1/2 **teaspoon pepper**
  6 **quail (1/3 to 1/2 pound *each*)**
1/2 **cup butter *or* margarine**
1/2 **pound fresh mushrooms, sliced**
  2 **cups chicken broth**
  2 **teaspoons minced fresh thyme *or* 3/4 teaspoon dried thyme**
Hot cooked noodles, optional

Combine 1/2 cup flour, salt and pepper; coat each quail. Melt butter in a skillet; brown the quail. Transfer to an ungreased 2-1/2-qt. baking dish. In the pan drippings, saute the mushrooms until tender. Add remaining flour and stir to make a smooth paste. Add broth and thyme, stirring constantly. Bring to a boil; boil for 1 minute or until thickened. Pour over the quail. Cover and bake at 350° for 40-

50 minutes or until tender and juices run clear. Serve over noodles if desired. **Yield:** 6 servings.

Grilled Lime Chicken

A wonderful citrusy marinade makes this chicken tangy and tasty. A few hours before dinner, simply marinate the chicken for a fuss-free meal later on.
—*Lisa Dougherty, Vacaville, California*

☑ Uses less fat, sugar or salt. Includes Nutritional Analysis and Diabetic Exchanges.

  8 boneless skinless chicken breast halves
1/2 cup lime juice
1/3 cup olive oil
  4 green onions, chopped
  4 garlic cloves, minced
  3 tablespoons chopped fresh dill, *divided*
1/4 teaspoon pepper

Pound chicken breasts to flatten. Combine lime juice, oil, onions, garlic, 2 tablespoons dill and pepper in a resealable plastic bag. Add chicken; seal and refrigerate 2-4 hours. Drain; discard marinade. Grill chicken, uncovered, over medium-hot heat for 12-15 minutes or until tender and juices run clear. Turn after 6 minutes. Sprinkle with remaining dill before serving. **Yield:** 8 servings. **Nutritional Analysis:** One serving equals 235 calories, 66 mg sodium, 73 mg cholesterol, 3 gm carbohydrate, 27 gm protein, 12 gm fat. **Diabetic Exchanges:** 3 lean meat, 1 vegetable, 1 fat.

Chicken Parmesan

With the convenience of boneless skinless chicken breasts, I rely on this recipe often. Oregano gives the coating a distinct, tasty flavor. —*Sharon Kelley Modesto, California*

1/2 cup grated Parmesan cheese
1/4 cup dry bread crumbs
  1 teaspoon dried oregano
  1 teaspoon dried parsley flakes
1/4 teaspoon paprika
1/4 teaspoon salt
1/4 teaspoon pepper
  6 boneless skinless chicken breast halves
1/4 cup butter *or* margarine, melted

In a large bowl, combine the first seven ingredients. Dip chicken in butter and then into crumb mixture. Place in a greased 15-in. x 10-in. x 1-in. baking pan. Bake, uncovered, at 400° for 20-25 minutes or until chicken is tender and juices run clear. **Yield:** 6 servings.

Crustless Swiss Quiche

(Pictured below)

I received this recipe from my mother-in-law, an all-around great cook. Everyone raves about her rich quiche when she serves it at card parties.
—*Marlene Kole, Highland Heights, Ohio*

1/2 cup butter *or* margarine
1/2 cup all-purpose flour
1-1/2 cups milk
2-1/2 cups cottage cheese
  1 teaspoon baking powder
  1 teaspoon salt
  1 teaspoon Dijon mustard
  9 eggs
  2 packages (one 8 ounces, one 3 ounces) cream cheese, softened
  3 cups (12 ounces) shredded Swiss cheese
1/3 cup grated Parmesan cheese

Melt butter in a medium saucepan. Stir in flour; cook and stir until bubbly. Gradually add milk; cook over medium heat, stirring occasionally, until sauce thickens. Remove from the heat; set aside to cool, about 15-20 minutes. Meanwhile, combine cottage cheese, baking powder, salt and mustard; set aside. In a large mixing bowl, beat the eggs. Slowly add cream cheese, cottage cheese mixture and cream sauce. Fold in Swiss and Parmesan cheeses. Pour into two greased 10-in. pie plates. Bake at 350° for 40 minutes or until a knife inserted near the center comes out clean. Serve immediately. **Yield:** 16-20 servings.

Pizza Meat Loaf

This is a fun and flavorful loaf that will please the palates of those who like pizza. The sauce and cheese really star. —Jim Hopkins, Whittier, California

    2 eggs
    1 jar (14 ounces) pizza sauce, *divided*
    1 cup (4 ounces) shredded mozzarella
      cheese
    1 cup seasoned bread crumbs
  1/4 teaspoon garlic salt
  1/8 teaspoon pepper
    2 pounds ground beef
  1/2 pound bulk Italian sausage

In a large bowl, beat eggs. Add 3/4 cup of pizza sauce, cheese, bread crumbs, garlic salt and pepper; mix well. Combine beef and sausage; add to egg mixture and mix well. Press into a 9-in. x 5-in. x 3-in. loaf pan. Bake at 350° for 1-1/4 hours. Drain. Spoon remaining pizza sauce over meat loaf; bake 15 minutes longer or until no pink remains and a meat thermometer reads 160°. Let stand 10 minutes before slicing. **Yield:** 6-8 servings.

Ranch Mac 'n' Cheese

(Pictured above)

I came up with the recipe for this creamy and satisfying macaroni and cheese, which has a special twist. My husband requests it often—it's hearty enough to serve as a main dish. —Michelle Rotunno
Independence, Missouri

    1 cup milk
  1/4 cup butter *or* margarine
    2 envelopes ranch salad dressing mix
    1 teaspoon lemon-pepper seasoning
    1 teaspoon garlic pepper
    1 teaspoon garlic salt
    1 cup cubed Colby cheese
    1 cup cubed Monterey Jack cheese
    1 cup (8 ounces) sour cream
  1/2 cup crushed saltines (about 15 crackers)
    1 pound elbow macaroni, cooked and
      drained
Grated Parmesan cheese

In a Dutch oven, combine the milk, butter, salad dressing mix, lemon pepper, garlic pepper, garlic salt, Colby and Monterey Jack cheese. Cook and stir over medium heat until cheese is melted and mixture begins to thicken. Fold in the sour cream. Add cracker crumbs and macaroni. Cook until heated through, stirring frequently. Sprinkle with Parmesan cheese. **Yield:** 6-8 servings.

Meal in a Mug

Noodles, beans and ground beef make this a warm hearty lunch. It's especially nice to serve during the colder months. —Geraldine Grisdale
Mt. Pleasant, Michigan

    1 pound ground beef
    2 cups water
    1 can (21 ounces) pork and beans,
      undrained
    1 can (14-1/2 ounces) diced tomatoes,
      undrained
    1 envelope sloppy joe mix
    1 cup uncooked elbow macaroni

In a large saucepan, brown ground beef; drain. Add water, pork and beans, tomatoes and sloppy joe mix. Bring to a boil; add macaroni and reduce heat. Cover and simmer for 10 minutes or until the macaroni is almost cooked. Pour into thermoses. **Yield:** 8 servings.

Buying Ground Beef

There are many choices when purchasing ground beef—ground sirloin (contains 15 percent fat), ground round (20 to 23 percent fat), ground chuck (23 to 30 percent fat) and ground beef (30 percent fat). The lower percentage of fat, the drier the cooked meat will be. The higher the percentage of fat, the more shrinkage there is after cooking.

Grilled Tarragon Chicken

Just a few simple seasonings is all that's needed to make grilled chicken moist and tasty. Mustard and tarragon make a great combination. —*Janie Thorpe*
Tullahoma, Tennessee

☑ Uses less fat, sugar or salt. Includes Nutritional Analysis and Diabetic Exchanges.

- **2 teaspoons Dijon mustard**
- **4 boneless skinless chicken breast halves**
- **1/4 teaspoon pepper**
- **1/3 cup butter *or* margarine, melted**
- **2 teaspoons lemon juice**
- **2 teaspoons minced fresh tarragon *or* 1/2 teaspoon dried tarragon**
- **1/2 teaspoon garlic salt**

Spread mustard on both sides of chicken; sprinkle with pepper. Cover and refrigerate at least 2 hours. Combine butter, lemon juice, tarragon and garlic salt. Grill chicken over hot heat until juices run clear, basting with butter mixture during last 3-5 minutes. **Yield:** 4 servings. **Nutritional Analysis:** One serving (prepared with margarine) equals 222 calories, 167 mg sodium, 73 mg cholesterol, 1 gm carbohydrate, 27 gm protein, 12 gm fat. **Diabetic Exchanges:** 4 lean meat.

— ♟ ♟ ♟ —

Smothered Meatballs

When I left home, I either had to learn to cook or eat convenience foods...I was too spoiled by Mom's delicious cooking to settle for that! —*Jerry Minerich*
Westminster, Colorado

- **2 slices bread, torn**
- **1-1/4 cups milk, *divided***
- **2 eggs, beaten**
- **1 teaspoon salt**
- **1/2 teaspoon poultry seasoning**
- **1/2 teaspoon pepper**
- **1 medium onion, finely chopped**
- **1 pound ground beef**
- **2 tablespoons vegetable oil**
- **1 can (10-3/4 ounces) condensed cream of mushroom soup, undiluted**

In a bowl, soak bread in 1/4 cup of milk for 2 minutes. Add eggs, salt, poultry seasoning, pepper and onion; mix well. Add beef; mix well. Shape into 1-in. balls. In a skillet, brown meatballs in oil; drain. Combine soup and the remaining milk; pour over meatballs. Stir until the sauce is heated. Pour into a 1-1/2-qt. baking dish. Bake, uncovered, at 350° for 25 minutes or until hot and bubbly. **Yield:** 4 servings.

Pork Tenderloin Diane

(Pictured above)

We have pork at least once a week, and this is one dish we especially enjoy. Moist tender pork "medallions" are served up in a savory sauce for a combination that's irresistible. I'm not sure where the recipe came from, but I'm glad I have it. —*Janie Thorpe*
Tullahoma, Tennessee

☑ Uses less fat, sugar or salt. Includes Nutritional Analysis and Diabetic Exchanges.

- **1 pork tenderloin (about 1 pound)**
- **1 tablespoon lemon-pepper seasoning**
- **2 tablespoons butter *or* margarine**
- **2 tablespoons lemon juice**
- **1 tablespoon Worcestershire sauce**
- **1 teaspoon Dijon mustard**
- **1 tablespoon minced fresh parsley**

Cut tenderloin into eight pieces; place each piece between two pieces of plastic wrap or waxed paper and flatten to 1/2-in. thickness. Sprinkle with lemon pepper. Melt butter in a large skillet over medium heat; cook pork for 3-4 minutes on each side or until no longer pink and juices run clear. Remove to a serving platter and keep warm. To the pan juices, add lemon juice, Worcestershire sauce and mustard; heat through, stirring occasionally. Pour over the pork and sprinkle with parsley. **Yield:** 4 servings. **Nutritional Analysis:** One serving (prepared with margarine) equals 214 calories, 491 mg sodium, 6 mg cholesterol, 1 gm carbohydrate, 18 gm protein, 14 gm fat. **Diabetic Exchanges:** 3 meat.

Breads, Rolls & Muffins

From muffins, biscuits and coffee cakes to quick breads, rolls and yeast breads, you can offer your family oven-fresh favorites around the clock.

— 🥄 🥄 🥄 —

BAKED GOODIES. Clockwise from upper left: Multigrain Buns (p. 103), Muenster Bread (p. 109), Pecan Cranberry Muffins (p. 108), Italian Cheese Twists (p. 98) and Lemon Blueberry Bread (p. 101).

and water; brush over the twists. Sprinkle with sesame seeds and/or Parmesan cheese. Bake at 375° for 10-12 minutes or until light golden brown. Serve warm. **Yield:** 2 dozen.

Zucchini-Oatmeal Muffins

As any cook with a booming zucchini crop knows, you can never have too many recipes calling for that abundant vegetable! —Shirlee Nelson, Marcus, Iowa

2-1/2 cups all-purpose flour
1-1/2 cups sugar
1/2 cup quick-cooking oats
1 tablespoon baking powder
1 teaspoon salt
1 teaspoon ground cinnamon
4 eggs, lightly beaten
3/4 cup vegetable oil
1-1/2 cups shredded peeled zucchini
1/2 cup raisins *or* chopped dates
1/2 cup chopped pecans

In a bowl, mix first six ingredients. Combine eggs and oil; stir into dry ingredients just until moistened. Fold in zucchini, raisins and pecans. Spoon into greased or paper-lined muffin cups. Bake at 400° for 20-25 minutes. Cool in pans for 5 minutes before removing to wire rack to cool completely. **Yield:** 1-1/2 dozen.

Italian Cheese Twists

(Pictured above and on page 96)

My family loves breadsticks, and this recipe was an immediate success. The breadsticks look delicate and fancy, but they aren't tricky to make using prepared bread dough. —Marna Heitz, Farley, Iowa

1 loaf (1 pound) frozen white bread dough, thawed
1/4 cup butter *or* margarine, softened
1/4 teaspoon garlic powder
1/4 teaspoon *each* dried basil, oregano and marjoram
3/4 cup shredded mozzarella cheese
1 egg
1 tablespoon water
2 tablespoons sesame seeds *and/or* grated Parmesan cheese

On a lightly floured surface, roll dough into a 12-in. square. Combine butter and seasonings; spread over dough. Sprinkle with mozzarella cheese. Fold dough into thirds. Cut crosswise into 24 strips, 1/2 in. each. Twist each strip twice; pinch ends to seal. Place 2 in. apart on a greased baking sheet. Cover and let rise in a warm place until almost doubled, about 30 minutes. In a small bowl, beat egg

---

Quick Bread Snack

When you make a quick bread, make an extra loaf. Slice the extra loaf into single servings, wrap them individually in plastic wrap and store them in the freezer. A frozen wrapped slice fits nicely into a lunch bag, and thaws in time for lunch.

Cranberry Nut Bread

Whenever I serve slices of this favorite treat, someone asks for the recipe. It's a moist, dark bread chockfull of old-fashioned, spicy goodness. —Maxine Smith, Owanka, South Dakota

2-1/2 cups halved fresh *or* frozen cranberries, *divided*
2/3 cup sugar
2 teaspoons grated orange peel
2-1/4 cups all-purpose flour
3/4 cup packed light brown sugar
1 tablespoon baking soda
1/2 teaspoon salt
2 teaspoons ground cinnamon

1/4 teaspoon ground cloves
2 eggs, lightly beaten
3/4 cup sour cream
1/4 cup butter *or* margarine, melted
1 cup chopped pecans

In a saucepan, combine 1-1/2 cups cranberries, sugar and orange peel. Bring to a boil; reduce heat and cook for 6-8 minutes or until the cranberries are soft. Remove from the heat; stir in the remaining berries and set aside. In a bowl, combine flour, brown sugar, baking soda, salt, cinnamon and cloves. Combine eggs, sour cream and butter; stir into dry ingredients until blended. Fold in cranberries and pecans. Pour into two greased 8-1/2-in. x 4-1/2-in. x 2-1/2-in. loaf pans. Bake at 350° for 55-60 minutes or until breads test done. Cool in pans for 10 minutes before removing to wire racks to cool completely. **Yield:** 2 loaves.

— ▼ ▼ ▼ —

Caraway Rye Bread

This pretty round bread's old-world flavor is so comforting and delicious. Just the right amount of caraway flavors the rye. —Connie Moore, Medway, Ohio

☑ Uses less fat, sugar or salt. Includes Nutritional Analysis and Diabetic Exchanges.

2 packages (1/4 ounce *each*) active dry yeast
1-1/2 cups warm water (110° to 115°), *divided*
3 tablespoons molasses
3 tablespoons butter *or* margarine, melted
1 tablespoon caraway seed
1 teaspoon salt
1-1/2 to 2 cups all-purpose flour
1-1/2 cups whole wheat flour
1 cup rye flour

In mixing bowl, dissolve yeast in 1/2 cup water. Add molasses, butter, caraway, salt and remaining water; mix well. Combine flours; add 3 cups to batter. Beat until smooth. Add enough remaining flour to form a firm dough. Turn onto a floured surface; knead until smooth and elastic, about 6-8 minutes. Place in greased bowl, turning once to grease top. Cover and let rise in a warm place until doubled, about 1 hour. Punch dough down; shape into a round loaf. Place on a greased baking sheet. Cover and let rise until doubled, about 30 minutes. Bake at 375° for 20-25 minutes or until golden brown. Transfer loaf to wire rack; cool. **Yield:** 1 loaf (16 slices). **Nutritional Analysis:** One slice equals 128 calories, 153 mg sodium, 0 cholesterol, 26 gm carbohydrate, 4 gm protein, 1 gm fat. **Diabetic Exchanges:** 2 starch.

Herbed Peasant Bread

(Pictured below)

The recipe for this beautiful, flavorful loaf came from our daughter-in-law, Karen. She's a great cook. Everyone who enjoys a slice of this moist bread asks me for the recipe. It's super used for a sandwich or just served with butter. —Ardath Effa, Villa Park, Illinois

1/2 cup chopped onion
3 tablespoons butter *or* margarine
1 cup plus 2 tablespoons warm milk (120° to 130°)
1 tablespoon sugar
1-1/2 teaspoons salt
1/2 teaspoon dill weed
1/2 teaspoon dried basil
1/2 teaspoon dried rosemary, crushed
1 package (1/4 ounce) active dry yeast
3 to 3-1/2 cups all-purpose flour
Melted butter *or* margarine

In a skillet over low heat, saute onion in butter until tender, about 8 minutes. Cool for 10 minutes. Place in a mixing bowl. Add milk, sugar, salt, herbs, yeast and 3 cups flour; beat until smooth. Add enough remaining flour to form a soft dough. Turn onto a floured surface; knead until smooth and elastic, about 6-8 minutes. Place in a greased bowl, turning once to grease top. Cover and let rise in a warm place until doubled, about 45 minutes. Punch the dough down. Shape into a ball and place on a greased baking sheet. Cover and let rise until doubled, about 45 minutes. Bake at 375° for 25-30 minutes. Remove to a wire rack; brush with melted butter. Cool. **Yield:** 1 loaf.

Bread's Ready—Fast!

OUR readers slice up these sweet and savory quick breads fresh from their ovens and have shared the recipes for you to enjoy.

— ▼ ▼ ▼ —

Cheddar-Dill Bread

(Pictured below)

With soup and salad, this savory cheese bread sparked with dill makes a terrific meal. —Karen Gardiner
Eutaw, Alabama

    2 cups self-rising flour*
    1 tablespoon sugar
  1/4 cup cold butter *or* margarine
    1 cup (4 ounces) shredded sharp cheddar
      cheese
    2 teaspoons dill weed
    1 egg
  3/4 cup milk

In a large bowl, combine flour and sugar. Cut in butter until crumbly; stir in the cheese and dill. In a small bowl, beat egg and milk; pour into dry ingredients and stir just until moistened. (Batter will be very thick.) Pour into a greased 8-in. x 4-in. x

2-in. loaf pan. Bake at 350° for 35-40 minutes or until bread tests done. Cool in pan 10 minutes before removing to a wire rack to cool completely. **Yield:** 1 loaf. ***Editor's Note:** As a substitute for self-rising flour, place 1 tablespoon baking powder and 1 teaspoon salt in a measuring cup. Add enough all-purpose flour to equal 2 cups.

— ▼ ▼ ▼ —

Dutch Apple Bread

(Pictured below)

This fruity streusel-topped bread is delightful for breakfast or brunch. Plus, it's a great make-ahead treat that freezes well. —June Formanek, Belle Plaine, Iowa

  1/2 cup butter *or* margarine, softened
    1 cup sugar
    2 eggs
    1 teaspoon vanilla extract
    2 cups all-purpose flour
    1 teaspoon baking soda
  1/2 teaspoon salt
  1/3 cup buttermilk
    1 cup chopped peeled apple

BEST BREADS. Cheddar-Dill and Dutch Apple Breads (shown above, left to right) are simple to stir up and big on taste.

1/3 cup chopped walnuts
TOPPING:
  1/3 cup all-purpose flour
    2 tablespoons sugar
    2 tablespoons brown sugar
  1/2 teaspoon ground cinnamon
    3 tablespoons cold butter *or* margarine

In a mixing bowl, cream butter and sugar. Beat in eggs and vanilla. Combine flour, baking soda and salt; stir into the creamed mixture alternately with buttermilk. Fold in apple and nuts. Pour into a greased 9-in. x 5-in. x 3-in. loaf pan. For topping, combine the first four ingredients; cut in butter until crumbly. Sprinkle over batter. Bake at 350° for 55-60 minutes or until bread tests done. Cool in pan 10 minutes before removing to a wire rack to cool completely. **Yield:** 1 loaf.

Lemon Bread

Family and friends often find this sunshiny-sweet bread baking in my kitchen. With its pound cake-like texture, it's wonderful with a steaming cup of tea or coffee. —Kathy Scott, Hemingford, Nebraska

  1/2 cup butter *or* margarine, softened
    1 cup sugar
    2 eggs
    2 tablespoons lemon juice
    1 tablespoon grated lemon peel
1-1/2 cups all-purpose flour
    1 teaspoon baking powder
  1/8 teaspoon salt
  1/2 cup milk
GLAZE:
    2 tablespoons lemon juice
  1/2 cup confectioners' sugar

In a mixing bowl, cream butter and sugar. Beat in eggs, lemon juice and peel. Combine flour, baking powder and salt; stir into creamed mixture alternately with milk. Pour into a greased 8-in. x 4-in. x 2-in. loaf pan. Bake at 350° for 45 minutes or until bread tests done. Combine glaze ingredients. Remove bread from pan; immediately drizzle with glaze. Cool on a wire rack. **Yield:** 1 loaf.

Apricot Walnut Bread

Orange juice and oat bran add flavor and texture to this recipe. And apricots make each slice nice and moist. —Diane Hixon, Niceville, Florida

✓ Uses less fat, sugar or salt. Includes Nutritional Analysis and Diabetic Exchanges.

    4 egg whites
  2/3 cup water
  1/2 cup orange juice
  1/4 cup vegetable oil
    1 teaspoon vanilla extract
  3/4 cup uncooked oat bran hot cereal
  1/2 cup chopped dried apricots
1-1/4 cups all-purpose flour
  1/2 cup packed brown sugar
    1 teaspoon baking powder
  1/2 teaspoon baking soda
  1/4 cup chopped walnuts

In a bowl, combine the first five ingredients. Stir in oat bran and apricots. Combine flour, brown sugar, baking powder and soda; stir into apricot mixture just until moistened. Fold in nuts. Pour into a greased 8-in. x 4-in. x 2-in. loaf pan. Bake at 350° for 50-55 minutes or until bread tests done. Cool in pan 10 minutes before removing to wire rack. **Yield:** 1 loaf (16 slices). **Nutritional Analysis:** One slice equals 141 calories, 42 mg sodium, 0 cholesterol, 20 gm carbohydrate, 4 gm protein, 5 gm fat. **Diabetic Exchanges:** 1 starch, 1 fat, 1/2 fruit.

Lemon Blueberry Bread

(Pictured on page 96)

Of all the quick breads we had growing up, this beautifully glazed, berry-studded loaf is the best. —Julianne Johnson, Grove City, Minnesota

  1/3 cup butter *or* margarine, melted
    1 cup sugar
    3 tablespoons lemon juice
    2 eggs
1-1/2 cups all-purpose flour
    1 teaspoon baking powder
  1/2 teaspoon salt
  1/2 cup milk
    2 tablespoons grated lemon peel
  1/2 cup chopped nuts
    1 cup fresh *or* frozen blueberries
GLAZE:
    2 tablespoons lemon juice
  1/4 cup sugar

In a mixing bowl, beat butter, sugar, juice and eggs. Combine flour, baking powder and salt; stir into egg mixture alternately with milk. Fold in peel, nuts and blueberries. Pour into a greased 8-in. x 4-in. x 2-in. loaf pan. Bake at 350° for 60-70 minutes or until bread tests done. Cool in pan for 10 minutes. Meanwhile, combine glaze ingredients. Remove bread from pan and drizzle with glaze. Cool on a wire rack. **Yield:** 1 loaf.

Quick Cherry Turnovers

(Pictured above)

These fruit-filled pastries are my family's favorite at breakfast. You can substitute other fillings for cherry.
—*Elleen Oberrueter, Danbury, Iowa*

> 1 tube (8 ounces) refrigerated crescent rolls
> 1 cup cherry pie filling
> 1/2 cup confectioners' sugar
> 1 to 2 tablespoons milk

Unroll dough and separate into eight triangles; make four squares by pressing the seams of two triangles together and rolling into shape. Place on an ungreased baking sheet. Spoon 1/4 cup pie filling in one corner of each square. Fold to make triangles; pinch to seal. Bake at 375° for 10-12 minutes or until golden. Mix sugar and enough milk to reach drizzling consistency. Drizzle over turnovers; serve warm. **Yield:** 4 servings.

━━━━ 🥤 🥤 🥤 ━━━━

Cardamom Holiday Bread

I have fond memories of coming home from school to find this bread cooling on a wire rack. I could hardly wait for a warm savory slice. —*Sheryl Olstad Rochester, New Hampshire*

> 2 packages (1/4 ounce *each*) active dry yeast
> 3/4 cup warm water (110° to 115°)
> 1 can (12 ounces) evaporated milk
> 1 cup sugar
> 1 teaspoon salt
> 1/2 cup butter *or* margarine, softened
> 4 eggs, beaten
> 1 to 1-1/2 teaspoons ground cardamom

> 7-1/2 to 8 cups all-purpose flour
> Confectioners' sugar glaze
> Candied cherries and sliced almonds

In a mixing bowl, dissolve yeast in water. Add milk, sugar, salt, butter, eggs, cardamom and 2 cups flour; beat until smooth. Add enough remaining flour to form a soft dough. Turn onto a floured surface; knead until smooth and elastic, about 6-8 minutes. Place in greased bowl, turning once to grease top. Cover and let rise in a warm place until doubled, about 1-1/2 hours. Punch dough down; let rest 10 minutes. Divide into nine portions; shape each into a 12-in. strip. Place three strips on a greased baking sheet and braid, sealing ends. Repeat with remaining strips. Cover and let rise until nearly doubled, about 45 minutes. Bake at 375° for 20-25 minutes or until golden. Transfer loaves to wire racks to cool. Glaze and decorate with cherries and almonds. **Yield:** 3 loaves.

━━━━ 🥤 🥤 🥤 ━━━━

Applesauce Muffins

These are such a popular item at the restaurant I own that I had it printed up on a card to share with guests.
—*Judy Noble, Findley Lake, New York*

> 1/2 cup butter *or* margarine, softened
> 1-1/2 cups sugar
> 2 eggs
> 2 cups all-purpose flour
> 1 teaspoon baking powder
> 1 teaspoon ground cinnamon
> 1/2 teaspoon baking soda
> 1/2 teaspoon ground cloves
> 1/4 teaspoon salt
> 1 cup applesauce

In a mixing bowl, cream butter and sugar. Add eggs, one at a time, beating well after each addition. Combine dry ingredients; add to the creamed mixture alternately with applesauce. Mix just until combined. Fill greased or paper-lined muffin cups two-thirds full. Bake at 350° for 20-25 minutes. Cool in pans for 5 minutes before removing to wire rack to cool completely. **Yield:** about 1-1/2 dozen.

Selecting Pecans

When selecting unshelled pecans, look for clean shells without holes or cracks. The heavier the nut, the meatier it will be. When selecting shelled pecans, pick plump nut meats that are uniform in color and size.

Multigrain Buns

(Pictured on page 96)

Delicious with a meal or to make a sandwich, these light and tasty rolls have a super nutty flavor.
—*Josie Drzewicki, Spirit River, Alberta*

    1 package (1/4 ounce) active dry yeast
    3 cups warm water (110° to 115°)
1-1/2 cups whole wheat flour
    1 cup old-fashioned oats
    1 egg plus 1 egg yolk
  1/4 cup sesame seeds
  1/4 cup salted sunflower kernels
  1/4 cup vegetable oil
    3 tablespoons butter *or* margarine, softened
    2 tablespoons sugar
1-1/2 teaspoons salt
    1 teaspoon caraway seed
  1/2 teaspoon vinegar
5-1/2 to 6 cups all-purpose flour
    2 tablespoons water
Additional oats

In a bowl, dissolve yeast in warm water. Add whole wheat flour, oats, 1 egg, sesame seeds, sunflower kernels, oil, butter, sugar, salt, caraway, vinegar and 2 cups all-purpose flour; beat until smooth. Add enough remaining flour to form a soft dough. Turn onto a floured surface; knead until smooth and elastic, about 6-8 minutes. Place in a greased bowl, turning once to grease top. Cover and let rise in a warm place until doubled, about 1 hour. Punch dough down. Shape into 18 round balls; roll each into a 4-1/2-in. circle. Place on greased baking sheets. Beat egg yolk with water; brush over buns. Sprinkle with oats. Cover and let rise until doubled, about 45 minutes. Bake at 350° for 20 minutes or until golden brown. Transfer buns to wire racks to cool. **Yield:** 1-1/2 dozen.

Pecan Waffles

(Pictured below)

I've tried for years to duplicate a delicious waffle I ate at a restaurant chain here in the South. This is the closest I've come, and they're crisp and nutty. Butter and maple syrup are my family's favorite toppings.
—*Susan Jansen, Smyrna, Georgia*

1-3/4 cups all-purpose flour
    1 tablespoon baking powder
  1/2 teaspoon salt
    2 eggs, *separated*
1-3/4 cups milk
  1/2 cup vegetable oil
    1 cup chopped pecans
Maple syrup

In a bowl, combine flour, baking powder and salt. Combine egg yolks, milk and oil; stir into dry ingredients. Beat egg whites until stiff; fold into batter. Sprinkle hot waffle iron with 2 tablespoons pecans. Pour 1/4 to 1/3 cup of batter over pecans and bake according to manufacturer's directions until golden brown. Repeat with remaining pecans and batter. Serve with syrup. **Yield:** 8-10 waffles (4-1/2 inches).

Say Yes to Yeasty Yummies

WHILE yeast breads may take some time to prepare, you'll agree the extra effort was worth it after one bite of these fresh-from-the-oven goodies.

— 🍞 🍞 🍞 —

Pineapple Sweet Rolls

(Pictured below)

A pan of these marvelous rolls makes any breakfast a holiday! Folks expect typical cinnamon rolls and are pleasantly surprised by these unusual treats.
—Pat Walter, Pine Island, Minnesota

    2 packages (1/4 ounce *each*) active dry
      yeast
1/2 cup warm water (110° to 115°)
1-1/2 cups warm milk (110° to 115°)
    6 tablespoons butter, melted
    1 cup sugar
    1 teaspoon salt
    2 eggs, beaten
    6 to 6-1/2 cups all-purpose flour
FILLING:
    1 tablespoon butter
    1 tablespoon all-purpose flour
1/2 cup orange juice
    2 tablespoons grated orange peel
    1 can (8 ounces) crushed pineapple, drained
1/3 cup sugar
1/8 teaspoon salt
GLAZE:
1/2 cup confectioners' sugar
    1 tablespoon orange juice

Dissolve yeast in water. Add milk, butter, sugar, salt, eggs and 1-1/3 cups flour; beat until smooth. Stir in enough remaining flour to form a soft dough. Turn onto a floured surface; knead until smooth and elastic, about 6-8 minutes. Place in a greased bowl, turning once to grease top. Cover and let rise in a warm place until doubled, about 1 hour. Mean-

YEAST BREAD BONUS. If you "knead" ideas for special loaves and raised-dough treats, why not try Peppery Cheese Bread, Pineapple Sweet Rolls and Homemade Egg Bread (shown above, clockwise from upper left)?

while, melt butter in a saucepan. Add remaining filling ingredients; bring to a boil, stirring constantly. Reduce heat; simmer 3-4 minutes or until thickened. Remove from heat; cool. Punch dough down; divide in half. Roll each half into a 15-in. x 12-in. rectangle; spread with filling. Roll up jelly-roll style starting with long side. Slice into 1-in. rolls. Place with cut side down in two greased 13-in. x 9-in. x 2-in. baking pans. Cover and let rise until doubled, about 1 hour. Bake at 350° for 20-25 minutes. Cool. Combine glaze ingredients; drizzle over rolls. **Yield:** 2-1/2 dozen.

Peppery Cheese Bread
(Pictured below left)

Savory slices of these round loaves will complement any meal. Or use this flavorful bread to liven up ordinary sandwiches.
—Sue Braunschweig
Delafield, Wisconsin

    1 package (1/4 ounce) active dry yeast
1/4 cup warm water (110° to 115°)
    1 cup (8 ounces) sour cream
    1 egg, beaten
    2 tablespoons sugar
    1 teaspoon salt
2-1/3 to 2-1/2 cups all-purpose flour
    1 cup (4 ounces) shredded cheddar cheese
1/2 teaspoon pepper

Dissolve yeast in water. Add the sour cream, egg, sugar, salt and 2/3 cup flour; beat until smooth. Stir in enough remaining flour to form a soft dough (dough will be sticky). Fold in cheese and pepper. Divide in half. Place in two greased 1-lb. coffee cans. Cover and let rise in a warm place until doubled, about 1 hour. Bake at 350° for 45-50 minutes. Remove from cans. **Yield:** 2 loaves.

Homemade Egg Bread
(Pictured at left)

People rave about this tender, delicate bread every time I serve it. The recipe makes two loaves...one for you and your family to enjoy and one to share.
—June Mullins, Livonia, Missouri

    2 packages (1/4 ounce *each*) active dry
      yeast
1/2 cup warm water (110° to 115°)
1-1/2 cups warm milk (110° to 115°)
1/4 cup sugar
    1 tablespoon salt

    3 eggs, beaten
1/4 cup butter *or* margarine, softened
    7 to 7-1/2 cups all-purpose flour
    1 egg yolk
    2 tablespoons water
Sesame seeds

Dissolve yeast in water. Add milk, sugar, salt, eggs, butter and 3-1/2 cups flour; mix well. Stir in enough remaining flour to form a soft dough. Turn onto a floured surface; knead until smooth and elastic, about 6-8 minutes. Place in greased bowl, turning once to grease top. Cover and let rise in warm place until doubled, 1-1/2 to 2 hours. Punch down. Cover and let rise until almost doubled, about 30 minutes. Divide into six portions. On a floured surface, shape each into a 14-in.-long rope. For each loaf, braid three ropes together on a greased baking sheet; pinch ends to seal. Cover and let rise until doubled, 50-60 minutes. Beat egg yolk and water; brush over loaves. Sprinkle with sesame seeds. Bake at 375° for 30-35 minutes. Transfer loaves to wire racks to cool. **Yield:** 2 loaves.

Elephant Ears

The reaction from those who eat these makes them worth the effort. They make quite an impression on the breakfast table.
—Suzanne McKinley
Lyons, Georgia

    1 package (1/4 ounce) active dry yeast
    1 cup warm water (110° to 115°)
    1 cup warm milk (110° to 115°)
    3 tablespoons sugar
    1 tablespoon salt
    3 tablespoons shortening
    4 to 4-1/2 cups all-purpose flour
Oil for deep-fat frying
TOPPING:
    1 cup sugar
    1 teaspoon ground cinnamon

Dissolve yeast in water. Add milk, sugar, salt, shortening and 2 cups flour; beat until smooth. Stir in enough remaining flour to form a soft dough. Turn onto a floured surface; knead until smooth and elastic, about 6-8 minutes. Place in a greased bowl, turning once to grease top. Cover and let rise in a warm place until doubled, about 1 hour. Punch down and shape into 15 ovals, 5-1/2 in. round by 1/8 in. thick. Heat 3-4 in. of oil to 375° in deep-fat fryer. Fry ovals, one at a time, for 3 minutes per side or until golden brown. Drain. Mix sugar and cinnamon; sprinkle over warm pastries. **Yield:** 15 servings.

Cheesy Potato Bread

(Pictured above)

Two crusty golden-brown loaves with terrific flavor and texture are what you'll get when you try this recipe. Potatoes and cheese make an unusual but delicious combination for a yeast bread. My family loves it served with soup or stew on cold days.
—*Deb Amrine, Grand Haven, Michigan*

>   2 packages (1/4 ounce *each*) active dry yeast
>   2 tablespoons sugar
> 1/2 cup warm water (110° to 115°)
>   1 cup half-and-half cream
>   5 tablespoons butter *or* margarine, melted, *divided*
>   1 tablespoon salt
> 1/8 teaspoon cayenne pepper
> 5-1/2 to 6 cups all-purpose flour
>   2 cups finely shredded peeled potatoes
>   1 cup (4 ounces) shredded cheddar cheese

In a large mixing bowl, dissolve the yeast and sugar in warm water; let stand until foamy, about 5 minutes. Add cream, 3 tablespoons butter, salt, cayenne pepper and 2-1/2 cups flour; beat on medium for 2 minutes. Stir in potatoes and enough remaining flour to form a soft dough. Turn onto a floured surface; knead until smooth and elastic, about 8-10 minutes. (Dough will feel slightly sticky.) Place in a greased bowl, turning once to grease top. Cover and let rise in a warm place until almost doubled, about 1 hour. Punch the dough down. Pat into a 1/2-in.-thick rectangle. Sprinkle cheese evenly over dough. Fold dough over the cheese and knead into dough. Shape into two round loaves; place in greased 9-in. round baking pans. Cover and let rise until doubled, about 45 minutes. Cut an X on top of each loaf; brush with remaining butter. Bake at 400° for 35-40 minutes or until golden brown. Remove from pans to cool on wire racks. **Yield:** 2 loaves.

Pumpkin Pancakes

Since my first love after teaching is cooking, I decided to combine the two into a career. I encourage kids in my kindergarten class to help prepare these pancakes.
—*Nancy Horsburgh, Everett, Ontario*

> 1 cup all-purpose flour
> 1 cup quick-cooking oats
> 2 tablespoons wheat germ
> 2 teaspoons sugar

2 teaspoons baking powder
1/2 teaspoon salt
Pinch ground cinnamon
1 cup milk
1 egg, lightly beaten
3/4 cup canned pumpkin
2 tablespoons vegetable oil
Chocolate chips *or* raisins, optional

In a bowl, combine the flour, oats, wheat germ, sugar, baking powder, salt and cinnamon. Combine milk, egg, pumpkin and oil; stir into dry ingredients just until moistened. Pour batter by 1/4 cupfuls onto a lightly greased hot griddle; turn when bubbles form on top of pancakes. Cook until second side is golden brown. Decorate with chocolate chips and raisins if desired. **Yield:** 10-12 pancakes.

Cranberry Canes

These confections are made from a recipe my mother handed down. I still think her breads are better than mine—even when we're using the same recipe!
—Darlene Markel, Sublimity, Oregon

FILLING:
1-1/2 cups chopped fresh *or* frozen cranberries
1/2 cup sugar
1/2 cup raisins
1/3 cup chopped walnuts
1/3 cup honey
DOUGH:
1 package (1/4 ounce) active dry yeast
1/4 cup warm water (110° to 115°)
4 cups all-purpose flour
1/4 cup sugar
1 teaspoon salt
1 cup cold butter *or* margarine
1 cup warm milk (110° to 115°)
2 eggs, lightly beaten
Confectioners' sugar icing, optional

In a saucepan, combine all filling ingredients; bring to a boil. Reduce heat and simmer, uncovered, for 5 minutes. Cool. For dough, dissolve yeast in water; set aside. In a large bowl, combine flour, sugar and salt. Cut in butter until mixture resembles coarse crumbs. Add yeast mixture, milk and eggs; stir to form a soft dough. Place in a greased bowl; cover with plastic wrap. Refrigerate at least 2 hours. Divide dough in half. On a well-floured surface, roll each half into an 18-in. x 15-in. rectangle. Spoon filling down the center of each rectangle widthwise. Fold into thirds so finished rectangles are 15 in. x 6 in. Cut each into 15 strips. Twist strips and shape into candy canes. Place on greased baking sheets. Bake at 375° for 15-18 minutes or un-

til golden. Cool. Frost with confectioners' sugar icing if desired. **Yield:** 30 rolls.

Monkey Bread

When my two boys hear I'm planning on making this bread, they're eager to help. This seems to taste twice as good when they've helped fix it. It's one of our favorites for breakfast or as a snack. —Carol Allen
McLeansboro, Illinois

1 package (3-1/2 ounces) cook and serve butterscotch pudding mix
3/4 cup sugar
1 tablespoon ground cinnamon
1/2 cup finely chopped pecans, optional
1/2 cup butter *or* margarine, melted
3 tubes (10 ounces *each*) refrigerated biscuits

In a plastic bowl with tight-fitting lid, combine pudding mix, sugar, cinnamon and pecans if desired. Pour the butter into a shallow bowl. Cut the biscuits into quarters. Dip several pieces into the butter, then place in bowl; cover and shake. Remove to a greased 10-in. fluted tube pan. Continue until all the biscuit pieces are coated. Bake at 350° for 30-35 minutes. Cool in pan for 30 minutes before inverting onto a serving plate. **Yield:** 10-12 servings.

Peanut Muffins

I was tired of buying chips and candy for my many grandchildren and great-grandchildren. I tried this recipe on them, and the kids loved it. These muffins are a wholesome snack. —Ruby Williams
Bogalusa, Louisiana

1-1/2 cups all-purpose flour
1/4 cup sugar
1 tablespoon baking powder
1/4 teaspoon salt
2 eggs, lightly beaten
1/2 cup butter *or* margarine, melted
1/2 cup milk
3/4 cup chopped dry roasted peanuts

In a large bowl, combine flour, sugar, baking powder and salt. Combine eggs, butter and milk; stir into the dry ingredients just until moistened. Fold in peanuts. Fill greased or paper-lined muffin cups two-thirds full. Bake at 400° for 15 minutes or until muffins test done. Cool in pan for 5 minutes before removing to a wire rack to cool completely. **Yield:** 1 dozen.

Pecan Cranberry Muffins

(Pictured below and on page 96)

When you want a little something extra for breakfast, serve these muffins—you'll get requests for seconds. I store them in the freezer and reheat them when we want them. —Suzanne McKinley, Lyons, Georgia

> 1-1/2 cups chopped fresh *or* frozen cranberries
> 1-1/4 cups sugar, *divided*
> 3 cups all-purpose flour
> 4-1/2 teaspoons baking powder
> 1/2 teaspoon salt
> 1/2 cup cold butter *or* margarine
> 2 eggs, lightly beaten
> 1 cup milk
> 1 cup chopped pecans
> 1 tablespoon grated lemon peel

In a bowl, toss cranberries with 1/4 cup sugar; set aside. Combine flour, baking powder, salt and remaining sugar. Cut in butter until the mixture resembles coarse crumbs. Combine eggs and milk; stir into flour mixture just until moistened. Fold in pecans, lemon peel and cranberries. Fill greased or paper-lined muffin cups two-thirds full. Bake at 400° for 20-25 minutes or until muffins test done. Cool in pan for 5 minutes before removing to wire rack to cool completely. **Yield:** about 1-1/2 dozen.

Butternut Squash Bread

This yeast bread is scrumptious served warm or toasted. A friend shared the recipe years ago. Squash gives each loaf a pretty golden color. —Agnes Miller, Marshall, Illinois

> 2 packages (1/4 ounce *each*) active dry yeast
> 1/2 cup warm water (110° to 115°)
> 1-1/4 cups mashed cooked butternut squash
> 1 cup warm milk (110° to 115°)
> 2 eggs, beaten
> 1/3 cup butter *or* margarine, melted
> 1/3 cup sugar
> 1 teaspoon salt
> 7 to 7-1/2 cups all-purpose flour

In a mixing bowl, dissolve yeast in water; let stand for 5 minutes. Add squash, milk, eggs, butter, sugar and salt; mix well. Gradually add 3-1/2 cups flour; beat until smooth. Add enough remaining flour to form a soft dough. Turn onto a floured surface; knead until smooth and elastic, about 6-8 minutes. Place in a greased bowl, turning once to grease top. Cover and let rise in a warm place until doubled, about 1 hour. Punch dough down. Shape into three loaves; place in greased 8-in. x 4-in. x 2-in. loaf pans. Cover and let rise until doubled, about 30 minutes. Bake at 375° for 25-30 minutes or until tops are golden. Remove from pans to cool on wire racks. **Yield:** 3 loaves.

Overnight Blueberry Coffee Cake

We have our own blueberry bushes that produce so heavily, I'm always looking for new ways to use them. This wonderful cake stars at "Welcome to Washington" breakfasts I serve summer company. —Marion Platt, Sequim, Washington

> 1 egg
> 1/2 cup plus 2 tablespoons sugar, *divided*
> 1-1/4 cups all-purpose flour
> 2 teaspoons baking powder
> 3/4 teaspoon salt
> 1/3 cup milk
> 3 tablespoons butter *or* margarine, melted
> 1 cup fresh blueberries

In a mixing bowl, beat egg and 1/2 cup sugar. Combine flour, baking powder and salt; add alternately with milk to sugar mixture, beating well after each addition. Stir in butter. Fold in berries. Pour into a greased 8-in. square baking pan; sprinkle with the remaining sugar. Cover and chill overnight. Remove from the refrigerator 30 minutes before baking. Bake at 350° for 30-35 minutes. **Yield:** 9 servings.

———— 🝆 🝆 🝆 ————

Muenster Bread

(Pictured at right and on page 96)

My sister and I won blue ribbons in 4-H with this bread many years ago. The recipe makes a beautiful, round golden loaf. With a layer of cheese peeking out of every slice, it's definitely worth the effort. —*Melanie Mero Ida, Michigan*

> 2 **packages (1/4 ounce *each*) active dry yeast**
> 1 **cup warm milk (110° to 115°)**
> 1/2 **cup butter *or* margarine, softened**
> 2 **tablespoons sugar**
> 1 **teaspoon salt**
> 3-1/4 **to 3-3/4 cups all-purpose flour**
> 1 **egg plus 1 egg yolk**
> 4 **cups (1 pound) shredded Muenster cheese**
> 1 **egg white, beaten**

In a large mixing bowl, dissolve yeast in milk. Add butter, sugar, salt and 2 cups flour; beat until smooth. Stir in enough remaining flour to form a soft dough. Turn onto a floured surface; knead until smooth and elastic, about 6-8 minutes. Place in a greased bowl, turning once to grease top. Cover and let rise in a warm place until doubled, about 1 hour. In a large bowl, beat egg and yolk; stir in cheese. Punch dough down; roll into a 16-in. circle. Place in a greased 9-in. round cake pan, letting dough drape over the edges. Spoon the cheese mixture into center of dough. Gather dough up over filling in 1-1/2-in. pleats. Gently squeeze pleats together at top and twist to make a top knot. Allow to rise 10-15 minutes. Brush loaf with egg white. Bake at 375° for 45-50 minutes. Cool on a wire rack for 20 minutes. Serve warm. **Yield:** 1 loaf.

———— 🝆 🝆 🝆 ————

Pine Nut Pancakes

When I was a youngster, pine nuts helped me earn a Boy Scout Cooking Merit Badge. I decided on pancakes for my project. The wild combination I put together was good then and still is today.
—*Ed Horkey, Ahwatukee, Arizona*

> 1-1/2 **cups buttermilk baking mix**
> 1 **cup puffed rice cereal**
> 1/3 **cup finely chopped banana**
> 1/3 **cup shredded peeled apple**
> 1/4 **cup raisins**
> 1/4 **cup pine nuts, toasted**
> 1 **egg**
> 3/4 **cup milk**
> 1/2 **teaspoon vanilla extract**

In a bowl, combine baking mix, cereal, banana, apple, raisins and pine nuts. In another bowl, beat egg, milk and vanilla; stir into the dry ingredients just until moistened. Pour batter by 1/4 cupfuls onto a lightly greased hot griddle; turn when bubbles form on top of pancakes. Cook until second side is golden brown. Serve immediately. **Yield:** about 10 pancakes.

Rising Yeast Dough

Yeast doughs rise best at an even temperature of 80° to 85°. Your oven is an ideal place to keep your dough warm and free from drafts.

The pilot light of a gas oven will provide enough warmth. If you don't have a pilot light or have an electric oven, turn on the oven to the lowest setting for 1 minute and then turn it off. Place the dough in a bowl on the center rack and close the oven door.

You can also place the dough in a cold oven with a pan of hot water below it. Whichever method you choose, always cover the dough with a towel to prevent it from drying out.

warm place until doubled, about 30 minutes. Punch dough down and press evenly into a greased 13-in. x 9-in. x 2-in. baking pan. With a very sharp knife, cut diagonal lines 1-1/2 in. apart completely through dough. Repeat in opposite direction, creating a diamond pattern. Cover and let rise in a warm place until doubled, about 1 hour. Redefine pattern by gently poking along cut lines with knife tip. Brush with 2 tablespoons melted butter. Bake at 375° for 15 minutes. Meanwhile, combine Parmesan cheese, basil, oregano and garlic powder. Brush bread with remaining butter; sprinkle with cheese mixture. Bake for 5 minutes. Loosely cover with foil and bake 5 minutes longer. Serve warm. **Yield:** 8-10 servings.

Golden French Toast

A combination of orange juice and cardamom make this oven-baked French toast extra special. It's a pretty dish to serve overnight guests. —*Karen Free Overland Park, Kansas*

  1/3 cup fresh orange juice
    1 teaspoon grated orange peel
    4 eggs
  1/2 teaspoon ground cardamom
  1/4 cup butter *or* margarine
   12 slices day-old French bread (cut 3/4 inch thick)
Maple syrup

In a bowl, combine orange juice, peel, eggs and cardamom; beat well. Melt butter in a 13-in. x 9-in. x 2-in. pan in the oven. Remove pan from the oven. Dip the bread on both sides in egg mixture; place in a single layer in pan. Bake at 450° for 10 minutes, turning once. Serve with syrup. **Yield:** 6 servings.

Spiced Applesauce Muffins

These muffins are moist and spicy with a cake-like texture. The batter keeps for 2 weeks in the refrigerator, so you can quickly bake muffins whenever you want. —*Linda Williams, LaFayette, Alabama*

    1 cup butter *or* margarine, softened
    2 cups sugar
    2 eggs
    1 teaspoon vanilla extract
    2 cups applesauce
    4 cups all-purpose flour
    2 teaspoons baking soda
    1 teaspoon ground cinnamon

Herbed Oatmeal Pan Bread

(Pictured above)

This beautiful, golden pan bread is especially good with a steaming bowl of homemade soup. The oats give it a distinctive flavor, and we really like the herb and Parmesan cheese topping. —*Karen Bourne Magrath, Alberta*

1-1/2 cups boiling water
    1 cup old-fashioned oats
    2 packages (1/4 ounce *each*) active dry yeast
  1/2 cup warm water (110° to 115°)
  1/4 cup sugar
    3 tablespoons butter *or* margarine, softened
    2 teaspoons salt
    1 egg, lightly beaten
    4 to 4-3/4 cups all-purpose flour
TOPPING:
  1/4 cup butter *or* margarine, melted, *divided*
    2 tablespoons grated Parmesan cheese
    1 teaspoon dried basil
  1/2 teaspoon dried oregano
  1/2 teaspoon garlic powder

In a small bowl, combine boiling water and oats; cool to 110°-115°. In a mixing bowl, dissolve yeast in warm water. Add sugar, butter, salt, egg, oat mixture and 2 cups of flour; beat until smooth. Add enough remaining flour to form a soft dough. Turn onto a floured surface; knead until smooth and elastic, about 6-8 minutes. Place in a greased bowl, turning once to grease top. Cover and let rise in a

1 teaspoon ground allspice
1/2 teaspoon ground cloves
1 cup chopped walnuts, optional
Cinnamon-sugar, optional

In a mixing bowl, cream butter and sugar. Add eggs and vanilla; mix well. Stir in applesauce. Combine flour, baking soda and spices; stir into creamed mixture. Fold in nuts. Fill greased or paper-lined muffin cups three-fourths full. Bake at 350° for 25 minutes or until muffins test done. Sprinkle with cinnamon-sugar if desired. Cool in pans for 5 minutes before removing to wire racks to cool completely. **Yield:** about 2 dozen.

— 🥤 🥤 🥤 —

Broccoli Corn Bread

I finally discovered a way to get my family to eat more broccoli—by tucking it into corn bread. This bread has a slightly sweet taste that completely hides the broccoli flavor. —Nila Towler, Baird, Texas

2 eggs
1 cup cottage cheese
1 package (10 ounces) frozen chopped broccoli, thawed
3/4 cup chopped onion
1/2 cup butter *or* margarine, melted, *divided*
2 packages (8-1/2 ounces *each*) corn bread/muffin mix

In a mixing bowl, lightly beat eggs. Add cottage cheese, broccoli, onion, 6 tablespoons butter and muffin mix; beat well. Pour remaining butter into a 10-in. ovenproof skillet; pour batter into skillet. Bake at 350° for 40-45 minutes or until golden. Cut into wedges and serve warm. **Yield:** 12-16 servings.

— 🥤 🥤 🥤 —

Valentine Coffee Cake

(Pictured at right)

Next Valentine's Day, shower your family with a gift from the heart...this festive coffee cake. Each slice is packed with almonds and maraschino cherries. —Dolores Skrout, Summerhill, Pennsylvania

4-1/2 to 5 cups all-purpose flour, *divided*
1/2 cup sugar
1-1/2 teaspoons salt
2 packages (1/4 ounce *each*) active dry yeast
1/2 cup milk
1/2 cup water
6 tablespoons butter *or* margarine, *divided*
2 eggs

FILLING:
3/4 cup packed dark brown sugar
1/2 cup chopped blanched almonds, toasted
1/3 cup chopped maraschino cherries
1 tablespoon all-purpose flour
2 teaspoons almond extract
GLAZE:
1-1/2 cups confectioners' sugar
2 tablespoons butter *or* margarine, softened
2 to 3 tablespoons milk
1/2 teaspoon vanilla extract

In a mixing bowl, combine 1-1/2 cups flour, sugar, salt and yeast. Heat milk, water and 4 tablespoons butter to 120°-130°. Gradually add to dry ingredients; beat on medium for 2 minutes. Add eggs and 1/2 cup flour; beat on high for 2 minutes. By hand, add enough remaining flour to form a soft dough. Turn onto a floured surface; knead until smooth and elastic, about 6-8 minutes. Place in a greased bowl, turning once to grease top. Cover and let rise in a warm place until doubled, about 1 hour. Punch dough down. Divide in half. Roll each half into a 26-in. x 8-in. rectangle. Melt remaining butter; brush over dough. Combine filling ingredients; sprinkle over butter. Roll up jelly-roll style from long end; pinch to seal. Place seam side down on greased nonstick baking sheets or baking sheets lined with parchment paper. Shape each roll into a heart; seal ends. Cut from outer edge two-thirds through cake every 1 in. and turn each section out. Cover and let rise until doubled, about 1 hour. Bake at 350° for 15-20 minutes or until golden. Remove immediately from baking sheets to wire racks. Cool completely; remove parchment paper if used. For glaze, cream sugar and butter. Stir in enough milk and vanilla until smooth. Drizzle over hearts. **Yield:** 2 coffee cakes.

Sweet and Savory Biscuits

FEW FOODS taste homier than fresh biscuits still warm from the oven! Five bakers invite you to try their quick and easy recipes, which range from luscious breakfast treats to zesty meal accompaniments.

— ♟ ♟ ♟ —

Quick Cheese Biscuits

(Pictured below)

Cheddar adds a burst of sunny flavor to these flaky biscuits. You can frequently find me in my kitchen making these tender treats. —Donna Engel
Portsmouth, Rhode Island

2 cups buttermilk baking mix
2/3 cup milk
1/2 cup shredded cheddar cheese
2 tablespoons butter *or* margarine, melted

1/2 teaspoon garlic powder

In a bowl, stir the baking mix, milk and cheese just until moistened. Drop by tablespoonfuls onto an ungreased baking sheet. Mix butter and garlic powder; brush over biscuits. Bake at 475° for 8-10 minutes or until golden brown. Serve warm. **Yield:** about 1-1/2 dozen.

— ♟ ♟ ♟ —

Upside-Down Orange Biscuits

(Pictured below)

I guarantee that the aroma of these biscuits baking is enough to get even the soundest sleeper out of bed. What a wonderful way to wake up!
—Kim Marie Van Rheenen, Mendota, Illinois

MOUTH-WATERING MORSELS. A big basket of tender biscuits like Quick Cheese Biscuits, Biscuits with Ham Butter and Upside-Down Orange Biscuits (shown above, clockwise from upper left) brings a comforting touch to the table.

2 cups all-purpose flour
1 tablespoon baking powder
1/2 teaspoon salt
3 tablespoons shortening
3/4 cup milk
2 tablespoons butter *or* margarine, softened
1/4 cup sugar
1 teaspoon ground cinnamon
TOPPING:
1/2 cup sugar
1/2 cup orange juice
3 tablespoons butter *or* margarine, melted
2 teaspoons grated orange peel

In a large bowl, combine flour, baking powder and salt; cut in shortening until mixture resembles coarse crumbs. Stir in milk just until moistened. Turn onto a lightly floured surface; knead gently 10-12 times. Roll into a 15-in. x 12-in. rectangle. Spread with butter. Combine the sugar and cinnamon; sprinkle over butter. Roll up jelly-roll style, starting from the short side. Cut into 12 equal slices. Place with cut side down in a greased 9-in. round baking pan. Combine topping ingredients; pour over biscuits. Bake at 450° for 20-25 minutes or until lightly browned. Cool in pan 5 minutes; invert onto a platter and serve warm. **Yield:** 1 dozen.

— ☕ ☕ ☕ —

Biscuits with Ham Butter

(Pictured at left)

Whether served as a finger food or a brunch dish, these tender and flaky biscuits are a great way to use up leftover ham. They always seem to disappear as soon as I remove them from the oven. —Andrea Bolden
Unionville, Tennessee

1-1/2 cups all-purpose flour
2 teaspoons baking powder
1/2 teaspoon salt
3/4 cup sour cream
1 egg, lightly beaten
1 cup cubed fully cooked smoked ham
1/2 cup butter *or* margarine, softened

In a bowl, combine flour, baking powder and salt; set aside. Combine sour cream and egg; mix well. Stir into dry ingredients just until moistened. Turn onto a lightly floured surface; knead gently 4-5 times. Roll to 1/2-in. thickness; cut with a 2-1/2-in. biscuit cutter. Place on a greased baking sheet. Bake at 425° for 10-12 minutes or until lightly browned. Meanwhile, in a blender or food processor, process ham until finely minced. Add butter and continue processing until well mixed. Spread over warm biscuits. **Yield:** 10 servings.

Glazed Cinnamon Biscuits

I make these easy cinnamon rolls as a breakfast treat on weekends. —Sue Gronholz, Columbus, Wisconsin

2 cups all-purpose flour
4 teaspoons baking powder
1/2 teaspoon salt
6 tablespoons butter *or* margarine, ***divided***
3/4 cup milk
1/4 cup sugar
1 teaspoon ground cinnamon
GLAZE:
1 cup confectioners' sugar
1 tablespoon butter *or* margarine, melted
1/8 teaspoon vanilla extract
5 to 6 teaspoons milk

In a large bowl, combine flour, baking powder and salt. Cut in 4 tablespoons of the butter until mixture resembles coarse crumbs. Stir in milk just until moistened. Turn onto a lightly floured surface; knead gently 8-10 times. Roll into an 11-in. x 8-in. rectangle about 1/2 in. thick. Melt remaining butter; brush 1 tablespoon over dough. Combine sugar and cinnamon; sprinkle over butter. Roll up jelly-roll style, starting with long edge. Cut into 12 equal slices. Place with cut side down in a greased 8-in. square baking pan. Brush with remaining butter. Bake at 450° for 18-20 minutes or until golden brown. Cool for 5 minutes. Combine confectioners' sugar, butter, vanilla and enough milk until smooth; spread over warm biscuits. Serve immediately. **Yield:** 1 dozen.

— ☕ ☕ ☕ —

Fluffy Whole Wheat Biscuits

Of all the different biscuit recipes I have on file, this is the most used. The golden biscuits are light and tasty! —Ruth Ann Stelfox, Raymond, Alberta

1 cup all-purpose flour
1 cup whole wheat flour
4 teaspoons baking powder
1 tablespoon sugar
3/4 teaspoon salt
1/4 cup cold butter *or* margarine
1 cup milk

In a medium bowl, combine flours, baking powder, sugar and salt; mix well. Cut in butter until mixture resembles coarse crumbs. Stir in milk just until moistened. Turn out onto a lightly floured surface; knead gently 8-10 times. Roll to 3/4-in. thickness; cut with a 2-1/2-in. biscuit cutter and place on an ungreased baking sheet. Bake at 450° for 10-12 minutes or until lightly browned. Serve warm. **Yield:** 1 dozen.

Cookies & Candies

Whether for Christmas gifts or special occasions throughout the year, these delectable cookies and candies will satisfy every sweet tooth.

SWEET TREATS. Clockwise from upper left: Pecan Delights (p. 117), Coconut Washboards (p. 131), Chocolate Raspberry Bars (p. 131), Three-Chocolate Fudge (p. 126) and Chocolate Malted Cookies (p. 132).

1-1/2 cups confectioners' sugar
2 cups (12 ounces) semisweet chocolate chips, melted

In a mixing bowl, cream butter and sugars. Add egg and vanilla; mix well. Combine flour, baking soda and salt; add to creamed mixture and mix well. Add oats, cornflakes and coconut. Shape into 1-in. balls and place 2 in. apart on greased baking sheets. Flatten with a glass dipped lightly in flour. Bake at 350° for 8-10 minutes or until lightly browned. Remove to wire racks to cool. For filling, beat cream cheese and sugar until smooth. Add the chocolate; mix well. Spread about 1 tablespoon on half of the cookies and top each with another cookie. Store in the refrigerator. **Yield:** about 2 dozen.

— 🍷 🍷 🍷 —

Sugar-Free Chocolate Fudge

I'm borderline diabetic, but I find it hard to resist sweets. I can indulge in this chocolaty fudge with little guilt. —Kaye Hartley, Jacksonville, Florida

✓ Uses less fat, sugar or salt. Includes Nutritional Analysis and Diabetic Exchanges.

2 packages (8 ounces *each*) cream cheese, softened
2 squares (1 ounce *each*) unsweetened chocolate, melted and cooled
Artificial sweetener equivalent to 1 cup sugar
1 teaspoon vanilla extract
1/2 cup chopped pecans

In a small mixing bowl, beat the cream cheese, chocolate, sweetener and vanilla until smooth. Stir in pecans. Pour into an 8-in. square baking pan lined with foil. Cover and refrigerate overnight. Cut into 16 squares. Serve chilled. **Yield:** 16 servings. **Nutritional Analysis:** One serving equals 147 calories, 84 mg sodium, 31 mg cholesterol, 5 gm carbohydrate, 3 gm protein, 14 gm fat. **Diabetic Exchanges:** 3 fat.

Chocolaty Double Crunchers

(Pictured above)

I first tried these crispy cookies at a family picnic when I was a child. Packed with oats, cornflakes and coconut, they quickly became a "regular" at our house. Years later, I still make them for my own family.
—Cheryl Johnson, Upper Marlboro, Maryland

1/2 cup butter *or* margarine, softened
1/2 cup sugar
1/2 cup packed brown sugar
1 egg
1/2 teaspoon vanilla extract
1 cup all-purpose flour
1/2 teaspoon baking soda
1/4 teaspoon salt
1 cup quick-cooking oats
1 cup crushed cornflakes
1/2 cup flaked coconut
FILLING:
2 packages (3 ounces *each*) cream cheese, softened

Caring for Candy

After spending precious time and ingredients making candy, you want to store it properly to keep it fresh. Most candies keep well for 2 to 3 weeks tightly covered in a cool, dry place. Don't store different candies in the same container or the candies' flavors will blend together. Fudge and caramels freeze well for up to 1 year. When removing candy from the freezer, let it come to room temperature before unwrapping and serving.

Pecan Delights

(Pictured on page 114)

A relative visiting from Oklahoma brought these and the recipe with her. Who can resist rich chewy caramel over crunchy pecans drizzled with sweet chocolate? These candies have become a holiday favorite to both make and eat! —Linda Jonsson, Marion, Ohio

2-1/4 cups packed brown sugar
  1 cup butter _or_ margarine
  1 cup light corn syrup
1/8 teaspoon salt
  1 can (14 ounces) sweetened condensed milk
  1 teaspoon vanilla extract
1-1/2 pounds whole pecans
  1 cup (6 ounces) semisweet chocolate chips
  1 cup (6 ounces) milk chocolate chips
  2 tablespoons shortening

In a large saucepan, combine the first four ingredients. Cook over medium heat until all the sugar is dissolved. Gradually add milk and mix well. Continue cooking until candy thermometer reads 248° (firm-ball stage). Remove from the heat; stir in vanilla until blended. Fold in the pecans. Drop by tablespoonfuls onto a greased waxed paper-lined baking sheet. Chill until firm. Melt chocolate chips and shortening in a microwave-safe bowl or double boiler. Drizzle over each cluster. Cool. **Yield:** about 4 dozen.

—— 🍳 🍳 🍳 ——

Cookie Dough Brownies

(Pictured at right)

When I take these rich brownies to any get-together, I carry the recipe, too, because it always gets requested. Children of all ages love the tempting "cookie dough" filling. This special treat is typically the first to be gone from the buffet table—even before the entrees!
—Wendy Bailey, Elida, Ohio

  2 cups sugar
1-1/2 cups all-purpose flour
1/2 cup baking cocoa
1/2 teaspoon salt
  1 cup vegetable oil
  4 eggs
  2 teaspoons vanilla extract
1/2 cup chopped walnuts, optional
FILLING:
1/2 cup butter _or_ margarine, softened
1/2 cup packed brown sugar
1/4 cup sugar
  2 tablespoons milk

  1 teaspoon vanilla extract
  1 cup all-purpose flour
GLAZE:
  1 cup (6 ounces) semisweet chocolate chips
  1 tablespoon shortening
3/4 cup chopped walnuts

In a mixing bowl, combine sugar, flour, cocoa and salt. Add oil, eggs and vanilla; beat at medium speed for 3 minutes. Stir in walnuts if desired. Pour into a greased 13-in. x 9-in. x 2-in. baking pan. Bake at 350° for 30 minutes or until brownies test done. Cool completely. For filling, cream butter and sugars in a mixing bowl. Add milk and vanilla; mix well. Beat in flour. Spread over the brownies; chill until firm. For glaze, melt chocolate chips and shortening in a saucepan, stirring until smooth. Spread over filling. Immediately sprinkle with nuts, pressing down slightly. **Yield:** 3 dozen.

Lemon Butter Cookies

(Pictured below)

These tender cutout cookies have a slight lemon flavor that makes them stand out from the rest. They're very easy to roll out compared to other sugar cookies I've worked with. I know you'll enjoy them as much as we do. —Judy McCreight, Springfield, Illinois

        1 cup butter (no substitutes), softened
        2 cups sugar
        2 eggs
    1/4 cup milk
        2 teaspoons lemon extract
    4-1/2 cups all-purpose flour
        2 teaspoons baking powder
    1/2 teaspoon salt
    1/4 teaspoon baking soda
    Colored sugar, optional

In a mixing bowl, cream butter and sugar. Beat in eggs, milk and extract. Combine flour, baking powder, salt and baking soda; gradually add to creamed mixture. Cover and chill for 2 hours. Roll out on a lightly floured surface to 1/8-in. thickness. Cut with a 2-in. cookie cutter dipped in flour. Place 2 in. apart on ungreased baking sheets. Sprinkle with colored sugar if desired. Bake at 350° for 8-9 minutes or until the edges just begin to brown. Remove to wire racks to cool. **Yield:** about 13 dozen.

Cutout Cookies with Ease

Here's a different way to prepare cutout cookies that makes it simple for children to help. Very lightly grease a cookie sheet and roll out your dough on it. Cut out as many cookies as possible with a bit of space between them, then peel away the scraps from around your cutouts. This method also works less flour into the dough.

Scott's Peanut Cookies

These cookies are packed with oatmeal and peanuts for a hearty, satisfying taste. —Scott Walter
Little Rock, Arkansas

        1 cup shortening
        1 cup sugar
        1 cup packed brown sugar
        2 eggs
    1-1/2 cups all-purpose flour
        1 teaspoon baking powder
        1 teaspoon baking soda
        3 cups quick-cooking oats
        1 cup salted peanuts

In a mixing bowl, cream shortening and sugars; beat in eggs. Combine flour, baking powder and baking soda; stir into creamed mixture. Add the oats and peanuts. Drop by heaping tablespoonfuls onto greased baking sheets. Slightly flatten cookies with a glass dipped in sugar. Bake at 350° for 7-10 minutes. Remove to wire racks to cool. **Yield:** 4 dozen.

———— ☕ ☕ ☕ ————

Apricot Bars

My family likes snacking on these rich-tasting bars. This recipe's one I've used and shared for many years. —Helen Cluts, Sioux Falls, South Dakota

        1 cup all-purpose flour
        1 teaspoon baking powder
    1/2 cup cold butter *or* margarine
        1 egg
        1 tablespoon milk
        1 cup apricot preserves
    TOPPING:
        1 egg
    2/3 cup sugar
    1/4 cup butter *or* margarine, melted
        1 teaspoon vanilla extract
        2 cups flaked coconut

In a bowl, combine the flour and baking powder. Cut in butter until the mixture resembles coarse crumbs. Beat the egg and milk; stir into flour mixture. Spread in a greased 9-in. square baking pan. Spread preserves over crust. Combine topping ingredients; carefully drop by tablespoonfuls over apricot layer. Bake at 350° for 25-30 minutes or until golden brown. Cool; cut into small bars. **Yield:** 2 to 2-1/2 dozen.

— 🥄 🥄 🥄 —

Double Chocolate Brownies

These rich, fudgy brownies can't be beat when you need dessert in a hurry. They look so pretty dusted with confectioners' sugar. —Sue Gronholz
Columbus, Wisconsin

1/2 cup butter *or* margarine
2 squares (1 ounce *each*) unsweetened chocolate
2 eggs
3/4 cup sugar
1/2 cup all-purpose flour
1 teaspoon baking powder
1 teaspoon vanilla extract
1/2 cup semisweet chocolate chips
Confectioners' sugar

In a microwave-safe bowl, combine butter and chocolate. Cook on high for 1-2 minutes or until melted; mix well. In a mixing bowl, beat eggs for 2-3 minutes or until light and foamy. Gradually add chocolate mixture, sugar, flour, baking powder and vanilla; mix well. Fold in chocolate chips. Pour into a greased 8-in. square microwave-safe baking dish. Cook on high for 3 minutes. Rotate a quarter turn and continue cooking for 3 minutes. Remove to a wire rack; cool for 10 minutes. Dust with confectioners' sugar. **Yield:** 1 dozen. **Editor's Note:** This recipe was tested in a 700-watt microwave.

— 🥄 🥄 🥄 —

Perfect Peppermint Patties

(Pictured above right)

Calling for just a few ingredients, this is one candy that's simple to prepare. I make lots of different candy at Christmas to give as gifts. It's time consuming, but worth it to see the delight it brings to people.
—Joanne Adams, Bath, Maine

1 package (1 pound) confectioners' sugar
3 tablespoons butter *or* margarine, softened
2 to 3 teaspoons peppermint extract
1/2 teaspoon vanilla extract
1/4 cup evaporated milk
2 cups (12 ounces) semisweet chocolate chips

2 tablespoons shortening

In a bowl, combine the first four ingredients. Add milk and mix well. Roll into 1-in. balls and place on a waxed paper-lined baking sheet. Flatten with a glass to 1/4 in. thickness; cover and freeze for 30 minutes. In a double boiler or microwave-safe bowl, melt chocolate chips and shortening. Dip patties; place on waxed paper to harden. **Yield:** about 5 dozen.

— 🥄 🥄 🥄 —

Peanut Butter Chocolate Chip Cookies

With just four ingredients, this recipe couldn't be easier. These moist cookies have a rich peanut flavor.
—Jeane Squires, Houston, Texas

1 cup peanut butter
1 cup sugar
1 egg, lightly beaten
1/2 cup miniature semisweet chocolate chips

In a mixing bowl, combine peanut butter, sugar and egg (batter will be stiff). Stir in the chocolate chips. Scoop level tablespoonfuls and roll into balls. Place on ungreased baking sheets and flatten with a fork. Bake at 350° for 15-18 minutes or until browned. Remove to wire racks to cool. **Yield:** 2 dozen. **Editor's Note:** This recipe does not use any flour.

These Cookies Say 'Christmas'

HOLIDAY BAKING means readying the rolling pin, bringing out the baking sheets and pulling out time-honored recipes for treats the family asks for every year.

We asked *Taste of Home* magazine readers to complete this sentence: "It wouldn't be Christmas at our house without _____ cookies." Here's how some of them responded.

Deluxe Sugar Cookies

(Pictured below)

Christmas cutouts signal the season for our family. Usually I "paint" these with colorful icing—or if time is short, I sprinkle them with colored sugar.
—Dawn Fagerstrom, Warren, Michigan

HOLIDAY SHAPES distinguish festive favorites featured here. Gingerbread Cutouts, Pecan Meltaways and Deluxe Sugar Cookies (shown above, clockwise from upper right) are sure to disappear fast!

1 cup butter *or* margarine, softened
1-1/2 cups confectioners' sugar
1 egg
1 teaspoon vanilla extract
1/2 teaspoon almond extract
2-1/2 cups all-purpose flour
1 teaspoon baking soda
1 teaspoon cream of tartar

In a mixing bowl, cream butter and sugar. Beat in egg and extracts. Combine flour, baking soda and cream of tartar; gradually add to the creamed mixture and mix well. Chill for at least 1 hour. On a surface lightly sprinkled with confectioners' sugar, roll out a quarter of the dough to 1/8-in. thickness. Cut into desired shapes with 2-in. cookie cutters. Place on ungreased baking sheets. Repeat with the remaining dough. Bake at 350° for 7-8 minutes or until the edges begin to brown. Remove to wire racks to cool. **Yield:** 5 dozen. **Editor's Note:** Cookies may be sprinkled with colored sugar before baking or frosted after being baked and cooled.

Pecan Meltaways

(Pictured at left)

These sugared, nut-filled balls are a Christmas tradition. They make an attractive addition to a plate of cookies. —Alberta McKay, Bartlesville, Oklahoma

1 cup butter *or* margarine, softened
1/2 cup confectioners' sugar
1 teaspoon vanilla extract
2-1/4 cups all-purpose flour
1/4 teaspoon salt
3/4 cup finely chopped pecans
Additional confectioners' sugar

In a mixing bowl, cream the butter, sugar and vanilla; mix well. Combine the flour and salt; add to creamed mixture. Stir in pecans. Chill. Roll dough into 1-in. balls and place on ungreased baking sheets. Bake at 350° for 10-12 minutes. Roll in confectioners' sugar while warm. Cool on wire racks; roll in sugar again. **Yield:** about 4 dozen.

Gingerbread Cutouts

(Pictured at left)

Baking is the tastiest part of my hobby of collecting gingerbread boys. I decorate these cookies to give as gifts. —LaJunta Malone, Camden, Alabama

1 cup butter *or* margarine, softened
1 cup sugar

1/2 cup dark corn syrup
1 teaspoon *each* ground cinnamon, nutmeg, cloves and ginger
2 eggs, beaten
1 teaspoon vinegar
5 cups all-purpose flour
1 teaspoon baking soda
Red-hot candies

In a large saucepan, combine the butter, sugar, corn syrup and spices; bring to a boil, stirring constantly. Remove from the heat and cool to lukewarm. Stir in eggs and vinegar. Combine the flour and baking soda; stir into sugar mixture to form a soft dough. Chill for several hours. On a lightly floured surface, roll dough to 1/4-in. thickness. Cut with a floured 2-1/2-in. gingerbread man cookie cutter and place on greased baking sheets. Use red-hots for eyes and buttons. Bake at 350° for 8-10 minutes. Remove to wire racks to cool. **Yield:** about 6 dozen.

Turtle Bars

This recipe of my mother's is a "must make" for the holidays. I always have good intentions of taking some to Christmas parties, but my family finishes them too soon! —Faye Hintz, Springfield, Missouri

2 cups all-purpose flour
1 cup packed brown sugar
1/2 cup butter *or* margarine, softened
1 cup pecan halves
TOPPING:
2/3 cup butter *or* margarine
1/2 cup packed brown sugar
1 cup (6 ounces) semisweet chocolate chips

In a mixing bowl, beat flour, sugar and butter on medium speed for 2-3 minutes. Press firmly into an ungreased 13-in. x 9-in. x 2-in. baking pan. Arrange pecans over crust. Combine butter and brown sugar in a heavy saucepan. Bring to a boil; boil for 1 minute, stirring constantly. Pour over pecans. Bake at 350° for 18-22 minutes or until bubbly. Sprinkle chocolate chips on top; let stand for 3 minutes. Spread chocolate but allow some chips to remain whole. Cool completely; cut into small squares. **Yield:** about 8 dozen.

Baking Sheet Basics

When making cookies and bars, use heavyweight metal baking sheets and pans with a light-colored dull finish. Dark-colored pans can overbrown the bottoms and sides of cookies and bars.

Peanut Butter Sandwich Cookies

(Pictured below)

I'm a busy mother of two children. I work in our school office and help my husband on our hog and cattle farm. When I find time to bake a treat, I like it to be special. The creamy filling gives traditional peanut butter cookies a new twist.
—Debbie Kokes
Tabor, South Dakota

        1 cup butter-flavored shortening
        1 cup creamy peanut butter
        1 cup sugar
        1 cup packed brown sugar
        1 teaspoon vanilla extract
        3 eggs
        3 cups all-purpose flour
        2 teaspoons baking soda
    1/4 teaspoon salt
FILLING:
    1/2 cup creamy peanut butter
        3 cups confectioners' sugar
        1 teaspoon vanilla extract
        5 to 6 tablespoons milk

In a mixing bowl, cream the shortening, peanut butter and sugars. Add vanilla and eggs, one at a time, beating well after each addition. Combine flour, baking soda and salt; gradually add to the creamed mixture. Shape into 1-in. balls and place 2 in. apart on ungreased baking sheets. Flatten to 3/8-in. thickness with a fork. Bake at 375° for 7-8 minutes or until golden. Remove to wire racks to cool. In a mixing bowl, beat peanut butter, confectioners' sugar, vanilla and enough milk to achieve desired frosting consistency. Spread on half of the cookies and top each with another cookie. **Yield:** about 4 dozen.

— 🍶 🍶 🍶 —

Marshmallow Puffs

With peanut butter, chocolate and marshmallows, these treats were very popular with our three children as they were growing up. Now I make them for our two grandchildren who also gobble them up.
—Dody Cagenello, Simsbury, Connecticut

    36 large marshmallows
1-1/2 cups semisweet chocolate chips
    1/2 cup chunky peanut butter
        2 tablespoons butter (no substitutes)

Line a 9-in. square pan with foil; butter the foil. Arrange marshmallows in pan. In a double boiler or microwave-safe bowl, melt chocolate chips, peanut butter and butter at 50% power. Pour and spread over the marshmallows. Chill completely. Cut between marshmallows. **Yield:** 3 dozen. **Editor's Note:** This recipe was tested in a 700-watt microwave.

— 🍶 🍶 🍶 —

Almond Biscotti

(Pictured on back cover)

I've learned to bake a double batch of these crisp dunking cookies, because one batch goes too fast!
—Mrs. H. Michaelsen, St. Charles, Illinois

    1/2 cup butter *or* margarine, softened
1-1/4 cups sugar, *divided*
        3 eggs
        1 teaspoon anise *or* vanilla extract
        2 cups all-purpose flour
        2 teaspoons baking powder
Dash salt
    1/2 cup chopped almonds
        2 teaspoons milk

In a mixing bowl, cream butter and 1 cup sugar. Add eggs, one at a time, beating well after each addition. Stir in anise or vanilla. Combine dry ingredients; add to creamed mixture. Stir in almonds. Line a baking sheet with foil and grease the foil. Di-

vide dough in half; spread into two 12-in. x 3-in. rectangles on foil. Brush with milk and sprinkle with remaining sugar. Bake at 375° for 15-20 minutes or until golden brown and firm to the touch. Remove from oven and reduce heat to 300°. Lift rectangles with foil onto wire rack; cool for 15 minutes. Place on a cutting board; slice diagonally 1/2 in. thick. Place slices with cut side down on ungreased baking sheets. Bake for 10 minutes. Turn cookies over; bake 10 minutes more. Turn oven off, leaving cookies in oven with door ajar to cool. Store in airtight container. **Yield:** 3-1/2 dozen.

Chewy Spice Cookies

This recipe fits the needs of those with special dietary restrictions and still delivers full flavor.
—Leah Peterson, Ashland, Missouri

☑ Uses less fat, sugar or salt. Includes Nutritional Analysis.

    1 cup packed brown sugar
  3/4 cup unsweetened applesauce
  1/4 cup molasses
Egg substitute to equal 1 egg
2-1/4 cups all-purpose flour
    2 teaspoons baking soda
    1 teaspoon ground ginger
    1 teaspoon ground cinnamon
  1/2 teaspoon ground cloves
Sugar

In a bowl, combine brown sugar, applesauce, molasses and egg substitute until well blended. Combine flour, baking soda and spices; stir into molasses mixture. Drop by teaspoonfuls 2 in. apart onto baking sheets that have been lightly coated with nonstick cooking spray. Sprinkle with sugar. Bake at 375° for 8-10 minutes. Remove to wire racks to cool. **Yield:** about 3-1/2 dozen. **Nutritional Analysis:** One cookie equals 56 calories, 15 mg sodium, trace cholesterol, 12 gm carbohydrate, 1 gm protein, trace fat.

Cranberry Date Bars

(Pictured above right)

I first discovered this recipe at Christmas a couple years ago, but it's a great way to use frozen cranberries throughout the year. It seems I'm always baking a batch of these moist bars for some event.
—Bonnie Nieter, Warsaw, Indiana

  1 package (12 ounces) fresh *or* frozen
    cranberries
  1 package (8 ounces) chopped dates

    2 tablespoons water
    1 teaspoon vanilla extract
    2 cups all-purpose flour
    2 cups old-fashioned oats
1-1/2 cups packed brown sugar
  1/2 teaspoon baking soda
  1/2 teaspoon salt
    1 cup butter *or* margarine, melted
GLAZE:
    2 cups confectioners' sugar
  1/2 teaspoon vanilla extract
    2 to 3 tablespoons orange juice

In a covered saucepan over low heat, simmer cranberries, dates and water for 15 minutes, stirring occasionally until the cranberries have popped. Remove from the heat; stir in vanilla and set aside. In a large bowl, combine the flour, oats, brown sugar, baking soda and salt. Stir in butter until well blended. Pat half into an ungreased 13-in. x 9-in. x 2-in. baking pan. Bake at 350° for 8 minutes. Spoon cranberry mixture over crust. Sprinkle with the remaining oat mixture. Pat gently. Bake at 350° for 25-30 minutes or until browned. Cool. Combine confectioners' sugar, vanilla and enough orange juice to achieve desired glaze consistency. Drizzle over bars. **Yield:** 3 dozen.

butter and vanilla; mix well. Stir in pecans. Spoon into shells. Bake at 325° for 25-30 minutes. Cool in pan on a wire rack. Decorate with maraschino cherries if desired. **Yield:** about 20.

— 🥢 🥢 🥢 —

Soft Sugar Cookies

I was born in Africa and grew up enjoying cardamom. Through the years, I've experimented with this herb in a variety of recipes. I hope you enjoy these old-fashioned sugar cookies. —Mabel Shirk
Fair Play, South Carolina

      1 cup butter *or* margarine, softened
2-1/4 cups sugar, *divided*
      2 eggs
      5 cups all-purpose flour
      1 teaspoon baking soda
   1/2 teaspoon baking powder
1-1/2 teaspoons ground cardamom, *divided*
   1/2 cup milk

In a large mixing bowl, cream butter and 2 cups sugar. Add eggs, one at a time, beating well after each addition. Combine the flour, baking soda, baking powder and 1 teaspoon cardamom; add to creamed mixture alternately with milk. In a small bowl, combine the remaining sugar and cardamom; dip rounded teaspoonfuls of dough into sugar mixture. Place on greased baking sheets. Bake at 375° for 10-12 minutes or until lightly browned. Remove to wire racks to cool. **Yield:** about 6 dozen.

— 🥢 🥢 🥢 —

Prune-Pecan Cookies

The prunes in this recipe are finely chopped so no one will need to know they appear in these crisp, lightly sweet cookies. —Lucille Dent, Galesburg, Michigan

✓ Uses less fat, sugar or salt. Includes Nutritional Analysis and Diabetic Exchanges.

    1 egg
    7 dried pitted prunes
 1/2 cup sugar
    1 cup all-purpose flour
 1/2 teaspoon baking soda
Pinch salt
24 pecan halves

In a blender, combine egg and prunes; cover and process until finely chopped. Pour into a mixing bowl. Add sugar. Combine the flour, baking soda and salt; add to prune mixture and mix well. Drop by rounded teaspoonfuls onto greased baking

Pecan Tarts

(Pictured above)

The flaky crust combined with a rich center makes these little tarts a satisfying snack to serve and eat. They look so appealing on a pretty platter and make a great finger-food dessert when you're entertaining. They also freeze well. —Jean Rhodes
Tignall, Georgia

    1 package (3 ounces) cream cheese, softened
 1/2 cup butter *or* margarine, softened
    1 cup all-purpose flour
 1/4 teaspoon salt
FILLING:
    1 egg
 3/4 cup packed dark brown sugar
    1 tablespoon butter *or* margarine, melted
    1 teaspoon vanilla extract
 2/3 cup chopped pecans
Maraschino cherry halves, optional

In a mixing bowl, beat cream cheese and butter; blend in flour and salt. Chill for 1 hour. Shape into 1-in. balls; press into the bottom and up the sides of greased mini-muffin cups. For filling, beat the egg in a small mixing bowl. Add brown sugar,

sheets. Top each cookie with a pecan half. Bake at 350° for 13-15 minutes or until golden brown. Remove to wire racks to cool. **Yield:** 2 dozen. **Nutritional Analysis:** One cookie equals 58 calories, 12 mg sodium, 9 mg cholesterol, 10 gm carbohydrate, 1 gm protein, 2 gm fat. **Diabetic Exchanges:** 1/2 starch, 1/2 fruit.

Hazelnut Shortbread

We have several acres of hazelnut trees here in the Willamette Valley, where the climate is perfect for this crop. Harvesttime is a big family event with everyone pitching in. I try to incorporate this wonderful flavorful nut into our recipes, and this cookie is always a hit.
—Karen Morrell, Canby, Oregon

  1 cup butter (no substitutes), softened
1/2 cup sugar
  2 tablespoons maple syrup *or* honey
  2 teaspoons vanilla extract
  2 cups all-purpose flour
1-1/4 cups finely chopped hazelnuts *or* filberts
1/2 cup semisweet chocolate chips

In a mixing bowl, cream butter and sugar. Add syrup and vanilla. Add flour and mix just until combined; fold in the nuts. Shape into two 1-1/2-in. rolls; wrap tightly in waxed paper. Chill for 2 hours or until firm. Cut into 1/4-in. slices and place 2 in. apart on ungreased baking sheets. Bake at 325° for 14-16 minutes or until edges begin to brown. Remove to wire racks to cool. Melt chocolate chips; drizzle over cookies. Allow chocolate to harden. **Yield:** about 6 dozen. **Editor's Note:** This recipe does not contain eggs.

Chocolate Thumbprints
(Pictured at right)

A group of friends had a weekly "movie night" during winters on Martha's Vineyard, and we'd take turns making a chocolate treat to share. These terrific cookies were an instant success.
—Laura Bryant German
West Warren, Massachusetts

1/2 cup butter *or* margarine, softened
2/3 cup sugar
  1 egg, *separated*
  2 tablespoons milk
  1 teaspoon vanilla extract
  1 cup all-purpose flour
1/3 cup baking cocoa
1/4 teaspoon salt

  1 cup finely chopped walnuts
FILLING:
1/2 cup confectioners' sugar
  1 tablespoon butter *or* margarine, softened
  2 teaspoons milk
1/4 teaspoon vanilla extract
 26 milk chocolate kisses

In a mixing bowl, beat butter, sugar, egg yolk, milk and vanilla until light and fluffy. Combine flour, cocoa and salt; gradually add to creamed mixture. Cover and chill 1 hour or until firm enough to roll into balls. Meanwhile, in a small bowl, lightly beat egg white. Shape dough into 1-in. balls; dip in egg white, then roll in nuts. Place on greased baking sheets. Make an indentation with thumb in center of each cookie. Bake at 350° for 10-12 minutes or until center is set. Combine the first four filling ingredients in a small bowl; mix until smooth. Spoon 1/4 teaspoon into each warm cookie; gently press a chocolate kiss in the center. Carefully remove from baking sheet to wire racks to cool. **Yield:** about 2 dozen.

Chocolate Chip Brownies

(Pictured below)

People love these very rich brownies so much that I never take them anywhere without bringing along several copies of the recipe to hand out. These treats are wonderful to take on a picnic because you don't have to worry about frosting melting. —Brenda Kelly
Ashburn, Virginia

    1 cup butter *or* margarine, softened
    3 cups sugar
    6 eggs
    1 tablespoon vanilla extract
2-1/4 cups all-purpose flour
  1/2 cup baking cocoa
    1 teaspoon baking powder
  1/2 teaspoon salt
    1 cup (6 ounces) semisweet chocolate chips
    1 cup (6 ounces) vanilla chips
    1 cup chopped walnuts

In a mixing bowl, cream butter and sugar. Add eggs and vanilla; mix well. Combine flour, cocoa, baking powder and salt; stir into creamed mixture just until blended (do not overmix). Pour into two greased 9-in. square baking pans. Sprinkle with

chips and nuts. Bake at 350° for 35-40 minutes or until a wooden pick inserted near the center comes out clean. Cool. **Yield:** 3-4 dozen.

Honey-Peanut Butter Cookies

When my husband wants a treat, he requests these cookies. Honey adds wonderful flavor to basic peanut butter cookies. —Lucile Proctor, Panguitch, Utah

  1/2 cup shortening
    1 cup creamy peanut butter
    1 cup honey
    2 eggs
    3 cups all-purpose flour
    1 cup sugar
1-1/2 teaspoons baking soda
    1 teaspoon baking powder
  1/2 teaspoon salt

In a mixing bowl, mix shortening, peanut butter and honey; beat in eggs. Combine flour, sugar, baking soda, baking powder and salt; add to peanut butter mixture and mix well. Roll into 1- to 1-1/2-in. balls and place on ungreased baking sheets. Flatten with a fork dipped in flour. Bake at 350° for 8-10 minutes. Remove to wire racks to cool. **Yield:** about 5 dozen.

Three-Chocolate Fudge

(Pictured on page 114)

I make this fudge at Christmastime to give to friends and neighbors. That tradition started years ago when I made more candy than my husband, three sons and I could eat, so we shared it. It's a tasty tradition I'm glad to continue. —Betty Grantham
Hanceville, Alabama

3-1/3 cups sugar
    1 cup butter *or* margarine
    1 cup packed dark brown sugar
    1 can (12 ounces) evaporated milk
   32 large marshmallows, halved
    2 cups (12 ounces) semisweet chocolate chips
    2 milk chocolate candy bars (7 ounces *each*), broken
    2 squares (1 ounce *each*) semisweet baking chocolate, chopped
    1 teaspoon vanilla extract
    2 cups chopped pecans

In a large saucepan, combine the first four ingredients. Cook and stir over medium heat until sugar is dissolved. Bring to a rapid boil; boil for 5 minutes, stirring constantly. Remove from the heat; stir in marshmallows until melted. Stir in chocolate chips until melted. Add chocolate bars and baking chocolate; stir until melted. Fold in vanilla and pecans; mix well. Pour into a greased 15-in. x 10-in. x 1-in. baking pan. Chill until firm. Cut into squares. **Yield:** 5-1/2 pounds.

Valentine Sugar Cookies

A touch of almond extract makes these delicious sugar cookies quite unique. I use this recipe throughout the year using different sizes and shapes of cutters.
—Renee Schwebach, Dumont, Minnesota

    1 **cup butter *or* margarine, softened**
1-1/2 **cups confectioners' sugar**
    1 **egg**
    1 **teaspoon vanilla extract**
    1 **teaspoon almond extract**
2-1/2 **cups all-purpose flour**
Colored sugar, optional

In a mixing bowl, cream butter and sugar; beat in egg and extracts. Stir in flour; mix well. Chill several hours. On a lightly floured surface, roll dough to 1/4-in. thickness; cut with a 2-1/2- or 3-in. heart-shaped cookie cutter. Place on ungreased baking sheets; sprinkle with sugar if desired. Bake at 375° for 8-10 minutes or until lightly browned. Remove to wire racks to cool. **Yield:** 3-1/2 dozen.

Frosted Pineapple Cookies

(Pictured above right)

These are the best pineapple cookies—sweet and moist with real tropical flavor. Because they are unique and look so pretty, these cookies are a hit whenever I serve them. People can't seem to eat just one!
—Mary DeVoe, Bradenton, Florida

    1 **can (8 ounces) crushed pineapple**
1/2 **cup shortening**
    1 **cup packed brown sugar**
    1 **egg**
    1 **teaspoon vanilla extract**
    2 **cups all-purpose flour**
1-1/2 **teaspoons baking powder**
1/4 **teaspoon baking soda**
1/4 **teaspoon salt**
1-1/2 **cups confectioners' sugar**

Drain pineapple, reserving 3 tablespoons juice. Set pineapple aside; set juice aside for frosting. In a mixing bowl, cream shortening and brown sugar. Add egg; mix well. Add pineapple and vanilla; mix well. Combine flour, baking powder, baking soda and salt; gradually add to the creamed mixture. Drop by teaspoonfuls 2 in. apart onto greased baking sheets. Bake at 325° for 17-20 minutes or until golden. Remove to wire racks to cool. For frosting, in a small bowl, combine confectioners' sugar with enough of the reserved pineapple juice to achieve a smooth spreading consistency. Frost cooled cookies. **Yield:** 3 dozen.

Cinnamon "Whippersnappers"

When you want a sweet treat without heating up the oven, make these in a snap on top of the stove.
—Kathy Scott, Hemingford, Nebraska

1/4 **cup butter *or* margarine**
    5 **cups miniature marshmallows**
1/2 **teaspoon ground cinnamon**
    4 **cups unseasoned croutons**
1/2 **cup chopped pecans**
1/2 **cup raisins**

Melt butter in a saucepan; add marshmallows and cinnamon. Cook and stir over low heat until marshmallows are melted; remove from heat. Add croutons, nuts and raisins; stir until well coated. Press into a greased 11-in. x 7-in. x 2-in. pan. Cool. Cut into bars. **Yield:** 2 dozen.

DANDY CANDY. Homemade confections like Macadamia Almond Brittle, Mocha Truffles and Coconut Yule Trees (shown above, clockwise from upper left) are a treat for the eyes and taste buds.

Macadamia Almond Brittle

(Pictured above)

This is a nuttier version of a basic brittle recipe. I added macadamia nuts—my favorites—and the brittle turned out tastier than ever. I love making this crisp snack because the results are impressive...and the job goes fast using the microwave. —Cheryl Miller
Fort Collins, Colorado

     1 cup sugar
 1/2 cup light corn syrup
 3/4 cup coarsely chopped macadamia nuts
 3/4 cup coarsely chopped almonds
     1 tablespoon butter *or* margarine
     2 teaspoons vanilla extract
     1 teaspoon baking soda

Combine sugar and corn syrup in a 1-1/2-qt. microwave-safe bowl. Microwave on high for 5 minutes. Stir in nuts. Microwave on high for 4-5 minutes longer or until a candy thermometer reads 300° (hard-crack stage). Quickly stir in butter, vanilla and baking soda until mixture is light and foamy. When bubbles subside, pour onto a greased cookie sheet, spreading as thinly as possible with a metal spatula. Cool completely; break into pieces. Store in an airtight container with waxed paper between layers. **Yield:** about 1 pound. **Editor's Note:** This recipe was tested in a 700-watt microwave.

Mocha Truffles

(Pictured at left)

Nothing compares to the melt-in-your-mouth flavor of these truffles...or to the simplicity of the recipe. Whenever I make them for my family or friends, they're quickly devoured. —Stacy Abell, Olathe, Kansas

- 2 packages (12 ounces *each*) semisweet chocolate chips
- 1 package (8 ounces) cream cheese, softened
- 3 tablespoons instant coffee granules
- 2 teaspoons water
- 1 pound dark chocolate confectionary coating

White confectionary coating, optional

In a microwave-safe bowl or double boiler, melt chocolate chips. Add cream cheese, coffee and water; mix well. Chill until firm enough to shape. Shape into 1-in. balls and place on a waxed paper-lined baking sheet. Chill for 1-2 hours or until firm. Melt chocolate coating in microwave-safe bowl or double boiler. Dip balls and place on waxed paper to harden. If desired, melt white coating and drizzle over truffles. **Yield:** about 5-1/2 dozen. **Editor's Note:** Truffles can be frozen for several months before dipping in chocolate. Thaw in the refrigerator before dipping.

Coconut Yule Trees

(Pictured at left)

People love these trees at Christmastime because they're so festive-looking and more fun than the standard holiday candy. If you like coconut, you'll love this recipe, too. I freeze the undecorated "trees" in an airtight container for up to a month. —Michelle Retterer, Marysville, Ohio

- 3 cups flaked coconut
- 2 cups confectioners' sugar
- 1/4 cup butter *or* margarine, softened
- 1/4 cup half-and-half cream
- 1 teaspoon almond extract
- 2 to 4 ounces dark chocolate confectionary coating

Green sugar and red-hot candies

In a large bowl, combine the first five ingredients; mix well. Drop by tablespoonfuls onto a waxed paper-lined baking sheet; cover and chill for 1 hour. Shape into trees; return to the baking sheet. In a double boiler or microwave-safe bowl, melt chocolate coating. Spoon over trunks of trees or dip trunks in chocolate coating; set aside to harden.

Decorate tops of trees with green sugar and red-hots. **Yield:** about 2 dozen.

Chocolate Peanut Butter Cookies

A few Christmases ago, I baked nine types of cookies over 2 days in a baking marathon that lasted into the night. These are a favorite anytime of year. —Bob Crabb, Scio, Oregon

- 1/2 cup creamy peanut butter
- 1/2 cup confectioners' sugar
- 1/2 cup packed brown sugar
- 1/4 cup sugar
- 1/2 cup butter *or* margarine, softened
- 6 ounces cream cheese, softened
- 1 egg
- 1 teaspoon vanilla extract
- 2 cups all-purpose flour
- 1/4 cup baking cocoa
- 1 teaspoon baking powder

FROSTING:
- 1 cup confectioners' sugar
- 2 ounces cream cheese, softened
- 2 tablespoons baking cocoa
- 1 to 2 tablespoons milk

In a small bowl, stir peanut butter and confectioners' sugar until smooth. Chill 15 minutes. Meanwhile, in a large bowl, beat sugars, butter and cream cheese until light and fluffy. Add egg and vanilla. Combine flour, cocoa and baking powder; add to cream cheese mixture and mix well. Roll into 1-in. balls. Place half of the balls 2 in. apart on a greased baking sheet. Make a depression in the center of each ball with your thumb; fill with 1 teaspoon of chilled peanut butter mixture. Flatten remaining balls and place on top, pressing edges to seal. Bake at 350° for 8-10 minutes. Remove to wire racks to cool. In a small bowl, mix confectioners' sugar, cream cheese, cocoa and enough milk to achieve desired frosting consistency. Frost cooled cookies. **Yield:** 2 dozen.

Confectionary Coating

Dark, milk or white chocolate confectionary coating is found in the baking section of most grocery stores. It is sometimes labled "almond bark" or "candy coating" and is often sold in bulk packages of 1 to 1-1/2 pounds. It is the product used for dipping chocolate. A substitute for 6 ounces chocolate coating would be 1 cup (6 ounces) semisweet, milk or white chocolate chips and 1 tablespoon shortening melted together.

Spice Cookies with Pumpkin Dip

(Pictured below)

My husband and two kids are sure to eat the first dozen of these cookies, warm from the oven, before the next tray is even done. A co-worker gave me the recipe for the pumpkin dip, which everyone loves with the cookies.
—Kelly McNeal, Derby, Kansas

  1-1/2 **cups butter *or* margarine, softened**
     2 **cups sugar**
     2 **eggs**
  1/2 **cup molasses**
     4 **cups all-purpose flour**
     4 **teaspoons baking soda**
     2 **teaspoons ground cinnamon**
     1 **teaspoon *each* ground ginger and cloves**
     1 **teaspoon salt**
Additional sugar
PUMPKIN DIP:
     1 **package (8 ounces) cream cheese, softened**
     1 **can (15 ounces) pumpkin pie mix**
     2 **cups confectioners' sugar**

  1/2 **to 1 teaspoon ground cinnamon**
  1/4 **to 1/2 teaspoon ground ginger**

In a mixing bowl, cream butter and sugar. Add eggs, one at a time, beating well after each addition. Add molasses; mix well. Combine flour, baking soda, cinnamon, ginger, cloves and salt; add to creamed mixture and mix well. Chill overnight. Shape into 1/2-in. balls; roll in sugar. Place 2 in. apart on ungreased baking sheets. Bake at 375° for 6 minutes or until edges begin to brown. Cool for 2 minutes before removing to a wire rack. For dip, beat cream cheese in a mixing bowl until smooth. Add pumpkin pie mix; beat well. Add sugar, cinnamon and ginger; beat until smooth. Serve with cookies. Store leftover dip in the refrigerator. **Yield:** about 20 dozen (3 cups dip).

Brown Sugar Icebox Cookies

(Pictured on page 148)

My daughters and I have been "fair-ly" successful competitors at county fairs and bake-offs for more than 20 years. This is one of those winning recipes. (You'll find three decadent desserts on page 148.)
—Eilene Bogar, Minier, Illinois

  1/2 **cup butter (no substitutes), softened**
     1 **cup packed brown sugar**
     1 **egg**
     1 **teaspoon vanilla extract**
  1-3/4 **cups all-purpose flour**
  1/2 **teaspoon baking soda**
  1/4 **teaspoon salt**
  2/3 **cup chopped pecans *or* flaked coconut**

Cream butter and brown sugar. Add egg and vanilla; mix well. Combine flour, baking soda and salt; gradually add to creamed mixture. Fold in pecans or coconut (dough will be sticky). Shape into two rolls and place on waxed paper; wrap tightly. Chill 4 hours or overnight. Cut into 1/4-in. slices. Place 2 in. apart on ungreased baking sheets. Bake at 375° for 7-10 minutes. Remove to wire racks to cool. **Yield:** about 3-1/2 dozen.

Chewy Granola Bars

For a satisfying snack that's both soft and crispy, try this recipe. These bars are a tempting, nutritious treat.
—Virginia Krites, Cridersville, Ohio

  1/2 **cup butter *or* margarine, softened**
     1 **cup packed brown sugar**
  1/4 **cup sugar**

2 tablespoons honey
1/2 teaspoon vanilla extract
1 egg
1 cup all-purpose flour
1 teaspoon ground cinnamon
1/2 teaspoon baking powder
1/4 teaspoon salt
1-1/2 cups quick-cooking oats
1-1/4 cups crisp rice cereal
1 cup chopped nuts
1 cup raisins *or* semisweet chocolate chips, optional

In a mixing bowl, cream butter and sugars. Add honey, vanilla and egg; mix well. Combine flour, cinnamon, baking powder and salt; gradually add to creamed mixture. Stir in oats, cereal and nuts. Add raisins or chocolate chips if desired. Press into a greased 13-in. x 9-in. x 2-in. baking pan. Bake at 350° for 25-30 minutes or until the top is lightly browned. **Yield:** 2 dozen.

Coconut Washboards

(Pictured on page 114)

My husband and I celebrated our 50th anniversary in 1994, and I've been making him these favorite cookies most of the years we've been married. Our great-grandchildren like to come over to munch on these chewy treats, too. —Tommie Sue Shaw
McAlester, Oklahoma

1/2 cup butter *or* margarine, softened
1/2 cup shortening
2 cups packed brown sugar
2 eggs
1/4 cup water
1 teaspoon vanilla extract
4 cups all-purpose flour
1-1/2 teaspoons baking powder
1/2 teaspoon baking soda
1/4 teaspoon salt
1 cup flaked coconut

In a mixing bowl, cream butter, shortening and brown sugar for 2 minutes or until fluffy. Add eggs; mix well. Gradually add water and vanilla; mix well. Combine flour, baking powder, baking soda and salt; add to the creamed mixture. Fold in coconut. Cover and refrigerate for 2-4 hours. Shape into 1-in. balls. Place 2 in. apart on greased baking sheets; flatten with fingers into 2-1/2-in. x 1-in. oblong shapes. Press lengthwise with a floured fork. Bake at 400° for 8-10 minutes or until lightly browned. Cool 2 minutes before removing to a wire rack. **Yield:** about 9 dozen.

Chocolate Raspberry Bars

(Pictured above and on page 114)

My family loves these rich, sweet bars. The chocolate and raspberry jam go together so well. I make a lot of cookies and bars, but these special treats are my favorite. They're so pretty served on a platter. —Kathy Smedstad, Silverton, Oregon

1 cup all-purpose flour
1/4 cup confectioners' sugar
1/2 cup cold butter *or* margarine
FILLING:
1/2 cup seedless raspberry jam
4 ounces cream cheese, softened
2 tablespoons milk
1 cup (6 ounces) vanilla chips, melted
GLAZE:
3/4 cup semisweet chocolate chips
2 tablespoons shortening

In a bowl, combine flour and confectioners' sugar; cut in butter until crumbly. Press into an ungreased 9-in. square baking pan. Bake at 375° for 15-18 minutes or until browned. Spread jam over warm crust. In a small mixing bowl, beat cream cheese and milk until smooth. Add vanilla chips; beat until smooth. Spread carefully over jam layer. Cool completely. Chill until set, about 1 hour. For glaze, melt chocolate chips and shortening; spread over filling. Chill for 10 minutes. Cut into bars; chill another hour. Store in the refrigerator. **Yield:** 3 dozen.

ever since. Everyone asks for the recipe once they have a taste. I make them for Christmas, picnics and charity auctions. They are so much better than store-bought caramels. —Marcie Wolfe, Williamsburg, Virginia

- **1 cup sugar**
- **1 cup dark corn syrup**
- **1 cup butter *or* margarine**
- **1 can (14 ounces) sweetened condensed milk**
- **1 teaspoon vanilla extract**

Line an 8-in. square pan with foil and butter the foil; set aside. Combine sugar, corn syrup and butter in a 3-qt. saucepan. Bring to a boil over medium heat, stirring constantly. Boil slowly for 4 minutes without stirring. Remove from the heat and stir in milk. Reduce heat to medium-low and cook until candy thermometer reads 238° (soft-ball stage), stirring constantly. Remove from the heat and stir in vanilla. Pour into prepared pan. Cool. Remove from pan and cut into 1-in. squares. Wrap individually in waxed paper; twist ends. **Yield:** 64 pieces.

Peanut Butter Snowballs

(Pictured above)

These creamy treats are a nice change from the typical milk chocolate and peanut butter combination. This recipe is also an easy one for children to help with. I prepare them for a bake sale at my granddaughter's school and put them in gift boxes I share with neighbors at Christmas. —Wanda Regula
Birmingham, Michigan

- **1 cup confectioners' sugar**
- **1/2 cup creamy peanut butter**
- **3 tablespoons butter *or* margarine, softened**
- **1 pound white confectionary coating**

In a mixing bowl, combine sugar, peanut butter and butter; mix well. Shape into 1-in. balls and place on a waxed paper-lined baking sheet. Chill for 30 minutes or until firm. Meanwhile, melt the white coating in a double boiler or microwave-safe bowl. Dip balls and place on waxed paper to harden. **Yield:** 2 dozen.

Creamy Caramels

I discovered this recipe in a local newspaper several years ago and have made these soft buttery caramels

Chocolate Malted Cookies

(Pictured on page 114)

These cookies are the next best thing to a good old-fashioned malted milk. With malted milk powder, chocolate syrup plus chocolate chips and chunks, these are the best cookies I've ever tasted...and with six kids, I've made a lot of cookies over the years.
—Teri Rasey-Bolf, Cadillac, Michigan

- **1 cup butter-flavored shortening**
- **1-1/4 cups packed brown sugar**
- **1/2 cup malted milk powder**
- **2 tablespoons chocolate syrup**
- **1 tablespoon vanilla extract**
- **1 egg**
- **2 cups all-purpose flour**
- **1 teaspoon baking soda**
- **1/2 teaspoon salt**
- **1-1/2 cups semisweet chocolate chunks**
- **1 cup (6 ounces) milk chocolate chips**

In a mixing bowl, combine shortening, brown sugar, malted milk powder, chocolate syrup and vanilla; beat for 2 minutes. Add egg. Combine the flour, baking soda and salt; gradually add to creamed mixture. Stir in chocolate chunks and chips. Shape into 2-in. balls; place 3 in. apart on ungreased baking sheets. Bake at 375° for 12-14 minutes or until golden brown. Cool for 2 minutes on pan before removing to wire racks to cool completely. **Yield:** about 1-1/2 dozen.

Crisp Sunflower Cookies

Kansas is the sunflower state, so I've come across many ways to put the hearty kernels to good use. Featuring sunflower kernels, oats and coconut, these crisp cookies are favored by all. —Karen Ann Bland
Gove, Kansas

```
3/4  cup shortening
  1  cup sugar
  1  cup packed brown sugar
  2  eggs
  1  teaspoon vanilla extract
  2  cups all-purpose flour
  1  teaspoon baking soda
1/2  teaspoon baking powder
1/2  teaspoon salt
  2  cups quick-cooking oats
  1  cup flaked coconut
  1  cup salted sunflower kernels
```

In a mixing bowl, cream shortening and sugars until light and fluffy. Add eggs and vanilla; mix well. Combine flour, baking soda, baking powder and salt; add to creamed mixture and mix well. Stir in the oats, coconut and sunflower kernels. Drop by teaspoonfuls onto greased baking sheets. Bake at 350° for 12-15 minutes or until golden brown. Remove to wire racks to cool. **Yield:** 5 dozen.

Frosted Ginger Cookies

(Pictured at right)

I work all day in an office, and I enjoy baking in the evening to relax. The wonderful aroma of these soft delicious cookies in our oven makes our house smell like home. —Jeanne Matteson
South Dayton, New York

```
1-1/2  cups butter or margarine
    1  cup sugar
    1  cup packed brown sugar
    2  eggs
  1/2  cup molasses
    2  teaspoons vanilla extract
4-1/2  cups all-purpose flour
    1  tablespoon ground ginger
    2  teaspoons baking soda
    2  teaspoons ground cinnamon
  1/2  teaspoon salt
  1/2  teaspoon ground cloves
```
FROSTING:
```
  1/3  cup packed brown sugar
  1/4  cup milk
    2  tablespoons butter or margarine
    2  cups confectioners' sugar
  1/2  teaspoon vanilla extract or caramel
       flavoring
```
Pinch salt

In a mixing bowl, cream butter and sugars. Add eggs, one at a time, beating well after each addition. Stir in molasses and vanilla; mix well. Combine dry ingredients; gradually add to creamed mixture. Drop by tablespoonfuls 2 in. apart onto ungreased baking sheets. Bake at 325° for 12-15 minutes or until cookies spring back when touched lightly (do not overbake). Remove to wire racks to cool. For frosting, in a medium saucepan, bring brown sugar, milk and butter to a boil; boil for 1 minute, stirring constantly. Remove from the heat (mixture will look curdled at first). Cool for 3 minutes. Add confectioner's sugar, vanilla and salt; mix well. Frost warm cookies. **Yield:** about 6 dozen.

Orange Taffy

This taffy has a satisfying tang that hits the tongue just before the sweetness. My mother-in-law gave me the recipe years ago. It takes time to wrap all the little candies, but the kids can help. It's a great way to involve them in the kitchen. —Christine Olson
Horse Creek, California

>   2 cups sugar
>   2 cups light corn syrup
>   1 can (6 ounces) frozen orange juice
>   concentrate, thawed
> Pinch salt
>   1 cup half-and-half cream
>   1/2 cup butter *or* margarine

In a heavy saucepan, combine first four ingredients. Cook and stir over medium heat until sugar is dissolved. Bring to a rapid boil and cook until a candy thermometer reads 245° (firm-ball stage). Add cream and butter; heat and stir until mixture reaches 245° again. Pour into a greased 15-in. x 10-in. x 1-in. pan; cool. When cool enough to handle, roll into 1-1/2-in. logs or 1-in. balls. Wrap individually in foil or waxed paper; twist ends. **Yield:** about 6 dozen.

Rolled Oat Cookies

(Pictured above)

I like to keep some of this dough in the freezer at all times since it's so handy to slice, bake and serve at a moment's notice. These wholesome cookies are super with a cup of coffee—in fact, we occasionally grab a few for breakfast when we're in a hurry.
—Kathi Peters, Chilliwack, British Columbia

>   1 cup butter *or* margarine
>   1 cup packed brown sugar
>   1/4 cup water
>   1 teaspoon vanilla extract
>   3 cups quick-cooking oats
> 1-1/4 cups all-purpose flour
>   1 teaspoon salt
>   1/4 teaspoon baking soda

In a mixing bowl, cream butter and brown sugar. Add water and vanilla; mix well. Combine dry ingredients; add to creamed mixture and mix well. Chill for 30 minutes. Shape into two 1-1/2-in. rolls; wrap tightly in waxed paper. Chill for 2 hours or until firm. Unwrap and cut into 1/2-in. slices. Place 2 in. apart on greased baking sheets. Bake at 375° for 12 minutes or until lightly browned. Remove to wire racks to cool. **Yield:** about 3-1/2 dozen.

─────── 🛆 🛆 🛆 ───────

Pumpkin Raisin Cookies

I got the recipe for these chewy cookies from my grandmother many years ago. Every time I prepare a batch, they're gobbled up in no time. —Carol Preston
Bloomington, Indiana

>   1/2 cup shortening
>   1 cup sugar
>   1 cup canned pumpkin
>   1 teaspoon vanilla extract
>   2 cups all-purpose flour
>   1 teaspoon baking powder
>   1 teaspoon baking soda
>   1 teaspoon ground cinnamon
> Dash salt
>   1 cup raisins
> FROSTING:
>   2 tablespoons butter *or* margarine
> 1-1/2 cups confectioners' sugar
>   2 tablespoons milk
>   1 teaspoon vanilla extract

In a mixing bowl, cream shortening and sugar. Add pumpkin and vanilla. Combine flour, baking powder, baking soda, cinnamon and salt; add to the creamed mixture and mix well. Fold in the raisins. Drop by teaspoonfuls onto greased baking sheets. Bake at 350° for 12-14 minutes or until lightly browned. Remove to wire racks to cool. For frosting, melt butter in a saucepan. Stir in the sugar, milk and vanilla until smooth. Frost cooled cookies. **Yield:** about 3 dozen.

Cheesecake Brownies

I was introduced to cooking at an early age by my grandmother. Now I cook everything from entrees to desserts. These bars won first place at a company picnic. —*James Harris, Columbus, Georgia*

   1 package (18-1/4 ounces) German
      chocolate cake mix
   1 egg, beaten
   1/2 cup butter *or* margarine, melted
   1 cup chopped nuts
TOPPING:
   1 package (8 ounces) cream cheese,
      softened
   1 cup sugar
   2 eggs, beaten
   1 teaspoon vanilla extract

In a mixing bowl, combine cake mix, egg, butter and nuts; mix well. Press into a greased 13-in. x 9-in. x 2-in. baking pan; set aside. Combine topping ingredients in another mixing bowl and beat until smooth. Carefully spread over batter. Bake at 350° for 30-35 minutes or until golden brown. Cool on a wire rack. Store in the refrigerator. **Yield:** about 2 dozen.

Homemade Candy Bars

I enter these treats, which are similar to Kit Kat bars, at the fair each year and win a blue ribbon. I've even had a judge ask how to make them! —*Karen Grant Tulare, California*

   8 ounces Waverly crackers, *divided*
   1 cup butter *or* margarine
   1/2 cup milk
   2 cups graham cracker crumbs
   1 cup packed brown sugar
   1/3 cup sugar
   2/3 cup creamy peanut butter
   1/2 cup milk chocolate chips
   1/2 cup butterscotch chips

Place a third of the crackers (about 25) in the bottom of an ungreased 13-in. x 9-in. x 2-in. pan. In a saucepan over medium-high heat, melt the butter. Add milk, graham cracker crumbs and sugars; bring to a boil. Boil, stirring constantly, for 5 minutes. Pour half of the mixture over crackers, carefully spreading to cover. Place half of the remaining crackers (about 25) on top. Spread with remaining sugar mixture. Top with remaining crackers. In a saucepan over low heat, stir the peanut butter and chips until melted and smooth. Spread over crackers. Chill until firm, about 1 hour. Cut into small squares. **Yield:** 3-4 dozen.

Christmas Hard Candy

(Pictured above)

When you make a batch of this beautiful jewel-toned candy, your whole house fills with wonderful scents of mint or cinnamon. My mom always makes this candy, and people request it every year. She puts it in clear jars with a holiday calico fabric on the lid. Now I've started making it, too. —*Jane Holman Moultrie, Georgia*

3-1/2 cups sugar
   1 cup light corn syrup
   1 cup water
   1/4 to 1/2 teaspoon cinnamon *or* peppermint
      oil*
   1 teaspoon red *or* green food coloring

In a large heavy saucepan, combine sugar, corn syrup and water. Cook on medium-high heat until candy thermometer reads 300° (hard-crack stage), stirring occasionally. Remove from the heat; stir in oil and food coloring, keeping face away from mixture as odor is very strong. Immediately pour onto a greased cookie sheet. Cool; break into pieces. Store in airtight containers. **Yield:** about 2 pounds. ***Editor's Note:** Cinnamon oil and peppermint oil are available in cake-decorating and candy supply stores.

Cakes, Pies & Desserts

**Bring your meals to a delectable close
with these eye-catching cakes, palate-pleasing
pies and tempting desserts.**

FANTASTIC FINISHES. Clockwise from upper left: White Christmas Cake (p. 152), Cherry Bavarian Cream (p. 147), Coconut Cream Pudding (p. 141), Strawberry-Pecan Pie (p. 157) and Pumpkin Sheet Cake (p. 143).

CRIMSON CROP. Tantalizing tart cherries lend lovely color and fresh tang to Cherry Almond Pie, Cherry Cobbler and Mini Cherry Cheesecakes (shown above, clockwise from upper left).

Cherry Almond Pie

(Pictured above)

I grew up in northern Michigan, where three generations of my family have been cherry producers. This traditional cherry pie makes a mouth-watering dessert that always gets rave reviews. —Ramona Pleva
Lincoln Park, New Jersey

> 4 cups pitted canned tart red cherries
> 3/4 cup sugar
> 1 tablespoon butter *or* margarine
> Pinch salt
> 1/4 cup cornstarch
> 1/3 cup cold water
> 1/4 teaspoon almond extract
> 1/4 teaspoon red food coloring, optional
> Pastry for double-crust pie (9 inches)

Drain cherries, reserving 2/3 cup juice; discard remaining juice. In a saucepan, combine reserved juice, cherries, sugar, butter and salt. In a small bowl, dissolve cornstarch in water; stir into cherry mixture. Bring to a boil over medium heat. Cook and stir until thickened and bubbly. Cook and stir 1 minute longer. Remove from the heat; stir in the almond extract and food coloring if desired. Cool. Place bottom pastry in a 9-in. pie plate. Add filling. Top with a lattice crust. Bake at 375° for 45-50 minutes or until crust is golden and filling is bubbly. **Yield:** 6-8 servings.

🍒 🍒 🍒

Cherry Cobbler

(Pictured above)

I've made this recipe for years, adapting it to suit our taste. It's a delicious way to use lots of cherries. I hope you enjoy this tart treat! —Peggy Burdick
Burlington, Michigan

> 5 cups pitted canned tart red cherries
> 1/3 cup sugar
> 1/3 cup packed brown sugar
> 2-1/2 tablespoons cornstarch
> 1 teaspoon ground cinnamon

1/4 teaspoon ground nutmeg
2-1/2 tablespoons lemon juice
TOPPING:
   1 cup all-purpose flour
   1 tablespoon sugar
   1 teaspoon baking powder
  1/4 teaspoon salt
   2 tablespoons cold butter *or* margarine
  1/3 to 1/2 cup milk

Drain cherries, reserving 1-1/4 cups juice; discard remaining juice. In a saucepan, combine sugars, cornstarch, cinnamon and nutmeg; stir in cherry and lemon juices. Bring to a boil, stirring occasionally; boil 2 minutes. Add cherries; pour into an ungreased 9-in. square baking pan. For topping, combine flour, sugar, baking powder and salt; cut in butter until crumbly. Stir in enough milk to moisten. Drop by tablespoonfuls over cherries. Bake at 450° for 10-13 minutes or until golden brown. **Yield:** 6-8 servings.

— ♟ ♟ ♟ —

✕ Mini Cherry Cheesecakes

(Pictured at left)

These individual cheesecakes make a festive dessert that's just right for cooks who don't have a lot of time for "fussy" recipes.
          —*Kay Keller*
          Morenci, Michigan

   1 cup vanilla wafer crumbs
   3 tablespoons butter *or* margarine, melted
   1 package (8 ounces) cream cheese, softened
1-1/2 teaspoons vanilla extract
   2 teaspoons lemon juice
  1/3 cup sugar
   1 egg
TOPPING:
   1 pound pitted canned tart red cherries
  1/2 cup sugar
   2 tablespoons cornstarch
Red food coloring, optional

In a bowl, combine crumbs and butter. Press gently into the bottom of 12 paper-lined muffin cups. In a mixing bowl, combine cream cheese, vanilla, lemon juice, sugar and egg; beat until smooth. Spoon into crusts. Bake at 375° for 12-15 minutes or until set. Cool completely. Drain cherries, reserving 1/2 cup juice; discard remaining juice. In a saucepan, combine reserved juice, cherries, sugar, cornstarch and food coloring if desired. Bring to a boil, stirring occasionally; boil for 1 minute. Cool; spoon over cheesecakes. Chill for at least 2 hours. **Yield:** 12 servings.

Peach Cream Pie

This yummy pie is sure a winner when fresh peaches are in season. The sour cream filling and cinnamon crumb topping complement the fruit flavor.
          —*Denise Goedeken, Platte Center, Nebraska*

1-1/2 cups all-purpose flour
  1/2 teaspoon salt
  1/2 cup cold butter *or* margarine
FILLING:
   4 cups fresh *or* frozen unsweetened sliced peaches
   1 cup sugar, *divided*
   2 tablespoons all-purpose flour
   1 egg
  1/2 teaspoon vanilla extract
  1/4 teaspoon salt
   1 cup (8 ounces) sour cream
TOPPING:
  1/3 cup sugar
  1/3 cup all-purpose flour
   1 teaspoon ground cinnamon
  1/4 cup cold butter *or* margarine

Combine flour and salt; cut in butter until crumbly. Press into a 9-in. pie plate. Place peaches in a bowl; sprinkle with 1/4 cup sugar. Combine flour, egg, vanilla, salt and remaining sugar; fold in sour cream. Stir into peaches; pour into crust. Bake at 400° for 15 minutes. Reduce heat to 350°; bake for 20 minutes. For topping, combine sugar, flour and cinnamon in a small bowl; cut in butter until crumbly. Sprinkle over the pie. Return oven temperature to 400°; bake 15 minutes longer. Cool. **Yield:** 6-8 servings.

— ♟ ♟ ♟ —

Easter Nests

My kids and I make a big batch of these sweet treats for ourselves and some to share. They're a hit at Easter dinner.   —*Faye Hintz, Springfield, Missouri*

   1 jar (7 ounces) marshmallow creme
  1/4 cup creamy peanut butter
   2 tablespoons butter *or* margarine, melted
   1 can (5 ounces) chow mein noodles
   1 cup pastel M&M's
Confectioners' sugar
Pastel peanut M&M's

In a mixing bowl, beat marshmallow creme, peanut butter and butter until smooth. Fold in noodles and M&M's. Chill until easy to handle. On waxed paper, form mixture by 1/3 cupfuls into 3-in. nests. Chill for 30 minutes. Dust with confectioners' sugar. Place several peanut M&M's in each nest. **Yield:** 9 servings.

Puddings Are Sure to Please

IT'S hard to come up with a dessert more comforting than homemade pudding! But these recipes are full of old-fashioned flavor.

— 🍴 🍴 🍴 —

Caramel Bread Pudding

(Pictured below)

My mom gave me the recipe for this simple-to-prepare pudding. It's a great way to use up day-old bread.
—*Tammie Peebles, Naples, Florida*

- **6 slices day-old bread, cut into 1/2-inch cubes**
- **1 cup hot water**
- **1 cup packed brown sugar**
- **4 eggs, lightly beaten**
- **2 cups warm milk**
- **1/2 cup sugar**
- **1/2 teaspoon vanilla extract**
- **1/2 teaspoon ground cinnamon**
- **1/8 teaspoon salt**

Place bread in a greased 2-qt. baking dish. Combine water and brown sugar; pour over bread. Combine remaining ingredients; pour over bread. Bake at 350° for 50-60 minutes or until a knife inserted near the center comes out clean. Serve warm or cold. **Yield:** 6-8 servings.

— 🍴 🍴 🍴 —

Ice Cream Pudding

(Pictured below)

No one will suspect you began with an instant pudding mix for this richly flavored treat. —*Wendy Masters Grand Valley, Oregon*

- **1 cup cold milk**
- **1 package (3.4 ounces) instant pudding mix, any flavor**
- **2 cups softened ice cream, any flavor**
- **Fresh fruit, optional**

In a mixing bowl, beat milk and pudding mix on low for 1 minute. Fold in ice cream until smooth. Spoon into dishes. Chill for at least 1 hour. Garnish with fruit if desired. **Yield:** 6 servings.

DOWN-HOME DESSERTS. One taste and you'll agree the proof's in the Caramel Bread and Ice Cream Pudding (shown above, top to bottom)!

Butterscotch Rice Pudding

When we married, my husband made sure to get the recipe for this delicious, comforting pudding from his mother.   —*Faye Hintz, Springfield, Missouri*

  3 **cups milk,** *divided*
  1/2 **cup uncooked long grain rice**
  1/2 **teaspoon salt**
  3/4 **cup packed brown sugar,** *divided*
  2 **tablespoons butter** *or* **margarine**
  2 **eggs,** *separated*
  1 **teaspoon vanilla extract**

In the top of double boiler, heat 2 cups milk to a gentle boil. Stir in rice and salt. Cover and cook over medium-low heat for 45 minutes, stirring occasionally. Remove from the heat; set aside. In a saucepan, heat 1/2 cup brown sugar, butter and remaining milk until simmering. In a small bowl, beat egg yolks. Add small amount of hot milk mixture to yolks; return to pan. Stir until smooth. Stir into rice mixture; cook and stir over medium heat for 5 minutes. Remove from heat; stir in vanilla. Pour into a greased 1-1/2-qt. baking dish; set aside. In a mixing bowl, beat egg whites until soft peaks form; gradually add remaining brown sugar, beating until stiff peaks form. Spread over rice mixture, sealing edges. Bake at 300° for 20-25 minutes. **Yield:** 6-8 servings.

— 🥄 🥄 🥄 —

Homemade Pudding

You can make pudding with this handy mix in no time. I'm always certain to have some in my cupboard.
—*Margery Bryan, Royal City, Washington*

PUDDING MIX:
2-3/4 **cups instant nonfat dry milk powder**
1-1/2 **cups sugar**
  3/4 **cup cornstarch**
  1 **teaspoon salt**
PUDDING:
2-1/4 **cups milk** *or* **water**
  1 **egg, beaten**
  1 **tablespoon butter** *or* **margarine**
1-1/2 **teaspoons vanilla extract**

Combine first four ingredients; store in an airtight container. For pudding, combine 1-1/4 cups of the mix and milk in a 2-qt. saucepan. Bring to a boil over medium heat, stirring occasionally; boil for 1 minute. Remove from the heat. Stir a small amount into egg; return to pan. Cook and stir over medium heat for 2 minutes. Remove from the heat; add butter and vanilla. Mix well. Pour into dishes; cover and chill for 2-3 hours. **Yield:** 4-5 servings (4 cups mix). **For chocolate pudding:** Add 3 table-spoons baking cocoa to 1-1/4 cups pudding mix before mixing with milk.

— 🥄 🥄 🥄 —

Coconut Cream Pudding

(Pictured on page 136)

A golden baked meringue makes the crowning touch to this mouth-watering dessert.   —*Verona Koehlmoos*
Pilger, Nebraska

1-1/4 **cups sugar,** *divided*
  1/4 **cup cornstarch**
  3 **cups milk**
  4 **eggs,** *separated*
  1 **cup flaked coconut**
  1 **teaspoon vanilla extract**

In a heavy saucepan, combine 3/4 cup sugar and cornstarch; stir in milk. Cook and stir over medium heat until thick and bubbly; cook and stir 2 minutes more. Remove from heat. Beat egg yolks. Stir 1 cup hot milk mixture into yolks; return to pan. Cook and stir over medium heat until gently boiling; cook and stir 2 minutes more. Remove from the heat; cool to lukewarm. Stir in coconut and vanilla. Pour into an ungreased 8-in. square baking dish. In a mixing bowl, beat egg whites until soft peaks form. Gradually add remaining sugar, beating until stiff peaks form. Spread over pudding, sealing edges. Bake at 350° for 10-15 minutes. Serve warm. **Yield:** 9 servings.

— 🥄 🥄 🥄 —

Old-Fashioned Banana Pudding

Peanuts add a pleasant crunch to this pudding. One bite will take you back to grandma's kitchen.
—*Edna Hoffman, Hebron, Indiana*

  3/4 **cup packed brown sugar**
  1/4 **cup all-purpose flour**
  2 **cups milk**
  2 **eggs, beaten**
  2 **tablespoons butter** *or* **margarine**
  1 **teaspoon vanilla extract**
  2 **medium ripe bananas, sliced**
  1/2 **cup chopped peanuts**

In a saucepan, combine sugar and flour. Gradually stir in milk; bring to a boil over medium heat, stirring constantly. Cook and stir 2 minutes. Stir a small amount into eggs; return to pan and mix well. Cook and stir over medium heat for 2-4 minutes. Remove from the heat; add butter, vanilla, bananas and peanuts. Pour into dishes. Chill. **Yield:** 4-6 servings.

Four-Fruit Pie

(Pictured above)

My husband likes this fruity combination almost as much as traditional apple pie—and that's saying something! I keep rhubarb, blueberries and raspberries in the freezer and always have apples on hand for this colorful dessert.
—Joan Rose
Langley, British Columbia

 1 cup sliced rhubarb
 1 cup chopped peeled apple
 1 cup blueberries
 1 cup raspberries
 1 teaspoon lemon juice
 3/4 cup sugar
 1/4 cup all-purpose flour
Pastry for double-crust pie (9 inches)
 2 tablespoons butter *or* margarine
Additional sugar, optional

In a large bowl, gently toss rhubarb, apple, berries and lemon juice. Combine sugar and flour; stir into the fruit and let stand for 30 minutes. Line a pie plate with bottom crust. Add filling; dot with butter. Roll out remaining pastry to fit top of pie; cut slits in top. Place over filling. Seal and flute edges. Bake at 400° for 50-60 minutes or until crust is golden brown and filling is bubbly. Sprinkle with sugar if desired. **Yield:** 6-8 servings.

———— 🝔 🝔 🝔 ————

Sugar-Free Apple Pie

*This pie is so delicious, you can't even detect the arti-*ficial sweetener. I always get rave reviews when I bring it to church potlucks.* *—Teresa Garlick*
Glendale, Arizona

☑ Uses less fat, sugar or salt. Includes Nutritional Analysis and Diabetic Exchanges.

 1/3 cup frozen apple juice concentrate
Artificial sweetener equivalent to 8 teaspoons sugar*
 2 teaspoons cornstarch
 1 teaspoon ground cinnamon
Pastry for double-crust pie (9 inches)
 8 cups thinly sliced peeled tart apples
 1 tablespoon margarine

Combine the first four ingredients. Line pie plate with bottom crust; add apples. Pour juice mixture over apples; dot with margarine. Roll out remaining pastry to fit top of pie; cut slits or an apple shape in top. Place over filling; seal and flute edges. Bake at 375° for 35 minutes. Increase temperature to 400°; bake 15-20 minutes longer or until apples are tender. **Yield:** 8 servings. *Editor's Note:* Sweet 'N Low or Sweet One are recommended for baking. **Nutritional Analysis:** One serving equals 337 calories, 233 mg sodium, 0 cholesterol, 45 gm carbohydrate, 2 gm protein, 17 gm fat. **Diabetic Exchanges:** 3 fat, 2 fruit, 1 starch.

———— 🝔 🝔 🝔 ————

German Chocolate Cheesecake Squares

When people ask about my all-time favorite recipe, I have a hard time deciding. But this recipe is definitely tops among sweets.
—Jerry Minerich
Westminster, Colorado

 1 package (1/4 ounce) active dry yeast
 1/2 cup warm water (110° to 115°)
 1/4 cup sugar
 1/2 teaspoon salt
 1 egg
 1/2 cup butter *or* margarine, softened
 2 to 2-1/2 cups all-purpose flour
FILLING:
 2 packages (8 ounces *each*) cream cheese, softened
 1 package (3 ounces) cream cheese, softened
 1/3 cup baking cocoa
 1 cup sugar
 3 eggs
 2 teaspoons vanilla extract
TOPPING:
 1/2 cup sugar
 1 egg
 1/2 cup evaporated milk
 1/4 cup butter *or* margarine

1 teaspoon vanilla extract
2/3 cup flaked coconut
1/2 cup chopped pecans

In a large mixing bowl, dissolve yeast in water. Add sugar, salt, egg, butter and 1 cup of flour; beat until smooth. Add enough remaining flour to form a soft dough. Turn onto a floured surface; knead until smooth and elastic, about 3-5 minutes. Place in a greased bowl, turning once to grease top. Cover and let rest for 20 minutes. Punch dough down. Press into the bottom and up the sides of a greased 15-in. x 10-in. x 1-in. baking pan. In a large mixing bowl, beat cream cheese until smooth; gradually add cocoa and sugar. Beat until fluffy. Beat in eggs, one at a time. Add vanilla. Pour into crust. Bake at 350° for 20-25 minutes or until crust is golden brown; cool. In a saucepan, combine first four topping ingredients; cook over low heat until thick, about 8-10 minutes, stirring constantly. Remove from the heat; stir in vanilla, coconut and nuts. Spread over cooled cake. Chill at least 1 hour. Store in the refrigerator. **Yield:** 3 dozen.

— 🛒 🛒 🛒 —

Breakfast Bread Pudding

I assemble this dish the day before our grandchildren come to visit. That way, I can have more fun time with them! —*Alma Andrews, Live Oak, Florida*

12 slices white bread, crusts removed and cubed
 1 package (8 ounces) cream cheese, cubed
12 eggs
 2 cups milk
1/3 cup maple syrup
1/4 teaspoon salt

Toss bread lightly with cream cheese cubes; place in a greased 13-in. x 9-in. x 2-in. baking pan. In a large mixing bowl, beat eggs. Add milk, syrup and salt; mix well. Pour over bread mixture. Cover and refrigerate 8 hours or overnight. Remove from refrigerator 30 minutes before baking. Bake, uncovered, at 375° for 40-45 minutes or until a knife inserted near the center comes out clean. Let stand 5 minutes before cutting. **Yield:** 6-8 servings.

— 🛒 🛒 🛒 —

Pumpkin Sheet Cake

(Pictured at right and on page 136)

The pastor at our church usually cuts his message short on carry-in dinner days when he knows this sheet cake is waiting in the fellowship hall. (I think he prays for leftovers since he gets to take them home!) This moist cake travels well and is also easy to prepare. —*Nancy Baker, Boonville, Missouri*

1 can (15 ounces) solid-pack pumpkin
2 cups sugar
1 cup vegetable oil
4 eggs, lightly beaten
2 cups all-purpose flour
2 teaspoons baking soda
1 teaspoon ground cinnamon
1/2 teaspoon salt
FROSTING:
1 package (3 ounces) cream cheese, softened
5 tablespoons butter *or* margarine, softened
1 teaspoon vanilla extract
1-3/4 cups confectioners' sugar
3 to 4 teaspoons milk
Chopped nuts

In a mixing bowl, beat pumpkin, sugar and oil. Add eggs; mix well. Combine flour, baking soda, cinnamon and salt; add to pumpkin mixture and beat until well blended. Pour into a greased 15-in. x 10-in. x 1-in. baking pan. Bake at 350° for 25-30 minutes or until cake tests done. Cool. For frosting, beat the cream cheese, butter and vanilla in a mixing bowl until smooth. Gradually add sugar; mix well. Add enough milk until frosting reaches desired spreading consistency. Frost cake. Sprinkle with nuts. **Yield:** 20-24 servings.

Cran-Raspberry Pie

Jewel-toned fruits team up to pack this pretty pie. This recipe is one our four grown children especially enjoy when they come home for family holiday meals.
—Verona Koehlmoss, Pilger, Nebraska

   2 cups chopped fresh *or* frozen cranberries
   1 package (12 ounces) unsweetened frozen raspberries
1-1/2 cups sugar
   2 tablespoons quick-cooking tapioca
 1/2 teaspoon almond extract
 1/4 teaspoon salt
Pastry for double-crust pie (9 inches)

In a bowl, gently stir cranberries, raspberries, sugar, tapioca, almond extract and salt. Line pie plate with bottom pastry; add filling. Top with a lattice crust. Bake at 375° for 15 minutes. Reduce heat to 350° and bake 35-40 minutes more or until bubbly. **Yield:** 6-8 servings.

——— ▼ ▼ ▼ ———

Peanut Squares

I've used this recipe for over 50 years. Our children and grandchildren look forward to these treats at Thanksgiving and Christmas.
—Mavis Larson Granger, Washington

   1 package (18-1/4 ounces) white cake mix
4-1/2 cups confectioners' sugar
 1/8 teaspoon salt
   1 teaspoon vanilla extract
   7 to 8 tablespoons milk
   1 jar (16 ounces) lightly salted dry roasted peanuts, finely chopped

Mix and bake cake according to package directions, using a greased 13-in. x 9-in. x 2-in. baking pan. Cool. Cut into 24 squares; set aside. In a medium bowl, combine sugar and salt. Add vanilla and enough milk to make a thin frosting. Frost top and sides of squares and immediately roll in peanuts. Place on wire racks to harden. **Yield:** 2 dozen.

——— ▼ ▼ ▼ ———

Blueberry Grunt

A tightly covered skillet will "grunt" while this traditional dessert cooks. It's said early settlers served this to the captain of the "Yankee Clipper".
—Iola Egle, McCook, Nebraska

   4 cups fresh blueberries
   1 cup sugar
   1 cup water
1-1/2 cups all-purpose flour
   2 teaspoons baking powder
   2 tablespoons grated orange peel
 1/2 teaspoon ground cinnamon
 1/4 teaspoon ground nutmeg
 1/4 teaspoon salt
 3/4 cup milk
Whipping cream, optional

In a skillet, combine blueberries, sugar and water; bring to a boil. Simmer, uncovered, for 20 minutes. In a bowl, combine the next six ingredients; stir in milk just until moistened (dough will be stiff). Drop by tablespoonfuls over blueberries. Cover and cook for 10-15 minutes or until dumplings are puffed and test done. Serve warm with cream if desired. **Yield:** 6-8 servings.

——— ▼ ▼ ▼ ———

Chocolate Almond Cake

(Pictured at right)

The first time I tried this recipe, I took the cake to a friend. She raved about it so much that I made one for my family.
—Sherri Gentry, Dallas, Oregon

 3/4 cup butter *or* margarine, softened
1-2/3 cups sugar
   2 eggs
 3/4 cup sour cream
   1 teaspoon vanilla extract
   1 teaspoon almond extract
   2 cups all-purpose flour
 2/3 cup baking cocoa
   2 teaspoons baking soda
 1/2 teaspoon salt
   1 cup buttermilk
FROSTING:
   5 tablespoons butter *or* margarine, softened
2-1/2 cups confectioners' sugar
   1 teaspoon vanilla extract
 1/2 teaspoon almond extract
   3 to 4 tablespoons milk
Sliced almonds, toasted

In a large mixing bowl, cream butter and sugar. Add eggs, one at a time, beating well after each addition. Add sour cream and extracts; mix well. Combine flour, cocoa, baking soda and salt; add to the creamed mixture alternately with buttermilk. Pour into a greased 10-in. fluted tube pan. Bake at 350° for 50-55 minutes or until cake tests done. Cool in pan for 10 minutes before removing to a wire rack. For frosting, cream butter, sugar and extracts in a small mixing bowl until smooth. Add enough milk until frosting reaches a desired spreading consistency. Frost cooled cake. Decorate with almonds. **Yield:** 12-16 servings.

FINALES FOR FALL. Chocolate Almond Cake, Coconut-Pecan Pie and Brownie Tarts (shown above, top to bottom) are tempting dessert ideas for autumn meals.

Brownie Tarts

(Pictured above)

I often take these bite-size chocolate goodies to potluck dinners for our country dance club. They're a no-fuss treat that are gobbled up in no time. —Sharon Wilkins Grande Pointe, Ontario

  1/2 **cup butter *or* margarine, softened**
     1 **package (3 ounces) cream cheese, softened**
     1 **cup all-purpose flour**
FILLING:
  1/2 **cup semisweet chocolate chips**
     2 **tablespoons butter *or* margarine**
  1/2 **cup sugar**
     1 **egg, beaten**
     1 **teaspoon vanilla extract**
  1/2 **cup chopped pecans, optional**
Maraschino cherry halves, optional

In a mixing bowl, cream the butter and cream cheese. Add flour; mix well. Chill for 1 hour. Shape into 1-in. balls. Place in ungreased miniature muffin cups; press into the bottom and up the sides to form a shell. For filling, melt chocolate chips and butter in a small saucepan. Remove from the heat; stir in sugar, egg and vanilla. Add the pecans if desired. Spoon into shells. Bake at 325° for 30-35 minutes or until a toothpick inserted near the center comes out clean. Cool 10 minutes before removing to a wire rack. Garnish with cherries if desired. **Yield:** 2 dozen.

Coconut-Pecan Pie

(Pictured above)

I grew up on a farm with lots of pecan trees. This pie really showcases that spectacular nut.
—Barbara Ann McKenzie, Keytesville, Missouri

     3 **eggs**
1-1/2 **cups sugar**
  1/2 **cup butter *or* margarine, melted**
     2 **teaspoons lemon juice**
     1 **teaspoon vanilla extract**
1-1/4 **cups flaked coconut**
  1/2 **cup coarsely chopped pecans**
     1 **unbaked pastry shell (9 inches)**

In a mixing bowl, beat eggs. Add sugar, butter, lemon juice and vanilla; mix well. Stir in coconut and pecans; pour into pie shell. Bake at 350° for 45-50 minutes or until set. Cool completely. Store in the refrigerator. **Yield:** 6-8 servings.

15 minutes before removing to a wire rack. Cool completely. Chill before slicing. Dust with confectioners' sugar if desired. **Yield:** 12-16 servings.

— ☕ ☕ ☕ —

Squash Pie

I adapted this dessert from a pumpkin pie recipe. Replacing the pumpkin for squash makes every bite even more delicious. —Joyce Jackson
Bridgetown, Nova Scotia

1-1/4 cups mashed cooked winter squash
  3/4 cup packed brown sugar
    2 tablespoons molasses
1-1/4 teaspoons ground cinnamon
  3/4 teaspoon salt
  3/4 teaspoon ground nutmeg
  3/4 teaspoon ground ginger
    3 eggs, beaten
    1 can (12 ounces) evaporated milk
    1 unbaked pastry shell (9 inches)
Whipped cream, optional

In a bowl, combine the first eight ingredients with a wire whisk. Stir in milk. Pour into pie shell. Bake at 450° for 10 minutes. Reduce heat to 350°; bake for 50-55 minutes or until a knife inserted near the center comes out clean. Cool. Serve with whipped cream if desired. **Yield:** 6-8 servings.

— ☕ ☕ ☕ —

Low-Fat Lemon Cheesecake

If you're looking for a cool, creamy dessert that even a diabetic can indulge in, try this recipe.
—Mary Merchant, Barre, Vermont

☑ Uses less fat, sugar or salt. Includes Nutritional Analysis and Diabetic Exchanges.

    1 cup graham cracker crumbs
    2 tablespoons reduced-fat margarine, melted
    3 packages (8 ounces *each*) light cream cheese, softened
    2 tablespoons all-purpose flour
  1/4 cup sugar
    3 tablespoons fresh lemon juice
  3/4 cup egg substitute
    1 carton (8 ounces) light nonfat lemon yogurt
Assorted fresh berries, optional

Combine cracker crumbs and margarine; press into bottom of an ungreased 9-in. springform pan. Set aside. Beat cream cheese, flour and sugar until light and fluffy. Gradually add lemon juice and egg substitute. Beat well. Fold in yogurt. Pour into crust. Cover loosely with foil. Bake at 350° for 60-70 min-

Golden Chocolate Cake

(Pictured above)

I'm always on the lookout for good dessert recipes. This moist cake is a favorite since it's chock-full of chocolate candy bars, pecans and coconut.
—Kay Hansen, Escondido, California

    1 package (18-1/4 ounces) yellow cake mix
    1 package (3.4 ounces) instant vanilla pudding mix
  1/2 cup vegetable oil
  1/2 cup water
    4 eggs
    1 cup (8 ounces) sour cream
    3 milk chocolate candy bars (1.55 ounces *each*), chopped
    1 cup (6 ounces) semisweet chocolate chips
    1 cup chopped pecans
    1 cup flaked coconut
Confectioners' sugar, optional

In a mixing bowl, combine cake and pudding mixes, oil, water and eggs; beat on low speed for about 30 seconds or until moistened. Beat 2 minutes on high. Blend in sour cream. Stir in candy bars, chocolate chips, pecans and coconut. Pour into a greased and floured 12-cup fluted tube pan. Bake at 350° for 60-65 minutes or until a toothpick inserted near the center comes out clean. Cool in pan

utes or until set. Cool to room temperature. Refrigerate. Garnish with berries if desired. **Yield:** 16 servings. **Nutritional Analysis:** One serving (without berries) equals 178 calories, 330 mg sodium, 25 mg cholesterol, 16 gm carbohydrate, 7 gm protein, 10 gm fat. **Diabetic Exchanges:** 1-1/2 fat, 1 starch, 1/2 meat.

───── ᵂ ᵂ ᵂ ─────

Cherry Bavarian Cream

(Pictured on page 136)

I especially like recipes for out-of-the-ordinary desserts. One bite and you'll agree this not-too-sweet treat is worth the extra effort. —Christina Till
South Haven, Michigan

    6 **egg yolks**
  1/2 **cup sugar**
    2 **cups warm milk (115° to 120°)**
    1 **tablespoon vanilla extract**
    2 **envelopes unflavored gelatin**
  1/4 **cup cold water**
Red food coloring, optional
    1 **cup whipping cream, whipped**
    2 **cups pitted tart red *or* bing cherries**
Fresh mint, optional

In the top of a double boiler, beat egg yolks and sugar with an electric mixer for 2 minutes. Gradually add milk and vanilla. Place over boiling water. Cook and stir constantly for 6-8 minutes or until mixture begins to coat the spoon. Pour into a large bowl; set aside. In a small bowl, sprinkle gelatin over water; let stand 2 minutes. Stir into egg mixture; tint with food coloring if desired. Set bowl over larger bowl filled with ice water. As soon as the cooked mixture begins to set up, fold in the cream and cherries. Pour into a 2-qt. serving bowl and refrigerate 4-6 hours or overnight. Garnish with mint if desired. **Yield:** 6-8 servings.

───── ᵂ ᵂ ᵂ ─────

Mud Pie

Desserts don't come much simpler to prepare than this swirly, chocolate mocha-flavored pie. The combination of chocolate and coffee is unbeatable.
—Debbie Jones, California, Maryland

    1 **quart coffee ice cream, softened**
    1 **chocolate cookie crust (9 inches)**
  1/2 **cup chocolate syrup**

Spread ice cream into crust; pour chocolate syrup on top and swirl with a knife. Cover and freeze for at least 2 hours. Serve frozen. **Yield:** 6-8 servings.

Washington Cream Pie

(Pictured below)

My mom made this cherry-topped cake every year for my uncle, who shares his birthday with George Washington! —Lyn Robitaille, East Hartland, Connecticut

    3 **eggs**
1-1/2 **cups sugar**
    2 **cups all-purpose flour**
    2 **teaspoons baking powder**
  1/2 **cup water**
FILLING:
    1 **cup sugar**
    2 **tablespoons cornstarch**
    2 **cups milk**
    2 **eggs, beaten**
    2 **tablespoons butter *or* margarine**
    1 **teaspoon vanilla extract**
    1 **can (21 ounces) cherry pie filling**
Whipped cream

In a mixing bowl, beat eggs on high for 3 minutes; gradually add sugar. Combine flour and baking powder; stir into egg mixture alternately with water. Beat on low for 1 minute. Pour into a greased 9-in. square baking pan. Bake at 375° for 25-30 minutes or until the cake tests done. Cool. Split cake into two layers. For filling, combine the sugar and cornstarch in a saucepan; stir in milk. Bring to a boil; cook for 2 minutes. Stir a small amount into eggs; mix well. Return all to pan. Cook and stir for 1 minute or until thick. Remove from the heat; cool slightly. Add the butter and vanilla; cool completely. Spread between cake layers. Cut into squares; top with pie filling and whipped cream. **Yield:** 9 servings.

Blue-Ribbon Bakers Share Prize-Winning Desserts

"MY DAUGHTERS, Claire, Amy, Jill and Lori, have always shared my love of baking," recalls Eilene Bogar of Minier, Illinois. "By their teens, the girls were turning out breads, pies and cakes.

"We decided to enter the county fair, and later, area bake-offs. We didn't always win, but over the years, we collected many ribbons. Best of all, we had a great time and met lots of good cooks."

Their idea for a cookbook including prize-winning recipes among other favorites became reality a few years ago, when the Minier Christian Church voted for a new building. "We decided to publish our very own cookbook, 'Baking—A Family Tradition', and share the profits with the church," relates Eilene. Three fa-

vorite recipes appear here. (You'll also find a recipe for Brown Sugar Icebox Cookies on page 130.)

Lemon Whipped Cream Torte features a creamy, refreshing filling in between light layers of moist sponge cake. It's a treat to make for special occasions.

For the chocolate lovers in your family, why not try Lovelight Chocolate Cake? "Jill was 15 years old when she won top honors at a local bake-off for this cake," says proud mom Eilene.

"It's not uncommon for us to have four different pies when our family gathers for a meal," admits Eilene. The addition of whipping cream makes Apple Cream Pie an irresistible change from other versions of this traditional dessert.

PRIZE-WINNING DESSERTS include Lemon Whipped Cream Torte, Apple Cream Pie, Lovelight Chocolate Cake and Brown Sugar Icebox Cookies (shown above, clockwise from upper left).

Lemon Whipped Cream Torte

(Pictured below left)

1/4 cup butter, softened
1/4 cup shortening
1-1/4 cups sugar, *divided*
2 teaspoons grated lemon peel
1/2 teaspoon vanilla extract
2 cups cake flour
1 tablespoon baking powder
1/4 teaspoon salt
3/4 cup milk
6 egg whites

FILLING:
1/2 cup sugar
1/3 cup all-purpose flour
1-3/4 cups milk
3 egg yolks, lightly beaten
1/4 cup lemon juice
1 teaspoon vanilla extract
1 teaspoon grated lemon peel
1 cup whipping cream, whipped

In a mixing bowl, cream butter, shortening and 1 cup sugar. Add lemon peel and vanilla; mix well. Combine flour, baking powder and salt. Gradually add to creamed mixture alternately with milk; set aside. Beat egg whites until soft peaks form. Gradually add remaining sugar, beating until stiff peaks form. Fold into the creamed mixture. Pour into three greased and waxed paper-lined 9-in. round cake pans. Bake at 350° for 15-20 minutes or until cake tests done. Cool for 10 minutes; remove from pans to a wire rack. For filling, combine sugar and flour in a saucepan. Gradually add milk; cook and stir until thickened and bubbly. Cook and stir 2 minutes more. Remove from heat. Gradually stir a little of the hot filling into the yolks; return all to the pan. Bring to a gentle boil. Cook and stir 2 minutes more. Remove from heat. Stir in lemon juice, vanilla and peel. Cover and cool. Fold in the cream. Spread between each layer and on top of cake. Cover and chill. **Yield:** 12-16 servings.

— ☕ ☕ ☕ —

Lovelight Chocolate Cake

(Pictured at left)

2 eggs, *separated*
1-1/2 cups sugar, *divided*
1-3/4 cups cake flour
3/4 teaspoon baking soda
3/4 teaspoon salt
1/3 cup vegetable oil
1 cup buttermilk, *divided*
2 squares (1 ounce *each*) semisweet chocolate, melted and cooled

FROSTING:
3 tablespoons butter, softened
1 package (3 ounces) cream cheese, softened
4 cups confectioners' sugar
3 to 4 tablespoons milk
2 squares (1 ounce *each*) semisweet chocolate, melted and cooled
1/2 teaspoon vanilla extract

Beat egg whites until soft peaks form. Gradually add 1/2 cup sugar, beating until stiff peaks form; set aside. In a mixing bowl, combine flour, baking soda, salt and remaining sugar. Add oil and 1/2 cup buttermilk; beat 1 minute. Add yolks, chocolate and remaining buttermilk; beat 1 minute. Fold in egg white mixture. Pour into two greased 9-in. round cake pans. Bake at 350° for 30-35 minutes or until cake tests done. Cool in pans 10 minutes before removing to a wire rack. For frosting, cream butter and cream cheese. Add sugar alternately with milk. Gradually add chocolate and vanilla; mix well. Frost cooled cake. Cover and chill. **Yield:** 10-12 servings.

— ☕ ☕ ☕ —

Apple Cream Pie

(Pictured at far left)

4 cups sliced peeled tart apples
1 unbaked pastry shell (9 inches)
1 cup sugar
1 cup whipping cream
3 tablespoons all-purpose flour
Ground cinnamon

Place apples in pie shell. Combine sugar, cream and flour; pour over the apples. Sprinkle with cinnamon. Bake at 400° for 10 minutes. Reduce heat to 375°; bake for 35-40 minutes or until pie is set in center. Cover crust edges with foil during the last 15 minutes if needed. Cool on a wire rack. Serve, or cover and refrigerate. **Yield:** 6-8 servings.

FAMILY BAKERS are Claire Logsdon (left), Eilene Bogar, Amy Freitag, Jill Kohl and Lori Groth (see story on opposite page).

TANTALIZING TASTES sprout up in company-tested goodies such as Turtle Cheesecake, Strawberry-Rhubarb Pie and Chocolate Coconut Cake (shown above, clockwise from upper left).

Strawberry-Rhubarb Pie

(Pictured above)

I cook the old-fashioned way, using locally grown berries and garden rhubarb for this favorite. It's a success every time I make it. —Helen Ward O'Key
Litchfield, Connecticut

> 3 cups chopped fresh *or* frozen rhubarb
> (1/2-inch pieces)
> 1 cup water
> 1 package (6 ounces) strawberry gelatin
> 1 cup sliced fresh *or* frozen strawberries
> 1 envelope whipped topping mix
> 1 graham cracker crust (9 inches)
Whole fresh strawberries

In a saucepan, bring rhubarb and water to a boil; remove from the heat. Add gelatin and stir until dissolved; cool. Stir in sliced strawberries; chill until it begins to thicken. Prepare whipped topping according to package directions; fold half into rhubarb mixture. Pour into crust. Chill 2 hours or until firm. Top with remaining whipped topping and whole strawberries. **Yield:** 6-8 servings.

— ♥ ♥ ♥ —

Turtle Cheesecake

(Pictured above)

Our guests love this rich, delicious make-ahead dessert. It turns out perfect every time and is impressive on the table. I'm proud to serve it to family and friends. —Jo Groth, Plainfield, Iowa

> 2 cups vanilla wafer crumbs
> 1/2 cup butter *or* margarine, melted
> 1 package (14 ounces) caramels
> 1 can (5 ounces) evaporated milk

2 **cups chopped pecans, toasted,** *divided*
4 **packages (8 ounces** *each***) cream cheese, softened**
1 **cup sugar**
2 **teaspoons vanilla extract**
4 **eggs**
1 **cup (6 ounces) semisweet chocolate chips, melted and slightly cooled**
Whipped cream, optional

Combine crumbs and butter; blend well. Press into the bottom and 2 in. up the sides of a 10-in. springform pan. Bake at 350° for 8-10 minutes or until set; cool. In a saucepan over low heat, melt caramels in milk, stirring until smooth. Cool 5 minutes. Pour into crust; top with 1-1/2 cups of pecans. In a mixing bowl, beat cream cheese until smooth. Add sugar and vanilla; mix well. Add eggs, one at a time, beating well after each addition. Add chocolate; mix just until blended. Carefully spread over pecans. Bake at 350° for 55-65 minutes or until filling is almost set. Cool to room temperature. Chill overnight. Garnish with remaining pecans and whipped cream if desired. **Yield:** 16 servings.

Chocolate Coconut Cake

(Pictured at left)

This recipe is doubly delicious because it pleases both chocolate and coconut lovers. It starts with a packaged cake mix for added convenience.
—Joanie Ward, Brownsville, Indiana

1 **package (18-1/4 ounces) chocolate cake mix with pudding**
1 **cup sugar**
1 **cup milk**
24 **large marshmallows**
1 **package (14 ounces) flaked coconut**
GLAZE:
1-1/2 **cups sugar**
1 **cup evaporated milk**
1/2 **cup butter** *or* **margarine**
2 **cups (12 ounces) semisweet chocolate chips**
1 **cup chopped almonds**

Mix cake according to package directions. Grease two 13-in. x 9-in. x 2-in. baking pans. Line bottom and sides of one pan with waxed paper; spray with nonstick cooking spray. Divide batter among pans. Bake at 350° for 15-20 minutes. Cool. In a saucepan, bring sugar and milk to a boil. Reduce heat to medium and stir in marshmallows until smooth. Add coconut. Spread over cake in pan without waxed paper. Using paper to hold, remove second cake from pan, carefully turn over and place on top of filling; remove paper. In another saucepan, bring sugar, milk and butter to a boil. Remove from heat; add chips and stir until smooth. Add almonds. Pour over cake; cool to room temperature. Chill overnight. **Yield:** 16-20 servings.

Grandma's Chocolate Pudding

My grandmother always made this creamy, very chocolaty pudding when we visited. Each spoonful takes me back in time to her cozy kitchen.
—Donna Hughes, Rochester, New York

1 **cup sugar**
1/2 **cup baking cocoa**
1/4 **cup all-purpose flour**
2 **cups water**
3/4 **cup evaporated milk**
1 **tablespoon vanilla extract**
Pinch salt

In a saucepan, combine sugar, cocoa and flour. Add water and milk; stir until smooth. Cook over medium heat, stirring constantly, until mixture comes to a boil. Cook until thick, about 1 minute. Remove from heat; stir in vanilla and salt. Cool to room temperature, stirring several times. Pour into a serving bowl or individual dishes. Serve warm or chilled. **Yield:** 4-6 servings.

Golden Apricot Pie

This pie is pretty as a picture and absolutely apricot in flavor. The fruit's golden-orange color beautifully shows through the lattice top. —Jo Martin Patterson, California

2 **packages (6 ounces** *each***) dried apricots**
2-3/4 **cups water**
Pastry for double-crust pie (9 inches)
1 **cup sugar**
3 **tablespoons cornstarch**
1/8 **teaspoon ground nutmeg**
1 **tablespoon butter** *or* **margarine**

In a saucepan, combine apricots and water; bring to a boil. Reduce heat and simmer for 20-22 minutes. Remove from the heat; cool. Place bottom pastry in a 9-in. pie plate. Drain apricots, reserving 3/4 cup liquid. Arrange apricots in pie shell. Combine sugar, cornstarch, nutmeg and reserved apricot liquid; mix well. Pour over apricots; dot with butter. Top with a lattice crust. Bake at 400° for 50-55 minutes or until crust is golden brown and filling is bubbly. **Yield:** 8 servings.

Chocolate Chiffon Cake

(Pictured below)

When I want to offer family and friends a dessert that really stands out from the rest, this is the cake I make. Beautiful high layers of rich sponge cake are drizzled with a succulent chocolate glaze. —Erma Fox
Memphis, Missouri

1/2 cup baking cocoa
3/4 cup boiling water
1-3/4 cups cake flour
1-3/4 cups sugar
1-1/2 teaspoons baking soda
1 teaspoon salt
1/2 cup vegetable oil
7 eggs, *separated*
2 teaspoons vanilla extract
1/4 teaspoon cream of tartar
ICING:
1/3 cup butter *or* margarine
2 cups confectioners' sugar
2 squares (1 ounce *each*) unsweetened chocolate, melted and cooled
1-1/2 teaspoons vanilla extract
3 to 4 tablespoons hot water
Chopped nuts, optional

In a bowl, combine cocoa and water until smooth; cool for 20 minutes. In a mixing bowl, combine flour, sugar, baking soda and salt. Add the oil, egg yolks, vanilla and cocoa mixture; beat until smooth. In another mixing bowl, beat egg whites and cream of tartar until stiff peaks form. Gradually fold in egg yolk mixture. Pour into an ungreased 10-in. tube pan. Bake on lowest rack at 325° for 60-65 minutes or until cake springs back when touched. Invert pan to cool; remove cake from pan. For icing, melt butter in medium saucepan. Remove from heat; stir in sugar, chocolate, vanilla and enough water to reach desired consistency; drizzle over cake. Sprinkle with nuts if desired. **Yield:** 16-20 servings.

— 🥤 🥤 🥤 —

Blueberry Custard Parfaits

When I pick or purchase fresh blueberries, this is the recipe I reach for when I get home. This light and refreshing dessert looks so pretty in parfait glasses.
—Mildred Stubbs, Hamlet, North Carolina

2 eggs, lightly beaten
1-1/2 cups milk
1/4 cup sugar
1/4 teaspoon salt
1 teaspoon vanilla extract
1 teaspoon grated lemon peel
1 teaspoon grated orange peel
1/4 teaspoon ground nutmeg
1/2 cup whipping cream
2 teaspoons confectioners' sugar
2 cups fresh blueberries

In a saucepan, combine eggs, milk, sugar and salt. Cook over medium-low heat, stirring constantly, until custard is slightly thickened and coats the back of a spoon, about 18 minutes. Remove from the heat. Add vanilla, peels and nutmeg; mix well. Cool for 30 minutes, stirring occasionally. In a small mixing bowl, whip the cream and sugar until stiff. Fold two-thirds into the custard. Layer custard and blueberries in parfait glasses. Garnish with remaining cream. Chill for 1 hour. **Yield:** 4 servings.

— 🥤 🥤 🥤 —

White Christmas Cake

(Pictured on page 136)

"Wow!" is the reaction from family and friends when they see and taste this lovely three-layer cake. White chocolate, coconut and pecans make the cake so delicious. —Nancy Reichert, Thomasville, Georgia

1/2 cup water
4 ounces white confectionary coating *or* vanilla chips

1 cup butter *or* margarine, softened
2 cups sugar
4 eggs, *separated*
1 tablespoon vanilla extract
2-1/2 cups all-purpose flour
1 teaspoon baking soda
1 cup buttermilk
1 cup flaked coconut
1 cup chopped pecans
FROSTING:
1 package (8 ounces) cream cheese, softened
1/2 cup butter *or* margarine, softened
1 teaspoon vanilla extract
1 package (1 pound) confectioners' sugar
1 tablespoon milk

In a saucepan, bring the water to a boil. Remove from the heat; stir in confectionary coating until melted. Cool for 20 minutes. Meanwhile, in a mixing bowl, cream butter and sugar. Add egg yolks; mix well. Beat in coating and vanilla. Combine flour and baking soda; add to creamed mixture alternately with buttermilk. Mix well. Stir in the coconut and pecans. Beat egg whites until stiff peaks form; fold into the batter. Pour into three greased and floured 8-in. square baking pans. Bake at 350° for 25-30 minutes or until cake tests done. Cool in pans 10 minutes; remove to wire rack to cool completely. Combine frosting ingredients in a mixing bowl; beat well. Frost tops of two layers; stack on serving plate with plain layer on top. Frost top and sides of cake. **Yield:** 10-12 servings.

🍶 🍶 🍶

Last-Minute Shortcake

This dessert is so quick because you make it in the microwave. Top single servings with fresh fruit.
—*Sharon Nichols, Brookings, South Dakota*

1 cup all-purpose flour
3 tablespoons sugar
1 teaspoon baking powder
1/4 teaspoon salt
1/4 cup cold butter *or* margarine
1 egg
1/3 cup milk
Fresh *or* frozen sliced strawberries, sweetened
Whipped cream

In a bowl, combine the first four ingredients; cut in the butter until crumbly. Beat the egg and milk; stir into flour mixture. Spoon into five individual microwave-safe 4-oz. custard cups. Place all of the cups in the microwave at once and cook on medium for 3 minutes. Cook on high for 2-3 minutes or until a toothpick inserted near the center comes

out clean. Serve warm or at room temperature with strawberries and whipped cream. **Yield:** 5 servings.
Editor's Note: This recipe was tested with a 700-watt microwave.

Sunshine Ice Cream Pie

(Pictured above)

Many people tell me this pretty, easy-to-make dessert tastes like the Dreamsicles they loved as children.
—*Bonnie Polson, Moravia, Iowa*

1 pint vanilla ice cream, softened
1 graham cracker crust (8 or 9 inches)
1 pint orange sherbet, softened
2 cups whipped topping
1 can (11 ounces) mandarin oranges, drained
2 tablespoons coconut, toasted

Spread ice cream into the crust; spread sherbet over ice cream. Freeze for at least 3 hours. Top with whipped topping. Cover and freeze. Remove pie from the freezer 30 minutes before serving; arrange oranges on top and sprinkle with coconut. **Yield:** 6-8 servings.

Homemade Graham Cracker Crusts

Combine 1-1/2 cups crumbs (24 squares), 1/4 cup sugar and 1/3 cup melted butter or margarine. Press onto the bottom and up sides of an ungreased 9-in. pie plate. Chill 30 minutes before filling or bake at 375° until lightly browned, about 8-10 minutes.

ungreased 10-in. springform pan; set aside. In a large mixing bowl, beat cream cheese and sugar until creamy. Add eggs, one at a time, beating well after each addition. Add extracts; beat just until blended. Pour into crust. Bake at 350° for 55 minutes or until center is almost set. Remove from the oven; let stand for 5 minutes. Combine sour cream, sugar and vanilla; spread over filling. Return to the oven for 5 minutes. Cool on a wire rack; chill overnight. Just before serving, sprinkle with almonds and remove sides of pan. Store in the refrigerator. **Yield:** 14-16 servings.

Luscious Almond Cheesecake

(Pictured above and on front cover)

I received this recipe along with a set of springform pans from a cousin at my wedding shower many years ago. It makes a heavenly cheesecake that my son, Tommy, often requests for his birthday cake.
—*Brenda Clifford, Overland Park, Kansas*

CRUST:
1-1/4 cups crushed vanilla wafers
  3/4 cup finely chopped almonds
  1/4 cup sugar
  1/3 cup butter *or* margarine, melted
FILLING:
    4 packages (8 ounces *each*) cream cheese, softened
1-1/4 cups sugar
    4 eggs
1-1/2 teaspoons almond extract
    1 teaspoon vanilla extract
TOPPING:
    2 cups (16 ounces) sour cream
  1/4 cup sugar
    1 teaspoon vanilla extract
  1/8 cup toasted sliced almonds

In a bowl, combine wafers, almonds and sugar; add the butter and mix well. Press into the bottom of an

Lemon Blueberry Pie

When blueberries are ripe, I find every possible way to enjoy them. This delicious tart proves the point!
—*Patricia Kile, Greentown, Pennsylvania*

    6 eggs, lightly beaten
    1 cup sugar
  1/2 cup butter *or* margarine
  1/3 cup fresh lemon juice
    2 teaspoons grated lemon peel
    1 pastry shell (9 inches), baked
    3 cups fresh blueberries
  1/3 cup sugar
  1/4 cup orange juice
    1 tablespoon cornstarch

In a saucepan, combine eggs, sugar, butter, lemon juice and peel; cook, stirring constantly, over medium-low heat until mixture thickens, about 20 minutes. Cool for 20 minutes, stirring occasionally. Pour into pie shell. In a saucepan, toss blueberries and sugar. Mix orange juice and cornstarch; add to blueberries. Cook over medium heat until mixture comes to a boil, about 8 minutes, stirring gently. Cook 2 minutes longer. Cool for 15 minutes, stirring occasionally. Spoon over lemon layer. Chill for 4-6 hours. **Yield:** 8 servings.

Blackberry Cake

Wild blackberries are plentiful here, so I started making this cake to put that pretty crop to good use. Everyone loves it. —*Doris Martin, Bostic, North Carolina*

    1 package (18-1/2 ounces) white cake mix with pudding
    1 package (3 ounces) black raspberry gelatin
    1 cup vegetable oil
  1/2 cup milk
    4 eggs

1 cup fresh *or* frozen blackberries
1 cup flaked coconut
1 cup chopped pecans
ICING:
  1/2 cup butter *or* margarine, softened
    1 pound confectioners' sugar
    4 to 5 tablespoons milk
  1/2 cup fresh *or* frozen blackberries, crushed
  1/2 cup flaked coconut
  1/2 cup chopped pecans

In a mixing bowl, combine cake mix, gelatin, oil and milk; mix until blended. Add eggs, one at a time, beating well after each addition. Fold in the blackberries, coconut and pecans. Pour into three greased 9-in. round baking pans. Bake at 350° for 25-30 minutes or until cake tests done; cool in pans 10 minutes before removing to wire racks. For icing, cream butter and sugar. Stir in enough milk to reach desired consistency. Fold in blackberries, coconut and pecans. Frost tops of two layers; stack on serving plate with plain layer on top. Frost top and sides of cake. **Yield:** 12-16 servings.

— 🥄 🥄 🥄 —

Lemon Sherbet

I try to make this sherbet often in summer because it's so refreshing. You won't believe how easy it is to put together. —*Elaine Shamblen, Seaside, Oregon*

  2 quarts half-and-half cream
  4 cups sugar
Juice of 8 lemons (about 2-1/4 cups)
  3 to 4 tablespoons grated lemon peel

In a large bowl, stir cream and sugar until sugar is dissolved. Slowly add lemon juice and peel; mix well. Pour into the cylinder of an ice cream freezer and feeze according to manufacturer's directions. **Yield:** about 2-1/2 quarts.

— 🥄 🥄 🥄 —

Ice Cream Sundae Dessert

When you want a change of pace from heavy sweets, this creamy ice cream dessert fills the bill. It makes a big batch to feed a group. —*Kimberly McKeever Shoreview, Minnesota*

  20 chocolate sandwich cookies, crushed
1/4 cup butter *or* margarine, softened
1/2 gallon vanilla *or* peppermint ice cream, softened
    1 carton (8 ounces) frozen whipped topping, thawed
    2 to 3 tablespoons chocolate syrup
1/4 cup chopped pecans

In a bowl, combine cookie crumbs and butter. Press into the bottom of a greased 13-in. x 9-in. x 2-in. pan. Carefully spread ice cream over crust. Spread whipped topping over ice cream. Drizzle chocolate syrup on top; sprinkle with pecans. Freeze until firm, about 2-4 hours. **Yield:** 12-16 servings.

— 🥄 🥄 🥄 —

Pecan Fudge Pie

(Pictured below)

This fudgy pie is the perfect showcase for crunchy pecans. It's a special chocolaty twist on traditional pecan pie. It slices beautifully, and one slice goes a long way. Top it with whipped cream and you won't wait long for compliments! —*Jacquelyn Smith Soperton, Georgia*

1-1/4 cups light corn syrup
  1/2 cup sugar
  1/3 cup baking cocoa
  1/3 cup all-purpose flour
  1/4 teaspoon salt
    3 eggs
    3 tablespoons butter *or* margarine, softened
1-1/2 teaspoons vanilla extract
    1 cup chopped pecans
    1 unbaked pastry shell (9 inches)
Whipped cream, optional

In a large mixing bowl, beat the first eight ingredients until smooth. Stir in pecans; pour into pie shell. Bake at 350° for 55-60 minutes or until set. Cool completely. Garnish with whipped cream if desired. **Yield:** 6-8 servings.

Banana Split Cream Puffs

(Pictured below)

These fruity cream puff "sandwiches" are a treat that our family has always found scrumptious.
—*Sandra McKenzie, Braham, Minnesota*

   1 cup water
 1/2 cup butter *or* margarine
   1 cup all-purpose flour
 1/4 teaspoon salt
   4 eggs
  12 scoops vanilla ice cream
   1 cup sliced fresh strawberries
   1 large *or* 2 medium bananas, thinly sliced
   1 can (8 ounces) pineapple tidbits, drained
 1/2 cup hot fudge sauce

In a saucepan over medium heat, bring water and butter to a boil. Add flour and salt all at once; stir until a smooth ball forms. Remove from the heat; let stand 5 minutes. Add eggs, one at a time, beating well after each addition. Beat until mixture is smooth and shiny, about 3 minutes. Drop by rounded tablespoonfuls onto a greased baking sheet. Bake at 400° for 30-35 minutes or until golden brown. Transfer to a wire rack. Immediately split puffs open; remove tops and set aside. Discard soft dough from inside. Cool puffs. Fill each with a scoop of ice cream and top with fruit. Drizzle with hot fudge sauce. Replace tops and serve immediately. **Yield:** 12 servings.

—— 📇 📇 📇 ——

Chocolate Dessert Waffles

(Pictured below)

These fun-to-eat waffles can be dressed up in their "sundae" best with vanilla ice cream and caramel sauce. —*Nanette Ehrsam, Wichita Falls, Texas*

 3/4 cup sugar
 1/2 cup vegetable oil
   2 eggs
   1 teaspoon vanilla extract
1-1/4 cups all-purpose flour
   6 tablespoons baking cocoa
   1 teaspoon baking powder
 1/2 teaspoon salt
 1/2 teaspoon ground cinnamon
Vanilla ice cream and caramel sauce, optional

In a bowl, combine sugar, oil, eggs and vanilla.

SUMMERTIME TREATS. Tempting desserts like Banana Split Cream Puffs, Apple Crumble Pie and Chocolate Dessert Waffles (shown below, clockwise from upper left) are impressive to serve yet simple to fix.

Combine dry ingredients. Add to sugar mixture; mix well. Bake in a preheated waffle iron according to manufacturer's directions; remove carefully. Do not overbake. Serve warm with vanilla ice cream and caramel sauce if desired. **Yield:** 3-4 servings.

— ❦ ❦ ❦ —

Apple Crumble Pie

(Pictured below left)

This lovely crumb-topped pie is easy to make. We like the chunky homemade apple filling. —*Vera Brouwer Maurice, Iowa*

　　5 cups cubed peeled tart apples
1/2 cup sugar
　　2 tablespoons all-purpose flour
　　1 teaspoon ground cinnamon
1/2 teaspoon ground nutmeg
　　1 unbaked pastry shell (9 inches)
TOPPING:
1/2 cup sugar
1/2 cup all-purpose flour
1/2 cup cold butter *or* margarine

In a bowl, combine the first five ingredients; spoon into pie shell. For topping, combine sugar and flour; cut in butter until mixture resembles coarse crumbs. Sprinkle over pie. Bake at 400° for 10 minutes. Reduce heat to 375°; bake for 40-45 minutes or until the topping is browned and apples are tender. Cover crust edges with foil during the last 15 minutes if needed. Cool completely before cutting. **Yield:** 6-8 servings.

— ❦ ❦ ❦ —

Rhubarb Torte

Each year when Grandmother asked what kind of birthday cake I'd like, my response was "Rhubarb Torte"! It's still a favorite today. —*Lois Heintz Hokne, Wisconsin*

1-3/4 cups all-purpose flour
　　1 teaspoon baking powder
　　2 egg yolks
1/2 cup shortening
　　2 tablespoons sugar
1/2 cup chopped walnuts
FILLING:
　　4 cups chopped fresh *or* frozen rhubarb
　　2 cups sugar
　　2 egg yolks
1/4 cup all-purpose flour
MERINGUE:
　　4 egg whites
1/2 cup sugar

　　1 teaspoon vanilla extract

Combine the first six ingredients with a fork until crumbly. Press into a greased 13-in. x 9-in. x 2-in. baking pan. Combine filling ingredients; mix well. Pour over crust. Bake at 350° for 50-60 minutes. In a mixing bowl, beat egg whites until stiff. Gradually add sugar and vanilla, beating well. Spread over hot filling. Return to the oven for 10-15 minutes or until lightly browned. **Yield:** 12-16 servings.

— ❦ ❦ ❦ —

Fresh Blueberry Tarts

These attractive individual treats deliver a burst of blueberry flavor. I appreciate their quick and easy convenience. —*Pat Habiger, Spearville, Kansas*

　　1 package (8 ounces) cream cheese, softened
1/4 cup packed light brown sugar
　　1 package (6 count) individual graham cracker tart shells
　　2 cups fresh blueberries, *divided*
　　3 tablespoons sugar
　　1 teaspoon fresh lemon juice
　　1 teaspoon grated lemon peel

In bowl, beat cream cheese and brown sugar until smooth. Spread in tart shells. In a bowl, mash 3 tablespoons blueberries with sugar, lemon juice and peel. Add remaining berries and toss. Spoon into tarts. Chill for 1 hour. **Yield:** 6 servings.

— ❦ ❦ ❦ —

Strawberry-Pecan Pie

(Pictured on page 136)

I stock up on locally grown berries for a treat like this pie, which pairs them with pecans. This recipe earned me a ribbon at a nearby strawberry festival. —*Becky Duncan, Leming, Texas*

1-1/2 cups sugar
1/4 cup all-purpose flour
　　1 teaspoon ground nutmeg
　　1 teaspoon ground cinnamon
　　2 cups chopped fresh strawberries
　　1 cup chopped pecans
Pastry for double-crust pie (9 inches)
　　1 to 2 tablespoons butter *or* margarine

In a bowl, combine sugar, flour, nutmeg and cinnamon. Add strawberries and pecans; toss gently. Line pie plate with bottom crust. Add filling; dot with butter. Top with a lattice crust. Bake at 375° for 50 minutes or until crust is golden brown and filling is bubbly. **Yield:** 6-8 servings.

TURN a simple meal into an occasion with homemade desserts like Chocolate Date Squares and Pineapple Bundt Cake (shown above, left to right).

Pineapple Bundt Cake

(Pictured above and on back cover)

Fruity and firm-textured, this beautiful cake is sure to impress. Folks are always surprised to find bits of moist pineapple in every bite. —*Fayne Lutz*
Taos, New Mexico

      1 cup butter *or* margarine, softened
1-1/2 cups sugar
      2 eggs
      2 egg whites
      2 teaspoons lemon extract
2-2/3 cups all-purpose flour
      1 teaspoon baking powder
      1 can (8 ounces) crushed pineapple,
         undrained
GLAZE:
      1 cup confectioners' sugar
   1/2 teaspoon lemon extract
      1 to 2 tablespoons milk

In a mixing bowl, cream butter and sugar. Add eggs, egg whites and extract; beat until fluffy, about 2 minutes. Combine flour and baking powder; gradually add to creamed mixture. Stir in pineapple. Pour into a greased 10-in. bundt pan. Bake at 350° for 55-60 minutes. Cool in pan 10 minutes

before removing to a wire rack. Cool. In a small bowl, combine sugar, lemon extract and enough milk to reach desired consistency. Drizzle over cake. **Yield:** 12-16 servings.

Chocolate Date Squares

(Pictured above and on back cover)

My mother-in-law used to send these moist bars to my husband when he was in the Army. They've become a favorite of our family. —*Pat Walter*
Pine Island, Minnesota

      2 cups chopped dates
      1 cup hot water
   2/3 cup shortening
      1 cup sugar
      2 eggs
1-1/2 cups all-purpose flour
      1 teaspoon baking soda
   1/2 teaspoon salt
TOPPING:
      1 cup (6 ounces) semisweet chocolate chips
   1/2 cup packed brown sugar
   1/2 cup chopped nuts

In a bowl, combine dates and water; set aside to cool (do not drain). In a mixing bowl, cream shortening and sugar. Add eggs, flour, baking soda and salt; mix well. Add dates. Pour into a greased and floured 13-in. x 9-in. x 2-in. baking pan. Combine the topping ingredients; sprinkle over batter. Bake at 350° for 40 minutes or until a toothpick inserted in the center comes out clean. **Yield:** 24 servings.

— 🍽 🍽 🍽 —

Cherry Oatmeal Crisp

A buttery oatmeal topping baked over a pie filling makes an easy, impressive dessert. —Lise Thomson
Magrath, Alberta

    1 can (21 ounces) cherry pie filling
3/4 cup packed brown sugar
3/4 cup all-purpose flour
3/4 cup old-fashioned oats
1/2 teaspoon ground cinnamon
1/4 teaspoon ground nutmeg
1/4 teaspoon salt
1/2 cup cold butter *or* margarine
Whipped cream *or* ice cream, optional

Spread pie filling into a greased 9-in. square baking pan. In a bowl, combine the next six ingredients. Cut in butter until the mixture resembles coarse crumbs; sprinkle over filling. Bake at 375° for 35-40 minutes or until golden brown. Serve with whipped cream or ice cream if desired. **Yield:** 6-8 servings.

— 🍽 🍽 🍽 —

Sugar-Free Star-Spangled Dessert

Each year, my diabetic mother-in-law makes this festive dessert for the Fourth of July. It takes some time to prepare, but the cool, creamy result makes it worthwhile. —Margaret Peterson, Rothschild, Wisconsin

☑ Uses less fat, sugar or salt. Includes Nutritional Analysis and Diabetic Exchanges.

BOTTOM LAYER:
    1 pint fresh *or* frozen blueberries
    2 cups water
    1 package (.6 ounce) sugar-free blueberry gelatin
    1 cup cold water
MIDDLE LAYER:
    1 envelope unflavored gelatin
1/2 cup cold water
    1 cup skim milk
    1 package (8 ounces) light cream cheese, softened
Artificial sweetener equivalent to 1/2 cup sugar

    1 teaspoon vanilla extract
TOP LAYER:
    1 package (.6 ounce) sugar-free raspberry gelatin
    2 cups boiling water
    2 cups cold water

In a saucepan, simmer blueberries and water over medium heat until berries are soft. Remove from heat; stir in blueberry gelatin until dissolved. Add cold water and mix well. Pour into a 13-in. x 9-in. x 2-in. pan. Chill until set, about 40 minutes. In a small bowl, sprinkle the unflavored gelatin over cold water; let stand for 1 minute. Heat milk but do not boil; add to softened gelatin and stir to dissolve. In a mixing bowl, beat cream cheese, artificial sugar and vanilla until smooth. Gradually beat in milk mixture. Spoon over bottom layer. Chill until set, about 30 minutes. Dissolve raspberry gelatin in boiling water; stir in cold water. Spoon over the middle layer. Chill until set, at least 2 hours. **Yield:** 16 servings. **Nutritional Analysis:** One serving equals 57 calories, 117 mg sodium, 8 mg cholesterol, 5 gm carbohydrate, 2 gm protein, 3 gm fat. **Diabetic Exchanges:** 1/2 fruit, 1/2 fat. **Editor's Note:** This dessert takes time since each layer must be set before the next is added.

— 🍽 🍽 🍽 —

Cranberry-Almond Apple Pie

This recipe is a family treasure from my grandmother. It's much better than everyday apple pie.
—Maxine Theriauit, Nashua, New Hampshire

    1 cup sugar
1/4 cup all-purpose flour
    3 tablespoons butter *or* margarine, melted
1/2 teaspoon ground nutmeg
1/8 teaspoon salt
    6 medium tart apples, peeled and thinly sliced
    1 cup fresh *or* frozen cranberries
    1 unbaked pastry shell (9 inches)
TOPPING:
1/2 cup packed brown sugar
1/3 cup all-purpose flour
1/2 teaspoon ground cinnamon
    3 tablespoons cold butter *or* margarine
1/3 cup sliced almonds, toasted

In a bowl, combine sugar, flour, butter, nutmeg and salt; mix well. Add apples and cranberries; stir gently. Pour into pie shell. In a small bowl, mix the brown sugar, flour and cinnamon; cut in butter until crumbly. Stir in almonds; sprinkle over filling. Bake at 350° for 1 hour or until apples are tender. **Yield:** 6-8 servings.

Country-Style Condiments

It's easy to stock up your pantry and refrigerator with the sure-to-please recipes in this chapter. These homemade salad dressings, jams, relishes, sauces and more make a nice addition to any meal.

FOODS YOU'LL RELISH. Clockwise from upper left: Freezer Cucumber Pickles (p. 162), Pear Cranberry Relish (p. 165), Pickled Mushrooms (p. 164), Blue Cheese Dressing (p. 162) and Cran-Raspberry Jam (p. 163).

Low-Fat Chocolate Sauce

Unlike most delicious desserts, this creamy sauce contains just a trace of fat. So I can satisfy my sweet tooth with little guilt. —Beverly Irick
Indianapolis, Indiana

✓ Uses less fat, sugar or salt. Includes Nutritional Analysis.

  1/2 **cup sugar**
    3 **tablespoons skim milk**
    1 **tablespoon baking cocoa**
    1 **tablespoon light corn syrup**
    1 **teaspoon vanilla extract**

In a saucepan, combine sugar, milk, cocoa and corn syrup. Bring to a boil; boil 1 minute. Remove from the heat; stir in vanilla. Best served immediately. Serve as a dip for fruit, or pour over frozen yogurt or angel food cake. **Yield:** 1/3 cup. **Nutritional Analysis:** One serving (1 tablespoon) equals 95 calories, 8 mg sodium, trace cholesterol, 24 gm carbohydrate, 1 gm protein, trace fat.

Blue Cheese Dressing

(Pictured below and on page 161)

I tasted this tangy dressing for the first time at a friend's house. She gave me the recipe, and now I make it every week. I always keep some in my refrigerator. It tastes better than bottled blue cheese dressing and is a snap to make. —Barbara Nowakowski
North Tonawanda, New York

1-1/2 **cups mayonnaise**
  1/2 **cup sour cream**
  1/4 **cup cider vinegar**
    4 **teaspoons sugar**
  1/2 **teaspoon ground mustard**
  1/2 **teaspoon garlic powder**
  1/2 **teaspoon onion powder**
    1 **package (4 ounces) blue cheese, crumbled**

In a bowl, combine the first seven ingredients. Stir in the blue cheese. Cover and chill at least 2 hours. Store in the refrigerator. **Yield:** 2 cups.

Freezer Cucumber Pickles

(Pictured on page 160)

When I first saw this recipe, I couldn't imagine freezing cucumbers would work. But they came out perfect! —Connie Goense, Pembroke Pines, Florida

    4 **pounds pickling cucumbers, sliced**
    8 **cups thinly sliced onions**
  1/4 **cup salt**
  3/4 **cup water**
    4 **cups sugar**
    2 **cups cider vinegar**

Combine cucumbers, onions, salt and water in two large bowls. Let stand at room temperature for 2 hours. Do not drain. Combine sugar and vinegar until sugar is dissolved; divide between two bowls. Pack into 1-pint freezer containers, leaving 1-in. headspace. Cover and freeze for up to 6 weeks. Thaw at room temperature for 4 hours before serving. **Yield:** 10 pints.

Low-Fat Italian Dressing

I found this recipe years ago and make it often. I prefer this homemade dressing to any store-bought variety. —Shonna Lee Leonard, Sackville, Nova Scotia

✓ Uses less fat, sugar or salt. Includes Nutritional Analysis and Diabetic Exchanges.

    5 **tablespoons frozen apple juice**
      concentrate, thawed
  1/4 **cup cider vinegar**
  1/4 **cup lemon juice**
    1 **garlic clove, minced**
  1/2 **teaspoon *each* onion powder, paprika,**
      ground mustard and dried oregano
  1/4 **teaspoon dried basil**
  1/8 **teaspoon dried thyme**
  1/8 **teaspoon dried rosemary, crushed**

In a jar with a tight-fitting lid, mix all ingredients.

Chill several hours or overnight. Shake well before serving. **Yield:** 3/4 cup. **Nutritional Analysis:** One serving (2 tablespoons) equals 30 calories, 6 mg sodium, 0 cholesterol, 8 gm carbohydrate, trace protein, trace fat. **Diabetic Exchanges:** 1/2 fruit.

Standish House Cranberry Relish

As a descendant of Myles Standish, I sponsored a dinner at my bed-and-breakfast a few years back to offer folks some holiday history and a taste of the foods offered at the first Thanksgiving. This relish was one of the menu items. —Norman Standish, Lanark, Illinois

- 3/4 cup orange *or* apple juice
- 2/3 cup sugar
- 1/4 teaspoon ground cinnamon
- 1/4 teaspoon ground nutmeg
- Dash ground cloves
    - 1 package (12 ounces) fresh *or* frozen cranberries
- 1/2 cup golden raisins
- 1/2 cup chopped pecans

In a saucepan, combine juice, sugar, cinnamon, nutmeg and cloves. Cook over medium heat, stirring frequently, until sugar is dissolved. Add cranberries and raisins; bring to a boil. Reduce heat; simmer 3-4 minutes or until cranberries pop. Remove from the heat; stir in nuts. Chill for several hours. **Yield:** about 3 cups.

Fresh Salsa

We like salsa with chips or with grilled meats. This recipe uses a lot of fresh tomatoes and keeps well for several days in the refrigerator.
                                          —Myra Innes
                                          Auburn, Kansas

☑ Uses less fat, sugar or salt. Includes Nutritional Analysis and Diabetic Exchanges.

- 4 cups chopped peeled fresh tomatoes
- 1/4 cup finely chopped onion
- 1 to 4 jalapeno peppers, seeded and finely chopped
- 1 tablespoon olive *or* vegetable oil
- 1 tablespoon vinegar
- 1 teaspoon ground cumin
- 1 teaspoon salt, optional
- 1 garlic clove, minced

In a bowl, combine all ingredients; mix well. Let stand for about 1 hour. Serve at room temperature. Store in a covered container in the refrigerator. **Yield:** 3-1/2 cups. **Nutritional Analysis:** One 1/4-cup serving (prepared without added salt) equals 22 calories, 2 mg sodium, 0 cholesterol, 3 gm carbohydrate, 1 gm protein, 1 gm fat. **Diabetic Exchanges:** 1 vegetable.

Cran-Raspberry Jam

(Pictured above and on page 160)

I'm sure to pick up extra bags of cranberries for the freezer in fall so that I can make this lovely, delicious jam all year-round. My kids love it on peanut butter sandwiches. Jars of this pretty ruby-colored jam also make great gifts.
                                          —Marjilee Booth
                                          Chino Hills, California

- 2 packages (10 ounces *each*) frozen sweetened raspberries, thawed
- 4 cups fresh *or* frozen cranberries
- 5 cups sugar
- 1 package (1-3/4 ounces) powdered fruit pectin

Drain the raspberries, reserving juice; add enough water to juice to measure 1-1/2 cups. Pour into a large kettle. Add raspberries, cranberries and sugar; bring to a full rolling boil, stirring constantly. Stir in pectin; return to a full rolling boil. Boil for 1 minute, stirring constantly. Remove from the heat; skim off any foam. Pour into hot jars, leaving 1/4-in. headspace. Adjust caps. Process for 15 minutes in a boiling-water bath. **Yield:** 6 half-pints.

Cranberry Butter

My sister and I came up with this recipe. It's a creamy, tangy spread that makes a nice addition to a breakfast buffet. —Bill Schultz, Walden, New York

> 1 can (16 ounces) whole-berry cranberry sauce
> 2 cups butter *or* margarine, softened
> 1 tablespoon grated orange peel

Combine all ingredients in a large mixing bowl; beat on high for 2 minutes or until creamy. Spoon into a crock or dish; cover and refrigerate. Serve on toast, English muffins or bagels. **Yield:** 3-1/2 cups.

Pickled Mushrooms

(Pictured above and on page 161)

These tangy mushrooms are a welcome addition to any meal or party buffet table. It doesn't take long for a whole bowlful to be devoured. I love to cook with fresh mushrooms—a crop our state is well known for.
—Sandra Johnson, Tioga, Pennsylvania

> 2/3 cup tarragon vinegar
> 1/2 cup vegetable oil
> 2 tablespoons water
> 1 tablespoon sugar
> 1-1/2 teaspoons salt
> 1 garlic clove, minced
> Dash hot pepper sauce
> 1 pound fresh mushrooms
> 1 medium onion, thinly sliced into rings
> Finely diced sweet red pepper

In a glass bowl, combine the first seven ingredients. Add mushrooms and onion; toss to coat. Cover and refrigerate 8 hours or overnight. Sprinkle with red pepper before serving. **Yield:** 4 cups.

Creamy Horseradish Sauce

My favorite way to use this sauce is on cold roast beef sandwiches. But it really complements a variety of foods. —Florence Palmer, Marshall, Illinois

> 1 cup whipping cream
> 1 cup mayonnaise
> 1/8 teaspoon salt
> 1/4 cup prepared horseradish

In a mixing bowl, whip cream until soft peaks form. Add mayonnaise and salt; blend thoroughly. Fold in horseradish. Chill until serving; use as a condiment with roast beef, corned beef, pork or sandwiches. **Yield:** 3-1/2 cups.

Highbush Cranberry Jam

Although not true cranberries, highbush cranberries also have tart red fruits that can be used in cooking. This is a lovely spread with mouth-watering tangy flavor. —Evelyn Gebhardt, Kasilof, Alaska

> 7-1/2 cups highbush cranberries
> 3/4 cup water
> 2 cups sugar
> 1 tablespoon grated orange peel
> 2 tablespoons orange juice
> 3/4 teaspoon ground allspice
> 1/2 teaspoon ground cinnamon
> 1/4 teaspoon ground nutmeg

In a large covered kettle, simmer cranberries and water for 20-25 minutes, stirring occasionally. Press berries through a strainer; discard skins. Strain mixture through a double layer of cheesecloth (juice will drip through; discard or set aside for another use). Measure 6 cups of the pulp that remains in the cheesecloth and place in the kettle. Add remaining ingredients. Simmer, uncovered, for 30-40 minutes, stirring frequently. Pour into freezer containers. Cool. Refrigerate or freeze. **Yield:** 3-4 half-pints.

Tarragon Butter

This seasoned butter is a delicious way to add great herb flavor and a hint of color to your favorite breads and vegetables. —Connie Moore, Medway, Ohio

> 1 cup butter *or* margarine, softened
> 2 tablespoons minced fresh tarragon *or* 2 teaspoons dried tarragon
> 2 tablespoons minced fresh parsley
> 1 teaspoon fresh *or* dried chives
> 1 garlic clove, minced
> Dash pepper

In a bowl, combine all ingredients. Store in refrigerator. Spread butter on French bread before toasting, season cooked vegetables or use when cooking fish. **Yield:** 1 cup.

— 🥄 🥄 🥄 —

Southwestern Seasoning Mix

I like to experiment with spices and this is one of my creations. There are so many different ways to put it to use. —Cheryl Miller, Fort Collins, Colorado

    1/4 cup chili powder
    1/4 cup onion powder
      2 tablespoons ground cumin
      2 tablespoons dried coriander
      2 tablespoons dried oregano
      2 tablespoons dried basil
      1 tablespoon dried thyme
      1 tablespoon garlic powder

Combine all ingredients. Store in an airtight container. Use as a seasoning for cooked vegetables, grilled meats or chip dips. **Yield:** 1 cup. **Editor's Note:** For use as a dip, combine 1 tablespoon mix with 1 cup sour cream and salt to taste. Chill for 1 hour.

— 🥄 🥄 🥄 —

Lazy-Day Cranberry Relish

While I'm busy with holiday bustle, this no-fuss ruby-red condiment can be simmering in my slow cooker. It's especially delicious served with turkey.
—June Formanek, Belle Plaine, Iowa

      2 cups sugar
      1 cup orange juice
      1 teaspoon grated orange peel
      4 cups fresh *or* frozen cranberries

In a slow cooker, combine sugar, orange juice and peel; stir until sugar is dissolved. Add the cranberries. Cover and cook on low for 6 hours. Mash the mixture. Chill several hours or overnight. **Yield:** 10-12 servings (3 cups).

— 🥄 🥄 🥄 —

Homemade Horseradish

Each year, I make a batch of this condiment. A little goes a long way. —Jan Roat, Red Lodge, Montana

      1 cup cubed peeled horseradish root
         (1/2-inch pieces)
    3/4 cup vinegar
      2 teaspoons sugar
    1/4 teaspoon salt

Combine all ingredients in a food processor or blender; cover and process until pureed. Carefully remove cover of processor or blender, keeping face away from container. Cover and store in the refrigerator. **Yield:** 1-1/4 cups.

— 🥄 🥄 🥄 —

Pear Cranberry Relish

(Pictured below and on page 160)

I created this recipe quite by accident one day when I had leftover pears and cranberries. It's now a traditional dish on our Thanksgiving and Christmas tables.
—Ann Rayas, Greenville, South Carolina

☑ Uses less fat, sugar or salt. Includes Nutritional Analysis and Diabetic Exchanges.

      3 cups fresh *or* frozen cranberries
    1/2 cup water
      5 large pears, peeled and cubed
      1 cup orange juice
      2 teaspoons grated orange peel
Artificial sweetener equivalent to 4 teaspoons sugar

In a large saucepan, simmer cranberries in water for 10-15 minutes or until tender. Add pears, orange juice and peel; simmer 15 minutes or until tender. Cool 15 minutes. Sprinkle with sweetener; stir well. Chill for 2 hours. **Yield:** 10 servings. **Nutritional Analysis:** One 1/3-cup serving equals 75 calories, 1 mg sodium, 0 cholesterol, 19 gm carbohydrate, 1 gm protein, trace fat. **Diabetic Exchanges:** 1 fruit.

Potluck Pleasers

Whether you're planning a menu for 10 or 100, you'll appreciate these large-quantity recipes. They come from experienced cooks, so they're guaranteed to satisfy your hungry crowd.

— 🏆 🏆 🏆 —

COOKING FOR A CROWD. Clockwise from upper left: Tarragon Chicken Casserole (p. 171), Parmesan Rolls (p. 168), Lime Gelatin Salad (p. 175), Fresh Broccoli Salad (p. 173) and Pumpkin Stew (p. 178).

Prize-Winning Potato Salad

With horseradish for tang, mayonnaise and sour cream for smoothness and bacon for crunch, you have a truly memorable potato salad. —*Ramona Hook Wysong Paducah, Kentucky*

16 **pounds baking potatoes, peeled, cooked and cubed**
32 **hard-cooked eggs, chopped**
 2 **pounds sliced bacon, cooked and crumbled**
16 **green onions, thinly sliced**
 4 **cups mayonnaise *or* salad dressing**
 4 **cups (32 ounces) sour cream**
 1 **cup prepared horseradish**
1/2 **cup chopped fresh parsley**
 2 **tablespoons salt**
 2 **tablespoons pepper**

Toss potatoes, eggs, bacon and onions. Combine remaining ingredients; mix until smooth. Toss with potato mixture. Chill several hours. **Yield:** 60-70 servings.

———— 🍷 🍷 🍷 ————

Date Nut Log

(Pictured below)

My mother served this dessert one year after a big holiday meal. We all thought it was delicious. Since then I've made it for various club meetings.
 —*Carla Hodenfield, Mandan, North Dakota*

40 **graham cracker squares, finely crushed, *divided***
24 **large marshmallows, snipped**
 8 **ounces dates, chopped**
 2 **cups chopped walnuts**

1-1/4 **cups whipping cream**
Whipped cream, optional

In a bowl, combine 2 cups of graham cracker crumbs, marshmallows, dates and walnuts. Stir in cream; mix thoroughly. Shape into a 14-in. x 3-in. log. Roll in remaining crumbs. Wrap tightly in plastic wrap or foil. Refrigerate at least 6 hours or overnight. Slice; garnish with whipped cream if desired. **Yield:** 10-12 servings.

———— 🍷 🍷 🍷 ————

Spicy Chicken Wings

This is a family recipe from a woman in our church. We increased the quantity to feed hungry teens at our annual gathering of over 100 students from the area.
 —*Gay Avery, Massena, New York*

 8 **packages (4 pounds *each*) frozen chicken wings**
 8 **cups soy sauce**
1/2 **cup to 2 cups hot pepper sauce**
 2 **cups water**
 2 **cups vegetable oil**
3/4 **cup cornstarch**
 8 **teaspoons ground ginger**
 4 **teaspoons minced garlic**

Place the frozen wings in a single layer on baking sheets that have been sprayed with nonstick cooking spray. Bake at 375° for 50-60 minutes or until chicken juices run clear. Meanwhile, combine the remaining ingredients in a saucepan; bring to a boil, stirring occasionally. Boil for 2 minutes or until thickened. Drain wings; transfer to large roasting pans. Cover with sauce. Bake, uncovered, for 60-70 minutes, stirring occasionally. **Yield:** about 13 dozen wings.

———— 🍷 🍷 🍷 ————

Parmesan Rolls

(Pictured on page 166)

My family just can't seem to get enough of these fun, cheesy rolls. They have a delightful texture from the cornmeal. —*Marietta Slater, Augusta, Kansas*

 2 **packages (1/4 ounce *each*) active dry yeast**
1/2 **cup warm water (110° to 115°)**
 1 **cup warm milk (110° to 115°)**
1/2 **cup grated Parmesan cheese**
1/3 **cup butter *or* margarine, melted**
 3 **tablespoons sugar**
 1 **teaspoon salt**
 1 **cup cornmeal**

2 eggs
4-1/2 to 5 cups all-purpose flour
TOPPING:
   1/4 cup butter *or* margarine, melted
   1/4 cup grated Parmesan cheese

In a large mixing bowl, dissolve yeast in water. Add milk, Parmesan cheese, butter, sugar, salt, cornmeal and eggs; mix well. Add 3 cups of flour and beat until smooth. Add enough remaining flour to form a soft dough. Turn onto a floured surface; knead until smooth and elastic, about 6-8 minutes. Place in a greased bowl, turning once to grease top. Cover and let rise in a warm place until doubled, about 1 hour. Punch dough down. Shape into 24 ovals; dip each into melted butter and Parmesan cheese. Place on greased baking sheets. Cover and let rise until doubled, about 30 minutes. Bake at 375° for 20-25 minutes or until golden brown. Remove from pans to cool on wire racks. **Yield:** 2 dozen.

Cheese 'n' Sausage Calzones

I love experimenting with recipes. Luckily, my husband likes to sample new foods! —Maryann Kipling Dayton, Ohio

   2 containers (15 ounces *each*) ricotta cheese
   4 cups (1 pound) shredded mozzarella cheese
   1 cup grated Parmesan cheese
   2 teaspoons dried oregano
   2 teaspoons dried basil
   1 cup finely chopped onion
   1 cup finely chopped green pepper
   2 garlic cloves, minced
   2 teaspoons vegetable oil
   2 pounds bulk Italian sausage
  10 loaves (1 pound *each*) frozen bread dough, thawed
   1/2 cup butter *or* margarine, melted
   2 jars (16 ounces *each*) spaghetti sauce, heated

In a large bowl, combine cheeses, oregano and basil; set aside. In a large skillet, saute the onion, green pepper and garlic in oil until tender; add to cheese mixture. In the same skillet, brown sausage; drain and stir into cheese mixture. Divide each loaf of dough into four portions; roll each into a 6-in. circle. Spoon 2 tablespoons of filling on half of one circle; fold dough over filling and seal edges. Repeat with remaining dough and filling. Brush with butter. Place on greased baking sheets. Bake at 350° for 25 minutes or until golden brown. Serve with spaghetti sauce for dipping. **Yield:** 40 servings.

Potluck Pockets

(Pictured above)

My husband taught me how to make these fun tasty sandwiches. They take little time to prepare, and we enjoy them all through the year. They don't last long on a buffet. —Debbie Jones, California, Maryland

   1 pound ground beef
   1/2 cup chopped onion
   1/2 cup chopped green pepper
   2 tablespoons Worcestershire sauce
   2 tablespoons soy sauce
   2 teaspoons garlic powder
   1 teaspoon ground cumin
   1/2 teaspoon Italian seasoning
   6 pita breads, halved
   2 medium tomatoes, diced
   3 cups shredded lettuce
SAUCE:
   1/2 cup soy sauce
   1/4 cup vinegar
   2 tablespoons Worcestershire sauce
   1/2 teaspoon onion powder
   1/2 teaspoon garlic powder
   1/2 teaspoon Italian seasoning
Dash pepper

In a skillet, brown beef, onion and green pepper; drain. Add Worcestershire sauce, soy sauce, garlic powder, cumin and Italian seasoning; mix well. Simmer for 5-10 minutes. In a small saucepan, bring all the sauce ingredients to a boil. Reduce heat and simmer for 5-10 minutes. Spoon meat mixture into pita halves; top with sauce, tomatoes and lettuce. **Yield:** 12 servings.

SATISFY HUNGRY APPETITES and lift spirits with such crowd-pleasers as Honey Party Buns and Corn Casserole (shown above).

Honey Party Buns

(Pictured above)

I use this recipe often for church get-togethers. Finger sandwiches are popular at these events, so I make these golden buns small and add sandwich toppings.
—*Ruth Linscott, Millfield, Ohio*

   1 **cup butter *or* margarine, cut into pieces**
1/2 **cup honey**
   2 **cups boiling water**
   2 **packages (1/4 ounce *each*) active dry yeast**
1/3 **cup warm water (110° to 115°)**
   2 **eggs, beaten**
   1 **teaspoon baking powder**
   1 **teaspoon salt**
3-1/2 **cups whole wheat flour**
   4 **to 4-1/2 cups all-purpose flour**
Sliced ham, cheese and lettuce, optional

Place butter and honey in a large mixing bowl; pour the boiling water over and set aside to cool to 110°-115°. In a small bowl, dissolve yeast in warm water; set aside. To honey mixture, add eggs, baking powder and salt. Add yeast mixture and whole wheat flour; beat until smooth. Stir in enough all-purpose flour to form a soft dough. Turn onto a floured surface; knead until smooth and elastic, about 8-10 minutes. Place in a greased bowl, turning once to grease top. Cover and let rise in a warm place until doubled, about 1 hour. Punch dough down; divide in half. On a lightly floured surface, roll each half to 1/2-in. thickness; cut with a 2-1/2-in. cutter. Place on greased baking sheets. Cover and let rise in a warm place until doubled, about 1 hour. Bake at 350° for 15-20 minutes or until golden brown. Remove from pans to cool on wire racks. Make into small sandwiches, if desired, by filling with ham, cheese and lettuce, or serve plain. **Yield:** 4-5 dozen.

Corn Casserole

(Pictured above)

For more than 30 years, I've been preparing this zippy side dish for all sorts of gatherings. In fact, whenever I'm invited to an event that involves food, it's "understood" that I'll bring this casserole.
—*Patricia Friend, Milledgeville, Georgia*

   1 **large onion, chopped**
   2 **medium green peppers, chopped**
1/2 **cup butter *or* margarine**
1/4 **cup all-purpose flour**
   2 **cups frozen *or* canned corn**

2 cups cooked long grain rice
1 can (14-1/2 ounces) diced tomatoes, undrained
4 hard-cooked eggs, chopped
2-1/2 cups (10 ounces) shredded sharp cheddar cheese, *divided*
2 tablespoons Worcestershire sauce
2 to 3 teaspoons hot pepper sauce
2 teaspoons salt
1 teaspoon pepper

In a large skillet, saute onion and peppers in butter until tender. Stir in flour. Remove from the heat; add remaining ingredients except for 1/2 cup cheese. Pour into a greased 2-1/2-qt. baking dish. Bake, uncovered, at 350° for 45 minutes. Top with remaining cheese; let stand 5 minutes. **Yield:** 10-12 servings.

— 🍷 🍷 🍷 —

Tarragon Chicken Casserole

(Pictured on page 166)

For a quick, hearty main dish that's ideal when the weather's warm, try this casserole. With cooked chicken, it bakes in just half an hour. People love the tasty sauce and cheese on top. —Bob Breno
Strongsville, Ohio

2 cans (10-3/4 ounces *each*) condensed cream of chicken soup, undiluted
2 cups half-and-half cream
4 teaspoons dried tarragon
1/2 teaspoon pepper
1 package (16 ounces) linguine *or* spaghetti, cooked and drained
6 cups cubed cooked chicken
1/2 cup grated Parmesan cheese
Paprika, optional

In a large bowl, combine soup, cream, tarragon and pepper. Stir in the linguine and chicken. Transfer to an ungreased 4-qt. baking dish. Sprinkle with the Parmesan cheese and paprika if desired. Bake, uncovered, at 350° for 30 minutes or until heated through. **Yield:** 12 servings.

— 🍷 🍷 🍷 —

Appetizer Meatballs

These are a favorite at parties and gatherings. The recipe is easy...and the meatballs can be made well ahead of time and frozen until needed. I think what makes them taste so good is the sauce. —Nathalie Wiedmann-Guest, Caledon, Ontario

1 cup (4 ounces) shredded mozzarella cheese

1/2 cup dry bread crumbs
1/4 cup finely chopped onion
2 tablespoons grated Parmesan cheese
1 tablespoon ketchup
2 teaspoons Worcestershire sauce
1 teaspoon Italian seasoning
1 teaspoon dried basil
1 teaspoon salt
1/4 teaspoon pepper
2 eggs, lightly beaten
2 pounds lean ground beef
SAUCE:
1 bottle (14 ounces) hot *or* regular ketchup
2 tablespoons cornstarch
1 jar (12 ounces) apple jelly
1 jar (12 ounces) currant jelly

In a bowl, combine the first 11 ingredients. Add beef; mix well. Shape into 1-in. balls. Place on a rack in a shallow roasting pan. Bake at 350° for 10-15 minutes. Remove the meatballs and rack; drain. Combine ketchup and cornstarch in roasting pan. Stir in jellies; add the meatballs. Cover and bake for 30 minutes. **Yield:** about 8 dozen.

— 🍷 🍷 🍷 —

Mexican Lasagna

This is one dish that is hearty enough to fill them up but tasty enough to keep them coming back for more! Flour tortillas are an interesting switch from lasagna noodles. —Roma Rogers, Oshkosh, Nebraska

18 pounds ground beef
3 cups chopped onion
18 envelopes taco seasoning mix
6 cans (15 ounces *each*) tomato sauce
6 cans (14-1/2 ounces *each*) diced tomatoes, undrained
32 to 40 flour tortillas (10 inches), cut into 2-inch strips
4-1/2 pounds cheddar cheese, shredded, *divided*

In several Dutch ovens over medium heat, brown beef and onion; drain. Add the taco seasoning, tomato sauce and tomatoes; bring to a boil. Reduce heat; cover and simmer for 10 minutes. Spoon about 2 cups each into six 13-in. x 9-in. x 2-in. baking pans. Top with a single layer of tortilla strips. Sprinkle with 1 cup cheese. Repeat layers two more times. Divide the remaining meat sauce among pans (each pan will have about 7 cups of sauce). Top with remaining tortillas. Cover and bake at 350° for 40 minutes or until bubbly. Uncover; sprinkle with remaining cheese. Return to the oven for 5-10 minutes or until the cheese melts. **Yield:** about 72 servings.

Festive Fruit Salad

(Pictured below)

This refreshing beautiful salad has become a favorite of everyone who's tried it. My bowl always comes home empty when I take this salad to a party or cookout. This recipe is a great way to take advantage of fresh fruit at its best.
—Gail Sellers
Savannah, Georgia

- 1 medium fresh pineapple
- 3 medium apples (1 red, 1 yellow and 1 green), cubed
- 1 small cantaloupe, cubed
- 1 large firm banana, sliced
- 1 pint strawberries, halved
- 1 pint blueberries
- 4 cups seedless red and green grapes
- 3 kiwifruit, peeled and sliced

DRESSING:
- 1 package (3 ounces) cream cheese, softened
- 1/2 cup confectioners' sugar
- 2 teaspoons lemon juice
- 1 carton (8 ounces) frozen whipped topping, thawed

Additional berries for garnish, optional

Peel and core pineapple; cut into cubes. Place in a 3- or 4-qt. glass serving bowl. Add remaining fruit and stir to mix. In a mixing bowl, beat the cream cheese until smooth. Gradually add sugar and lemon juice; mix well. Fold in whipped topping. Spread over fruit. Garnish with additional berries if desired. Store leftovers in the refrigerator. **Yield:** 16-20 servings.

Wild Rice Dressing

This colorful dish makes an attractive addition to any buffet table. Everyone comments on the wonderful combination of bread, sausage, rice and fruit.
—Shirley Werner, Twin Falls, Idaho

- 2-1/2 cups chopped celery
- 2-1/2 cups chopped onion
- 2 tablespoons poultry seasoning
- 1/2 cup butter *or* margarine
- 1 pound bulk pork sausage, cooked and crumbled
- 10 cups cubed crustless day-old white bread
- 6 cups cooked wild rice
- 4 cups chopped apples
- 1 cup chopped walnuts
- 1 cup chopped fresh parsley
- 1 cup chopped fresh *or* frozen cranberries
- 2 cups chicken broth
- 1/2 cup orange juice
- 2 tablespoons brown sugar

In a large skillet, saute celery, onion and poultry seasoning in butter until vegetables are tender; transfer to a large bowl. Add all remaining ingredients; mix well. Place in two greased 6-qt. Dutch ovens. Cover and bake at 350° for 50 minutes; uncover and bake 10 minutes longer. **Yield:** 35 (3/4-cup) servings.

———— 🛒 🛒 🛒 ————

Golden Cheese Soup

This is my adaptation of a recipe served at a popular local restaurant. The large serving size comes in handy for large family gatherings and church socials.
—Marilyn Hillam, Brigham City, Utah

- 2-1/2 cups chopped onion
- 1-1/4 cups butter *or* margarine
- 1-1/4 cups all-purpose flour
- 1-1/4 cups cornstarch
- 2-1/2 teaspoons paprika
- 5 teaspoons salt
- 2-1/2 teaspoons pepper
- 5 quarts chicken broth
- 5 quarts milk
- 5 cups chopped carrots, cooked
- 5 cups chopped celery, cooked
- 10 cups (2-1/2 pounds) shredded sharp cheddar cheese
- 2-1/2 cups chopped fresh parsley

In a large Dutch oven over medium heat, saute onion in butter until tender. Combine flour, cornstarch, paprika, salt and pepper; stir into pan until a smooth paste forms. Gradually add broth, stirring constantly. Bring to a boil; cook and stir for 2 minutes or until thickened. Gradually add milk, stirring constantly. Add carrots, celery and cheese. Cook and stir over low heat until cheese is melted and soup is heated through. Add parsley just before serving. **Yield:** 50 (1-cup) servings.

🍷 🍷 🍷

Big Batch Cookies

It's nice to offer a little homemade taste when feeding a hungry horde. These cookies also freeze well, so you can make them when time allows. —Diana Dube Rockland, Maine

 1 pound (2 cups) butter *or* margarine, softened
1-1/2 cups sugar
1-1/2 cups packed brown sugar
 4 eggs, lightly beaten
 1 tablespoon vanilla extract
 5 cups all-purpose flour
 1 tablespoon baking soda
 1 teaspoon salt
 1 pound (3-3/4 cups) chopped walnuts
 2 packages (10 ounces *each*) peanut butter chips

In a large mixing bowl, cream butter and sugars. Add eggs and vanilla; mix well. Combine flour, baking soda and salt; add to creamed mixture and mix well. Fold in the nuts and chips. Drop by rounded teaspoonfuls onto ungreased baking sheets. Bake at 350° for 10-12 minutes or until lightly browned. Remove to wire racks to cool. **Yield:** 12 dozen.

🍷 🍷 🍷

Fresh Broccoli Salad
(Pictured on page 166)

This unique salad is pretty with the broccoli, mushrooms, red onion and olives. It has a great crunch, and the dressing is quick to make. —Marilyn Fields Groveland, California

✓ Uses less fat, sugar or salt. Includes Nutritional Analysis and Diabetic Exchanges.

 2 pounds fresh broccoli, cut into bite-size pieces
 1 package (12 ounces) fresh mushrooms, sliced
 2 small red onions, thinly sliced into rings
 1 can (2-1/4 ounces) sliced ripe olives, drained
1-1/2 cups Italian salad dressing
 1/3 cup shredded Parmesan cheese

Combine all ingredients in a large bowl; toss to mix

well. Cover and chill for at least 2 hours. **Yield:** 12 servings. **Nutritional Analysis:** One serving (prepared with fat-free salad dressing) equals 66 calories, 182 mg sodium, 3 mg cholesterol, 9 gm carbohydrate, 5 gm protein, 2 gm fat. **Diabetic Exchanges:** 2 vegetable, 1/2 fat.

Italian Sausage Sandwiches
(Pictured above)

When my wife and I have friends over, we love to serve these sandwiches. This is a convenient recipe, since it can be prepared the day before and reheated. —Mike Yaeger, Brookings, South Dakota

20 Italian sausages
 4 large green peppers, thinly sliced
1/2 cup chopped onion
 1 can (12 ounces) tomato paste
 1 can (15 ounces) tomato sauce
 1 cup water
 1 tablespoon sugar
 4 garlic cloves, minced
 2 teaspoons dried basil
 1 teaspoon dried oregano
 1 teaspoon salt
20 sandwich buns
Shredded mozzarella cheese, optional

In a large Dutch oven, brown sausages a few at a time; discard all but 2 tablespoons drippings. Saute peppers and onion in drippings until crisp-tender; drain. Return sausages to pan along with tomato paste, tomato sauce, water, sugar, garlic, basil, oregano and salt; bring to a boil. Reduce heat; cover and simmer for 30 minutes. Serve on buns. Top with cheese if desired. **Yield:** 20 servings.

Cookie Sheet Apple Pie
(Pictured above)

I belong to several volunteer service groups, and this dessert has been a real time-saver when there's a large crowd to be fed. It serves more than an ordinary pie with about the same amount of effort.
—Bertha Jeffries, Great Falls, Montana

3-3/4 cups all-purpose flour
1-1/2 teaspoons salt
3/4 cup shortening
3 eggs, lightly beaten
1/3 cup milk
8 cups sliced peeled tart apples
1-1/2 cups sugar
1 teaspoon ground cinnamon
1/2 teaspoon ground nutmeg
1 cup crushed cornflakes
1 egg white, beaten

In a bowl, combine flour and salt. Cut in shortening until mixture resembles coarse crumbs. Add eggs and milk; mix to form dough. Chill for 20 minutes. Divide dough in half; roll one half to fit the bottom and sides of a greased 15-in. x 10-in. x 1-in. baking pan. Arrange apples over crust. Combine sugar, cinnamon, nutmeg and cornflakes; sprinkle over apples. Roll remaining dough to fit top of pan and place over apples. Seal edges; cut slits in top. Brush with egg white. Bake at 400° for 15 minutes. Reduce heat to 350°; bake for 25-30 minutes or until golden. **Yield:** 16-20 servings.

"Trash Bag" Taco Salad

I use this recipe for church functions and patio parties and assign each guest an ingredient. This simple and economical crowd-pleaser makes cleanup a breeze. —Margie Dodd, Choctaw, Oklahoma

3 pounds ground beef
3 envelopes taco seasoning mix
3 heads lettuce, shredded
3 cups (12 ounces) shredded cheddar cheese
3 cups chopped tomatoes
2 cups chopped onion
3 cans (4-1/4 ounces *each*) chopped *or* sliced ripe olives, drained
2 cans (15 ounces *each*) ranch-style *or* chili beans, drained
1 package (16 ounces) corn chips
1 bottle (16 ounces) Catalina salad dressing
1 jar (12 ounces) salsa

Brown beef; drain. Add taco seasoning and prepare according to package directions. Cool. Toss with remaining ingredients in a large plastic bag or container. **Yield:** 40-50 servings.

—— 🏆 🏆 🏆 ——

Fiesta Rice

This delicious dish is filled with eye-appealing colors and taste that makes even a large batch disappear fast. It's easy to assemble and pop into the oven.
—Rita Wilken, Bloomfield, Nebraska

2 cups chopped onion
1/4 cup butter *or* margarine
4 cups uncooked long grain rice
2 cans (6 ounces *each*) small whole pitted ripe olives, drained
2 cans (28 ounces *each*) diced tomatoes, undrained
1 cup chopped green pepper
1 tablespoon salt
1 to 2 teaspoons chili powder
1 teaspoon dried oregano
1/2 teaspoon pepper
4 cups water
3 cups (12 ounces) shredded cheddar cheese

In a skillet over medium heat, saute the onion in butter until tender. Transfer to a large bowl. Stir in the next eight ingredients. Divide between two ungreased 13-in. x 9-in. x 2-in. baking pans. Stir 2 cups of water into each pan. Cover and bake at 350° for 1-1/2 hours. Uncover; sprinkle with cheese. Return to the oven for 5-10 minutes or until cheese is melted. **Yield:** 30-36 servings.

Strawberry Spinach Salad for a Bunch

The unusual combination of ingredients makes a re-freshing salad people can't stop eating.
—*Polly Bloom, Whitefish Bay, Wisconsin*

  5 pounds fresh spinach, torn
  8 pints fresh strawberries, sliced
  5 cucumbers, thinly sliced
  3 cups sliced green onions
  1 cup snipped fresh mint, optional
 32 ounces bottled ranch salad dressing

Toss spinach, strawberries, cucumber, onions and mint if desired. Just before serving, add dressing and toss. **Yield:** 50-60 servings.

— 🥄 🥄 🥄 —

Lime Gelatin Salad

(Pictured on page 166)

I've made this refreshing recipe hundreds of times over the past 20 years! It can be a salad or dessert.
—*Louise Harding, Newburgh, New York*

  1 package (6 ounces) lime gelatin
  1 cup boiling water
  1 package (8 ounces) cream cheese, softened
1/2 teaspoon vanilla extract
  1 can (15 ounces) mandarin oranges, drained
  1 can (8 ounces) crushed pineapple, drained
  1 cup lemon-lime soda
1/2 cup chopped pecans
  1 carton (8 ounces) frozen whipped
    topping, thawed, *divided*

Dissolve gelatin in water. In a mixing bowl, beat cream cheese until fluffy. Add gelatin mixture; beat until smooth. Stir in vanilla, fruit, soda and pecans. Chill until mixture mounds slightly when dropped from a spoon. Fold in three-fourths of whipped topping. Pour into a 13-in. x 9-in. x 2-in. dish. Chill for 4 hours or until firm. Cut into squares; garnish with remaining whipped topping. **Yield:** 16-20 servings.

— 🥄 🥄 🥄 —

Church Supper Chili

This recipe was created for church suppers. It's a simple meal when served with cheese and crackers.
—*Vera Tollefsen, Whitefish Bay, Wisconsin*

 21 pounds ground beef, browned and drained
  9 cans (16 ounces *each*) pork and beans
  9 cans (16 ounces *each*) kidney beans,
    rinsed and drained
  9 cans (28 ounces *each*) diced tomatoes,
    undrained
  9 cans (29 ounces *each*) tomato sauce

  3 pounds onions, finely chopped
7-1/2 cups finely chopped celery with leaves
  9 large green peppers, finely chopped
  9 bay leaves
  2 tablespoons salt
  5 tablespoons chili powder
  1 tablespoon paprika
  1 tablespoon pepper
  1 tablespoon ground cumin
  1 tablespoon cayenne pepper

Combine all of the ingredients in three large kettles. Cover and cook on medium heat for 2-3 hours. Remove bay leaves. **Yield:** 75 servings (18 quarts).

— 🥄 🥄 🥄 —

Summer Squash Salad

(Pictured below)

This dish is inexpensive to prepare and a great way to put fresh produce to use.
—*Diane Hixon*
Niceville, Florida

  4 cups julienned zucchini
  4 cups julienned yellow squash
  2 cups sliced radishes
  1 cup vegetable oil
1/3 cup cider vinegar
  2 tablespoons Dijon mustard
  2 tablespoons snipped fresh parsley
1-1/2 teaspoons salt
  1 teaspoon dill weed
1/2 teaspoon pepper

In a bowl, toss the zucchini, squash and radishes. In a small bowl or jar with tight-fitting lid, combine all remaining ingredients; shake or mix well. Pour over vegetables. Cover and refrigerate for at least 2 hours. **Yield:** 12-16 servings.

Peanut Butter Bars

I got this recipe when working as a school cafeteria manager years ago. These bars were so popular with the kids that we'd have to make extra or we'd run out.
—Sarah Thomas, Roanoke, Virginia

12 eggs
6 cups sugar
3 cups packed brown sugar
2 cups peanut butter
1 cup shortening
2 tablespoons vanilla extract
8 cups all-purpose flour
3 tablespoons baking powder
2 teaspoons salt
Confectioners' sugar

Cream the eggs, sugars, peanut butter, shortening and vanilla until smooth. Combine flour, baking powder and salt; gradually add to creamed mixture and mix well. Press into three greased 15-in. x 10-in. x 1-in. baking pans. Bake at 350° for 20-25 minutes or until top is golden brown. Cool. Dust with confectioners' sugar. **Yield:** about 8 dozen.

— 🍴 🍴 🍴 —

Pistachio Ambrosia

(Pictured below)

For a fruity, satisfying dessert, we like this smooth and creamy pudding. Since the recipe makes a big batch, it's nice for a potluck. —Carol Lynn Chizzoniti
Holbrook, New York

2 cans (17 ounces *each*) fruit cocktail
2 cans (20 ounces *each*) pineapple chunks
2 cans (11 ounces *each*) mandarin oranges
4 packages (3.4 ounces *each*) instant pistachio pudding mix
2 cups (16 ounces) sour cream
1 carton (12 ounces) frozen whipped topping, thawed
Chopped pecans, optional

Drain fruit cocktail, pineapple and oranges, reserving 3 cups juice. Set fruit aside; pour juice into a 4-qt. bowl. Add pudding mix and mix until smooth. Stir in sour cream. Add whipped topping and mix until smooth. Fold in fruit; chill for several hours. Just before serving, top with pecans if desired. **Yield:** 16-20 servings.

— 🍴 🍴 🍴 —

Mincemeat Coffee Cake

For years my grandmother and I would have a contest to see whose mincemeat coffee cake was the best (our families voted). After years of losses, I modified my original recipe and finally won! —Ed Layton
Absecon, New Jersey

2 packages (1/4 ounce *each*) active dry yeast
1-1/4 cups warm milk (110° to 115°), *divided*
1/2 cup sugar
1/2 cup butter *or* margarine, softened
2 eggs, beaten
2 teaspoons salt
1 teaspoon ground cinnamon
1/8 teaspoon *each* ground allspice, cloves and mace
5 to 5-1/2 cups all-purpose flour
1-1/2 cups prepared mincemeat
Confectioners' sugar

In a large bowl, dissolve yeast in 1/2 cup milk. Add sugar, butter, eggs, salt, cinnamon, allspice, cloves, mace, 2-1/2 cups flour and the remaining milk; beat until smooth. Stir in enough remaining flour to form a soft dough. Turn onto a floured surface; knead until smooth and elastic, about 6-8 minutes. Place in a greased bowl, turning once to grease top. Cover and let rise in a warm place until doubled, about 1 hour. Punch dough down; let rest 10 minutes. Turn onto a lightly floured surface. Roll into a 16-in. x 12-in. rectangle. Spread mincemeat to within 1 in. of edges. Roll up from one long side. Pinch seams; join and seal ends to form a circle. Place in a greased 10-in. fluted tube pan. Cover and let rise until nearly doubled, about 30 minutes. Bake at 375° for 40-45 minutes or until golden brown. Cool 10 minutes in pan before removing to a wire rack. Just before serving, dust with confectioners' sugar. **Yield:** 12-16 servings.

Calico Salad

When our daughter got married, I took it upon myself to prepare all the food for her wedding reception. This make-ahead salad was easy to prepare and serve.
—*Meg Wilkins, Dublin, California*

- 12 packages (16 ounces *each*) frozen peas, thawed
- 12 packages (16 ounces *each*) frozen corn, thawed
- 12 cans (8 ounces *each*) sliced water chestnuts, drained
- 3 cups sliced green onions with tops
- 6 cups mayonnaise *or* salad dressing
- 2-1/4 cups milk
- 2-1/4 cups grated Parmesan cheese
- 3/4 cup lemon juice
- 2 tablespoons salt
- 1-1/2 teaspoons pepper
- 3 jars (4 ounces *each*) sliced pimientos, drained
- 6 cups slivered almonds, toasted

In large bowls or containers, mix peas, corn, water chestnuts and onions. Combine the mayonnaise, milk, Parmesan cheese, lemon juice, salt and pepper; pour over vegetables. Add pimientos and mix well. Chill for several hours or overnight. Before serving, add almonds and toss. **Yield:** 140 servings.

— 🍷 🍷 🍷 —

Turkey Salad for 50

This refreshing salad always pleases at church functions and special luncheons. Red grapes, celery and eggs add color, while almonds add a little crunch.
—*Helen Lord-Burr, Oshkosh, Wisconsin*

- 18 cups diced cooked turkey (about one 14-pound turkey)
- 8 cups thinly sliced celery
- 8 cups seedless grapes
- 18 hard-cooked eggs, diced
- 2 cups slivered almonds, toasted

DRESSING:
- 1 quart mayonnaise *or* salad dressing
- 1 pint (16 ounces) whipping cream, whipped
- 1/4 cup lemon juice
- 1/4 cup sugar
- 1 teaspoon salt
- 1/2 teaspoon pepper

In one large bowl or several smaller bowls, combine turkey, celery, grapes, eggs and almonds. Combine dressing ingredients; mix until smooth. Pour over salad and stir gently. Chill until serving. **Yield:** 50 servings.

Harvest Sugar Cookies

(Pictured above)

Rich buttery cookies like these never last long at a party or potluck. I got this recipe from a friend in Texas years ago and have used it many times since. I use pumpkin- and leaf-shaped cookie cutters to celebrate autumn "tastefully".
—*Lynn Burgess Rolla, Missouri*

- 3/4 cup butter *or* margarine, softened
- 1 cup sugar
- 2 eggs
- 1 teaspoon vanilla extract
- 2-3/4 cups all-purpose flour
- 1 teaspoon baking powder
- 1/2 teaspoon salt

Frosting* *or* additional sugar, optional

In a mixing bowl, cream butter and sugar. Add eggs and vanilla; beat until light and fluffy. Combine flour, baking powder and salt; gradually add to creamed mixture and mix well. Chill for 1 hour or until firm. On a lightly floured surface, roll the dough to 1/4-in. thickness. Cut with pumpkin or leaf cookie cutters or others of your choice. Using a floured spatula, place cookies on greased baking sheets. Sprinkle with sugar if desired (or frost baked cookies after they have cooled). Bake at 375° for 8-10 minutes or until lightly browned. Cool on wire racks. **Yield:** 6-7 dozen (2-1/2-inch cookies). ***Editor's Note:** For a richer color, tint frosting with food coloring paste available at kitchen and cake decorating supply stores.

No-Fuss Chicken

(Pictured above)

This recipe could hardly be simpler to prepare. No one will know you used convenient ingredients like a bottle of salad dressing and onion soup mix.
—Marilyn Dick, Centralia, Missouri

  1 bottle (16 ounces) Russian *or* Catalina
     salad dressing
 2/3 cup apricot preserves
  2 envelopes onion soup mix
 16 boneless skinless chicken breast halves
Hot cooked rice

In a bowl, combine salad dressing, preserves and soup mix. Place chicken in two ungreased 11-in. x 7-in. x 2-in. baking pans; top with dressing mixture. Cover and bake at 350° for 20 minutes; baste. Bake, uncovered, 20 minutes longer or until chicken juices run clear. Serve over rice. **Yield:** 16 servings.

— 🏺 🏺 🏺 —

Pumpkin Stew

(Pictured on page 166)

This special stew is the meal our two kids look forward to each fall because we only get to enjoy it when the fresh pumpkins come out of the garden.
—Donna Mosher, Augusta, Montana

  2 pounds beef stew meat, cut into 1-inch
     cubes
  3 tablespoons vegetable oil, *divided*

  1 cup water
  3 large potatoes, peeled and cut into 1-inch
     cubes
  4 medium carrots, sliced
  1 large green pepper, cut into 1/2-inch pieces
  4 garlic cloves, minced
  1 medium onion, chopped
  2 teaspoons salt
1/2 teaspoon pepper
  2 tablespoons beef bouillon granules
  1 can (14-1/2 ounces) diced tomatoes,
     undrained
  1 pumpkin (10 to 12 pounds)

In a Dutch oven, brown meat in 2 tablespoons oil. Add water, potatoes, carrots, green pepper, garlic, onion, salt and pepper. Cover and simmer for 2 hours. Stir in bouillon and tomatoes. Wash pumpkin; cut a 6- to 8-in. circle around top stem. Remove top and set aside; discard seeds and loose fibers from inside. Place pumpkin in a shallow sturdy baking pan. Spoon stew into pumpkin and replace the top. Brush outside of pumpkin with remaining oil. Bake at 325° for 2 hours or just until the pumpkin is tender (do not overbake). Serve stew from pumpkin, scooping out a little pumpkin with each serving. **Yield:** 8-10 servings.

— 🏺 🏺 🏺 —

Hearty Macaroni Salad

With chicken, ham and tiny shrimp, this recipe makes a hearty warm-weather salad. The dill adds a nice twist. It's great to serve for a luncheon.
—Mary Selner, Green Bay, Wisconsin

  2 cups cubed cooked chicken
  2 cups cubed fully cooked ham
  2 cups cooked salad shrimp
  1 package (7 ounces) elbow macaroni,
     cooked and drained
  1 celery rib, sliced
1/4 cup diced green pepper
1/4 cup diced sweet red pepper
1/4 cup diced onion
  1 teaspoon salt
1/2 teaspoon pepper
DRESSING:
1/2 cup mayonnaise
1/2 cup sour cream
  2 tablespoons vinegar
1/2 teaspoon sugar
  2 teaspoons minced fresh dill *or* 1 teaspoon
     dill weed

In a large bowl, toss the chicken, ham, shrimp, macaroni, celery, peppers, onion, salt and pepper. In a small bowl, combine all dressing ingredients;

mix well. Pour over salad and toss. Cover and chill for 3-4 hours. **Yield:** 10-12 servings.

— 🝙 🝙 🝙 —

Garlic Cheese Bread

Meals for crowds need to be simple to prepare, hot and filling. This is a favorite. —Mike Marratzo
Florence, Georgia

     6 cups grated Parmesan cheese
     1 cup dried oregano
     1 cup dried parsley flakes
     3 cups butter _or_ margarine, softened
    12 garlic cloves, minced
     3 cups vegetable oil
    18 loaves French bread, cut into 1/2-inch
        slices
    18 pounds mozzarella cheese, shredded

Combine Parmesan, oregano and parsley; mix well and set aside. In a large mixing bowl, beat butter and garlic. Gradually beat in oil until smooth. Spread over one side of bread. Place with buttered side up in greased large shallow baking pans. Top each slice with 1/4 cup mozzarella. Sprinkle with Parmesan mixture. Bake at 400° for 10-12 minutes or until the cheese is melted and top is lightly browned. Serve warm. **Yield:** about 150 servings (2 slices each).

— 🝙 🝙 🝙 —

Sloppy Joes for 100

I use this recipe at a church dinner every year, and we always sell out. It's a delicious main dish for any gathering. —Linda Cailteux, Clifton, Illinois

    20 pounds ground beef
     4 large onions, chopped
     4 large green peppers, chopped
     4 cups chopped celery
     1 cup packed brown sugar
     1 cup spicy brown mustard
     4 cups ketchup
     2 cans (12 ounces _each_) tomato paste
     4 cans (15 ounces _each_) tomato sauce
     6 to 8 cups water
     1 cup vinegar
   2/3 cup Worcestershire sauce
   100 hamburger buns

In a large Dutch oven, brown the beef, onions, peppers and celery in batches until meat is browned. Remove with a slotted spoon to a large roaster; add the next eight ingredients. Cover and simmer for 3-4 hours. Serve on buns. **Yield:** 100 servings (12 quarts).

Fruit Cocktail Bars

(Pictured below)

My mother passed this recipe on to me. The moist bars have a delightful fruity taste, perfect for potlucks in winter and spring when fresh fruit is limited and expensive. —Linda Tackman, Escanaba, Michigan

   1-1/2 cups sugar
       2 eggs
       1 can (17 ounces) fruit cocktail, undrained
       1 teaspoon vanilla extract
   2-1/4 cups all-purpose flour
   1-1/2 teaspoons baking soda
       1 teaspoon salt
   1-1/3 cups flaked coconut
       1 cup chopped walnuts
GLAZE:
     1/2 cup sugar
     1/4 cup butter _or_ margarine
       2 tablespoons milk
     1/4 teaspoon vanilla extract

In a mixing bowl, cream sugar and eggs. Add fruit cocktail and vanilla; mix well. Combine the flour, baking soda and salt; add to the creamed mixture and mix well. Pour into a greased 15-in. x 10-in. x 1-in. baking pan. Sprinkle with coconut and walnuts. Bake at 350° for 20-25 minutes or until cake tests done. Cool for 10 minutes. In a saucepan, bring sugar, butter and milk to a boil. Remove from the heat; add vanilla and mix well. Drizzle over cake. Cool. Cut into bars. **Yield:** 2 to 2-1/2 dozen.

Country White Bread

Anytime is the right time for a comforting slice of homemade bread. These loaves are especially nice since the crust stays so tender. —Joanne Shew Chuk
St. Benedict, Saskatchewan

    2 packages (1/4 ounce *each*) active dry yeast
    2 cups warm water (110° to 115°)
1/2 cup sugar
    1 tablespoon salt
    2 eggs, beaten
1/4 cup vegetable oil
6-1/2 to 7 cups all-purpose flour

In a large mixing bowl, dissolve yeast in water. Add sugar, salt, eggs, oil and 3 cups of flour; beat until smooth. Stir in enough remaining flour to form a soft dough. Turn onto a floured surface; knead until smooth and elastic, about 6-8 minutes. Place in a greased bowl, turning once to grease top. Cover and let rise in a warm place until doubled, about 1 hour. Punch dough down. Divide in half and shape into loaves. Place in two greased 9-in. x 5-in. x 3-in. loaf pans. Cover and let rise until doubled, about 1 hour. Bake at 375° for 25-30 minutes or until golden brown. Remove from pans to cool on wire racks. **Yield:** 2 loaves.

— 🍶 🍶 🍶 —

Catalina Spinach Salad

(Pictured below)

My husband enjoys this colorful crisp salad. The tangy homemade dressing is economical and easy to fix.
—Joyce Cutbirth, Meridian, Idaho

1/2 cup vegetable oil
1/4 cup ketchup
1/4 cup cider *or* red wine vinegar

1/4 cup finely chopped onion
    3 tablespoons sugar
    2 teaspoons Worcestershire sauce
1/2 teaspoon salt
    2 packages (10 ounces *each*) spinach, torn
    2 large tomatoes, diced
    2 cans (8 ounces *each*) sliced water
       chestnuts, drained
    2 cups chow mein noodles
    2 hard-cooked eggs, chopped
   12 bacon strips, cooked and crumbled

Combine the first seven ingredients in a jar with tight-fitting lid; shake well. Combine remaining ingredients in a large salad bowl; add dressing and toss. Serve immediately. **Yield:** 6-8 servings.

— 🍶 🍶 🍶 —

Pecan Pie for a Crowd

Honey gives these pies a different yet delicious flavor. I sometimes add chocolate for a special twist.
—Louise Covington, Bennettsville, South Carolina

   12 eggs, beaten
    1 cup dark brown sugar
    5 cups sugar
    2 cups dark corn syrup
1-1/3 cups honey
    1 cup butter *or* margarine, melted
    3 tablespoons vanilla extract
   12 to 15 cups chopped pecans
    8 unbaked pastry shells (9 inches *each*)

In large mixing bowls, combine the first seven ingredients; mix well. Add the pecans. Pour 2-1/4 cups filling into each pie shell. Bake at 300° for 40-50 minutes. **Yield:** 64 servings. **Editor's Note:** To make chocolate pecan pies, melt 3 cups semisweet chocolate chips and add to the batter before adding pecans.

— 🍶 🍶 🍶 —

Vegetable Beef Soup for 50

Do you cringe at the thought of making soup for a crowd? This wonderfully seasoned soup with a rich broth is really quite easy. —Elsie Schimmer
Grand Island, Nebraska

    8 pounds boneless beef chuck, cut into
       1/2-inch cubes
    1 cup all-purpose flour
    1 tablespoon salt
    2 teaspoons pepper
1/2 cup vegetable oil
    4 garlic cloves, minced
    2 bay leaves

2 teaspoons dried thyme
6 quarts water
4 cans (15 ounces *each*) tomato sauce
1 can (46 ounces) tomato juice
12 beef bouillon cubes
2 cups medium pearl barley
2 pounds potatoes, peeled and cubed
1-1/2 pounds carrots, sliced
1 pound chopped cabbage
1 pound onions, chopped
1 package (16 ounces) frozen green beans
1 package (16 ounces) frozen peas

Toss beef with flour, salt and pepper. In a large Dutch oven, brown the meat in batches in oil; drain. Transfer to a large stockpot or soup kettle; add garlic, bay leaves, thyme, water, tomato sauce and juice, bouillon and barley. Bring to a boil. Reduce heat; cover and simmer 1 hour. Add vegetables; bring to a boil. Reduce heat; cover and simmer 1-1/2 to 2 hours or until vegetables and meat are tender. Remove bay leaves. **Yield:** 50 servings.

Garden Casserole

(Pictured at right)

This cheesy casserole includes a sunny medley of eggplant, zucchini and tomatoes. —*Phyllis Hickey Bedford, New Hampshire*

2 pounds eggplant, peeled
5 teaspoons salt, *divided*
1/4 cup olive *or* vegetable oil
2 medium onions, finely chopped
2 garlic cloves, minced
2 medium zucchini, sliced 1/2 inch thick
5 medium tomatoes, peeled and chopped
2 celery ribs, sliced
1/4 cup minced fresh parsley
1/4 cup minced fresh basil *or* 1 tablespoon dried basil
1/2 teaspoon pepper
1/2 cup grated Romano cheese
1 cup Italian bread crumbs
2 tablespoons butter *or* margarine, melted
1 cup (4 ounces) shredded mozzarella cheese

Cut eggplant into 1/2-in.-thick slices; sprinkle both sides with 3 teaspoons salt. Place in a deep dish; cover and let stand for 30 minutes. Rinse with cold water; drain and dry on paper towels. Cut into 1/2-in. cubes and saute in oil until lightly browned, about 5 minutes. Add onions, garlic and zucchini; cook 3 minutes. Add tomatoes, celery, parsley, basil, pepper and remaining salt; bring to a boil. Reduce heat; cover and simmer for 10 minutes. Remove from the heat; stir in Romano cheese. Pour

into a greased 13-in. x 9-in. x 2-in. baking dish. Combine crumbs and butter; sprinkle on top. Bake, uncovered, at 375° for 15 minutes. Sprinkle with mozzarella cheese. Return to the oven for 5 minutes or until cheese is melted. **Yield:** 12 servings.

Spicy Applesauce Cake

For a "picnic perfect" dessert, this moist delicious cake travels and slices very well. With chocolate chips, walnuts and raisins, it's a real crowd-pleaser. —*Marian Platt, Sequim, Washington*

2 cups all-purpose flour
1-1/2 cups sugar
1 tablespoon baking cocoa
1-1/2 teaspoons baking soda
1 teaspoon *each* ground cinnamon, nutmeg, allspice and cloves
1 teaspoon salt
1/2 cup shortening
2 cups applesauce
2 eggs, lightly beaten
1/2 cup semisweet chocolate chips
1/2 cup chopped walnuts
1 cup raisins
TOPPING:
1/2 cup semisweet chocolate chips
1/2 cup chopped walnuts
2 tablespoons brown sugar

In a mixing bowl, combine dry ingredients. Add shortening, applesauce and eggs; beat until well mixed. Stir in chocolate chips, walnuts and raisins. Pour into a greased 13-in. x 9-in. x 2-in. baking pan. Combine topping ingredients and sprinkle over batter. Bake at 350° for 35-40 minutes or until cake tests done. **Yield:** 20-24 servings.

Cooking for One or Two

These perfectly portioned recipes— featuring delectable entrees, side dishes, desserts and more— deliciously prove good things really do come in small packages!

SMALL SERVINGS. Clockwise from upper left: Broccoli Cheddar Soup, Busy Day Salad and Sweet Cornmeal Muffins (p. 192), Orange-Glazed Chicken, Herbed Rice and French Peas (p. 184), Ham Steak with Lemon, Small-Batch Potato Salad and Biscuits for Two (p. 190) and Baked Eggs and Ham and Apple Turnover (p. 188).

Singling Out Good Food

DINING for one *does* have its benefits. You can cook what you like and not worry whether anyone else will eat it…and you always eat in good company! Two terrific cooks helped us assemble a mighty good meal for one. (You'll find more singular sensations on the following pages.)

Diane Madonna of Brunswick, Ohio is married and a mother. But years ago, she relied on recipes for one. "I had just graduated from college and was living in an apartment," she reports.

"A friend gave me this recipe for Orange-Glazed Chicken," Diane continues. "It's a sweet and tangy way to dress up a chicken breast."

For a succulent side dish, John Davis of Mobile, Alabama suggests Herbed Rice. "A few years ago, I put together a special cookbook for folks who cook for themselves," informs John. "This is one of my favorite recipes in the book."

John also shares his recipe for French Peas. "I'm always on the lookout for side dishes that go with nearly any main meal. This medley of peas, onions and mushrooms fills the bill," he states.

Orange-Glazed Chicken

✓ Uses less fat, sugar or salt. Includes Nutritional Analysis and Diabetic Exchanges.

    1 tablespoon all-purpose flour
1/2 teaspoon salt, optional
1/4 teaspoon pepper
    1 boneless skinless chicken breast half
    2 teaspoons vegetable oil
1/2 teaspoon orange marmalade
Dash ground nutmeg
1/2 cup orange juice

Combine flour, salt if desired and pepper; coat chicken breast. In a skillet, heat oil on medium; brown chicken. Spread marmalade on top of chicken; sprinkle with nutmeg. Add orange juice and simmer for 10-15 minutes or until the chicken juices run clear. **Yield:** 1 serving. **Nutritional Analysis:** One serving (without added salt) equals 370 calories, 71 mg sodium, 83 mg cholesterol, 23 gm carbohydrate, 31 gm protein, 17 gm fat. **Diabetic Exchanges:** 4 lean meat, 1 fat, 1 fruit, 1/2 starch.

Herbed Rice

✓ Uses less fat, sugar or salt. Includes Nutritional Analysis and Diabetic Exchanges.

1/4 cup uncooked long grain rice
    1 green onion with top, cut into 1-inch pieces
    1 tablespoon butter *or* margarine
1/8 teaspoon *each* dried tarragon, thyme, basil, parsley flakes and pepper
1/2 cup chicken broth
Salt to taste, optional

In a small saucepan, cook rice and onion in butter until onion is tender. Add the seasonings; cook for

1 minute. Add broth and salt if desired; bring to a boil. Cover and simmer for 15 minutes or until liquid is absorbed and rice is tender. **Yield:** 1 serving. **Nutritional Analysis:** One serving (prepared with margarine and low-sodium broth and without added salt) equals 284 calories, 129 mg sodium, 0 cholesterol, 39 gm carbohydrate, 5 gm protein, 12 gm fat. **Diabetic Exchanges:** 2-1/2 starch, 2 fat.

French Peas

✓ Uses less fat, sugar or salt. Includes Nutritional Analysis and Diabetic Exchanges.

1 teaspoon butter *or* margarine
2 teaspoons water
2 medium fresh mushrooms, thinly sliced
1/2 cup frozen peas
2 thin onion slices
Pinch salt, optional

Melt butter in a small saucepan; add all remaining ingredients. Cover and cook until the peas are tender, stirring occasionally. **Yield:** 1 serving. **Nutritional Analysis:** One serving (prepared with margarine and without added salt) equals 104 calories, 104 mg sodium, 0 cholesterol, 13 gm carbohydrate, 4 gm protein, 1 gm fat. **Diabetic Exchanges:** 1 starch, 1 fat.

TIRED of eating chicken the same old way? The "one"-derful meal featured here will likely liven up your taste buds!

As a widow, Alvena Franklin of Coldwater, Michigan cooks for only herself much of the time. "Chicken breast halves are perfect when cooking for one... just wrap and freeze them individually, then thaw and cook one at a time," conveys Alvena.

Her Stuffed Chicken Breast features a flavorful stuffing that adds flair to ordinary chicken.

"I've learned to scale down recipes for casseroles that I served often when our four kids were still at home," states Alvena.

"I still bake four loaves of bread at a time," she confesses. "But I freeze three until I need them. I also freeze vegetables from my garden in small portions so I can enjoy them all winter."

Alvena sometimes serves sauteed summer squash with the chicken. Or, she'll pair the chicken with her Scalloped Potatoes for One.

If a fish dinner is more to your liking, try Steamed Fish and Vegetables from Marilyn Newcomer of Menifee, California. "Everyone who tries this dish is amazed at how simple it is to prepare," reports Marilyn. "Plus, it's tasty and low in fat."

— 🍴 🍴 🍴 —

✗ Stuffed Chicken Breast

    1 bone-in chicken breast half
1/8 teaspoon *each* salt and pepper
    1 tablespoon chopped onion
    1 tablespoon chopped celery
    1 tablespoon butter *or* margarine
1/8 teaspoon *each* dried thyme, basil and
        parsley flakes
    2 slices day-old white bread, cubed
    2 tablespoons chicken broth

Place chicken with skin side down in a 15-in. x 12-in. piece of heavy-duty foil. Sprinkle with salt and pepper; set aside. In a skillet, saute onion and celery in butter until soft; stir in seasonings, bread and broth. Place in cavity of chicken; fold foil over and fold in edges twice, forming a pouch. Place in a small baking pan. Bake at 375° for 45 minutes. Open foil and bake 5 minutes more or until chicken is tender, juices run clear and stuffing is lightly browned. **Yield:** 1 serving.

— 🍴 🍴 🍴 —

Scalloped Potatoes for One

(Not pictured)

✓ Uses less fat, sugar or salt. Includes Nutritional Analysis and Diabetic Exchanges.

    1 small potato, peeled and sliced
1/3 cup milk
    1 garlic clove, minced
1/4 teaspoon salt, optional
1/8 teaspoon pepper
1/2 teaspoon butter *or* margarine
    1 to 2 tablespoons shredded cheddar cheese

In a small saucepan, combine potato slices, milk, garlic, salt if desired and pepper; bring to a boil. Pour into a buttered 10-oz. custard cup. Sprinkle with cheese. Bake, uncovered, at 375° for 35 minutes or until potatoes are tender. **Yield:** 1 serving. **Nutritional Analysis:** One serving (prepared with skim milk and margarine and without added salt) equals 179 calories, 131 mg sodium, 12 mg

cholesterol, 24 gm carbohydrate, 8 gm protein, 6 gm fat. **Diabetic Exchanges:** 1 starch, 1/2 meat, 1/2 fat, 1/2 skim milk.

--- 🍶 🍶 🍶 ---

Steamed Fish and Vegetables

(Not pictured)

✓ Uses less fat, sugar or salt. Includes Nutritional Analysis and Diabetic Exchanges.

1 whitefish fillet (4 ounces)
1/2 cup thinly sliced carrot
1/2 cup thinly sliced zucchini
2 teaspoons lemon juice
1/2 teaspoon dried parsley flakes
1/2 teaspoon lemon-pepper seasoning
1/4 teaspoon dill weed

Place fish in a 15-in. x 12-in. piece of heavy-duty foil. Add vegetables; sprinkle with juice, parsley, lemon pepper and dill. Fold foil over and fold in edges twice, forming a pouch. Place in a small baking pan. Bake at 450° for 15-20 minutes or until vegetables are tender and fish flakes easily with fork. Carefully open foil to allow steam to escape. **Yield:** 1 serving. **Nutritional Analysis:** One serving equals 226 calories, 768 mg sodium, 78 mg cholesterol, 11 gm carbohydrate, 23 gm protein, 10 gm fat. **Diabetic Exchanges:** 3 lean meat, 1 vegetable.

THE MOST IMPORTANT meal of the day needn't be ho-hum. Instead of cold cereal, plain toast or day-old doughnuts, enjoy a great breakfast or brunch with these rise-and-shine ideas.

From Center, Texas, Carolyn Crump shares her recipe for Baked Eggs and Ham. "I give this dish Southwestern flair and zip by using cheese flavored with jalapeno peppers," informs Carolyn. "But regular cheddar cheese also produces tasty results."

For an old-fashioned apple pastry without all the leftovers, try Phyllis Fahey's Apple Turnover recipe. Says the Fergus Falls, Minnesota cook, "My mother made this all the years she lived alone. Now I make it for myself or my husband as a sweet treat."

Rita Winterberger of Huson, Montana passes along her recipe for hearty Cinnamon-Raisin Oatmeal. "This simple breakfast is my favorite on cool mornings," explains Rita. "I especially like the fact that it's easy to prepare."

— 🍵 🍵 🍵 —

Baked Eggs and Ham

      1/4 cup seasoned croutons
        2 tablespoons chopped fully cooked ham
        1 tablespoon butter *or* margarine, melted
        2 eggs
        1 tablespoon shredded cheddar cheese
Fresh fruit, optional

In a greased shallow 2-cup baking dish, toss the croutons, ham and butter. Break the eggs carefully on top. Sprinkle with cheese. Bake, uncovered, at 350° for 15-18 minutes or until eggs reach desired doneness. Serve with fresh fruit if desired. **Yield:** 1 serving.

— 🍵 🍵 🍵 —

Apple Turnover

      1/4 cup all-purpose flour
Pinch salt
        4 teaspoons shortening
        1 tablespoon ice water
        1 medium tart apple, peeled and sliced
        1 teaspoon sugar
      1/8 teaspoon ground cinnamon
Milk
GLAZE:
        2 tablespoons confectioners' sugar
        1 teaspoon corn syrup
Pinch salt
      1/2 teaspoon hot water

In a small bowl, combine flour and salt; cut in shortening until mixture resembles coarse crumbs. Sprinkle with ice water and toss with a fork. Form into a ball. On a lightly floured surface, roll dough into a 7-in. circle. Place apple slices on half of the circle; sprinkle with sugar and cinnamon. Fold dough over filling, sealing edges with fingers or pressing with a fork. Brush with milk. Prick top with a fork. Place on a greased baking sheet. Bake at 375° for 25-30 minutes or until golden brown. Combine glaze ingredients until smooth; drizzle over turnover. **Yield:** 1 serving.

Cinnamon-Raisin Oatmeal

(Not pictured)

✓ Uses less fat, sugar or salt. Includes Nutritional Analysis and Diabetic Exchanges.

- **1/4 cup quick-cooking oats**
- **1/4 cup Grape-Nuts cereal**
- **1/4 cup raisins**
- **1 tablespoon brown sugar**
- **1 teaspoon ground cinnamon**
- **1 cup milk**
- **Cream *or* additional milk, optional**

In a microwave-safe cereal bowl, combine the first six ingredients. Microwave on high for 3 minutes. Serve with cream or milk if desired. **Yield:** 1 serving. **Nutritional Information:** One serving (prepared with skim milk and 1 teaspoon brown sugar) equals 395 calories, 325 mg sodium, 4 mg cholesterol, 83 gm carbohydrate, 15 gm protein, 3 gm fat. **Diabetic Exchanges:** 3 starch, 2 fruit, 1 skim milk.

Cooking for 'Just the Two of Us'

IT'S SAID that "good things come in twos"…but finding good recipes that work well for just two people isn't always easy. So, here and on the following pages, we provide recipes that are perfect for serving two people.

When you have a taste for ham but don't want to have lots of leftovers, reach for the Ham Steak with Lemon recipe from Lorraine Carr of Seattle, Washington. Individual ham slices make just the right amount and take just minutes to cook.

Since their kids left home some years ago, June Schwanz of Saukville, Wisconsin has been relying on smaller-portioned recipes. "Small-Batch Potato Salad conveniently calls for canned potatoes, so I can make it at a moment's notice," informs June.

Most biscuit recipes have a large yield. But Sylvia McCoy of Lees Summit, Missouri shares a recipe for fluffy Biscuits for Two she got from a friend.

Steaming mugs of smooth Cozy Hot Chocolate are a nice anytime beverage that Marie Hattrup of The Dalles, Oregon enjoys with husband, Ken.

— 🍶 🍶 🍶 —

Ham Steak with Lemon

  2 **slices fully cooked ham (1/2 inch thick)**
  1 **lemon, halved**
  3 **tablespoons brown sugar**
  2 **teaspoons prepared mustard**

Broil ham slices 5 in. from the heat for 5 minutes. Meanwhile, slice one lemon half; set aside. Grate peel from the other half and squeeze 1 tablespoon juice into a bowl. Add peel, brown sugar and mustard to juice. Turn ham over; brush with the lemon mixture. Top with lemon slices. Broil 3-4 minutes more or until ham is heated through. **Yield:** 2 servings.

— 🍶 🍶 🍶 —

Small-Batch Potato Salad

  4 **bacon strips**
  1 **tablespoon cornstarch**
1/3 **cup sugar**
1/2 **cup water**
1/4 **cup vinegar**
1/2 **teaspoon salt**
1/4 **teaspoon pepper**
  1 **can (15 ounces) sliced potatoes, drained**
Minced fresh parsley

In a skillet, cook bacon until crisp. Drain, reserving 2 tablespoons of drippings. Crumble bacon and set aside. Add cornstarch and sugar to drippings; stir until smooth. Add water, vinegar, salt and pepper; cook and stir over medium heat for 3-4 minutes or until thickened and bubbly. Stir in potatoes and bacon. Cook for 2-3 minutes or until heated through. Serve warm or at room temperature. Garnish with parsley. **Yield:** 2 servings.

Biscuits for Two

    1 cup all-purpose flour
2-1/2 teaspoons baking powder
    1 teaspoon sugar
  1/2 teaspoon salt
  1/8 teaspoon cream of tartar
  1/4 cup shortening
  1/2 cup milk

In a bowl, combine dry ingredients. Cut in short-ening until mixture resembles coarse crumbs. Stir in milk. Turn onto a floured surface; knead 1 min-ute. Roll or pat dough to 1/2-in. thickness. Cut with a floured 2-1/2-in. biscuit cutter. Place on a greased baking sheet. Bake at 450° for 10-12 minutes. **Yield:** 4 biscuits.

Cozy Hot Chocolate

(Not pictured)

    2 tablespoons baking cocoa
    2 tablespoons sugar
  1/4 cup water
    2 cups milk
  1/2 teaspoon vanilla extract
Whipped cream
Ground cinnamon, optional

In a saucepan, mix the cocoa and sugar; add wa-ter. Bring to a boil, stirring constantly; boil for 1 minute. Reduce heat; add milk and heat through. Remove from the heat and stir in vanilla. Pour in-to 2 cups; top with whipped cream and sprinkle with cinnamon if desired. **Yield:** 2 servings.

SMALL on yield but big on meal satisfaction, these recipes are geared to suit two-at-the-table.

Broccoli Cheddar Soup comes from Cheryl McRae of West Valley, Utah. "Husband Eric and I eat dinner together to spend some quality time together," explains Cheryl. "This cheesy soup is proof that soup doesn't need to be made in big batches to be good."

From Lancaster, California, Bettie Walker shares her recipe for Busy Day Salad, a tasty refreshing meal for two. "With our children gone from home now, I spend a lot of time trying to convert recipes I made for our large family into recipes for just my husband, Lee, and me. We really enjoy this salad," she reports.

Kirkwood, Missouri cook Marie Kramer shares, "My husband, Axtell, was a fan of the cornmeal muffins from a restaurant we visited. I found a similar recipe and cut it down to serve two. Sweet Cornmeal Muffins are his favorite."

— ☕ ☕ ☕ —

Broccoli Cheddar Soup

- 1/4 cup chopped onion
- 1/4 cup butter *or* margarine
- 1/4 cup all-purpose flour
- 1/4 teaspoon salt
- 1/4 teaspoon pepper
- 3/4 cup chicken broth
- 1-1/2 cups milk
- 1 cup chopped cooked fresh *or* frozen broccoli
- 1/2 cup shredded cheddar cheese

In a saucepan, saute the onion in butter until tender. Stir in flour, salt and pepper; cook and stir until smooth and bubbly. Add broth and milk all at once; cook and stir until the mixture boils and thickens. Add broccoli. Simmer, stirring constantly, until heated through. Remove from the heat and stir in cheese until melted. **Yield:** 2 servings.

— ☕ ☕ ☕ —

Busy Day Salad

- 4 cups torn lettuce
- 1/4 cup julienned fully cooked ham
- 1/4 cup julienned salami
- 2 hard-cooked eggs, sliced

DRESSING:
- 1/4 cup mayonnaise *or* salad dressing
- 4 teaspoons ketchup
- 2 teaspoons sweet pickle relish
- 2 teaspoons chopped green onion
- 1/2 teaspoon lemon juice
- 1/4 teaspoon salt

On a serving plate or two individual plates, arrange lettuce, ham, salami and eggs. In a small bowl, combine dressing ingredients; mix well. Serve with salad. **Yield:** 2 servings.

— ☕ ☕ ☕ —

Sweet Cornmeal Muffins

☑ Uses less fat, sugar or salt. Includes Nutritional Analysis and Diabetic Exchanges.

2 tablespoons sugar
4 teaspoons vegetable oil
1 egg, beaten *or* egg substitute equivalent
2 tablespoons milk
1/4 cup cornmeal
1/4 cup all-purpose flour
1/2 teaspoon baking powder
Pinch salt

In a bowl, combine sugar, oil, egg and milk; mix well. In another bowl, combine dry ingredients; stir in sugar mixture just until moistened. Pour into four muffin cups that have been lined with papers or coated with nonstick cooking spray. Bake at 400° for 15-18 minutes or until lightly browned. **Yield:** 4 muffins. **Nutritional Analysis:** One muffin (prepared with egg substitute and skim milk) equals 153 calories, 87 mg sodium, trace cholesterol, 20 gm carbohydrate, 4 gm protein, 6 gm fat. **Diabetic Exchanges:** 1-1/2 starch, 1 fat.

WHEN you have the taste for fowl but don't want to hassle with the leftovers from a whole turkey or chicken, you can depend on this super smaller-yield holiday dinner.

Stuffed Cornish Hens is a delightful recipe shared by Wanda Jean Sain of Hickory, North Carolina. "With a golden and flavorful stuffing, these tender hens are a special-occasion entree for just the two of us," assures Wanda Jean.

Alongside the Cornish hens, Wanda typically serves her Simple Green Salad with homemade dressing. "It's nice to make up a fresh garden salad that is perfect for one meal," she says.

Scalloped Sweet Potatoes from Marjorie Wilkerson is a comforting blend of apples, pecans and sweet potatoes with a smaller yield that won't leave you with a big pan of leftovers.

Another pair of "empty nesters", Marjorie and husband Daryl live in Dighton. Kansas. "We've been married over 40 years now and have three grown boys," says Marjorie. "I enjoy cooking and baking but have had to scale back a bit since the boys are gone. These sweet potatoes are one of our favorite dishes."

— 🍴 🍴 🍴 —

Stuffed Cornish Hens

    2 tablespoons finely chopped onion
1/3 cup uncooked long grain rice
    4 tablespoons butter *or* margarine,
       divided
1/2 cup condensed cream of celery soup
3/4 cup water
    1 tablespoon lemon juice
    1 teaspoon dried chives
    1 teaspoon dried parsley flakes
    1 chicken bouillon cube
    2 Cornish game hens (1 to 1-1/4 pounds
       each)
Salt and pepper to taste
1/2 teaspoon dried tarragon

In a skillet, cook and stir onion and rice in 2 tablespoons butter until rice is browned. Add the soup, water, lemon juice, chives, parsley and bouillon; bring to a boil. Reduce heat; cover and simmer for 25 minutes or until rice is tender and liquid is absorbed. Remove from heat and cool slightly. Sprinkle hen cavities with salt and pepper; stuff with rice mixture. Place with breast side up on a rack in an ungreased 13-in. x 9-in. x 2-in. baking pan. Melt remaining butter and add tarragon; brush some over the hens. Cover loosely and bake at 375° for 30 minutes. Uncover and bake 30 minutes more or until tender, basting frequently with tarragon butter. **Yield:** 2 servings.

Simple Green Salad

    2 tablespoons olive *or* vegetable oil
    2 tablespoons cider *or* red wine vinegar
1/2 teaspoon Italian seasoning
1/2 teaspoon sugar
1/4 teaspoon salt
1/8 teaspoon garlic powder
1/8 teaspoon pepper
    2 to 3 cups torn lettuce

Combine first seven ingredients in a small bowl; drizzle over lettuce and serve. **Yield:** 2 servings.

—— 🥤 🥤 🥤 ——

Scalloped Sweet Potatoes

1 large sweet potato, peeled and sliced
1 large apple, peeled and sliced
1/3 cup dry bread crumbs

1/3 cup light corn syrup
1/8 teaspoon salt
1 tablespoon butter *or* margarine
1 tablespoon chopped pecans

In a greased 1-qt. baking dish, layer half the sweet potato slices, apple slices and crumbs. Repeat layers. Pour corn syrup over top; sprinkle with salt. Dot with butter; sprinkle with nuts. Cover; bake at 400° for 35 minutes. **Yield:** 2 servings.

'My Mom's Best Meal'

Six cooks recall special times when they prepare a meal often served by their own moms.

FOODS EVOKE MEMORIES. Clockwise from upper left: Birthday Bonanza (p. 214), Finger-Lickin' Fixin's (p. 202), Down-on-the-Farm Dinner (p. 218) and Meat-and-Potatoes Meal (p. 210).

Her mom's traditional Southern dishes made a lasting impression on this cook.

By Mary McGuire, Graham, North Carolina

MY MOTHER (Irene Isley, above) has a reputation for good cooking in our community. It's no wonder she's often asked to bring some of her best dishes to various potlucks and gatherings. I'm proud to say that she's been an inspiration for me in the kitchen my whole life.

Although Mom would often serve salmon when I was growing up, what I looked forward to most were special occasions when she would treat the family to her wonderful Salmon Croquettes. (It was my job to debone the salmon.) Topped with a specially seasoned tartar sauce, each bite is so delicious.

With the croquettes, Mom would be certain to serve Hush Puppies, an absolute "must" on most dinner tables in the South. Crisp and brown, they're an extra-special treat. We'd eat every one, often as they were cool enough to handle.

Another typical Southern dish is coleslaw, and we sure enjoyed Mom's version. Her Marinated Slaw smelled so good while marinating that it was hard for us to wait to dig in. We were always thankful the recipe made a big batch!

And Mom's best meal wouldn't be complete without her signature Coconut Pie. A rich slice of this succulent pie is true comfort food that brings back fond memories of spending time with Mom in the kitchen.

Of all the lessons I learned from Mom through the years, the most important thing I remember is to add tender loving care to everything I cook.

PICTURED AT LEFT: Salmon Croquettes, Hush Puppies, Marinated Slaw and Coconut Pie (recipes are on the next page).

crumbs. Heat oil in a deep-fat fryer to 365°. Fry croquettes, a few at a time, for 2 to 2-1/2 minutes or until golden brown. Drain on paper towels; keep warm. Combine tartar sauce ingredients in a medium saucepan; cook over medium-low heat until heated through and slightly thickened. Serve warm with croquettes. **Yield:** 4-6 servings.

Hush Puppies

Mom is well known for her wonderful hush puppies. Her recipe is easy to prepare and gives tasty results. The chopped onion adds to the great flavor.

    1 cup yellow cornmeal
    1/4 cup all-purpose flour
1-1/2 teaspoons baking powder
    1/2 teaspoon salt
    1 egg, beaten
    3/4 cup milk
    1 small onion, finely chopped
Oil for deep-fat frying

In a medium bowl, combine cornmeal, flour, baking powder and salt; mix well. Add the egg, milk and onion; stir just until mixed. Heat oil in a deep-fat fryer or electric skillet to 365°. Drop bat-

Salmon Croquettes

Mom frequently served salmon when I was a girl. Learning the ropes in the kitchen as I grew up, I got the chore of deboning the salmon. I didn't mind, because these light crisp croquettes are absolutely delicious.

    1 can (14-3/4 ounces) pink salmon, drained, bones and skin removed
    1 cup evaporated milk, *divided*
1-1/2 cups cornflake crumbs, *divided*
    1/4 cup dill pickle relish
    1/4 cup finely chopped celery
    2 tablespoons finely chopped onion
Oil for deep-fat frying
TARTAR SAUCE:
    2/3 cup evaporated milk
    1/4 cup mayonnaise
    2 tablespoons dill pickle relish
    1 tablespoon finely chopped onion

In a medium bowl, combine salmon, 1/2 cup milk, 1/2 cup crumbs, relish, celery and onion; mix well. With wet hands, shape 1/4 cupfuls into cones. Dip into remaining milk, then into remaining

ter by teaspoonfuls into oil. Fry 2 to 2-1/2 minutes or until golden brown. Drain on paper towels. Serve warm. **Yield:** 4-6 servings.

Marinated Slaw

This is a delectable dish that looks as good as it tastes. Mother usually saved this recipe for special occasions, but when she did make it, we sure enjoyed it. The best part is the mouth-watering dressing that even tempted us while it cooked.

> 8 cups shredded cabbage (1-1/2 to 2 pounds)
> 2 tablespoons chopped pimientos
> 1/2 cup chopped green pepper
> 3/4 cup chopped onion
> 1 cup sugar
> 1 cup vinegar
> 1/2 cup water
> 1 tablespoon mustard seed

In a large bowl, combine the cabbage, pimientos, green pepper and onion. Toss lightly; set aside. Combine remaining ingredients in a medium saucepan; bring to a boil. Reduce heat; simmer, uncovered, for 20-25 minutes or until slightly thickened. Pour over cabbage mixture. Cover and refrigerate 4 hours or overnight. Slaw will keep in the refrigerator for several days. **Yield:** 8-10 servings.

Coconut Pie

Watching my mother cook from scratch, I hardly knew that anything was available "pre-made" until I'd left home. One of Mom's best desserts is her creamy old-fashioned coconut pie. (I use a convenient store-bought crust.) A rich slice is true comfort food.

> 1-1/2 cups milk
> 1 cup sugar
> 3/4 cup flaked coconut
> 2 eggs, beaten
> 3 tablespoons all-purpose flour
> 1 tablespoon butter *or* margarine, melted
> 1/4 teaspoon vanilla extract
> 1 unbaked pie shell (9 inches)

In a large bowl, place milk, sugar, coconut, eggs, flour, butter and vanilla; stir until combined. Pour into pie shell. Bake at 350° for 50 minutes or until a knife inserted near the center comes out clean. Cool to room temperature. Refrigerate leftovers. **Yield:** 6-8 servings.

Perfect Pie Crust

To prevent the fluted edges of pies from browning too much while baking, first cut out and discard the round center of a foil pie plate. Then set the round rim on top of the pie so it covers the edges.

Mom made every delicious meal a culinary adventure for this reader's taste buds.

By Judy Clark, Elkhart, Indiana

A CHERISHED memory of growing up, shared by my two sisters, my brother and I, is coming home from church on Sunday to the wonderful aroma of Tangy Spareribs baking in the oven. Mom's recipe for the nicely seasoned sauce is finger-licking-good!

Along with the ribs, Mom (Thelma Arnold, above) served tender baked potatoes topped with creamy butter and extra rib sauce, garden peas and golden Icebox Butterhorns.

Mom had just the right touch when mixing up the dough for these rich, buttery rolls. The result was a melt-in-your-mouth wonder!

This recipe is especially appealing because the dough is made the night before. The next day, just shape the rolls, let rise and bake. There were usually no rolls left over to enjoy at another meal.

We were always too full for dessert at the end of the meal. But by mid-afternoon, we were ready for one of our favorite dessert combinations—Cheery Cherry Cookies and Homemade Frozen Custard.

Mom's creamy custard is better than any other I've tried. And generous scoops of it were perfectly paired with the eye-catching cherry cookies.

Mom taught us girls that cooking is an adventure, not a chore. To her, a high compliment from family or guests was a look of delight at a first mouthful.

Eating delicious meals like this, all four of us kids would tell you we grew up enjoying a privileged childhood filled with happy memories.

PICTURED AT LEFT: Tangy Spareribs, Icebox Butterhorns, Cheery Cherry Cookies and Homemade Frozen Custard (recipes are on the next page).

Tangy Spareribs

I'll never forget the wonderful aroma of these spareribs when I was growing up. They have a real old-fashioned flavor. Who can resist when that mouth-watering homemade barbecue sauce clings to every morsel?

       4 to 5 pounds pork spareribs
       1 medium onion, finely chopped
     1/2 cup finely chopped celery
       2 tablespoons butter *or* margarine
       1 cup ketchup
       1 cup water
     1/4 cup lemon juice
       2 tablespoons vinegar
       2 tablespoons brown sugar
       1 tablespoon Worcestershire sauce
     1/2 teaspoon ground mustard
     1/8 teaspoon pepper
     1/8 teaspoon chili powder

Cut ribs into serving-size pieces; place on a rack in a shallow roasting pan. Bake, uncovered, at 350° for 1 hour. Meanwhile, in a medium saucepan, saute onion and celery in butter for 4-5 minutes or until tender. Add remaining ingredients; mix well. Bring to a boil; reduce heat. Cook and stir until slightly thickened, about 10 minutes. Remove from the heat. Drain fat from roasting pan. Pour sauce over ribs. Bake 1-1/2 hours longer or until meat is tender. **Yield:** 6-8 servings.

Icebox Butterhorns

If you'd like a roll that melts in your mouth, you have to try Mom's recipe. She has just the right touch when she's mixing up this dough. The rolls smell absolutely heavenly as they bake to a golden brown.

       1 package (1/4 ounce) active dry yeast
       2 tablespoons warm water (110° to 115°)
       2 cups warm milk (110° to 115°)
     1/2 cup sugar
       1 egg, beaten
       1 teaspoon salt
       6 cups all-purpose flour
     3/4 cup butter *or* margarine, melted
Additional melted butter

In a large mixing bowl, dissolve yeast in water. Add milk, sugar, egg, salt and 3 cups flour; beat until smooth. Beat in butter and remaining flour (dough will be slightly sticky). Do not knead. Place in a greased bowl, turning once to grease top. Cover and refrigerate overnight. Punch dough down and divide in half. On a floured surface, roll each half into a 12-in. circle. Cut each circle into 12 pie-shaped wedges. Beginning at the wide end, roll up each wedge. Place rolls, point side down, 2 in. apart on greased baking sheets. Cover and let rise in a warm place until doubled, about 1 hour. Bake at 350° for 15-20 minutes or until golden brown. Immediately brush tops with melted butter. **Yield:** 2 dozen.

Cheery Cherry Cookies

With a tall glass of ice-cold milk, a couple of these cherry cookies really hit the spot for dessert or as a snack. The coconut, pecans and bits of cherries provide a fun look and texture.

- 3/4 cup butter *or* margarine, softened
- 1 cup packed brown sugar
- 1 egg
- 2 tablespoons milk
- 1 teaspoon vanilla extract
- 2 cups all-purpose flour
- 1/2 teaspoon salt
- 1/2 teaspoon baking soda
- 1/2 cup maraschino cherries, well drained and chopped
- 1/2 cup chopped pecans
- 1/2 cup flaked coconut

In a mixing bowl, cream butter and brown sugar; beat in the egg, milk and vanilla. Combine flour, salt and baking soda; gradually add to creamed mixture. Fold in cherries, pecans and coconut. Drop by teaspoonfuls 3 in. apart onto ungreased baking sheets. Bake at 375° for 10-12 minutes or until golden brown. Cool on wire racks. **Yield:** 4 dozen.

Homemade Frozen Custard

My siblings and I had a hard time finding room for dessert after Mom's meals, but when we were ready, we could count on a creamy bowl of frozen custard.

- 4 cups milk
- 4 eggs
- 1-1/4 cups sugar
- 1/3 cup cornstarch
- 1/8 teaspoon salt
- 1 can (14 ounces) sweetened condensed milk
- 2 tablespoons vanilla extract

In a large heavy saucepan, bring milk to a boil. Meanwhile, beat eggs; add sugar, cornstarch and salt. Mix well. Gradually add a small amount of hot milk; return all to the saucepan. Cook and stir constantly for 6-8 minutes or until mixture thickens and coats a spoon. Gradually stir in condensed milk and vanilla; mix well. Chill for 3-4 hours. Pour into the cylinder of an ice cream freezer and freeze according to manufacturer's directions. **Yield:** about 1-1/2 quarts.

Avoid Drop Disasters

To help keep drop cookie dough from flattening too much during baking, always cool baking sheets completely between batches.

Down-home foods cooked on the wood-burning stove made family feel like royalty.

By Willa Govoro, St. Clair, Missouri

I'M in my 80's, but I still remember so clearly the delicious meals Mom prepared on her old wood-burning stove.

Sunday dinner was always special. Mom (Ellen Gibson, above) set out her good dishes and flatware on the big oak table.

My brother and sister and I couldn't wait to dig into her comforting Chicken and Dumplings, which filled the house with a wonderful aroma while simmering on the back of the stove.

Tender chicken and succulent dumplings are covered with a creamy gravy, while carrots and celery add a little bit of color.

A big bowl of her Old-Fashioned Green Beans got passed around until it was scraped clean. Bacon adds a little zip and brown sugar adds a touch of sweetness. You'll appreciate the short list of ingredients in this reliable recipe.

To round out the meal, Mother's Dinner Rolls were set on the table fresh from the oven. With their wonderfully light texture and slightly sweet dough, we could never eat just one.

For dessert, Mom would present a lovely Orange Dream Cake featuring citrus and coconut. Even full from the hearty meal, we'd still manage to devour thick slices of this refreshing sweet delight.

Although our family didn't have much money back then, Mom always made satisfying and balanced meals. And she instilled in me the joy of cooking for others, which I never lost.

PICTURED AT LEFT: Chicken and Dumplings, Old-Fashioned Green Beans, Mother's Dinner Rolls and Orange Dream Cake (recipes are on the next page).

Chicken and Dumplings

On Sundays, Mom set our big round oak table with a snowy white cloth and her fine dishes and tableware. On the old wood stove, pushed way back to simmer slowly, was a big pot of chicken and dumplings in a thick gravy. I can still taste it.

- 1 cup all-purpose flour
- 2 broiler-fryer chickens (2-1/2 to 3 pounds *each*), cut up
- 2 tablespoons vegetable oil
- 3 celery ribs, cut into 1-inch pieces
- 3 medium carrots, cut into 1-inch pieces
- 1/4 cup chopped fresh parsley
- 2 teaspoons salt
- 1 teaspoon garlic powder
- 1 teaspoon dried thyme
- 1/2 teaspoon pepper
- 8 to 12 cups water

DUMPLINGS:
- 2 cups all-purpose flour
- 2 teaspoons baking powder
- 2 eggs, beaten

GRAVY:
- 1/4 cup all-purpose flour
- 1/2 cup water

Place flour in a bowl or bag; add the chicken pieces and dredge or shake to coat. In a large skillet, brown chicken in oil; drain. Place in an 8-qt. Dutch oven. Add celery, carrots, parsley and seasonings. Add enough water to cover chicken; bring to a boil. Reduce heat; cover and simmer until chicken is almost tender, about 45-50 minutes. Remove 1 cup of broth to use for dumplings; cool, then add flour, baking powder and eggs. Mix well to form a stiff batter; drop by tablespoonfuls into simmering broth. Cover and simmer for 15-20 minutes. Remove chicken and dumplings to a serving dish and keep warm. For gravy, remove 4 cups broth and vegetables to a large saucepan; bring to a boil. Combine flour and water; mix well. Stir into vegetable mixture. Cook over medium heat, stirring constantly, until thickened and bubbly. Pour over chicken and dumplings. Serve immediately. **Yield:** 6-8 servings. **Editor's Note:** Any remaining chicken broth can be frozen for future use.

— 🝐 🝐 🝐 —

Old-Fashioned Green Beans

Mom would prepare home-grown green beans using this recipe, and did they ever taste good. The bacon provides rich flavor and the brown sugar a touch of sweetness. This is one irresistible side dish.

- 6 bacon strips, cut into 1/2-inch pieces
- 2 pounds fresh green beans
- 3 tablespoons brown sugar
- 1/2 cup water

In a large skillet, cook bacon over medium heat until crisp-tender, about 5 minutes. Add beans, brown sugar and water. Stir gently; bring to a boil. Reduce heat; cover and simmer for 15 minutes or until beans are crisp-tender. Remove to a serving bowl with a slotted spoon. **Yield:** 6-8 servings.

Orange Dream Cake

We tried to save room for a big slice of this pretty cake. The flavor of orange and lemon really comes through. With a heavenly whipped cream frosting, this cake is a delightful end to a terrific meal.

2/3 cup butter *or* margarine, softened
1-1/3 cups sugar
2/3 cup fresh orange juice
3 tablespoons fresh lemon juice
1 teaspoon grated orange peel
1 teaspoon grated lemon peel
2 eggs
2 cups cake flour
2 teaspoons baking powder
1 teaspoon salt
FROSTING:
1 cup flaked coconut
1/4 cup sugar
2 tablespoons fresh orange juice
1 tablespoon fresh lemon juice
4 teaspoons grated orange peel, *divided*
1 cup whipping cream, whipped

In a large mixing bowl, cream butter and sugar. Add juices and peel; mix well (mixture may appear curdled). Add eggs, one at a time, beating well after each addition. Sift flour with baking powder and salt; add to creamed mixture and mix well. Pour into two greased and floured 8-in. cake pans. Bake at 375° for 25-30 minutes or until cake tests done. Cool in pans for 10 minutes before removing to a wire rack to cool completely. For frosting, combine coconut, sugar, juices and 3 teaspoons peel; mix well. Let stand for 10-15 minutes or until sugar is dissolved. Fold in whipped cream. Spread between cake layers and over the top. Sprinkle with remaining orange peel. Chill for at least 1 hour. Store in the refrigerator. **Yield:** 10-12 servings.

Mother's Dinner Rolls

These tender rolls will melt in your mouth. Mom would set out her big square-footed honey bowl with them— some sweet butter and a drizzle of honey on these rolls is a special treat.

2 packages (1/4 ounce *each*) active dry yeast
1 cup warm water (110° to 115°)
1 cup boiling water
1 cup shortening
3/4 cup sugar
1 teaspoon salt
2 eggs, beaten
7-1/2 to 8 cups all-purpose flour

In a small bowl, dissolve yeast in warm water. Meanwhile, in a large mixing bowl, combine boiling water, shortening, sugar and salt. Allow to stand 3-4 minutes or until shortening is melted and sugar is dissolved. Add the yeast mixture and eggs; mix well. Add 2 cups of flour; beat until smooth. Add enough remaining flour to form a soft dough (do not knead). Place in a greased bowl, turning once to grease top. Cover and refrigerate overnight. Turn dough onto a floured surface. Pinch off a piece and form a 2-1/2-in. ball. Roll into a 5-in. rope; shape into a knot. Repeat with remaining dough. Place on a greased baking sheet. Cover and let rise in a warm place until doubled, about 30 minutes. Bake at 350° for 20-25 minutes or until golden brown. **Yield:** 2-1/2 dozen.

Cooked with love, this memorable family meal includes old-fashioned recipes and goodness you, too, will savor.

By Darlis Wilfer, Phelps, Wisconsin

LIFE wasn't as busy back when my two sisters, one brother and I were growing up.

Our mom (Lorraine Justman, above) took pride in her family, home and cooking. She always had delicious meals on the table for Dad and us kids. When we came home from school, the house had a heavenly aroma.

We sat together around the table, thanked the Lord for our blessings, ate a warm filling meal and took time to "share our day" with one another.

One of Mom's specialties was her savory Porcupine Meatballs. The addition of rice adds a nice texture to the meatballs simmering in a lovely, rich tomato sauce.

With that delightful dish, she often served creamy Baked Mashed Potatoes. This comforting casserole featuring potatoes, sour cream and green onions is especially nice because it can be made ahead of time. So there are less dishes to put together at the last minute.

My brother would dig into the meatballs and potatoes first. But we girls started with Spinach Apple Salad. A slightly sweet dressing brings out the natural flavors of spinach and apples for a true taste sensation.

No matter how much food we piled onto our plate, we all saved room for Mom's wonderful Lazy Daisy Cake. It's an old-fashioned cake with excellent caramel and coconut topping.

Through the years, Mom has been an inspiration to me and my daughters as well. We're sure this meal will soon be a favorite at your house, too.

PICTURED AT LEFT: Porcupine Meatballs, Baked Mashed Potatoes, Spinach Apple Salad and Lazy Daisy Cake (recipes are on the next page).

Porcupine Meatballs

These well-seasoned meatballs in a rich tomato sauce are one of my mom's best main dishes. I used to love this meal when I was growing up. I made it at home for our children, and now my daughters make it for their families as well.

    1/2 cup uncooked long grain rice
    1/2 cup water
    1/3 cup chopped onion
      1 teaspoon salt
    1/2 teaspoon celery salt
    1/8 teaspoon pepper
    1/8 teaspoon garlic powder
      1 pound ground beef
      2 tablespoons vegetable oil
      1 can (15 ounces) tomato sauce
      1 cup water
      2 tablespoons brown sugar
      2 teaspoons Worcestershire sauce

In a bowl, combine the first seven ingredients. Add beef and mix well. Shape into 1-1/2-in. balls. In a large skillet, brown meatballs in oil; drain. Combine tomato sauce, water, brown sugar and Worcestershire sauce; pour over meatballs. Reduce heat; cover and simmer for 1 hour. **Yield:** 4-6 servings.

Baked Mashed Potatoes

This is one comforting side dish that you can prepare ahead. My brother was always quick to dive into these creamy and fluffy potatoes when Mom served them with dinner. My sisters and I kept our eyes on him to be sure we'd get our fair share.

      4 large potatoes, peeled and quartered
    1/4 cup milk
    1/2 teaspoon salt
      2 tablespoons butter *or* margarine, melted, *divided*
      1 egg, beaten
      1 cup (8 ounces) sour cream
      1 cup small-curd cottage cheese
      5 green onions, finely chopped
    1/2 cup crushed butter-flavored crackers

Cook potatoes until tender; drain. Place in a large bowl. Add milk, salt and 1 tablespoon butter; beat until light and fluffy. Fold in egg, sour cream, cottage cheese and onions. Place in a greased 1-1/2-qt. baking dish. Combine the cracker crumbs and remaining butter; sprinkle over potato mixture. Bake, uncovered, at 350° for 20-30 minutes or until crumbs are lightly browned. **Yield:** 4-6 servings. **Editor's Note:** This dish can be made ahead and refrigerated. Remove from the refrigerator 30 minutes before baking. Sprinkle with crumbs and bake as directed.

Spinach Apple Salad

Whenever Mom made this salad, it was the first thing on my plate. With spinach, apples, raisins and a light dressing, this beautiful harvest salad is a feast for the eyes as well as the palate.

> 2 tablespoons cider vinegar
> 2 tablespoons vegetable oil
> 1/4 teaspoon salt
> 1/4 teaspoon sugar
> 1 cup diced unpeeled apple
> 1/4 cup chopped sweet onion
> 1/4 cup raisins
> 2 cups torn fresh spinach
> 2 cups torn romaine

In a small bowl, combine vinegar, oil, salt and sugar; mix well. Add apple, onion and raisins; toss lightly to coat. Cover and let stand for 10 minutes. Just before serving, combine spinach and romaine in a large salad bowl; add dressing and toss. **Yield:** 4-6 servings.

Lazy Daisy Cake

We couldn't wait until Mom sliced this old-fashioned cake with its caramel-like frosting, loaded with chewy coconut. Even after one of Mom's delicious meals, one piece of this cake wasn't enough.

> 4 eggs
> 2 cups sugar
> 2 teaspoons vanilla extract
> 2 cups all-purpose flour
> 2 teaspoons baking powder
> 1/2 teaspoon salt
> 1 cup milk
> 1/4 cup butter *or* margarine
> **FROSTING:**
> 1-1/2 cups packed brown sugar
> 3/4 cup butter *or* margarine, melted
> 1/2 cup half-and-half cream
> 2 cups flaked coconut

In a mixing bowl, beat eggs, sugar and vanilla until thick, about 4 minutes. Combine flour, baking powder and salt; add to egg mixture and beat just until combined. In a saucepan, bring milk and butter to a boil, stirring constantly. Add to batter and beat until combined. Pour into a greased 13-in. x 9-in. x 2-in. baking pan. Bake at 350° for 35-40 minutes or until cake tests done. Combine frosting ingredients; spread over warm cake. Broil until lightly browned, about 3-4 minutes. **Yield:** 16-20 servings.

*She only had one
birthday wish each year–
that Mom would prepare her
best meal for the occasion.
Mom never failed to make
that dream come true.*

By Dianne Esposite, New Middletown, Ohio

ONE OF Mom's best meals is the one my three brothers and I always requested for our birthday dinners when we were growing up. We could hardly wait for those days to come around on the calendar. (Even today when we get together, we ask her to make this memorable meal.)

Each of these treasured recipes was handed down from our great-grandmother, so the entire family has been enjoying this delicious meal for generations. And it's no wonder.

We started out with hearty slices of Swiss Steak. Smothered in mushrooms, celery and onion, it really stands out from any other versions I've tried through the years.

Crisp and golden, Mom's Potato Pancakes are an old-fashioned favorite I know I'll never tire of. I think it's the touch of onion that adds just the right amount of additional flavor. These potato pancakes always seemed to disappear too fast from the plate.

Also eaten up quickly was the Creamy Coleslaw. Carrots and green pepper make a nice addition. Because it needs to be prepared ahead and refrigerated, it's a perfect side dish for a busy cook.

The only way to bring Mom's meal to a fantastic finish was to dish out generous helpings of her Peach Crisp. Try topping it with sweetened whipped cream or vanilla ice cream for an even bigger indulgence.

Mom didn't leave Dad out of the meal preparation. He was employed to grate the potatoes and cabbage!

PICTURED AT LEFT: Swiss Steak, Mom's Potato Pancakes, Creamy Coleslaw and Peach Crisp (recipes are on the next page).

Mom's Potato Pancakes

These old-fashioned pancakes are fluffy inside and crispy on the outside. Grated onion adds nice flavor. Mom got this recipe from Grandma, so we've enjoyed it for years.

- 4 **cups shredded peeled potatoes (about 4 large)**
- 1 **egg, lightly beaten**
- 3 **tablespoons all-purpose flour**
- 1 **tablespoon grated onion**
- 1 **teaspoon salt**
- 1/4 **teaspoon pepper**

Vegetable oil

Rinse potatoes in cold water; drain well. Place in a large bowl. Add egg, flour, onion, salt and pepper; mix well. In a skillet, heat 1/4 in. of oil over medium heat. Drop batter by 1/3 cupfuls into hot oil. Flatten to form a pancake. Fry until golden brown; turn and brown the other side. Drain on paper towels. Serve immediately. **Yield:** 6 servings.

Swiss Steak

Mom was always glad to prepare this tender, flavorful dish for a birthday dinner when one of my three brothers or I'd ask her for it. Now my family enjoys this entree when I make it for them.

- 1/4 **cup all-purpose flour**
- 1 **teaspoon salt**
- 1/4 **teaspoon pepper**
- 1-1/2 **to 2 pounds beef round steak, trimmed**
- 2 **tablespoons vegetable oil**
- 1 **cup chopped celery**
- 1 **cup chopped onion**
- 1/2 **pound fresh mushrooms, sliced**
- 1 **cup water**
- 1 **garlic clove, minced**
- 1 **tablespoon steak sauce**

Combine the flour, salt and pepper. Cut steak into serving-size pieces; dredge in the flour mixture. In a skillet, brown steak in oil. Drain and place in a 2-1/2-qt. casserole. Top with celery, onion and mushrooms. Combine water, garlic and steak sauce; pour over vegetables. Cover and bake at 350° for 1-1/2 hours or until the meat is tender. **Yield:** 6 servings.

Keeping Fried Foods Warm

When foods need to be cooked in stages (such as the potato pancakes above), you can easily keep each batch warm until the entire recipe is cooked. After frying, drain the food on paper towels and then place on an ovenproof platter. Cover loosely with foil and place in a 200° oven until the entire recipe is completed.

1 cup all-purpose flour
1/2 cup packed brown sugar
1/4 teaspoon salt
1/2 cup cold butter *or* margarine
FILLING:
   2 cans (16 ounces *each*) sliced peaches
   1 cup sugar
1/4 cup cornstarch
TOPPING:
1-1/2 cups rolled oats
1/2 cup packed brown sugar
1/4 cup all-purpose flour
   5 tablespoons cold butter *or* margarine

In a bowl, combine flour, brown sugar and salt. Cut in butter until crumbly. Pat into a greased 9-in. square baking pan. Bake at 350° for 15 minutes. Meanwhile, drain the peaches and reserve juice in a medium saucepan. Add the sugar and cornstarch; bring to a boil, stirring constantly. Boil for 2 minutes or until thickened. Remove from the heat; stir in peaches. Pour into crust. For topping, combine oats, brown sugar and flour. Cut in the butter until crumbly. Sprinkle over filling. Bake at 350° for 25-30 minutes or until golden and bubbly. **Yield:** 6-8 servings.

Creamy Coleslaw

This colorful coleslaw is another longtime family favorite. Cabbage, carrots and green pepper are blended with a tasty dressing that gets its zest from a hint of mustard.

   3 to 4 cups shredded cabbage
   1 cup shredded carrots
   1 cup thinly sliced green pepper
1/2 cup mayonnaise *or* salad dressing
1/4 cup lemon juice
   1 to 2 tablespoons sugar
   1 tablespoon prepared mustard
   1 teaspoon celery seed
   1 teaspoon salt

In a large salad bowl, toss cabbage, carrots and green pepper. In a small bowl, combine the remaining ingredients. Pour over the cabbage mixture and toss to coat. Chill for at least 2-3 hours. **Yield:** 6-8 servings.

Peach Crisp

A hearty serving of this sweet and tart treat is a mouth-watering way to end one of Mom's meals. With the comforting crust, fruit filling and crunchy topping, this dessert is as lovely as it is delicious.

To capture the comforts of farm life, her mother would make family and friends a down-home Midwestern dinner featuring meat loaf.

By Linda Nilsen, Anoka, Minnesota

MY MOTHER was a busy teacher when my younger brother and I were children. She was always on the go. But that didn't stop her from making luscious meals for our family…or from teaching me the importance of offering family and friends delicious foods made with love.

We lived in California, but Mom was from a Swedish Minnesota farm family. When she got homesick for the farm, she'd make hearty meals with Midwestern flair. We always looked forward to those meals more than any others she prepared!

I especially remember Mom's Best Meat Loaf. The zesty seasoning featuring horseradish gives the meat a little zip. And the wonderful aroma while baking was unbeatable. Now I often capture that mouthwatering fragrance in my own kitchen.

Creamed Peas and Potatoes is an old-fashioned, hearty side dish that also adds appealing color to the table. My mom and her cousin came up with this original recipe for Favorite French Dressing many years ago. We'd look forward to a big green salad served with this tangy dressing. Mom got lots of requests for this recipe.

To top off her meal, Mom liked to prepare a special traditional dessert from an old recipe, which has been handed down in the family. Swedish Creme is thick, rich, beautiful and tasty.

I guarantee your family will favor this mouth-watering menu no matter where you live!

PICTURED AT LEFT: Mom's Best Meat Loaf, Creamed Peas and Potatoes, Favorite French Dressing and Swedish Creme (recipes are on the next page).

In a large bowl, combine the first 11 ingredients; add beef and mix well. Press into an ungreased 8-1/2-in. x 4-1/2-in. x 2-1/2-in. loaf pan. Bake at 350° for 1 hour. Drizzle top of loaf with ketchup; bake 15 minutes more or until no longer pink and a meat thermometer reads 160°. **Yield:** 6-8 servings.

Creamed Peas and Potatoes

Nothing beats this comforting side dish to go with Mom's meat loaf. The peas and potatoes combined with a creamy white sauce make a hearty dish.

- 4 medium red potatoes, cubed
- 1 package (10 ounces) frozen peas
- 1 teaspoon sugar
- 2 tablespoons butter *or* margarine
- 2 tablespoons all-purpose flour
- 1/2 teaspoon salt
- 1/4 teaspoon white pepper
- 1-1/2 cups milk
- 2 tablespoons minced fresh dill

Place potatoes in a saucepan; cover with water and cook until tender. Cook peas according to package directions, adding the sugar. Meanwhile, melt butter in a saucepan; add flour, salt and pepper to form a paste. Gradually stir in milk. Bring to a boil; boil for 1 minute. Add dill; cook until thickened and bubbly. Drain potatoes and peas; place in a serving bowl. Pour sauce over and stir to coat. Serve immediately. **Yield:** 6-8 servings.

Mom's Best Meat Loaf

This is no ordinary meat loaf—the recipe is so good it's been passed down in our family for three generations. The zesty seasoning gives the flavor a spark. I remember Mom's delicious meals. She loved to serve this meat loaf.

- 1 cup milk
- 1 egg, lightly beaten
- 3/4 cup soft bread crumbs
- 1 medium onion, chopped
- 1 tablespoon chopped green pepper
- 1 tablespoon ketchup
- 1-1/2 teaspoons salt
- 1 teaspoon prepared horseradish
- 1 teaspoon sugar
- 1 teaspoon ground allspice
- 1 teaspoon dill weed
- 1-1/2 pounds lean ground beef
- Additional ketchup

Swedish Creme

This thick creamy dessert is a great finale to one of Mom's hearty meals. It has just a hint of almond flavor and looks spectacular with bright-red berries on top. The recipe calls for either fresh or frozen raspberries, making this a perfect year-round treat.

    2 cups whipping cream
    1 cup plus 2 teaspoons sugar, *divided*
    1 envelope unflavored gelatin
    1 teaspoon vanilla extract
    1 teaspoon almond extract
    2 cups (16 ounces) sour cream
    1 cup fresh *or* frozen red raspberries, crushed

In a saucepan, combine cream and 1 cup sugar. Cook and stir constantly over low heat until candy thermometer reads 160° or steam rises from pan (do not boil). Stir in gelatin until dissolved; add extracts. Cool for 10 minutes. Whisk in sour cream. Pour into eight dessert glasses or small bowls; chill at least 1 hour. Before serving, combine raspberries and remaining sugar; spoon over each serving. **Yield:** 8 servings.

Favorite French Dressing

My mom and her cousin developed this tangy dressing many years ago. It really perks up salad greens and holds together well once mixed. Everyone wants the recipe once they try it.

        1 cup vinegar
      3/4 cup sugar
      1/4 cup grated onion
    1-1/2 teaspoons salt
    1-1/2 teaspoons ground mustard
    1-1/2 teaspoons paprika
        1 bottle (12 ounces) chili sauce
        1 cup vegetable oil

In a bowl or jar with tight-fitting lid, mix vinegar, sugar and onion. Combine salt, mustard, paprika and 2 tablespoons chili sauce to form a paste. Add remaining chili sauce and mix well. Pour into vinegar mixture; add oil and mix or shake well. Store in the refrigerator. **Yield:** 3-1/2 cups.

Thermometer Testing

It is recommended to test your candy thermometer before each use by bringing water to a boil; the thermometer should read 212°. Adjust your recipe temperature up or down based on your test.

Editors' Meals

Taste of Home magazine is edited by 1,000 cooks across North America. On the following pages, six of those cooks share a favorite meal that you and yours are sure to enjoy!

SURE-FIRE FAVORITES. Clockwise from upper left: Thanksgiving Meal with a Twist (p. 244), Can't-Miss Cookout Cuisine (p. 236), Christmas Eve Festivities (p. 224) and Down-Home Chicken Dinner (p. 232).

On Christmas Eve, she treats the family to a festive traditional dinner in a joy-filled farmhouse.

By Marge Clark, West Lebanon, Indiana

AS our four grown sons and their families arrive here at Oak Hill Farm on Christmas Eve, candles glow and the house is fragrant with the aroma of dinner in the oven and the scent of holiday decorations. First I serve mugs of orange juice or cranberry juice cocktail with cinnamon stick stirrers, then a hot appetizer before all of us sit down to dinner.

We all love ham and potatoes, so I dress them up for the holiday! Apricot Baked Ham gets a tangy-sweet taste from the fruity glaze, which also adds a beautiful "finish" to the meat.

I prepare my Stuffed Baked Potatoes up to a week before our dinner, wrap them well and freeze them to thaw (still wrapped) the morning of Christmas Eve. Everyone loves their smooth texture and rich flavor.

Ruby Red Raspberry Salad is beautiful to serve, and we think the combination of raspberry, cherry, cranberry and pineapple flavors is fabulous.

I also serve homemade rolls with strawberry jam, a green salad with herb dressing and herbed breadsticks.

For our crowd, I usually make traditional pecan pie along with another favorite like Cranberry Sauce Cake. The moist beautifully textured cake stirs up in a wink.

As I spend satisfying hours in the kitchen preparing for Christmas, I recall my childhood and how I loved watching my mother roll out pie dough, beat cake batter by hand and knead the dough for perfect pan icebox rolls.

I've learned lots of shortcuts through the years. However, at holiday time—more than any other time—I seek out old family favorite recipes to prepare and serve. I hope this tradition will live on for many, many years.

🥄 🥄 🥄

PICTURED AT LEFT: Apricot Baked Ham, Stuffed Baked Potatoes, Ruby Red Raspberry Salad and Cranberry Sauce Cake (recipes are on the next page).

Their flavorful cheesy filling goes so nicely with juicy slices of glazed ham.

    3 **large baking potatoes (1 pound** *each***)**
1-1/2 **teaspoons vegetable oil, optional**
  1/2 **cup sliced green onions**
  1/2 **cup butter** *or* **margarine,** *divided*
  1/2 **cup half-and-half cream**
  1/2 **cup sour cream**
    1 **teaspoon salt**
  1/2 **teaspoon white pepper**
    1 **cup (4 ounces) shredded cheddar cheese**
Paprika

Rub potatoes with oil if desired; pierce with a fork. Bake at 400° for 1 hour and 20 minutes or until tender. Allow potatoes to cool to the touch. Cut in half lengthwise; carefully scoop out pulp, leaving a thin shell. Place pulp in a large bowl. Saute onions in 1/4 cup butter until tender. Add to potato pulp along with half-and-half cream, sour cream, salt and pepper. Beat until smooth. Fold in cheese. Stuff potato shells and place in a 13-in. x 9-in. x 2-in. baking pan. Melt remaining butter; drizzle over the potatoes. Sprinkle with paprika. Bake at 350° for 20-30 minutes or until heated through. **Yield:** 6 servings. **Editor's Note:** Potatoes may be stuffed ahead of time and refrigerated or frozen. Allow additional time for reheating.

Apricot Baked Ham

Ham is a super choice for a holiday meal because once you put it in the oven, it practically takes care of itself until dinnertime. I serve it because everyone in my family loves it! The sugary crust makes the ham beautiful to serve.

  1/2 **fully cooked bone-in ham (5 to 7 pounds)**
   20 **whole cloves**
  1/2 **cup apricot preserves**
    3 **tablespoons ground mustard**
  1/2 **cup packed light brown sugar**

Score the surface of the ham with shallow diamond-shaped cuts. Insert cloves in cuts. Combine preserves and mustard; spread over ham. Pat brown sugar over apricot mixture. Place ham on a rack in a roasting pan. Bake at 325° for 20 minutes per pound or until ham is heated through and thermometer reads 140°. **Yield:** 10-14 servings.

— 🍳 🍳 🍳 —

Stuffed Baked Potatoes

These special potatoes are a hit with my whole family, from the smallest grandchild on up. I prepare them up to a week in advance, wrap them well and freeze.

Ruby Red Raspberry Salad

A refreshing and attractive side dish, this salad adds a festive touch to your holiday table. Children especially like this slightly sweet gelatin salad brimming with raspberries and pineapple.

    1 package (3 ounces) raspberry gelatin
    2 cups boiling water, *divided*
    1 package (10 ounces) sweetened frozen
      raspberries
1-1/2 cups sour cream
    1 package (3 ounces) cherry gelatin
    1 can (20 ounces) crushed pineapple,
      drained
    1 can (16 ounces) whole-berry cranberry
      sauce
Lettuce leaves
Mayonnaise *or* salad dressing, optional
Mint leaves, optional

Dissolve raspberry gelatin in 1 cup boiling water. Add raspberries and stir until berries are thawed and separated. Pour into a 13-in. x 9-in. x 2-in. pan; chill until set. Carefully spread with sour cream; chill. Dissolve cherry gelatin in remaining boiling water. Add pineapple and cranberry sauce; mix well. Allow to thicken slightly. Carefully spoon over sour cream mixture; chill. Cut into squares and serve on lettuce leaves. If desired, top each with a dollop of mayonnaise and garnish with a mint leaf. **Yield:** 12-16 servings.

Cranberry Sauce Cake

This moist cake is so easy to make because it mixes in one bowl. Slice it at the table so everyone can see how beautiful it is.

    3 cups all-purpose flour
1-1/2 cups sugar
    1 cup mayonnaise*
    1 can (16 ounces) whole-berry cranberry
      sauce
    1/3 cup orange juice
    1 tablespoon grated orange peel
    1 teaspoon baking soda
    1 teaspoon salt
    1 teaspoon orange extract
    1 cup chopped walnuts
ICING:
    1 cup confectioners' sugar
    1 to 2 tablespoons orange juice

In a mixing bowl, combine flour, sugar, mayonnaise, cranberry sauce, orange juice and peel, baking soda, salt and extract; mix well. Fold in walnuts. Cut waxed or parchment paper to fit the bottom of a 10-in. tube pan. Spray the pan and paper with nonstick cooking spray. Pour batter into paper-lined pan. Bake at 350° for 60-70 minutes or until the cake tests done. Cool 10 minutes in pan before removing to a wire rack. Combine confectioners' sugar and enough orange juice to achieve desired consistency; drizzle over the warm cake. **Yield:** 12-16 servings. ***Editor's Note:** It is not recommended to use light or low-fat mayonnaise products for this recipe.

Her crowd-pleasing brunch can be prepared a day ahead to brighten Easter or any special morning.

By Mary Anne McWhirter, Pearland, Texas

AFTER CHURCH on Easter Sunday, my family likes to sit down to a leisurely brunch, to which we invite relatives or special friends.

The greatest thing about this economical menu is that most of the dishes can be made ahead of time.

The aroma of ham and green onions sauteing for my Scrambled Egg Casserole creates a savory sneak preview of this delicious dish, which is assembled entirely the night before.

In the morning, I simply pop it into the oven and then enjoy time with family and guests.

Wrapping the Pigs in a Blanket can be done in a jiffy using handy convenience foods.

The fruity base for refreshing Banana Brunch Punch is also made ahead and frozen. Just take it out of the freezer an hour before serving and blend the soda and pineapple juice with the thawing mixture.

Cream Cheese Coffee Cake is so delicious and looks impressive…but don't be fooled—it's quick and easy to make. In fact, you simply cut "X" shapes across the top of the cheese-filled yeast-dough loaves to create the attractive braided effect.

Fresh or frozen berries add fruity festivity to my Blueberry Streusel Muffins, light-textured and pretty with their sweet golden topping. They can be made several days ahead and frozen.

To complete the meal, I serve fresh fruit such as grapefruit halves topped with fresh strawberries. You can use a variety of fruits in season, arranging a colorful plate for the buffet.

I hope to one day own and operate a bed-and-breakfast…I'll certainly treat guests to my Easter brunch. Meantime, I hope our favorite-meal menu will soon become a favorite of yours!

PICTURED AT LEFT: Scrambled Egg Casserole, Pigs in a Blanket, Banana Brunch Punch, Cream Cheese Coffee Cake and Blueberry Streusel Muffins (recipes are on the next page).

Pigs in a Blanket

(Pictured on page 229)

This simple recipe uses refrigerated crescent rolls and pre-cooked breakfast links.

**1 tube (8 ounces) refrigerated crescent rolls
1 package (12 ounces) smoked sausage links**

Separate the dough into eight triangles. Place a sausage on wide end of each triangle and roll up. Place, tip down, on an ungreased baking sheet. Bake at 400° for 10-15 minutes or until golden brown. **Yield:** 8 servings.

— ▼ ▼ ▼ —

Scrambled Egg Casserole

There's nothing nicer than a delicious egg dish you can prepare the night before.

**1/2 cup butter *or* margarine, *divided*
2 tablespoons all-purpose flour
1/2 teaspoon salt
1/8 teaspoon pepper
2 cups milk
1 cup (4 ounces) shredded process
American cheese
1 cup cubed fully cooked ham
1/4 cup sliced green onions
12 eggs, beaten
1 can (4 ounces) sliced mushrooms, drained
1-1/2 cups soft bread crumbs
Additional sliced green onions, optional**

In a medium saucepan, melt 2 tablespoons butter. Add flour, salt and pepper; cook and stir until bubbly. Gradually stir in milk; cook until thickened and bubbly, stirring constantly. Remove from heat. Add cheese; mix well and set aside. In a large skillet, saute ham and onions in 3 tablespoons but-

ter until onions are tender. Add eggs; cook and stir until they begin to set. Add mushrooms and cheese sauce; mix well. Pour into a greased 11-in. x 7-in. x 2-in. baking dish. Melt remaining butter; toss with bread crumbs. Sprinkle over top of casserole. Cover and refrigerate 2-3 hours or overnight. Remove from refrigerator 30 minutes before baking. Bake, uncovered, at 350° for 25-30 minutes or until top is golden brown. Sprinkle with onions if desired. **Yield:** 6-8 servings.

Banana Brunch Punch

A cold glass of refreshing punch really brightens a brunch. It's nice to serve a crisp beverage like this.

**6 medium ripe bananas
1 can (12 ounces) frozen orange juice
concentrate, thawed
3/4 cup lemonade concentrate
3 cups warm water, *divided*
2 cups sugar, *divided*
1 can (46 ounces) pineapple juice
3 bottles (2 liters *each*) lemon-lime soda
Orange slices, optional**

In a blender or food processor, cover and process bananas, orange juice and lemonade until smooth. Remove half of the mixture and set aside. Add 1-1/2 cups of warm water and 1 cup sugar to mixture in blender; blend until smooth. Place in a large freezer container. Repeat with remaining banana mixture, water and sugar; add to container. Cover and freeze until solid. One hour before serving, take punch base out of freezer. Just before serving, place in a large punch bowl. Add pineapple juice and soda; stir until well blended. Garnish with orange slices if desired. **Yield:** 60-70 servings (10 quarts).

Cream Cheese Coffee Cake

These impressive loaves really sparkle on the buffet. You can't just eat one slice of this treat.

> 1 cup (8 ounces) sour cream
> 1/2 cup sugar
> 1/2 cup butter *or* margarine
> 1 teaspoon salt
> 2 packages (1/4 ounce *each*) active dry yeast
> 1/2 cup warm water (110° to 115°)
> 2 eggs, beaten
> 4 cups all-purpose flour

FILLING:
> 2 packages (8 ounces *each*) cream cheese, softened
> 3/4 cup sugar
> 1 egg, beaten
> 2 teaspoons vanilla extract
> 1/8 teaspoon salt

GLAZE:
> 2-1/2 cups confectioners' sugar
> 1/4 cup milk
> 1 teaspoon vanilla extract

Toasted sliced almonds, optional

In a saucepan, combine sour cream, sugar, butter and salt. Cook over medium-low heat, stirring constantly, for 5-10 minutes or until well blended. Cool to room temperature. In a mixing bowl, dissolve yeast in water. Add sour cream mixture and eggs; mix well. Gradually stir in flour. (Dough will be very soft.) Cover and refrigerate overnight. Next day, combine filling ingredients in a mixing bowl until well blended. Turn dough onto a floured surface; knead 5-6 times. Divide into four equal portions. Roll each portion into a 12-in. x 8-in. rectangle. Spread 1/4 of the filling on each to within 1 in. of edges. Roll up jelly-roll style from long side; pinch seams and ends to seal. Place, seam side down, on greased baking sheet. Cut six X's on top of loaves. Cover and let rise until nearly doubled, about 1 hour. Bake at 375° for 20-25 minutes or until golden brown. Cool on wire racks. Combine the first three glaze ingredients; drizzle over loaves. Sprinkle with almonds if desired. Store in the refrigerator. **Yield:** 20-24 servings.

Blueberry Streusel Muffins

It's a joy to set out a basket of these moist muffins!

> 1/4 cup butter *or* margarine, softened
> 1/3 cup sugar
> 1 egg, beaten
> 2-1/3 cups all-purpose flour
> 4 teaspoons baking powder
> 1/2 teaspoon salt
> 1 cup milk
> 1 teaspoon vanilla extract
> 1-1/2 cups fresh *or* frozen blueberries

STREUSEL:
> 1/2 cup sugar
> 1/3 cup all-purpose flour
> 1/2 teaspoon ground cinnamon
> 1/4 cup cold butter *or* margarine

In a mixing bowl, cream butter and sugar. Add egg; mix well. Combine flour, baking powder and salt; add to the creamed mixture alternately with milk. Stir in vanilla. Fold in blueberries. Fill 12 greased or paper-lined muffin cups two-thirds full. In a small bowl, combine sugar, flour and cinnamon; cut in butter until crumbly. Sprinkle over muffins. Bake at 375° for 25-30 minutes or until browned. **Yield:** 1 dozen.

*A heritage of
good home cooking
flavors this cook's
versatile menu that's
perfect for family
or company.*

By Schelby Thompson, Dover, Delaware

MIXING and matching good recipes to come up with a special menu—like the flavorful meal featured here—is a real pleasure for me.

My husband, Steve, and I like a wide range of foods and enjoy entertaining. We also try to introduce our two young girls to different dishes on a regular basis. Their enthusiastic reaction to this menu told me I was on the right track!

The Parmesan Chicken recipe was given to me by a college friend. It's easy to prepare, yet pretty enough to serve company.

When fixing the chicken for just our family, I'll often cut the chicken into "fingers" and decrease the baking time by about 20 minutes.

Onion-Roasted Potatoes are quick and simple, and they taste mild enough for those who are not onion lovers. The flavor blends well with a variety of meats, making this a versatile side dish for any meal.

Because I never acquired a taste for anchovies, I created a version of Caesar Salad that eliminates this traditional ingredient without losing any of the wonderful flavor.

Although Raspberry Linzer Cookies take a bit of extra effort, they're well worth it! Spreading the dough on a large plate will decrease the chilling time, and rolling the dough between sheets of waxed paper reduces countertop mess.

"Fancy" hardly describes my down-home cooking style, which combines solid basics that I learned from my mother with a generous amount of experimentation on my part.

Whether guests are due or you're cooking for just the family, this home-style supper is sure to satisfy.

❦ ❦ ❦

PICTURED AT LEFT: Parmesan Chicken, Onion-Roasted Potatoes, Caesar Salad and Raspberry Linzer Cookies (recipes are on the next page).

chicken is no longer pink and juices run clear. **Yield:** 6-8 servings.

——— 🍷 🍷 🍷 ———

Onion-Roasted Potatoes

Slightly crisp on the outside and tender on the inside, these potatoes are a hit with my family. This side dish is one of my favorites because the soup mix glazes the potatoes so nicely, and it's very simple to prepare.

   2 pounds red potatoes, sliced 1/2 inch
       thick
 1/3 cup vegetable oil
   1 envelope onion soup mix

Combine all ingredients in a large plastic bag; shake until well coated. Empty bag into an ungreased 13-in. x 9-in. x 2-in. baking pan. Cover and bake at 350° for 35 minutes, stirring occasionally. Uncover and bake 15 minutes longer or until potatoes are tender. **Yield:** 6-8 servings.

Parmesan Chicken

The savory coating on this chicken has the satisfying flavor of Parmesan cheese. It's easy enough to be a family weekday meal, yet impressive enough to serve to guests. When I make this chicken for dinner, we never have leftovers.

 1/2 cup butter *or* margarine, melted
   2 teaspoons Dijon mustard
   1 teaspoon Worcestershire sauce
 1/2 teaspoon salt
   1 cup dry bread crumbs
 1/2 cup grated Parmesan cheese
   6 to 8 boneless skinless chicken breast
       halves

In a pie plate or shallow bowl, combine butter, mustard, Worcestershire sauce and salt. In a plastic bag, combine crumbs and Parmesan cheese. Dip chicken in butter mixture, then shake in crumb mixture. Place in an ungreased 13-in. x 9-in. x 2-in. baking pan. Drizzle with any remaining butter mixture. Bake at 350° for 40-45 minutes or until

Grating Parmesan Cheese

If you buy a chunk of Parmesan cheese to grate on your own, use the finest section on your grating tool. Or cut the cheese into 1-inch cubes and process 1 cup of cubes at a time on high in your food processor or blender until finely grated.

1 cup butter *or* margarine, softened
1-1/4 cups sugar, *divided*
2 eggs, *separated*
2-1/2 cups all-purpose flour
1/4 teaspoon salt
Confectioners' sugar
1/2 cup ground almonds
3/4 cup raspberry preserves

In a mixing bowl, cream butter. Gradually add 2/3 cup sugar, beating until light and fluffy. Add egg yolks, one at a time, beating well after each addition. Combine flour and salt; gradually add to creamed mixture and mix well. Shape dough into a ball; chill for 30-45 minutes or until firm. On a surface dusted with confectioners' sugar, roll half of the dough to 1/8-in. thickness; cut with a 2-1/2-in. round cookie cutter. Repeat with remaining dough, using a 2-1/2-in. doughnut cutter so the center is cut out of each cookie. Beat egg whites until frothy. Combine almonds and remaining sugar. Brush each cookie with egg white and sprinkle with the almond mixture. Place on greased baking sheets. Bake at 350° for 6-8 minutes or until lightly browned. Remove immediately to wire racks to cool completely. Spread 2 teaspoons of raspberry preserves over the plain side of solid cookies. Place cookies with centers cut out, almond side up, on top of the preserves, making a sandwich. **Yield:** about 2 dozen.

Caesar Salad

(Also pictured on front cover)

This crunchy refreshing salad has a zippy zesty dressing that provides a burst of flavor with each bite. It's a great salad to perk up any spring or summer meal.

1 large bunch romaine, torn
3/4 cup olive *or* vegetable oil
3 tablespoons cider *or* red wine vinegar
1 teaspoon Worcestershire sauce
1/2 teaspoon salt
1/4 teaspoon ground mustard
1 large garlic clove, minced
1/2 fresh lemon
Dash pepper
1/4 to 1/2 cup shredded Parmesan cheese
Caesar-flavored *or* garlic croutons

Place romaine in a large salad bowl. Combine the next six ingredients in a blender; cover and process until smooth. Pour over lettuce and toss. Squeeze lemon juice over lettuce. Sprinkle with pepper, Parmesan cheese and croutons. Serve immediately. **Yield:** 6-8 servings.

Raspberry Linzer Cookies

These wonderful cookies require a bit of extra effort to make and assemble, but the delight on the faces of family and friends when I serve them makes it all worthwhile.

When family members pitch in, preparing this summery feast is light work for this cook, who shares her can't-miss party menu.

By Jeri Dobrowski, Beach, North Dakota

WE LIKE having company during grilling season, and I often serve this delicious "standby" menu.

The whole family pitches in to prepare these favorite dishes, which are perfect for warm-weather entertaining—preparation is quick and easy, and the results are impressive.

The aroma of Teriyaki Finger Steaks grilling never fails to draw guests (following their noses!) out into our backyard, where they find my husband, Rob, at the grill.

I slice and marinate the sirloin ahead of time. The thin strips of meat cook nicely on skewers, and the fluffy Herbed Rice Pilaf is a perfect accompaniment to their hearty grilled flavor.

Our summertime favorite, Strawberry-Glazed Fruit Salad, is something son Brian usually stirs up prior to the party.

This is a great recipe for eager young cooks because it's simple but delicious. Bright fresh berries, pineapple chunks and banana slices appeal to the eye as well as the palate.

Chocolate Almond Cheesecake is one of daughter Jennifer's specialties, adapted from a 4-H cooking class recipe. One taste told us this dessert was bound to be a favorite for some time to come.

Its rich chocolate flavor is mellowed to perfection with cream cheese and whipped cream topping. (In my opinion, nothing substitutes for the taste of real whipping cream in a special dessert like this one.)

Since much of the preparation for these recipes can be done in advance, we don't have to spend a lot of time in the kitchen when we're hosting guests. Leftovers of these dishes are super the next day, so I intentionally plan to make extra!

🍴 🍴 🍴

PICTURED AT LEFT: Teriyaki Finger Steaks, Herbed Rice Pilaf, Strawberry-Glazed Fruit Salad and Chocolate Almond Cheesecake (recipes are on the next page).

Teriyaki Finger Steaks

When these flavorful skewered steaks are sizzling on the grill, the aroma makes everyone around stop what they're doing and come to see what's cooking. The tasty marinade is easy to make.

☑ Uses less fat, sugar or salt. Includes Nutritional Analysis and Diabetic Exchanges.

2 pounds boneless sirloin steak
1/2 cup soy sauce
1/4 cup vinegar
2 tablespoons brown sugar
2 tablespoons minced onion
1 tablespoon vegetable oil
1 garlic clove, minced
1/2 teaspoon ground ginger
1/8 teaspoon pepper

Trim fat from steak and slice lengthwise into 1/2-in. strips; place in a large glass bowl. Combine all remaining ingredients; pour over meat and toss gently. Cover and refrigerate for 2-3 hours. Drain, discarding marinade. Loosely thread meat strips onto metal or soaked wooden skewers. Grill over medium-hot heat, turning often, for 7-10 minutes or until meat reaches desired doneness. Remove from skewers and serve. **Yield:** 6 servings. **Nutritional Analysis:** One serving (prepared with low-sodium soy sauce) equals 190 calories, 725 mg sodium, 62 mg cholesterol, 6 gm carbohydrate, 24 gm protein, 7 gm fat. **Diabetic Exchanges:** 3 lean meat, 1/2 starch.

Herbed Rice Pilaf

This savory side dish has been a family favorite for years. Our daughter, Jennifer, is an expert with this recipe, which is a great help for a busy working mom like me. We sure enjoy this rice dish in the summer with a grilled entree.

1 cup uncooked long grain rice
1 cup chopped celery
3/4 cup chopped onion
1/4 cup butter *or* margarine
2-1/2 cups water
1 package (2 to 2-1/2 ounces) chicken noodle soup mix
2 tablespoons minced fresh parsley
1/2 teaspoon dried thyme
1/4 teaspoon rubbed sage
1/4 teaspoon pepper
1 tablespoon chopped pimientos, optional

In a large skillet, cook the rice, celery and onion in butter, stirring constantly, until rice is browned. Stir in the next six ingredients; bring to a boil. Reduce heat; cover and simmer for 15 minutes. Stir in the pimientos if desired. Remove from the heat and let stand, covered, for 10 minutes. **Yield:** 6 servings.

Strawberry-Glazed Fruit Salad

I first tasted this delightful salad at a friend's house when she served it with dinner. It tastes so good made with fresh strawberries. After sampling it, no one would ever believe how incredibly easy it is to prepare.

1 quart fresh strawberries, halved
1 can (20 ounces) pineapple chunks, drained
4 firm bananas, sliced
1 jar *or* pouch (16 ounces) strawberry glaze

In a large bowl, gently toss strawberries, pineapple and bananas; fold in the glaze. Chill for 1 hour. **Yield:** 6-8 servings. **Editor's Note:** Strawberry glaze can often be found in the produce section of your grocery store.

Chocolate Almond Cheesecake

My family enjoys a good meal, but we all save room for dessert when this cheesecake is part of the menu. Its rich chocolate flavor is so satisfying when we're craving something sweet and creamy.

1-1/4 cups graham cracker crumbs
1-1/2 cups sugar, *divided*
1/2 cup plus 2 tablespoons baking cocoa, *divided*
1/4 cup butter *or* margarine, melted
2 packages (8 ounces *each*) cream cheese, softened
1 cup (8 ounces) sour cream
3 eggs
1-1/2 teaspoons almond extract, *divided*
1 cup whipping cream
1/4 cup confectioners' sugar
1/4 cup sliced almonds, toasted

Combine crumbs, 1/4 cup sugar, 2 tablespoons cocoa and butter; mix well. Press into the bottom of a 9-in. springform pan; chill. In a mixing bowl, beat the cream cheese, sour cream and remaining sugar until smooth. Add eggs, one at a time, beating well after each addition. Stir in 1 teaspoon of extract and remaining cocoa. Pour into crust. Bake at 350° for 45-50 minutes or until the center is almost set. Cool completely. Refrigerate at least 8 hours. In a mixing bowl, whip cream until it mounds slightly. Add confectioners' sugar and remaining extract; continue whipping until soft peaks form. Spread evenly over cheesecake. Sprinkle with almonds. Store in refrigerator. **Yield:** 12 servings.

A visit to the family farm means fresh air, fun and great food when she prepares these dishes to satisfy hungry appetites.

By Page Alexander, Baldwin City, Kansas

EACH SUMMER, my husband, Monte, and I plan a weekend when our two grown children, their families and a few other relatives can come out to our farm for some fun and good food.

With the crops maturing, flowers blooming and our garden bearing fresh produce, there couldn't be a better time for a family gathering!

Barbecued Brisket is cooked slowly to its tender best. The meat absorbs the delicious sweet-tart flavor from the sauce as it tenderizes.

A friend told me how to roast the brisket, but the sauce is my own concoction. While it's easy to use bottled sauce in a recipe like this, you can make your own with just a little extra effort.

With the beef, I serve Special Potato Salad, a recipe shared by daughter-in-law Lisa. This salad is a little different from any other I'd made and has a wonderful creamy dressing. Red onion and celery add color and crunch. My nieces say it's a perfect addition to any picnic or barbecue.

Layered Fruit Salad goes well with any meat entree and is especially refreshing on a hot day. Its simple citrus dressing seems to bring out the flavor of each fruit in the medley. Be sure to serve this colorful salad in a clear glass bowl or trifle dish if you have one.

After a big meal, a slice of Meringue Berry Pie really hits the spot. This dessert's crispy nutty crust, ice cream filling, tangy fruit and sweet sauce make it a summer delight.

As we all sit back after dinner, everyone says how glad they are to come to our place for a visit. I'll often send each family home with a jar of blackberry jelly I've made using wild fruit growing on our property.

The next time your family's coming, I hope you'll consider trying one of my favorite recipes.

PICTURED AT LEFT: Barbecued Brisket, Special Potato Salad, Layered Fruit Salad and Meringue Berry Pie (recipes are on the next page).

Barbecued Brisket

For a mouth-watering main dish to star in a summer meal, this brisket can't be beat. Baked slowly, the meat gets nice and tender, and picks up the sweet and tangy flavor of the barbecue sauce.

```
    1 beef brisket (3 to 4 pounds)*
1-1/4 cups water, divided
  1/2 cup chopped onion
    3 garlic cloves, minced
    1 tablespoon vegetable oil
    1 cup ketchup
    3 tablespoons cider or red wine vinegar
    2 tablespoons lemon juice
    2 tablespoons brown sugar
    1 tablespoon Worcestershire sauce
    2 teaspoons cornstarch
    1 teaspoon paprika
    1 teaspoon chili powder
  1/4 teaspoon salt
  1/4 teaspoon pepper
  1/4 teaspoon liquid smoke
```

Place brisket in a large Dutch oven. Add 1/2 cup water. Cover and bake at 275° for 2 hours. Meanwhile, in a medium saucepan, saute onion and garlic in oil until tender. Add ketchup, vinegar, lemon juice, brown sugar, Worcestershire sauce, cornstarch, paprika, chili powder, salt, pepper and remaining water. Simmer, uncovered, for 1 hour, stirring occasionally. Add liquid smoke; mix well. Drain drippings from Dutch oven. Pour sauce over meat. Cover and bake 1-2 hours longer or until meat is tender. **Yield:** 6-8 servings. ***Editor's Note:** This is a fresh beef brisket, not corned beef.

Special Potato Salad

Vinegar and yogurt give this salad a refreshing tang that's unlike typical potato salads with heavy creamy dressings. My family loves the crispness of the onion and celery, and the heartiness that comes from the eggs and crumbled bacon.

```
2-1/2 pounds red potatoes
    2 tablespoons cider or red wine vinegar
    1 tablespoon olive or vegetable oil
    1 tablespoon Dijon mustard
  1/2 teaspoon dried basil
  1/2 teaspoon pepper
  1/4 teaspoon salt
  1/2 cup plain yogurt
  1/4 cup sour cream
    1 teaspoon garlic salt
  3/4 cup chopped red onion
  1/2 cup diced celery
    4 bacon strips, cooked and crumbled
    2 hard-cooked eggs, chopped
```

In a saucepan, cook potatoes in boiling salted water until tender. Meanwhile, in a large bowl, combine vinegar, oil, mustard, basil, pepper and salt; mix well. Drain potatoes; cut into 1-in. chunks and add to vinegar and oil mixture while still warm. Toss to coat; cool completely. In another bowl, combine yogurt, sour cream and garlic salt. Add onion, celery, bacon and eggs; mix well. Add to potato mixture; toss gently. Cover and chill for several hours. **Yield:** 6-8 servings.

cream in a meringue crust make each slice absolutely irresistible.

 1/2 **cup sugar,** *divided*
 1/4 **cup toasted slivered almonds, ground**
   2 **tablespoons cornstarch**
   2 **egg whites**
 1/8 **teaspoon cream of tartar**
SAUCE AND TOPPING:
 1/2 **cup sugar**
   1 **tablespoon cornstarch**
 1/3 **cup water**
   1 **pint fresh** *or* **frozen raspberries**
   1 **quart vanilla ice cream**
   2 **cups fresh mixed berries**

In a small bowl, combine 1/4 cup sugar, almonds and cornstarch; mix well. In a small mixing bowl, beat egg whites at high speed until foamy. Add cream of tartar; continue beating until soft peaks form. Gradually add remaining sugar; beat until stiff peaks form. Fold in almond mixture. Spread over the bottom and sides of a greased 9-in. pie plate. Bake at 275° for 1 to 1-1/2 hours or until light golden brown. Turn off oven; do not open door. Let cool in oven for 1 hour. Remove from oven and cool completely. Meanwhile, for sauce, combine sugar and cornstarch in a medium saucepan. Gradually stir in water; mix until smooth. Add raspberries; bring to a boil over medium heat, stirring constantly. Boil 1 minute or until thickened; set aside. Cool. To serve, scoop ice cream onto meringue; top with mixed berries and sauce. Serve immediately. Store leftovers in the freezer. **Yield:** 6-8 servings.

Layered Fruit Salad

This colorful salad is a real eye-catcher, and it tastes as good as it looks. Fresh fruit is always a welcome side dish with a summer meal. The addition of oranges and grapefruit gives this salad a different twist.

 1/2 **cup orange juice**
 1/4 **cup lemon juice**
 1/4 **cup packed brown sugar**
 1/2 **teaspoon grated orange peel**
 1/2 **teaspoon grated lemon peel**
   1 **cinnamon stick**
   2 **cups pineapple chunks**
   1 **cup seedless red grapes**
   2 **medium bananas, sliced**
   2 **medium oranges, peeled and sectioned**
   1 **medium grapefruit, peeled and sectioned**
   1 **pint strawberries, sliced**
   2 **kiwifruit, peeled and sliced**

In a medium saucepan, combine the first six ingredients; bring to a boil. Reduce heat; simmer, uncovered, for 5 minutes. Remove from the heat; cool completely. Meanwhile, layer fruit in a glass serving bowl. Remove cinnamon stick from the sauce; pour sauce over fruit. Cover and chill for several hours. **Yield:** 6-8 servings.

— 🥄 🥄 🥄 —

Meringue Berry Pie

A hot day calls for a cool dessert like this tempting pie. Fresh berries and a sweet raspberry sauce over ice

He treats his family to a Thanksgiving dinner that takes the turkey—and some heat!—out of the kitchen.

By Ken Churches, San Andreas, California

WHY DO I cook our Thanksgiving turkey on the grill? First, that makes it easier to accommodate the other foods that fill the oven.

Second, since traffic in the kitchen is usually congested, things are considerably cooler when the item that cooks the longest is parked on the patio.

My wife, Cindy, and our three children insist on adding a third reason to my delight. They believe the bird truly benefits from my special marinade.

My Marinated Thanksgiving Turkey is the result of experimenting and listening to comments from family and guests. When I got to the point that I received consistent compliments about its great flavor and juiciness, I decided I'd better write down the recipe.

A stuffed bird doesn't cook well on the grill. So I prepare my Unstuffing separately and cook it indoors. Italian sausage makes it extra hearty and zesty. The dressing's tasty anytime—I keep a plastic bag in the freezer to collect leftover bits and pieces of bread, and when the bag gets full, I make dressing!

In addition to mashed potatoes, I also fix Ken's Sweet Potatoes. Since I don't have much of a sweet tooth, I rarely fix sweet side dishes, but this traditional treat has appealing taste and color.

Fall Pear Pie showcases one of the many fruits our state grows so bountifully. Guests often say it's a delicious alternative to other holiday pies. An egg wash gives the crust a shine, and cream poured through slits in the top crust adds richness to the filling.

After savoring our holiday meal, we like to catch up on news of family and friends.

If you've never cooked a turkey on the grill, perhaps my recipe will tempt you to try—if not for Thanksgiving, maybe at some other time.

PICTURED AT LEFT: Marinated Thanksgiving Turkey, Unstuffing, Ken's Sweet Potatoes and Fall Pear Pie (recipes are on the next page).

Marinated Thanksgiving Turkey

My family enjoys this turkey because it cooks up tender, tasty and golden-brown. The marinade flavors the meat very well. I like grilling it since it adds that tempting barbecued flavor.

1-1/2 **cups chicken broth**
    2 **cups water**
    1 **cup soy sauce**
  2/3 **cup lemon juice**
    2 **garlic cloves, minced**
1-1/2 **teaspoons ground ginger**
    1 **teaspoon pepper**
    1 **turkey (12 to 13 pounds)**

Combine the first seven ingredients; reserve 1 cup for basting. Pour remaining marinade into a 2-gal. resealable plastic bag. Add the turkey and seal bag; turn to coat. Refrigerate overnight, turning several times. Drain and discard marinade. Heat grill according to manufacturer's directions for indirect cooking or roast in a conventional oven*. Tuck wings under turkey and place with breast side down on grill rack. Cover and grill for 1 hour. Add 10 briquettes to coals; turn the turkey breast side up. Brush with reserved marinade. Cover and cook for 2 hours, adding 10 briquettes to maintain heat and brushing with marinade every 30 minutes until meat thermometer reads 185°. Cover and let stand 20 minutes before carving. **Yield:** 8 servings. ***Conventional Roasting Method:** Place turkey on a rack in a large roaster. Bake, uncovered, at 325° for 4 to 4-1/2 hours or until meat thermometer reads 185°. Baste frequently with reserved marinade. When turkey begins to brown, cover lightly with a tent of aluminum foil.

Ken's Sweet Potatoes

This simple recipe turns plain sweet potatoes into a wonderful holiday side dish. The raisins add a nice touch, and the sweet syrup makes the potatoes taste extra-special.

    8 **medium sweet potatoes**
1-1/4 **cups packed brown sugar**
  1/2 **cup apple juice**
  1/2 **cup water**
  1/2 **cup raisins**
  1/4 **cup butter *or* margarine**

Cook and peel potatoes; allow to cool. Slice and place in a greased 2-1/2-qt. baking dish. In a small saucepan, combine remaining ingredients; bring to a boil, stirring frequently. Pour over the

potatoes. Bake, uncovered, at 350° for 45 minutes, basting occasionally. **Yield:** 8 servings.

— 🍽 🍽 🍽 —

Unstuffing

With sausage, mushrooms, celery and the perfect blend of seasonings, this moist dressing is irresistible. This recipe gets its name since it bakes separately from the turkey, which I do on the grill.

      1/2 **pound bulk Italian sausage**
      1/4 **cup butter *or* margarine**
      1/2 **pound fresh mushrooms, sliced**
      3/4 **cup chopped celery**
        1 **medium onion, chopped**
        1 **teaspoon poultry seasoning**
      1/2 **teaspoon salt**
      1/4 **teaspoon pepper**
        6 **cups unseasoned stuffing croutons *or* dry**
            bread cubes
2-1/2 to 3 **cups chicken broth**

In a large skillet, brown sausage; drain. Add butter, mushrooms, celery and onion; saute 2-3 minutes or until onion is tender. Stir in poultry seasoning, salt and pepper. Transfer to a large bowl; add croutons and enough broth to moisten. Place in a greased 2-qt. baking dish. Cover and bake at 350° for 30 minutes. Uncover and bake 10 minutes more. **Yield:** 8 servings.

Fall Pear Pie

A wide slice of this festive fruity pie is a great end to a delicious meal. The mellow flavor of pears is a refreshing alternative to the more common pies for the holidays. It's nice to serve a dessert that's a little unexpected.

    8 **cups thinly sliced peeled pears**
  3/4 **cup sugar**
  1/4 **cup quick-cooking tapioca**
  1/4 **teaspoon ground nutmeg**
Pastry for double-crust pie (9 inches)
    1 **egg, lightly beaten**
  1/4 **cup whipping cream, optional**

In a large bowl, combine pears, sugar, tapioca and nutmeg. Line a pie plate with bottom crust; add pear mixture. Roll out remaining pastry to fit top of pie; cut large slits in top. Place over filling; seal and flute edges. Brush with egg. Bake at 375° for 55-60 minutes or until the pears are tender. Remove to a wire rack. Pour cream through slits if desired. **Yield:** 8 servings.

Time's Ripe for Pears

You can't judge a pear by its color when it comes to ripeness. Bartletts will turn from green to yellow, but winter pears like Anjou, Bosc and Comice remain nearly the same shade. Instead, apply gentle pressure at the base of the stem. If it yields slightly, the pear is ripe and juicy. To speed ripening, store pears in a brown paper bag at room temperature.

Meals in Minutes

Mix and match these family-favorite recipes from fellow busy cooks to create countless meals that go from start to finish in less than 30 minutes.

＿＿ ☕ ☕ ☕ ＿＿

QUICK AND EASY. Clockwise from upper left: Oven Entree Blooms with Brief Recipes (p. 254), Fall Feast Will Harvest Compliments (p. 260), Hot Dogs with Fixin's Is a Grand-Slam Hit (p. 258) and Spicy Supper Kindles Family Memories (p. 252).

Delicious Dinner Warms Heart and Soul

IF HOLIDAY hustle and bustle keeps your time in the kitchen to a minimum, a satisfying fast-to-fix meal is the perfect gift to give yourself and your family!

The complete-meal menu here is made up of favorite recipes shared by three great cooks. You can have everything ready to serve in about 30 minutes.

Salisbury Steak is shared by Carol Callahan of Rome, Georgia. "This meat dish can be made in 25 minutes," she assures, "or made ahead and reheated with the gravy in the microwave."

Continues Carol, "I often double the recipe and freeze one batch of cooked steaks and gravy for an even faster meal on an especially busy night."

Quick Carrots is a versatile colorful side dish from Florence Jacoby. This Granite Falls, Minnesota cook reports that the carrots and green onions are a flavorful combination your family is sure to enjoy.

Banana Pudding Dessert comes from Hazel Merrill of Greenville, South Carolina. "This creamy dessert with mild banana taste is 'comfort food' that tastes like you fussed," Hazel says.

— 🥤 🥤 🥤 —

Salisbury Steak

☑ Uses less fat, sugar or salt. Includes Nutritional Analysis and Diabetic Exchanges.

   1 **egg white, lightly beaten**
1/3 **cup chopped onion**
1/4 **cup crushed saltines**
   2 **tablespoons milk**
   1 **tablespoon prepared horseradish**
1/4 **teaspoon salt, optional**
1/8 **teaspoon pepper**
   1 **pound lean ground beef**
   1 **jar (12 ounces) beef gravy**
1-1/4 **to 1-1/2 cups sliced fresh mushrooms**
   2 **tablespoons water**
Hot cooked noodles, optional

In a bowl, combine the egg white, onion, crumbs, milk, horseradish, salt if desired and pepper. Add beef; mix well. Shape into four oval patties. Fry in a skillet over medium heat for 10-12 minutes or until cooked through, turning once. Remove patties and keep warm. Add gravy, mushrooms and water to skillet; heat for 3-5 minutes. Serve over patties and noodles if desired. **Yield:** 4 servings. **Nutri-**

tional **Analysis:** One serving (prepared with low-fat gravy and skim milk and without salt or noodles) equals 248 calories, 205 mg sodium, 66 mg cholesterol, 9 gm carbohydrate, 25 gm protein, 12 gm fat. **Diabetic Exchanges:** 3 meat, 1/2 starch, 1/2 vegetable.

— 🥤 🥤 🥤 —

Quick Carrots

   2 **cups fresh *or* frozen sliced carrots**
   1 **tablespoon butter *or* margarine**
   2 **tablespoons sliced green onions**
   1 **tablespoon water**
1/4 **teaspoon salt**
Chopped fresh parsley

In a saucepan, combine the first five ingredients. Cover and simmer for 8-10 minutes or until the carrots are crisp-tender. Sprinkle with parsley. **Yield:** 4 servings.

— 🥤 🥤 🥤 —

Banana Pudding Dessert

1-1/4 **cups cold water**
   1 **can (14 ounces) sweetened condensed milk**
   1 **package (3.4 ounces) instant vanilla pudding mix**
   2 **cups whipped topping**
 24 **to 32 vanilla wafers**
   3 **large firm bananas, sliced**

In a large bowl, combine water, milk and pudding mix; beat on low speed for 2 minutes. Chill for 5 minutes. Fold in the whipped topping. In individual dessert dishes, layer wafers, pudding, bananas and more pudding. Top each with a wafer. Chill until serving. **Yield:** 6-8 servings.

Vivid Veggies

For lovely looking vegetable dishes, add a bit of vinegar to the water when cooking. This trick helps all vegetables keep their fresh, bright color.

Spicy Supper Kindles Family Memories

SPENDING TIME in the kitchen preparing an elaborate meal is a joyful task for those who love to cook. But some days you need to pull together a satisfying meal in just minutes.

You don't need to resort to frozen pizza or fast food when the clock is ticking closer to dinnertime. With these family favorites from three great cooks, a wholesome, hearty meal is within reach!

As an added bonus, you can have this complete meal ready to serve in about 30 minutes.

Quick Chili comes from Jean Ward of Montgomery, Texas, who's made this mild-tasting and hearty main dish for more than 30 years to the delight of her family and friends.

Canned soup and beans are the secrets to the recipe's rapid preparation. For even faster meal making, brown, drain and freeze the ground beef when time allows. When ready to use, just combine frozen cooked beef with the other ingredients and simmer as directed.

South-of-the-Border Sandwiches, shared by Karen Byrd of Las Vegas, Nevada, are fun and filling with a tasty combination of ingredients. "My mom and her dear friend, Betty, came up with this recipe many years ago, and I'm still using it," Karen relates. "Of course with seven kids in the family, Mom would have to double and sometimes triple the recipe!"

Adds Karen, "My mom grew up in Wisconsin. But after she and Dad moved here in the 1950's, she quickly learned from her mother-in-law how to prepare many Mexican dishes. In fact, I recall eating beans and tortillas almost every night with dinner."

Peanut Butter Sundaes are a peanutty change of pace from the traditional ice cream sundae with chocolate sauce, assures Susan Mowery of Newville, Pennsylvania. This delicious recipe proves that even a quick meal doesn't have to go without dessert.

A little bit of this sauce goes a long way to please every sweet tooth in your family. For a little variation, sprinkle some chocolate chips on top.

— 🥄 🥄 🥄 —

Quick Chili

☑ Uses less fat, sugar or salt. Includes Nutritional Analysis and Diabetic Exchanges.

1 pound ground beef
1 can (10-3/4 ounces) condensed tomato soup, undiluted
1 can (15 ounces) chili beans in gravy, undrained
2 to 3 teaspoons chili powder
1/2 cup water, optional

In a saucepan, brown the ground beef; drain. Add soup, beans and chili powder. Reduce heat. Cover and simmer for 20 minutes. Add water if a thinner soup is desired. **Yield:** 4 servings. **Nutritional Analysis:** One serving (prepared with lean ground beef and low-fat tomato soup) equals 344 calories, 341 mg sodium, 108 mg cholesterol, 24 gm carbohydrate, 31 gm protein, 5 gm fat. **Diabetic Exchanges:** 3 meat, 1-1/2 starch.

— 🥄 🥄 🥄 —

South-of-the-Border Sandwiches

2 hard-cooked eggs, chopped
1 tablespoon chopped green chilies
1/3 cup salsa
1 green onion, sliced
2 tablespoons sliced ripe olives
Dash *each* salt, pepper and ground cumin
1 cup (4 ounces) shredded cheddar cheese
4 French *or* submarine rolls, split

In a large bowl, mix eggs, chilies, salsa, onion, olives and seasonings. Fold in cheese. Spoon 1/2 cup onto bottom of rolls. Replace tops; wrap each sandwich tightly in foil. Bake at 350° for 20 minutes. **Yield:** 4 servings.

— 🥄 🥄 🥄 —

Peanut Butter Sundaes

1 cup sugar
1/2 cup water
1/2 cup creamy peanut butter
Vanilla ice cream
Salted peanuts, optional

In a saucepan, combine sugar and water. Bring to a boil; boil 1 minute or until sugar is dissolved. Remove from the heat; stir in peanut butter. Place in a blender; cover and blend on high until smooth. Cool slightly; pour over ice cream. Sprinkle with peanuts if desired. Refrigerate any leftovers. **Yield:** 1-1/2 cups sauce.

Oven Entree Blooms With Brief Recipes

AS WARM, mild weather beckons you and your family outdoors, even those who love to cook may not want to spend a lot of time in the kitchen. At times like that, you need a tasty menu you can pull together in just a matter of minutes!

The appealing meal here is made up of family-tested and -approved recipes from three time-conscious cooks. You can have everything ready to serve in about 30 minutes.

Special Pork Chops from LaDane Wilson have zesty flair and are a snap to prepare. "I work 9 hours a day, so I need delicious and simple recipes like this one," shares this Alexander City, Alabama cook. "My husband thinks I work hard fixing meals, but these chops are good and easy. In summer, I can my own salsa and use some to top these chops."

Golden Potatoes make even canned potatoes taste terrific. The cheesy seasoning creates a puffy golden coating, making these an attractive addition to the table. This fancy-looking side dish comes from Carla Cagle of Marceline, Missouri.

Broccoli-Mushroom Medley is a fresh flavorful vegetable dish shared by Cherie Sechrist of Red Lion, Pennsylvania. "People will think you fussed when you offer this elegant skillet side dish," Cherie says.

— 🍶 🍶 🍶 —

Special Pork Chops

6 to 8 boneless pork loin chops (1/3 inch thick)
1 tablespoon vegetable oil
1 jar (16 ounces) salsa

In an ovenproof skillet, brown the pork chops in oil; drain any fat. Pour salsa over chops. Bake, uncovered, at 350° for 25 minutes or until pork juices run clear. **Yield:** 4-6 servings.

— 🍶 🍶 🍶 —

Golden Potatoes

2 cans (16 ounces *each*) whole white potatoes, drained
1/4 cup butter *or* margarine, melted
1/2 teaspoon seasoned salt
2 to 3 tablespoons grated Parmesan cheese
1 tablespoon minced fresh parsley

Place potatoes in an ungreased 8-in. square baking dish. Pour butter over potatoes. Sprinkle with seasoned salt, cheese and parsley. Bake, uncovered, at 350° for 25 minutes or until lightly browned. **Yield:** 4-6 servings.

— 🍶 🍶 🍶 —

Broccoli-Mushroom Medley

☑ Uses less fat, sugar or salt. Includes Nutritional Analysis and Diabetic Exchanges.

1-1/2 pounds fresh broccoli, cut into florets
1 teaspoon lemon juice
1 teaspoon salt, optional
1 teaspoon sugar
1 teaspoon cornstarch
1/4 teaspoon ground nutmeg
1 cup sliced fresh mushrooms
1 medium onion, sliced into rings
1 to 2 garlic cloves, minced
3 tablespoons vegetable oil

Steam broccoli for 1-2 minutes or until crisp-tender. Rinse in cold water and set aside. In a bowl, combine lemon juice, salt if desired, sugar, cornstarch and nutmeg; set aside. In a large skillet or wok over high heat, stir-fry mushrooms, onion and garlic in oil for 3 minutes. Add broccoli and lemon juice mixture; stir-fry for 1-2 minutes. Serve immediately. **Yield:** 6 servings. **Nutritional Analysis:** One serving (prepared without salt) equals 88 calories, 22 mg sodium, 0 cholesterol, 10 gm carbohydrate, 4 gm protein, 5 gm fat. **Diabetic Exchanges:** 2 vegetable, 1 fat.

Bushel of Broccoli Tips

To select good broccoli, look for tight compact bud clusters with uniform dark green or purplish color. The stems should be tender, slightly moist and lighter green than the buds. Avoid clusters with soft or slippery spots.

For optimum flavor and nutrition, wash broccoli but don't soak it in water. Use fresh broccoli as soon as possible. To cook broccoli, use just a bit of water and a short cooking time for the best results.

Give Plain Spaghetti Dinner a Tasty Twist

THINK YOU can't serve your family a wholesome meal with an Italian twist because time in the kitchen is often too short? Put away that jar of prepared spaghetti sauce and think again!

It's easy to offer a homemade meal in minutes with these delicious dishes from three busy cooks. This quick menu goes from start to finish in less than 30 minutes!

Spaghetti with Sausage and Peppers comes from Ginger Harrell of El Dorado, Arkansas. "Smoked turkey sausage is a wonderful change of pace from traditional Italian sausage and ground beef sauces," relates Ginger. "And with fresh peppers and onion, this dish is not only quick, but economical, too."

While you likely don't have time to make bread from scratch on hurried days, you can dress up fresh store-brought bread in a jiffy with a few simple ingredients. "Slices of delicious Poppy Seed French Bread bake up crisp with a poppy seed and Parmesan cheese coating," informs Leavenworth, Washington cook Ruth Andrewson, who shares the recipe.

Strawberry Delight from Lyons, Georgia's Suzanne McKinely is a cool and creamy dessert that gets a head start with a purchased graham cracker crust.

"I often substitute other berries," Suzanne shares. "You can also use different pudding flavors."

— 🥤 🥤 🥤 —

Spaghetti with Sausage and Peppers

1 pound smoked turkey sausage, cut into 1/4-inch slices
2 medium green peppers, thinly sliced
2 medium sweet red peppers, thinly sliced
1 medium onion, halved and thinly sliced
2 cans (14-1/2 ounces *each*) diced tomatoes, undrained
3 garlic cloves, minced
6 to 8 drops hot pepper sauce
1 teaspoon paprika
1/2 teaspoon salt
1/4 teaspoon cayenne pepper
1/2 cup chicken broth
2 tablespoons cornstarch
1 package (12 ounces) spaghetti, cooked and drained

In a Dutch oven, brown sausage. Add peppers and onion; saute for 2 minutes. Add tomatoes, garlic, hot pepper sauce, paprika, salt and cayenne pepper; cook and stir until the vegetables are tender. Combine broth and cornstarch; add to sausage mixture. Bring to a boil. Cook and stir until thickened. Add spaghetti; cook for 5 minutes, stirring occasionally. **Yield:** 6-8 servings.

— 🥤 🥤 🥤 —

Poppy Seed French Bread

1/4 cup butter *or* margarine, softened
1/2 cup grated Parmesan cheese
1-1/2 tablespoons poppy seeds
8 slices French bread (1 inch thick)

Combine butter, Parmesan cheese and poppy seeds; spread on both sides of each piece of bread. Place on a baking sheet. Bake at 350° for 12-16 minutes, turning once. **Yield:** 6-8 servings.

— 🥤 🥤 🥤 —

Strawberry Delight

2 cups frozen whole strawberries, thawed
Red food coloring, optional
1 package (3.4 ounces) instant vanilla pudding mix
1 carton (12 ounces) frozen whipped topping, thawed
1 graham cracker crust (9 inches)
1/2 cup flaked coconut, toasted

In a mixing bowl, crush strawberries. Add food coloring if desired. Beat in pudding mix until smooth. Fold in whipped topping. Pour into crust; sprinkle with coconut. Chill until serving. Store leftovers in the refrigerator. **Yield:** 6-8 servings.

Toasting Coconut

Recipes often call for toasted coconut. To prepare, spread the flaked coconut on a baking sheet and bake at 350° until light golden brown, stirring often. Timing will depend on how finely the coconut is shredded and the weight of your baking pan. Generally coconut will toast in 6-10 minutes, but keep a close watch to prevent burning.

Hot Dogs with Fixin's Is A Grand-Slam Hit

WHETHER you're planning a gathering for friends before the big game or a family picnic in the backyard, keeping the kitchen cool during food preparation is key on warm summer days.

Of course, all that fresh air will likely build big appetites. So you need a fast-to-fix, nutritious meal that satisfies everyone.

The complete-meal menu here is made up of favorites from three great cooks, combined in our test kitchen. You can have everything ready to serve in only half an hour!

Chili Dogs made with a super zesty sauce are a fun summer main dish, says Linda Rainey from her Monahans, Texas home. "I got the recipe for the hearty sauce more than 20 years ago from an aunt who lived in Chicago," Linda comments. "We love it at home or on a picnic."

Vicky Rader of Mullinville, Kansas also shares an all-in-the-family favorite. "My aunt traveled the world over and brought the recipe for Tomato Avocado Salad back with her from the Middle East," relates Vicky. "It's so colorful and simple to make."

Lemonade Pie is a refreshing dessert perfect for a summer meal. From Wilma Rusk of Bringhurst, Indiana, this cool, creamy sweet/tart pie hits the spot on a hot day…and you don't have to heat the oven to make it! With its ease of preparation, this recipe is a great way to get kids helping in the kitchen.

Chili Dogs

- 1 pound ground beef
- 1 garlic clove, minced
- 1 cup tomato juice
- 1 can (6 ounces) tomato paste
- 2 tablespoons chili powder
- 1 teaspoon hot pepper sauce
- 1 teaspoon salt
- 1/4 teaspoon pepper
- 8 hot dogs, cooked
- 8 hot dog buns
Chopped onion and shredded cheddar cheese, optional

In a large skillet, brown beef and garlic; drain. Stir in next six ingredients. Simmer, uncovered, for 20 minutes. Serve over hot dogs on buns. Top with onion and cheese if desired. **Yield:** 8 servings.

Tomato Avocado Salad

- 2 ripe avocados, peeled and sliced
- 2 large tomatoes, cut into wedges
- 1 medium onion, cut into wedges
- 1 cup Italian salad dressing
Lettuce leaves, optional

In a bowl, combine the avocados, tomatoes and onion; add dressing and stir to coat. Chill for 20-30 minutes. Serve over lettuce if desired. **Yield:** 6-8 servings.

Lemonade Pie

- 1 can (14 ounces) sweetened condensed milk
- 3/4 cup lemonade concentrate
- 2 to 3 drops yellow food coloring, optional
- 1 carton (8 ounces) frozen whipped topping, thawed
- 1 graham cracker crust (8 inches)
Lemon slices and fresh mint, optional

In a large bowl, combine milk, lemonade and food coloring if desired. Fold in the whipped topping; spoon into crust. Chill until serving. If desired, garnish with lemon slices and mint. **Yield:** 6-8 servings.

Avocado Advice

When purchasing avocados, think about how you'll be using them. If you'll be slicing and chopping them, look for ripe avocados that are slightly firm. If you'll be mashing the pulp, select very ripe avocados that feel soft. Avoid bruised fruit.

Refrigerate avocados and use within a few days after they're first purchased. To speed the ripening process of very firm avocados, place them in a brown paper bag.

To seed an avocado, cut lengthwise through the fruit around the seed. Separate the halves by twisting them in opposite directions; remove seed. Peel each half and slice. Or scoop out the pulp.

Fall Feast Will Harvest Compliments

WHEN cooler days signal the start of the busy pre-holiday season, even dedicated cooks can't always spend as much time as usual in the kitchen. Then hearty, fast-to-fix meals come in handy.

The complete-meal menu here is made up of favorites from three busy cooks, combined in our test kitchen. You can have everything ready to serve in only half an hour!

Turkey in Curry Sauce is a delicious fall entree with a hint of curry flavor and crunchy nuts. "You can whip up this main dish in just minutes using leftover turkey," reports Lucile Proctor of Panguitch, Utah.

Peas with Mushrooms, from Mary Dennis of Bryan, Ohio, is a savory side dish with a fresh taste, even though it calls for convenient frozen peas.

Rich Chocolate Mousse will get raves for its big chocolate taste. The recipe comes from Florence Palmer of Marshall, Illinois, who remarks, "I love to serve this impressive dessert because people think I went to a lot of trouble. Actually, it's easy to make."

Turkey in Curry Sauce

1/2 cup chopped onion
1/4 cup butter *or* margarine
1/4 cup all-purpose flour
1 can (14-1/2 ounces) chicken broth
1 cup half-and-half cream
2 to 3 teaspoons curry powder
2 cups diced cooked turkey
2 tablespoons chopped pimientos
Hot cooked rice
1/2 cup chopped peanuts

In a saucepan, saute onion in butter until tender. Add flour to form a smooth paste. Gradually stir in broth; bring to a boil. Boil for 1-2 minutes or until thickened. Reduce heat. Add half-and-half cream and curry; mix well. Add turkey; heat through. Stir in pimientos. Serve over rice; sprinkle with peanuts. **Yield:** 4 servings.

Peas with Mushrooms

✓ Uses less fat, sugar or salt. Includes Nutritional Analysis and Diabetic Exchanges.

1/2 pound fresh mushrooms, sliced
2 tablespoons sliced green onions
1 tablespoon butter *or* margarine
1/4 teaspoon dried marjoram
1/4 teaspoon salt, optional
1/8 teaspoon pepper
Dash ground nutmeg
1 package (10 ounces) frozen peas, cooked

In a skillet over medium heat, saute the mushrooms and onions in butter for 3-5 minutes. Add marjoram, salt if desired, pepper and nutmeg; mix well. Add peas and heat through. **Yield:** 4 servings. **Nutritional Analysis:** One serving (prepared with margarine and without added salt) equals 95 calories, 117 mg sodium, 0 cholesterol, 10 gm carbohydrate, 4 gm protein, 3 gm fat. **Diabetic Exchanges:** 1 vegetable, 1/2 starch, 1/2 fat.

Rich Chocolate Mousse

8 squares (1 ounce *each*) semisweet chocolate
3 tablespoons confectioners' sugar
3 tablespoons hot strong coffee
3 egg yolks
1 carton (8 ounces) frozen whipped topping, thawed, *divided*

In a double boiler over simmering water, melt chocolate. Remove top pan from heat; stir in sugar and coffee. Add one yolk at a time, stirring until smooth. Place top pan over boiling water; cook and stir for 3-4 minutes or until thick. Pour into bowl; chill 6-8 minutes. Fold in 3 cups whipped topping. Spoon into dishes. Top with remaining whipped topping. **Yield:** 4 servings.

Poultry Pointers

The next time you roast a whole turkey or turkey breast, set aside 2 cups diced, cooked meat for this meal. Let cool completely and place in an airtight container. To prevent the turkey from drying out, cover with a damp paper towel; refrigerate for 3 to 4 days. For longer storage, freeze up to 3 months.

Meals on a Budget

With these six economical entrees, you can serve your family wholesome, hearty meals for just pennies a person.

FRUGAL AND FLAVORFUL. Clockwise from upper left: Ham Loaves, Au Gratin Potatoes and Orange Buttermilk Salad (p. 266); Chicken Rice Casserole, Homemade Seasoned Rice Mix and Soft Breadsticks (p. 264); Hearty Minestrone, Pop-Up Rolls and Apple Nut Crunch (p. 274); Budget Macaroni and Cheese, Vegetable Salad and Great-Grandma's Ginger Cake (p. 268).

Feed Your Family for $1.09 a Plate!

EVEN at today's prices, you can feed your family for just pennies a person.

The frugal yet flavorful meal here is from two great cooks, who estimate the total cost at just $1.09 per setting.

In fact, the Chicken Rice Casserole main course—from Marcia Hostetter of Canton, New York—can be doubly thrifty because of the Homemade Seasoned Rice Mix. After using the cup of it the casserole calls for, you can use the remainder of the rice mix as a gift for family and friends (as in the photo at right) or as a side dish with meat another day.

Soft Breadsticks come from Hazel Fritchie of Palestine, Illinois, who's been making them for 30 years.

— 🏆 🏆 🏆 —

Homemade Seasoned Rice Mix

    3 **cups uncooked long grain rice**
    6 **teaspoons chicken bouillon granules**
 1/4 **cup dried parsley flakes**
    2 **teaspoons onion powder**
 1/2 **teaspoon garlic powder**
 1/4 **teaspoon dried thyme**

Combine all ingredients in a storage container with a tight-fitting lid. **Yield:** 3-1/2 cups. **Editor's Note:** To prepare rice as a side dish, combine 2 cups water and 1 tablespoon butter in a saucepan; bring to a boil. Stir in 1 cup mix. Reduce heat; cover and simmer for 15-20 minutes. **Yield:** 6 servings.

— 🏆 🏆 🏆 —

Chicken Rice Casserole

2-1/2 cups cubed cooked chicken
1-1/2 cups frozen mixed vegetables
    1 cup Homemade Seasoned Rice Mix
       (recipe above)
 1/2 cup chopped onion
    1 can (4 ounces) mushroom stems and
       pieces, drained
    1 can (10-3/4 ounces) condensed cream of
       chicken soup, undiluted

    2 cups water
 1/4 teaspoon onion salt
 1/4 teaspoon dried thyme
 1/4 cup crushed potato chips

In a greased 2-qt. casserole, combine chicken, vegetables, rice mix, onion and mushrooms. Combine soup, water, onion salt and thyme; mix well. Pour over the rice mixture; stir. Cover and bake at 375° for 55-65 minutes or until the rice is tender, stirring occasionally. Sprinkle with potato chips. **Yield:** 6 servings.

— 🏆 🏆 🏆 —

Soft Breadsticks

(Also pictured on front cover)

1 package (1/4 ounce) active dry yeast
1 cup warm water (110° to 115°)
3 tablespoons sugar
1 teaspoon salt
1/4 cup vegetable oil
3 cups all-purpose flour
Cornmeal
1 egg white
1 tablespoon water
Coarse salt, optional

In a mixing bowl, dissolve yeast in water. Add sugar, salt and oil; stir until dissolved. Add 2 cups of flour; beat until smooth. Add enough remaining flour to form a soft dough. Turn onto a floured surface; knead until smooth and elastic, about 6-8 minutes. Place in a greased bowl, turning once to grease top. Cover and let rise in a warm place until doubled, about 1 hour. Punch dough down and divide into 12 portions. Roll each portion into a 10-in. x 1/2-in. strip. Place 1 in. apart on a greased baking sheet sprinkled with cornmeal. Let rise, uncovered, until doubled, about 45-60 minutes. Beat egg white and water; brush over breadsticks. Sprinkle with coarse salt if desired. Place baking sheet on middle rack of oven; place a large shallow pan filled with boiling water on lowest rack. Bake at 400° for 10 minutes. Brush again with egg white. Bake 5 minutes more or until golden brown. **Yield:** 1 dozen. **Nutritional Analysis:** One breadstick (prepared without coarse salt) equals 178 calories, 194 mg sodium, 0 cholesterol, 29 gm carbohydrate, 4 gm protein, 5 gm fat. **Diabetic Exchanges:** 2 starch, 1 fat.

Feed Your Family for $1.42 a Plate!

WHEN feeding a hungry horde, meat-and-potatoes meals are the mouth-watering mainstays in kitchens across the country.

Just ask Carol Van Sickle, the Versailles, Kentucky cook who often puts together this low-budget menu for a group of family and friends.

With the hearty ingredients packed into every bite, it will surely satisfy hungry appetites. But best of all, Carol estimates that this economical dinner costs just $1.42 per setting.

Ham Loaves are a delicious way to dress up ham, and they also freeze well. Au Gratin Potatoes are real comfort food with their creamy cheese sauce. For a refreshing, slightly sweet side dish, Carol serves Orange Buttermilk Salad.

"Most everything in this meal can be prepared the day ahead, so I can enjoy the meal with no last-minute fuss in the kitchen," adds Carol. She and her husband are originally from Pennsylvania and have two grown daughters.

This satisfying spread goes to show you don't have to forgo flavor when eating inexpensively.

Ham Loaves

- 4 eggs, lightly beaten
- 1 cup milk
- 4 cups dry bread crumbs
- 2 pounds ground pork
- 2 pounds ground fully cooked ham
- 1-1/2 cups packed brown sugar
- 3/4 cup water
- 1/2 cup vinegar
- 1 teaspoon ground mustard

In a bowl, combine eggs, milk and crumbs. Add pork and ham; mix well. Shape into 12 ovals, using 1 cup of mixture for each. Place in an ungreased 15-in. x 10-in. x 1-in. baking pan. Combine brown sugar, water, vinegar and mustard; pour over the loaves. Bake, uncovered, at 350° for 1 hour and 15 minutes or until a meat thermometer reads 160-170°, basting every 15-20 minutes. **Yield:** 12 servings.

Au Gratin Potatoes

- 8 cups cubed peeled potatoes
- 1/4 cup butter *or* margarine
- 2 tablespoons all-purpose flour
- 3/4 teaspoon salt
- 1/8 teaspoon pepper
- 1-1/2 cups milk
- 1 pound process American cheese, cubed
Minced fresh parsley

In a large saucepan, cook potatoes in boiling water until tender. Drain and place in a greased 2-1/2-qt. baking dish. In a saucepan, melt butter. Add the flour, salt and pepper; stir to form a smooth paste. Gradually add milk, stirring constantly. Bring to a

boil; boil and stir for 1 minute. Add cheese; stir just until melted. Pour over potatoes. Cover and bake at 350° for 45-50 minutes or until bubbly. Sprinkle with parsley. **Yield:** 12 servings.

Orange Buttermilk Salad

1 **can (20 ounces) crushed pineapple, undrained**
1 **package (6 ounces) orange gelatin**
2 **cups buttermilk**
1 **carton (8 ounces) frozen whipped topping, thawed**

In a saucepan, bring pineapple to a boil. Remove from the heat; add gelatin and stir until dissolved. Add buttermilk and mix well. Cool to room temperature. Fold in whipped topping. Pour into an 11-in. x 7-in. x 2-in. dish. Refrigerate several hours or overnight. Cut into squares. **Yield:** 12 servings.

"Buttermilk" Made Easy

As a substitute for each cup of buttermilk, place 1 tablespoon of lemon juice or vinegar in a measuring cup. Add milk to measure 1 cup. Let stand for 5 minutes before using in the recipe.

Feed Your Family for $1.37 a Plate!

AFTER a long day, there's nothing like sitting down to an old-fashioned, down-home dinner featuring flavorful "comfort" foods.

Three busy cooks show how easy it is to assemble a million-dollar meal for just $1.37 per person.

Budget Macaroni and Cheese is a quick and creamy main dish shared by Debbie Carlson of San Diego, California. "I've tried many macaroni and cheese recipes, but this is my favorite," she says.

Vegetable Salad from Pat Scott of Delray Beach, Florida is a super combination of crunchy fresh vegetables coated with a tangy marinade.

Even a budget meal can include dessert, points out Teresa Pelkey of Cherry Valley, Massachusetts, who sent her old-fashioned recipe for Great-Grandma's Ginger Cake.

Budget Macaroni and Cheese

- 1 package (7 ounces) elbow macaroni
- 3 tablespoons butter *or* margarine
- 3 tablespoons all-purpose flour
- 1/4 teaspoon salt
- Dash pepper
- 1 cup milk
- 1 cup (4 ounces) shredded cheddar cheese

Cook the macaroni according to package directions. Drain; set aside and keep warm. In a saucepan over medium-low heat, melt butter. Add flour, salt and pepper; stir to make a smooth paste. Gradually add milk, stirring constantly. Heat and stir until thickened. Remove from the heat; stir in cheese until melted. Pour over macaroni and mix well. **Yield:** 4 servings.

Vegetable Salad

- 2 cups broccoli florets
- 2 cups cauliflowerets
- 4 large mushrooms, sliced
- 1 celery rib, sliced

- 1 medium green *or* sweet red pepper, diced
- 1/4 cup chopped onion
- 1/3 cup vegetable oil
- 1/4 cup sugar
- 1/4 cup vinegar
- 1/4 teaspoon salt
- 1-1/2 teaspoons poppy seeds

In a large bowl, combine all of the vegetables. Combine remaining ingredients in a jar with tight-fitting lid; shake well. Pour over vegetables and toss. Cover and chill 6-8 hours. **Yield:** 4 servings.

Great-Grandma's Ginger Cake

2-1/4 cups all-purpose flour
   1 teaspoon baking soda
   1 teaspoon ground ginger
   1 teaspoon ground cinnamon
 1/2 teaspoon salt
Dash ground cloves
 1/2 cup sugar
 1/2 cup shortening
 2/3 cup molasses
   1 egg
 3/4 cup boiling water
Whipped topping

Combine flour, baking soda, ginger, cinnamon, salt and cloves; set aside. In a mixing bowl, cream sugar and shortening; beat in molasses and egg. Stir in the dry ingredients alternately with water; mix well. Pour into a greased 9-in. square baking pan. Bake at 350° for 35-40 minutes. Cool completely. Cut into squares; top with a dollop of whipped topping. Leftovers will keep several days in an airtight container. **Yield:** 9 servings.

Feed Your Family for $1.33 a Plate!

EAT WELL economically at today's prices? You can! Three great cooks will help you plan a penny-pinching pizza party for your family, friends or a bunch of hungry kids.

This savory Italian-style supper can be prepared for just $1.33 per setting.

Homemade Pizza, a hearty, zesty main dish with a crisp, golden crust, is shared by Marianne Edwards of Lake Stevens, Washington. Feel free to use whatever toppings your family enjoys.

Italian Salad from Regina Bianchi of Bessemer, Pennsylvania is super for summer with a light dressing and a nice combination of fresh ingredients.

Even an inexpensive meal doesn't have to go without dessert, points out Leona Luecking of West Burlington, Iowa, who sends her extra-easy recipe for Berries in Custard Sauce.

—— 🝞 🝞 🝞 ——

Homemade Pizza

     1 package (1/4 ounce) active dry yeast
     1 teaspoon sugar
1-1/4 cups warm water (110° to 115°)
   1/4 cup vegetable oil
     1 teaspoon salt
3-1/2 cups all-purpose flour
   1/2 pound ground beef
     1 small onion, chopped
     1 can (15 ounces) tomato sauce
     1 tablespoon dried oregano
     1 teaspoon dried basil
     1 medium green pepper, diced
     2 cups (8 ounces) shredded mozzarella
       cheese

In large bowl, dissolve yeast and sugar in water; let stand for 5 minutes. Add oil and salt. Stir in flour, a cup at a time, to form soft dough. Turn onto a floured surface; knead until smooth and elastic, about 2-3 minutes. Place in greased bowl, turning once to grease top. Cover and let rise in a warm place until doubled, about 45 minutes. Meanwhile, brown beef and onion; drain. Punch dough down; divide in half. Press each into a greased 12-in.

pizza pan. Combine the tomato sauce, oregano and basil; spread over each crust. Top with beef mixture, green pepper and cheese. Bake at 400° for 25-30 minutes or until crust is lightly browned. **Yield:** 2 pizzas (6 servings).

—— 🝞 🝞 🝞 ——

Italian Salad

1/2 cup olive *or* vegetable oil
1/4 cup cider *or* red wine vinegar
  2 garlic cloves, minced
  1 teaspoon sugar
1/2 teaspoon dried oregano
1/2 teaspoon salt

1/4 teaspoon pepper
1 small head lettuce, torn
1/2 cup sliced green onions
1/2 cup chopped celery
1/2 cup shredded mozzarella cheese
1 can (2-1/4 ounces) sliced ripe olives, drained
1 medium tomato, cut into wedges
2 tablespoons shredded Parmesan cheese

In a jar with tight-fitting lid, combine the first seven ingredients; shake well and set aside. In a large bowl, combine lettuce, onions, celery, mozzarella cheese, olives and tomato. Just before serving, add the dressing and toss. Sprinkle with Parmesan cheese. **Yield:** 6 servings.

Berries in Custard Sauce

1 cup milk
1 egg, lightly beaten
2 tablespoons sugar
Pinch salt
1/2 teaspoon vanilla extract
3 cups fresh blueberries, raspberries and strawberries

In saucepan, scald milk. Combine egg and sugar in a bowl; stir in small amount of hot milk. Return all to saucepan. Cook over low heat, stirring constantly, until mixture thickens slightly and coats a spoon, about 15 minutes. Remove from heat; stir in salt and vanilla. Chill at least 1 hour. Serve over berries. **Yield:** 6 servings.

Feed Your Family for $1.35 a Plate!

WHETHER she's looking to prepare an everyday meal for family or a special-occasion supper for friends, Norma Erne of Albuquerque, New Mexico reaches for this delicious dinner that's fit for a king.

But don't think you have to break the bank to prepare this flavor-filled, frugal meal in your own kitchen. That's because Norma estimates a mere cost of just $1.35 per setting.

Individual Meat Loaves are a fun way to serve an old standby. Says Norma, "I've made this hearty entree many times over the years, and it's always so good." Plus, these single-serving loaves bake much faster than one large loaf.

Zucchini Corn Medley, with its creamy cheese sauce and zippy taste, turns abundant garden vegetables into a comforting side dish.

Spiced Peaches are a delightful end to this delicious meal. "This is a super summer dessert because peaches are plentiful. The sweet chilled fruit topped with sour cream and brown sugar is so refreshing," Norma assures. When fresh peaches aren't available, use canned peach halves with tasty results.

Individual Meat Loaves

1 can (5 ounces) evaporated milk
1 egg, lightly beaten
3/4 cup quick-cooking oats
1/4 cup chopped onion
1 teaspoon salt
1/4 teaspoon pepper
1-1/2 pounds ground beef
1/3 cup ketchup
1 tablespoon brown sugar
1 tablespoon prepared mustard

In a bowl, combine the first six ingredients. Add beef and mix well. Shape into six loaves, about 4 in. x 2-1/2 in. Place in an ungreased 13-in. x 9-in. x 2-in. baking dish. Combine ketchup, sugar and mustard; spoon over loaves. Bake, uncovered, at 350° for 35-45 minutes or until a meat thermometer reads 160° and no pink remains. **Yield:** 6 servings.

Zucchini Corn Medley

5 medium zucchini, cut into 1/2-inch chunks
1/2 cup water
1/2 teaspoon salt
1 package (10 ounces) frozen corn
1 can (4 ounces) chopped green chilies
2 tablespoons butter *or* margarine
2 tablespoons all-purpose flour
1/4 teaspoon ground mustard
1/4 teaspoon salt
1/4 teaspoon pepper
1 cup milk
1/2 cup shredded sharp cheddar cheese

In a saucepan over medium heat, cook zucchini

in water and salt until just tender, about 6 minutes. Add corn; cook for 1 minute. Drain. Stir in chilies; pour into a greased 1-1/2-qt. shallow baking dish. Melt butter in a saucepan; stir in flour and seasonings until smooth and bubbly. Stir in milk; bring to a boil, stirring constantly. Boil 3-4 minutes or until thickened. Remove from the heat and stir in cheese until melted. Pour over vegetables. Bake, uncovered, at 350° for 20 minutes or until bubbly. **Yield:** 6 servings.

— 🥤 🥤 🥤 —

Spiced Peaches

1/2 cup sugar

1/2 cup water
1/4 cup vinegar
8 to 10 whole cloves
1 cinnamon stick
6 fresh peaches, peeled and halved
1/2 cup sour cream
2 tablespoons brown sugar

In a large saucepan, bring the first five ingredients to a boil. Reduce heat; simmer for 10 minutes. Add peaches; simmer for about about 10 minutes or until heated through. Discard cinnamon stick; pour into a shallow baking dish. Cover and chill 8 hours or overnight. Drain. Spoon peaches into serving dishes; garnish with a dollop of sour cream and sprinkle with brown sugar. **Yield:** 6 servings.

Feed Your Family for 80¢ a Plate!

DINNER for less than a buck? Three budget-conscious cooks prove that it's amazing but true! They estimate that the total cost for the "soup"-er supper featured here is just 80¢ per serving.

Hearty Minestrone is a fresh-tasting main dish that gets its zesty flavor from Italian sausage. "When you want to use up your garden bounty of zucchini, try this soup," advises Victor, New York cook Donna Smith. If your family likes food extra spicy, use hot bulk Italian sausage instead.

For lightly sweet, biscuit-like rolls that are anything but dry, you can't beat simple Pop-Up Rolls. "With just four basic ingredients that are mixed in one bowl, they're so easy to make," assures Judi Brinegar of Liberty, North Carolina.

Even an inexpensive meal doesn't have to go without a delectable dessert. Hazel Fritchie of Palestine, Illinois shares an old family recipe for Apple Nut Crunch, which smells wonderful as it bakes.

Hearty Minestrone

- 1 pound bulk Italian sausage
- 2 cups sliced celery
- 1 cup chopped onion
- 6 cups chopped zucchini
- 1 can (28 ounces) diced tomatoes, undrained
- 1-1/2 cups chopped green pepper
- 1-1/2 teaspoons Italian seasoning
- 1-1/2 teaspoons salt
- 1 teaspoon dried oregano
- 1 teaspoon sugar
- 1/2 teaspoon dried basil
- 1/4 teaspoon garlic powder

In a large saucepan, brown the sausage. Remove with a slotted spoon to paper towel to drain, reserving 1 tablespoon of drippings. Saute celery and onion in the drippings for 5 minutes. Add sausage and remaining ingredients; bring to a boil. Reduce heat; cover and simmer for 20-30 minutes or until the vegetables are tender. **Yield:** 9 servings.

Pop-Up Rolls

- 1-1/2 cups self-rising flour*
- 3/4 cup milk
- 3 tablespoons sugar
- 1-1/2 tablespoons mayonnaise

In a bowl, stir together all ingredients until thoroughly combined. Fill greased muffin cups half full. Bake at 375° for 18-20 minutes or until lightly browned. **Yield:** 9 rolls. ***Editor's Note:** As a substitute for *each* cup of self-rising flour, place 1-1/2 teaspoons baking powder and 1/2 teaspoon salt in a measuring cup. Add all-purpose flour to measure 1 cup. For 1/2 cup self-rising flour, place 3/4 teaspoon

baking powder and 1/4 teaspoon salt in a measuring cup. Add all-purpose flour to measure 1/2 cup.

—— 🥤 🥤 🥤 ——

Apple Nut Crunch

1 egg
3/4 cup sugar
1/3 cup all-purpose flour
1 teaspoon baking powder
1/8 teaspoon ground cinnamon
1/2 cup chopped peeled apple
1/2 cup chopped walnuts
1 teaspoon vanilla extract
2-1/4 cups ice cream

In a mixing bowl, beat the egg. Combine sugar, flour, baking powder and cinnamon. Add to egg; beat until smooth. Fold in apple, nuts and vanilla. Spoon into a greased 8-in. square baking pan. Bake at 350° for 25-30 minutes or until cake tests done. Cool. Serve with ice cream. **Yield:** 9 servings.

Out of Batter?

If all muffin cups aren't filled with batter, fill the empty ones with some water to ensure even baking.

Getting in the Theme of Things

These fun and flavor-filled meals–featuring theme-related menus, decorating ideas and activities—will make your galas grand.

———— 🍴 🍴 🍴 ————

PARTYTIME PLANS. Clockwise from upper left: Brunch Helps Welcome Bundle of Joy (p. 284), Southwest Fare Sets Fiesta Mood (p. 288), Fishy Celebration Reels in Finny Fun (p. 286) and Spring into "Carrot Patch" Menu (p. 282).

Let It Snow at Cheery Winter Party

By Lynne Peterson, Salt Lake City, Utah

January has always been a bit of a letdown for me—holiday festivities are over, decorations are put away and life quiets down…sometimes too much!

So I decided to brighten up the dark wintry month with a "Let It Snow" theme dinner party.

Planning to entertain four couples my husband and I enjoy spending time with turned out to be a boost for my morale. Plus, our guests said they were delighted to be invited out at a time of year when many people are "holed up"!

I summoned our guests with homemade invitations featuring a smiling snowman and "Let It Snow" on the front, and details of the time and place inside.

An assortment of cute snowmen figures I'd made or

collected formed centerpieces. At each place, I tucked a napkin and the silverware into a colorful knit glove and set a favor of a felt snowman holding a roll of wintergreen Life Savers. Later, I gave the men the snowmen and the women a pair of gloves to take home.

Beginning with a shrimp cocktail, the meal I served was elegant but easy. Cheese soup warmed our palates for the main course of Chicken Kiev.

Along with the chicken, I served mixed vegetables and homemade spinach noodles. You could substitute purchased noodles or another side dish.

As I mixed up my grandmother's Buttery Crescents earlier on the day of the party, memories of her teaching me to make them brightened my kitchen.

For a dessert that looked frosty but didn't make us shiver, I settled on festive Snowflake Cake.

Planning a polar party and spending a warm evening with friends really took the chill off the post-holiday season for me. I hope these ideas and recipes do the same for you!

— 🥄 🥄 🥄 —

Chicken Kiev

A favorite aunt shared this special recipe with me. It makes attractive individual servings.

      1/4 **cup butter** *or* **margarine, softened**
        1 **tablespoon grated onion**
        1 **tablespoon minced fresh parsley**
      1/2 **teaspoon garlic powder**
      1/2 **teaspoon dried tarragon**
      1/4 **teaspoon pepper**
        6 **boneless skinless chicken breast halves**
        1 **egg**
        1 **tablespoon milk**
        1 **envelope seasoned chicken coating mix**

Combine butter, onion, parsley, garlic powder, tarragon and pepper. Shape mixture into six pencil-thin strips about 2 in. long; place on waxed paper. Freeze until firm, about 30 minutes. Flatten each chicken breast to 1/4 in. Place one butter strip in the center of each chicken breast. Fold long sides over butter; fold ends up and secure with a toothpick. In a bowl, beat egg and milk; place coating mix in another bowl. Dip chicken in milk, then roll in coating mix. Place chicken, seam side down, in a greased 13-in. x 9-in. x 2-in. baking pan. Bake, uncovered, at 425° for 35-40 minutes or until juices run clear. Remove toothpicks before serving. **Yield:** 6 servings.

— 🥄 🥄 🥄 —

Buttery Crescents

My grandmother taught me how to make these rolls when I was a new bride.

        2 **packages (1/4 ounce** *each***) active dry yeast**
        2 **cups warm milk (110° to 115°)**
    6-1/2 **to 7 cups all-purpose flour**
        2 **eggs, lightly beaten**
      1/4 **cup butter** *or* **margarine, melted and cooled**
        3 **tablespoons sugar**
        1 **teaspoon salt**
    Additional melted butter *or* **margarine, optional**

In a large mixing bowl, dissolve yeast in milk. Add 4 cups flour, eggs, butter, sugar and salt; beat until smooth. Add enough remaining flour to form a soft dough. Turn onto a floured surface; knead until smooth and elastic, about 6-8 minutes. Place in a greased bowl, turning once to grease top. Cover and let rise in a warm place until doubled, about 1 hour. Punch the dough down and divide into thirds. Roll each portion into a 12-in. circle; cut each circle into 12 wedges. Roll up wedges from the wide end and place with pointed end down on greased baking sheets. Cover and let rise until doubled, about 30 minutes. Bake at 400° for 12-14 minutes or until golden brown. Brush with butter if desired. **Yield:** 3 dozen.

— 🥄 🥄 🥄 —

Snowflake Cake

The coconut sprinkled on this old-fashioned white cake gives the impression of fresh snow.

        2 **eggs plus 4 egg yolks**
    1-1/2 **cups sugar**
        1 **cup milk**
      1/2 **cup butter** *or* **margarine**
    2-1/2 **cups all-purpose flour**
        1 **tablespoon baking powder**
        1 **teaspoon vanilla extract**
      1/2 **cup chopped nuts, optional**
    FROSTING:
    1-3/4 **cups sugar**
      1/2 **cup water**
        4 **egg whites**
      1/2 **teaspoon cream of tartar**
        1 **teaspoon vanilla extract**
        2 **cups flaked coconut**

In a mixing bowl, beat eggs, yolks and sugar until light and fluffy, about 5 minutes. In a saucepan, heat milk and butter until butter is melted. Combine flour and baking powder; add to egg mixture alternately with milk mixture. Beat until well mixed. Add vanilla. Fold in nuts if desired. Pour into three greased 9-in. round baking pans. Bake at 350° for 15-18 minutes or until cakes test done. Cool in pans 10 minutes before removing to a wire rack to cool completely. For frosting, in a saucepan, bring sugar and water to a boil. Boil 3-4 minutes or until a candy thermometer reads 242° (firm-ball stage). Meanwhile, beat egg whites and cream of tartar in a mixing bowl until foamy. Slowly pour in hot sugar mixture and continue to beat on high for 6-8 minutes or until stiff peaks form. Add vanilla. Frost the tops of two cake layers and sprinkle with coconut; stack on a cake plate with plain layer on top. Frost sides and top of cake; sprinkle with coconut. Refrigerate for several hours. **Yield:** 12-16 servings.

Put on the Green for St. Pat's Day

By Gloria Warczak, Cedarburg, Wisconsin

Celebrating St. Patrick's Day with festive food served at a gaily decorated table is a good way to chase away any late-winter doldrums!

In the past, we've had guests arrive at our annual Irish theme party with a case of the "blahs". But after an evening of fun, food and music, they left smiling.

I set my St. Patrick's Day table with a white tablecloth and kelly-green runners. Paper napkins and holiday paper plates add green to each place setting.

The chandelier is decked with a foil shamrock garland. I sprinkle foil clovers across the tablecloth and glue others to white index cards as place cards.

A green glass bowl holds my centerpiece of green and white silk roses, green and white paper carnations and glittery shamrocks.

After our guests arrive, we toast the occasion with sparkling Leprechaun Lime Punch. Later, with Irish music playing in the background, I serve an authentic Irish menu.

The tender, flavorful corned beef is complemented by a colorful medley of vegetables in addition to the traditional cabbage. Husband Pat and I have a large garden and love fresh vegetables.

If you've never made Irish Soda Bread, you'll be pleasantly surprised how easy it is to mix up and shape this raisin-studded loaf.

Shamrock Pie is actually a lemon meringue pie—a few drops of green food coloring transform its color. It's a refreshing dessert no matter the season.

Our guests tell me it's no blarney that my efforts to set the holiday theme make these tried-and-true favorites taste even better.

I like to believe that's true and hope that my ideas might bring a little luck o' the Irish to your table.

—— ☕ ☕ ☕ ——

Leprechaun Lime Punch

With sherbet, soda and a blend of juices, this punch is a refreshing way to welcome folks into your home.

      1 can (46 ounces) lime citrus drink
      2 cans (12 ounces *each*) frozen limeade concentrate, thawed
  1/4 cup sugar
  1/4 cup lime juice
      1 carton (1 quart) lime sherbet, softened
      1 bottle (2 liters) white soda
Lime slices, optional

In a punch bowl, combine citrus drink, limeade, sugar, lime juice and sherbet; stir until smooth and sugar is dissolved. Add soda; stir to mix. Float lime slices on top of punch if desired. Serve immediately. **Yield:** 20-24 servings (1 gallon).

—— ☕ ☕ ☕ ——

Corned Beef and Mixed Vegetables

A colorful medley of vegetables adds a special twist to a traditional corned beef dinner. It's a festive combination to serve family or guests.

      1 corned beef brisket (3 to 4 pounds), trimmed
      6 to 8 small red potatoes
      3 medium carrots, cut into 2-inch pieces
      3 celery ribs, cut into 2-inch pieces
      2 tablespoons chopped celery leaves
      2 turnips, peeled and cut into wedges
      1 medium head cabbage, cut into 6 to 8 wedges
  1/2 pound fresh green beans
      3 to 4 ears fresh corn, halved

Place corned beef and enclosed seasoning packet in an 8-qt. Dutch oven. Cover with water and bring to a boil. Reduce heat; cover and simmer for 2 hours or until meat is tender. Add potatoes, carrots, celery, celery leaves and turnips; return to a boil. Reduce heat; cover and simmer for 20 minutes. Add cabbage, beans and corn; return to a boil. Reduce heat; cover and simmer 15-20 minutes or until vegetables are tender. **Yield:** 6-8 servings.

Irish Soda Bread

This recipe makes a beautiful high loaf of bread dotted with sweet raisins. Whenever I prepare this, it doesn't last long at our house.

      2 cups all-purpose flour
      2 tablespoons brown sugar
      1 teaspoon baking powder
  1/2 teaspoon baking soda
  1/4 teaspoon salt
      3 tablespoons cold butter *or* margarine
      2 eggs, *divided*
  3/4 cup buttermilk
  1/3 cup raisins

In a bowl, combine the flour, brown sugar, baking powder, baking soda and salt. Cut in butter until crumbly. Combine 1 egg and buttermilk; stir into the flour mixture just until moistened. Fold in raisins. Knead on a floured surface for 1 minute. Shape into a round loaf; place on a greased baking sheet. Cut a 1/4-in.-deep cross in top of loaf. Beat remaining egg; brush over loaf. Bake at 375° for 30-35 minutes or until golden brown. **Yield:** 6-8 servings.

—— ☕ ☕ ☕ ——

Shamrock Pie

Guests may wonder if the dessert has been touched by a leprechaun when they see the green layer in my lemon meringue pie.

      1 cup sugar
  1/4 cup cornstarch
  1-1/2 cups water
      3 egg yolks, lightly beaten
  1/4 cup lemon juice
      1 tablespoon butter *or* margarine
  1-1/2 teaspoons grated lemon peel
      5 to 6 drops green food coloring
      1 pastry shell (9 inches), baked
MERINGUE:
      3 egg whites
  1/3 cup sugar

Combine the sugar, cornstarch and water in a saucepan; stir until smooth. Bring to a boil, stirring constantly. Boil for 2 minutes or until thickened. Stir a small amount into egg yolks; return all to the pan. Cook and stir for 1 minute. Remove from heat; stir in lemon juice, butter, lemon peel and food coloring until smooth. Pour into crust. For meringue, beat egg whites until foamy. Gradually add sugar and beat until stiff peaks form. Spread over hot filling, sealing to the edges. Bake at 350° for 10-15 minutes or until lightly brown. Cool. **Yield:** 6-8 servings.

Spring into "Carrot Patch" Menu

By Grace Yaskovic, Branchville, New Jersey

Coming up with a novel idea for our monthly theme luncheon group in April had me stumped at first. We've been getting together for many years, and I didn't want to repeat anything that had been done before.

Then *carrots* came to mind! They're colorful, versatile and fit a spring mood without duplicating other Easter themes.

With carrots' reputation as "rabbit food", my table decorations were off to a hopping start. I collected all the bunnies I had and borrowed a few more. I was delighted to find carrot candles and carrot-shaped bags filled with orange jelly beans to use as favors. Set on

a pastel print tablecloth, my "carrot patch" looked fresh, fun and whimsical.

In our group, the hostess provides the main course and assigns recipes for other members to bring to the party. The meal I planned was well-"rooted"!

Crunchy carrot sticks with dip whet appetites for more to come. Next was Creamy Carrot Soup, a pretty puree with hints of rosemary and ginger.

Carrot Pilaf, featuring shredded carrots with rice, and Zesty Carrot Bake were perfect accompaniments to the herb-roasted chicken I prepared.

Also on our outstanding orange menu were a carrot quick bread and a marinated sliced carrot salad.

"Save room for dessert!" I cautioned, knowing carrot cookies and Moist Carrot Cake were waiting in the wings. Guests were surprised to learn this cake calls for a can of tomato soup!

Producing a theme around a popular garden "ingredient" turned out to be both tasty and a lot of fun.

— 🥄 🥄 🥄 —

Creamy Carrot Soup

People are amazed by this soup's bright color and are hooked by the deliciously different flavor.

- 1 cup chopped onion
- 1/4 cup butter *or* margarine
- 4-1/2 cups sliced carrots (1/4 inch thick)
- 1 large potato, peeled and cubed
- 2 cans (14-1/2 ounces *each*) chicken broth
- 1 teaspoon ground ginger
- 2 cups whipping cream
- 1 teaspoon dried rosemary, crushed
- 1/2 teaspoon salt
- 1/8 teaspoon pepper

In a 5-qt. Dutch oven, saute onion in butter until tender. Add carrots, potato, broth and ginger. Cover and cook over medium heat for 30 minutes or until vegetables are tender. Cool 15 minutes. Puree in small batches in a blender or food processor until smooth. Return all to saucepan; add remaining ingredients. Cook over low heat until heated through. **Yield:** 6-8 servings (2-1/2 quarts).

— 🥄 🥄 🥄 —

Carrot Pilaf

A few simple ingredients give ordinary rice a mouthwatering makeover.

✓ Uses less fat, sugar or salt. Includes Nutritional Analysis and Diabetic Exchanges.

- 1 cup shredded carrots
- 1/2 cup chopped onion
- 1 tablespoon butter *or* margarine
- 1 cup uncooked long grain rice
- 1 can (14-1/2 ounces) chicken broth
- 1 teaspoon lemon-pepper seasoning

In a saucepan, saute carrots and onion in butter until tender. Add rice and stir to coat. Stir in broth and lemon pepper; bring to a boil. Reduce heat; cover and simmer 20 minutes or until rice is tender. **Yield:** 6 servings. **Nutritional Analysis:** One serving (prepared with margarine and low-sodium broth) equals 137 calories, 36 mg sodium, 0 cholesterol, 28 gm carbohydrate, 3 gm protein, 1 gm fat. **Diabetic Exchanges:** 1-1/2 starch, 1 vegetable.

Zesty Carrot Bake

For a fun vegetable dish, try these tender carrots in a sauce that gets its zip from horseradish.

- 1 pound carrots, cut into 1/2-inch slices
- 3/4 cup mayonnaise
- 1/3 cup water
- 2 tablespoons minced onion
- 1 tablespoon prepared horseradish
- 1/4 teaspoon pepper
- 1/2 cup dry bread crumbs
- 2 tablespoons butter *or* margarine, melted
- 1/2 cup shredded sharp cheddar cheese

On stovetop or in a microwave oven, cook carrots until tender. Place in a 1-qt. baking dish; set aside. In a small bowl, combine the next five ingredients; mix well. Pour over carrots. Combine bread crumbs and butter; sprinkle on top. Bake, uncovered, at 350° for 25-30 minutes. Sprinkle with cheese. Bake 2-3 minutes more or until the cheese is melted. **Yield:** 6 servings.

— 🥄 🥄 🥄 —

Moist Carrot Cake

This flavorful cake with rich frosting always gets raves.

- 1/2 cup shortening
- 1 cup sugar
- 1 can (10-3/4 ounces) condensed tomato soup, undiluted
- 1 egg
- 2 cups all-purpose flour
- 1-1/2 teaspoons baking soda
- 1 teaspoon ground cinnamon
- Dash salt
- 1 cup shredded carrots
- 1/2 cup chopped walnuts
- 1/2 cup raisins *or* dried currants, optional
- FROSTING:
- 1 package (8 ounces) cream cheese, softened
- 3 cups confectioners' sugar
- 1 teaspoon vanilla extract
- 1 tablespoon milk
- Chopped walnuts, optional

In a large mixing bowl, cream shortening and sugar. Add soup and egg; mix well. Combine flour, baking soda, cinnamon and salt; beat into creamed mixture. Stir in the carrots, walnuts and raisins or currants if desired. Pour into a greased 10-in. fluted tube pan. Bake at 350° for 45-50 minutes or until cake tests done. Cool in pan 10 minutes before removing to a wire rack to cool completely. In another mixing bowl, combine the first four frosting ingredients; beat until smooth. Frost cake; top with walnuts if desired. **Yield:** 12-16 servings.

Brunch Helps Welcome Bundle of Joy

By Joyce Leach, Armstrong, Iowa

When a good friend of mine had her first baby at age 39, it was cause for celebration! So I planned a Saturday morning brunch shower for her and her darling little Megan.

I love to entertain, but a full-time job puts some limitations on my time. However, by "bottling up" some bright ideas, I was able to easily create a pretty-in-pink baby shower brunch.

Colorful, festive paper goods quickly got me started on a theme. I found adorable paper plates and matching napkins with a pastel baby theme. A simple centerpiece with balloons and pastel carnations gave a novel nursery look to the table.

Because we were celebrating the birth of a girl, I chose pink place mats and had some fun putting pink on the menu, too.

Fruity pink punch served in small glass baby bottles really got guests giggling! I found I could slip a sturdy plastic drinking straw in alongside the nipple. I also glued miniature baby bottles to pink nut cups filled with pastel candies and nuts.

For the main dish, I served Asparagus Ham Quiche. This easy "crustless" recipe mixes ham and Swiss cheese with frozen asparagus. The wonderful aroma of this inviting entree whetted my guests' appetites as they arrived at the door.

My salad, Cherry Fluff, contained a mix of fruit, coconut and nuts in a creamy dressing. By combining all the ingredients in one bowl and refrigerating overnight, it couldn't be easier to prepare.

Cookies Make Impression

Baby Shower Sugar Cookies, cut with footprint and handprint cutters, were simply sprinkled with pink and blue colored sugar. (Look for these clever cutouts at hardware stores or kitchen specialty shops.)

Two simple games kept the mood festive throughout the party. When guests arrived, I gave each one a diaper-sized safety pin. Anyone caught crossing her legs had to give her pin to the person who first spotted her doing so. Later, the person with the most pins won a prize.

Also, I'd asked everyone to bring a handful of pennies and a baby picture of herself. Anyone caught saying "baby" during the shower had to put a penny in a piggy bank I'd bought for Megan. Meantime, we had a lot of laughs guessing who was who as we passed around those baby pictures!

Even though Megan slept through much of the shower, she seemed to know all this hoopla was in her honor. And her mom couldn't thank me enough for the memorable morning.

I'm happy to share my baby shower theme, hoping fellow cooks can build on my ideas. (Of course, you can switch to blue if appropriate!)

Asparagus Ham Quiche

This fantastic brunch dish is easy to make, has such a nice blend of flavors and looks so inviting. With the eggs, asparagus, ham and Swiss cheese baking into one hearty pie, I can greet my guests without last-minute fussing in the kitchen. The recipe can be cut in half if entertaining a smaller crowd.

  2 packages (10 ounces *each*) frozen cut asparagus, thawed
  1 pound fully cooked ham, chopped
  2 cups (8 ounces) shredded Swiss cheese
1/2 cup chopped onion
  6 eggs
  2 cups milk
1-1/2 cups buttermilk baking mix
  2 tablespoons dried vegetable flakes
1/4 teaspoon pepper

In two greased 9-in. pie plates, layer the asparagus, ham, cheese and onion. In a bowl, beat eggs. Add remaining ingredients and mix well. Divide in half and pour over asparagus mixture in each pie plate. Bake at 375° for 30 minutes or until a knife inserted near the center comes out clean. **Yield:** 12 servings.

Cherry Fluff

Chunky tart cherries, coconut, pecans and pineapple give substance to this lightly sweet make-ahead salad. With its pastel color and fluffy look, it's perfect for a baby shower.

  1 carton (8 ounces) frozen whipped topping, thawed
  1 can (20 ounces) crushed pineapple, drained
  1 can (21 ounces) cherry pie filling
  1 can (14 ounces) sweetened condensed milk
1/2 cup flaked coconut
1/2 cup chopped pecans

Combine all ingredients in a large bowl; mix well. Chill overnight. **Yield:** 12-16 servings.

Baby Shower Sugar Cookies

To celebrate the pitter-patter of tiny feet (or any occasion), crisp buttery sugar cookies like these are a hit, hands down! They cut wonderfully into delicate shapes and look festive decorated with pink and blue sugar. (Or, if you have time, bake plain cookies. Let cool and decorate with pink and blue tinted frosting.)

  1 cup butter *or* margarine, softened
1-1/2 cups sugar
  1 egg
  1 teaspoon vanilla extract
1/2 teaspoon almond extract
2-1/2 cups all-purpose flour
  1 teaspoon baking soda
  1 teaspoon cream of tartar
Pink and blue colored sugar

In a mixing bowl, cream butter and sugar. Add egg and extracts; mix well. Combine flour, baking soda and cream of tartar; add to creamed mixture and mix well. Shape into a ball. Chill for 1-2 hours. On a lightly floured surface, roll out dough to 1/8-in. thickness; cut into small hands and feet or desired shapes. Place on greased baking sheets. Sprinkle with colored sugar. Bake at 375° for 6-8 minutes or until edges are light brown. Cool on wire racks. **Yield:** 5-6 dozen.

Pack a Punch

The next time you serve punch, fruit juices or lemonade at a party, make ice cubes from the drinks. This will prevent the beverages from becoming watered down.

Fishy Celebration Reels in Finny Fun

By Elizabeth LeBlanc , Bourg, Louisiana

At our home, a "lucky" birthday (also called a golden birthday)—when your age matches the date—is always a little more special.

How would we celebrate when our oldest son, Philip, became a teen on the 13th of the month? Knowing what an avid fisherman he is lured me to a theme.

After fishing all morning, husband Mark and Philip returned home to see the table decorated with a fishing hat complete with baits and a jar of gummy worms as the centerpiece. I'd even found a fishing-bait print tablecloth.

We enjoyed Saucy Fish Sandwiches made with frozen fillets. Plus, our refreshing Tropical Fish Punch was complete with "swimming" fish-shaped ice cubes.

I made them by freezing punch in the same plastic fish candy mold I used to make the Chocolate Fish Lol-lipops. These fun treats were a hit with kids of all ages!

After the lunch table was cleared, everyone had to guess how many gummy worms were in the container and how many baits were on the fishing hat, which I'd hidden from sight. The person with the closest guess won those items as a prize.

We also had a casting contest in the backyard, using a target in a wading pool. Then it was time for Philip to go on another sort of fishing trip. Clues directed him to 13 gifts wrapped in fish-motif paper, hidden throughout the house, yard and garage.

A "Fishy" Red Velvet Cake, topped with red candy fish and candles, was the party's finale.

Turning 13 proved to be fun for Philip and all of us. We hope you get "hooked" on the idea and plan a "reel" great party of your own!

Saucy Fish Sandwiches

The golden cornmeal breading coats the fillets nicely, and the sauce is tangy.

1 cup mayonnaise
1/3 cup ketchup
1 teaspoon dried parsley flakes
1 teaspoon dried minced onion
1/2 teaspoon Worcestershire sauce
1/4 to 1/2 teaspoon hot pepper sauce
1/8 teaspoon garlic powder
1/2 cup all-purpose flour
1/2 cup yellow cornmeal
1 teaspoon salt
1/8 teaspoon pepper
1/8 teaspoon cayenne pepper
1 egg
1/2 cup milk
6 panfish *or* cod fillets (about 1 pound)
Vegetable oil
6 hamburger buns, split
Lettuce leaves

In a small bowl, combine the first seven ingredients; cover and chill at least 1 hour. In a shallow bowl, combine the next five ingredients. Beat egg and milk. Cut fish to fit buns; dip fillets into egg mixture, then coat with flour mixture. In a large skillet, fry fish in a small amount of oil for 5-10 minutes or until it flakes easily with a fork and is golden brown on both sides. Serve on buns with lettuce and sauce. **Yield:** 6 servings.

—— 🐟 🐟 🐟 ——

Tropical Fish Punch

This versatile, tasty drink works well for any occasion.

1 envelope unsweetened tropical punch soft drink mix
2 quarts water
3/4 cup sugar
1 can (46 ounces) pineapple juice, chilled
1 liter ginger ale, chilled

In large pitcher, combine drink mix, water and sugar; stir until dissolved. Chill. Just before serving, pour into punch bowl; add pineapple juice and ginger ale. **Yield:** 18 servings (about 4-1/2 quarts).

—— 🐟 🐟 🐟 ——

Chocolate Fish Lollipops

A netful of compliments will come your way as soon as guests dive into these crispy, chocolaty lollipops.

6 ounces milk chocolate confectionary coating *or* dipping chocolate

3/4 cup crisp rice cereal, slightly crushed
Fish candy mold *or* candy mold of your choice
Lollipop sticks

Melt chocolate in a double boiler over simmering water; stir in cereal. Fill each cavity of fish candy mold three-fourths full. Press a lollipop stick into the chocolate; top with a small amount of chocolate. Place in the freezer until firm, about 15 minutes. Remove from mold. **Yield:** about 6 servings.

—— 🐟 🐟 🐟 ——

"Fishy" Red Velvet Cake

Based on an old-fashioned recipe, this "reel" unusual birthday cake will steal the show at your party.

1 cup butter *or* margarine, softened
1-1/2 cups sugar
2 eggs
1 teaspoon vanilla extract
1 teaspoon butter flavoring
1 bottle (1 ounce) red food coloring, optional
2-1/2 cups cake flour
2 tablespoons baking cocoa
1 teaspoon baking soda
1 cup buttermilk
1 teaspoon vinegar
FLUFFY FROSTING:
1-1/2 cups milk
1/2 cup all-purpose flour
1-1/2 cups butter *or* margarine, softened
1-1/2 cups sugar
1-1/2 teaspoons vanilla extract
1-1/2 teaspoons butter flavoring
Gummy fish and worms, optional

In a large mixing bowl, cream butter and sugar until fluffy. Add eggs, one at a time, beating well after each addition. Beat in vanilla, butter flavoring and food coloring if desired. Combine flour, cocoa and baking soda. Combine buttermilk and vinegar. Add flour mixture alternately with buttermilk mixture to creamed mixture. Pour into three greased and floured 9-in. round cake pans. Bake at 350° for 15-20 minutes or until toothpick inserted near the center comes out clean. Cool in pans 10 minutes before removing to a wire rack to cool completely. For frosting, whisk together milk and flour in a saucepan. Cook over medium heat, stirring constantly, for 5 minutes or until thick; cool. In a mixing bowl, cream butter. Gradually add sugar; beat well. Gradually add cooled milk mixture and beat for 4 minutes or until light and fluffy. Add vanilla and butter flavoring; mix well. Frost cooled cake. Decorate with gummy fish and worms if desired. **Yield:** 12-16 servings.

Southwest Fare Sets Fiesta Mood

By Dean Schrock, Jacksonville, Florida

A vacation to Arizona and Mexico sparked the idea to plan a "Southwest Fiesta" when I returned home. I was so impressed with the region's landscape, colors and flavors that I wanted to share my enthusiasm with friends.

I've often helped others plan gatherings, but it had been awhile since I'd hosted one myself. This theme was the perfect impetus.

On the buffet tables, I draped a serape and poncho I'd picked up on my trip. Their bold primary colors were so easy to work with. I found bright paper plates

and used different hues of paper napkins to wrap the utensils, which I "potted" in a clay planter.

I also fanned napkins on the table and wove some through a willow basket to hold crisp tortilla shells on the "taco table", where guests could fix their own.

The zippy Spiced Olives are best made a week in advance—they really reach perfection at 10 days.

Besides tacos, the zesty blend of chicken, jalapenos and cheese in the Southwest Roll-Ups also awakened guests' taste buds.

Beef and Pepper Medley is an original recipe devised when I bought a deli salad that needed a lot of help. I "doctored it up", and the flavor was so much improved that I jotted down what I'd added.

Of all the foods on my buffet, the biggest hit was Festive Corn Bread Salad. Locally grown sweet onions were perfect for this dish. Dessert was a plate of homemade cookies.

If you're due for a party and in the mood for easy, casual, colorful entertaining, maybe my recipes and decorating ideas will get you started!

Spiced Olives

Double or triple this zippy recipe…you won't regret it!

1 jar (7 ounces) stuffed olives
1/2 cup tomato juice
1 tablespoon olive *or* vegetable oil
1/2 to 1 teaspoon crushed red pepper flakes
2 garlic cloves, minced
1/2 teaspoon dried basil
1/2 teaspoon dried oregano

Drain the olives, discarding juice, and return to the jar. In a small bowl, combine remaining ingredients. Pour over olives; cover and refrigerate for 3-10 days, turning jar daily. Drain before serving. **Yield:** 1-1/2 cups.

Southwest Roll-Ups

Taste buds tingle when I serve these tempting tortillas. Cut in half, they're easy to eat by hand.

2 tablespoons salsa
1 to 2 jalapeno peppers, seeded
1 garlic clove
2 tablespoons chopped onion
1 can (16 ounces) refried beans
1/2 teaspoon ground cumin
1 tablespoon chopped fresh cilantro *or* parsley
1 cup cubed cooked chicken
1 cup (4 ounces) shredded cheddar cheese, *divided*
10 to 12 flour tortillas (6 inches)
Sour cream and additional salsa, optional

Place the first eight ingredients and 1/2 cup cheese in a food processor; blend until smooth. Spread evenly over tortillas. Roll up and place seam side down in a greased 13-in. x 9-in. x 2-in. baking dish. Cover and bake at 350° for 20 minutes or until heated through. Sprinkle with remaining cheese; let stand until cheese is melted. Serve with sour cream and salsa if desired. **Yield:** 10-12 servings.

Beef and Pepper Medley

For a meaty dish that packs as much visual punch as it does flavor, try this refreshing salad. Colorful peppers and onion add crunch, and the dressing is tangy.

2 tablespoons garlic powder
2 tablespoons cracked black pepper
1 eye of round beef roast (about 4 pounds)
2 large green peppers, julienned
2 large sweet red peppers, julienned
2 large sweet onions, cut into thin wedges
DRESSING:
2/3 cup olive *or* vegetable oil
1/2 cup cider *or* red wine vinegar
2 tablespoons Dijon mustard
2 garlic cloves, minced
1/2 teaspoon crushed red pepper flakes
1/2 teaspoon salt

Combine garlic powder and pepper; rub over all sides of roast. Place on a rack in a shallow roasting pan. Preheat oven to 500°. Place roast in oven and reduce heat to 350°. Bake for 1-1/2 to 2 hours or until meat reaches desired doneness. Chill for 30-40 minutes or until meat is cool enough to handle. Cut into 3-in. x 1/4-in. x 1/4-in. strips. Place in a large salad bowl; add peppers and onions. Combine dressing ingredients in a jar with tight-fitting lid; shake well. Pour over salad and toss to coat. Cover and refrigerate overnight. Serve cold. **Yield:** 10-12 servings.

Festive Corn Bread Salad

The unusual combination of ingredients in this lightly sweet, fresh-tasting salad brought the guests at my Southwestern theme party back for seconds.

5 cups cubed corn bread *or* 6 corn bread muffins
3 cups diced fresh tomatoes
1 cup diced sweet onion
1 cup diced green pepper
1 pound sliced bacon, cooked and crumbled
1/4 cup sweet pickle relish
1 cup mayonnaise
1/4 cup sweet pickle juice
Shredded Parmesan cheese

Place corn bread cubes in a large salad bowl (or crumble muffins into bowl). Combine tomatoes, onion, green pepper, bacon and relish; add to corn bread. Combine mayonnaise and pickle juice; mix well. Pour over vegetables. Sprinkle with Parmesan cheese. Chill until serving. **Yield:** 10-12 servings.

General Recipe Index

This handy index lists every recipe by food category and/or major ingredient, so you can easily locate recipes.

Low-Fat Lemon Cheesecake, 146
Shamrock Pie, 281

MARSHMALLOWS
Caramel Marshmallow Delights, 10
Chocolate Coconut Cake, 151
Cinnamon "Whippersnappers", 127
Crispy Coconut Balls, 9
Date Nut Log, 168
Easter Nests, 139
Marshmallow Puffs, 122
Three-Chocolate Fudge, 126

MEAT LOAVES & MEATBALLS
Best Meat Loaf, 91
Country Meat Loaf, 69
Favorite Meat Loaf, 77
Ham Loaves, 266
Individual Meat Loaves, 272
Mexi-Italian Spaghetti, 71
Mom's Best Meat Loaf, 220
Pizza Meat Loaf, 94
Porcupine Meatballs, 212
Smothered Meatballs, 95
Spaghetti and Meatballs, 74
Swedish Meatballs, 81

MEAT PIES & PIZZA
Cheese 'n' Sausage Calzones, 169
Farmhouse Pork and Apple Pie, 83
Homemade Pizza, 270
Matt's Mexican Pizza, 19
Party Pizzas, 20
Pheasant Potpie, 78
Southwest Appetizer Pizza, 17
Spaghetti Pie, 72

MICROWAVE RECIPES
Coconut Yule Trees, 129
Double Chocolate Brownies, 119
Fish Fillets with Stuffing, 76
Ginger-Orange Squash, 62
Macadamia Almond Brittle, 128
Marshmallow Puffs, 122
Matt's Mexican Pizza, 19
Microwave Clam Chowder, 41
Mocha Truffles, 129
Nacho Cheese Dip, 16
Perfect Peppermint Patties, 119
Turkey Stroganoff, 81

MUFFINS
Applesauce Muffins, 102
Blueberry Streusel Muffins, 231
Peanut Muffins, 107
Pecan Cranberry Muffins, 108
Spiced Applesauce Muffins, 110
Sweet Cornmeal Muffins, 192
Zucchini-Oatmeal Muffins, 98

MUSHROOMS
Broccoli-Mushroom Medley, 255

Grilled Mushrooms, 61
Mushroom Beef Skillet, 80
Mushroom-Chicken Stir-Fry, 86
Peas with Mushrooms, 261
Pickled Mushrooms, 164
Quail in Mushroom Gravy, 92
Salisbury Steak, 251
Savory Rye Snacks, 9
Turkey Stroganoff, 81
Unstuffing, 247

NUTS *(also see Peanut Butter)*
Almond Biscotti, 122
Almond Chicken Salad, 32
Apple Nut Crunch, 275
Apricot Walnut Bread, 101
Big Batch Cookies, 173
Cherry Almond Pie, 138
Chewy Granola Bars, 130
Chocolate Almond Cake, 144
Chocolate Almond Cheesecake, 239
Chocolate Thumbprints, 125
Cinnamon "Whippersnappers", 127
Coconut-Pecan Pie, 145
Cranberry-Almond Apple Pie, 159
Cranberry Nut Bread, 98
Crunchy Granola, 13
Date Nut Log, 168
Favorite Snack Mix, 10
Luscious Almond Cheesecake, 154
Macadamia Almond Brittle, 128
Nutty Tuna Sandwiches, 43
Peanut Muffins, 107
Peanut Squares, 144
Pecan Cranberry Muffins, 108
Pecan Delights, 117
Pecan Fudge Pie, 155
Pecan Meltaways, 121
Pecan Pie for a Crowd, 180
Pecan Tarts, 124
Pecan Waffles, 103
Pine Nut Pancakes, 109
Pistachio Ambrosia, 176
Prune-Pecan Cookies, 124
Scott's Peanut Cookies, 118
Strawberry-Pecan Pie, 157
Trail Mix, 14
Turtle Bars, 121
Turtle Cheesecake, 150
Valentine Coffee Cake, 111

OATS
Cherry Oatmeal Crisp, 159
Chewy Granola Bars, 130
Chocolaty Double Crunchers, 116
Cinnamon-Raisin Oatmeal, 189
Crisp Sunflower Cookies, 133
Crunchy Granola, 13
Herbed Oatmeal Pan Bread, 110
Multigrain Buns, 103

Pumpkin Pancakes, 106
Rolled Oat Cookies, 134
Scott's Peanut Cookies, 118
Zucchini-Oatmeal Muffins, 98

OLIVES
Beef and Olive Spread, 18
Cheesy Olive Snacks, 13
Spiced Olives, 289
Warm Olive Dip, 21

ONIONS
French Onion Soup, 45
Onion-Roasted Potatoes, 234

ORANGE
Ginger-Orange Squash, 62
Golden French Toast, 110
Orange Avocado Salad, 33
Orange Buttermilk Salad, 267
Orange Dream Cake, 209
Orange-Glazed Chicken, 184
Orange Taffy, 134
Strawberry-Orange Chicken Salad, 34
Sunshine Ice Cream Pie, 153
Upside-Down Orange Biscuits, 112

PASTA & NOODLES *(also see Spaghetti)*
Beef Noodle Soup, 48
Broccoli-Pasta Side Dish, 60
Budget Macaroni and Cheese, 268
Cajun Chicken Pasta, 71
Cheese-Stuffed Shells, 86
Four-Cheese Lasagna, 77
Hearty Macaroni Salad, 178
Light Tuna Noodle Casserole, 82
Meal in a Mug, 94
Ranch Mac 'n' Cheese, 94
Spinach Noodles, 63
Tarragon Chicken Casserole, 171
Tarragon Pasta Salad, 37
Vegetable Noodle Casserole, 64
Venison Pot Roast, 87

PEACHES
Peach Cream Pie, 139
Peach Crisp, 217
Spiced Peach Salad, 28
Spiced Peaches, 273

PEANUT BUTTER
Big Batch Cookies, 173
Chocolate Peanut Butter Cookies, 129
Coconut Snacks, 16
Easter Nests, 139
Homemade Candy Bars, 135
Honey-Peanut Butter Cookies, 126
Lunch Box Special, 50
Marshmallow Puffs, 122
Peanut Butter Bars, 176
Peanut Butter Chocolate Chip Cookies, 119

Issue-by-Issue Index

Do you have a favorite dish from a specific Taste of Home issue but can't recall the recipe's actual name? You'll easily find it in this categorized listing of recipes by issue.

DECEMBER/JANUARY

APPETIZERS & BEVERAGES
Appetizer Meatballs, 171
Cheese Crisps, 12
Cinnamon Candy Popcorn, 16
Crispy Coconut Balls, 9
Matt's Mexican Pizza, 19
Savory Rye Snacks, 9
Spicy Chicken Wings, 168
Sugar-Free Holiday Nog, 15
Trail Mix, 14

BREADS
Buttery Crescents, 279
Cardamom Holiday Bread, 102
Cranberry Canes, 107
Cranberry Nut Bread, 98
Golden French Toast, 110
Mincemeat Coffee Cake, 176
Monkey Bread, 107
Pecan Cranberry Muffins, 108
Pecan Waffles, 103
Soft Breadsticks, 264
Spiced Applesauce Muffins, 110

CAKES
Cranberry Sauce Cake, 227
Snowflake Cake, 279

CANDIES
Christmas Hard Candy, 135
Coconut Yule Trees, 129
Creamy Caramels, 132
Macadamia Almond Brittle, 128
Marshmallow Puffs, 122
Mocha Truffles, 129
Orange Taffy, 134
Peanut Butter Snowballs, 132
Pecan Delights, 117
Perfect Peppermint Patties, 119
Sugar-Free Chocolate Fudge, 116
Three-Chocolate Fudge, 126

CONDIMENTS
Favorite French Dressing, 221
Lazy-Day Cranberry Relish, 165

COOKIES & BARS
Apricot Bars, 118
Big Batch Cookies, 173
Deluxe Sugar Cookies, 120
Gingerbread Cutouts, 121
Pecan Meltaways, 121
Pecan Tarts, 124
Scott's Peanut Cookies, 118
Soft Sugar Cookies, 124
Turtle Bars, 121

DESSERTS
Banana Pudding Dessert, 251
Date Nut Log, 168
Ice Cream Sundae Dessert, 155

Swedish Creme, 221
Washington Cream Pie, 147
White Christmas Cake, 152

MAIN DISHES
Apricot Baked Ham, 226
Chicken Kiev, 279
Chicken Rice Casserole, 264
Easy Oven Stew, 79
Mexi-Italian Spaghetti, 71
Mom's Best Meat Loaf, 220
Orange-Glazed Chicken, 184
Quail in Mushroom Gravy, 92
Salisbury Steak, 251
Turkey Biscuit Stew, 76

PIES
Cranberry-Almond Apple Pie, 159
Cran-Raspberry Pie, 144
Pecan Fudge Pie, 155

SALADS
Cherry Cranberry Salad, 36
Lime Gelatin Salad, 175
Ruby Red Raspberry Salad, 227
Sour Cream Cucumbers, 32
Turkey Curry Salad, 25
Turkey Salad for 50, 177

SIDE DISHES
Cardamom Sweet Potatoes, 61
Creamed Peas and Potatoes, 220
Far North Wild Rice Casserole, 58
French Peas, 185
Herbed Rice, 184
Homemade Seasoned Rice Mix, 264
Potato Pie, 62
Quick Carrots, 251
Stuffed Baked Potatoes, 226

SOUPS & SANDWICHES
Basic Turkey Soup, 49
Creamy Vegetable Soup, 44
Dill Pickle Soup, 42
Potato-Leek Soup, 41
Toasted Turkey Sandwiches, 48

FEBRUARY/MARCH

APPETIZERS & BEVERAGES
Banana Brunch Punch, 230
Beef and Olive Spread, 18
Buttermilk Shakes, 12
Chocolate-Dipped Fruit, 14
Cozy Hot Chocolate, 191
Ham and Cheese Bread, 12
Leprechaun Lime Punch, 281

BREADS
Apricot Walnut Bread, 101
Biscuits for Two, 191
Blueberry Streusel Muffins, 231
Broccoli Corn Bread, 111

Cheddar-Dill Bread, 100
Cheesy Potato Bread, 106
Cream Cheese Coffee Cake, 231
Dutch Apple Bread, 100
Irish Soda Bread, 281
Lemon Blueberry Bread, 101
Lemon Bread, 101
Valentine Coffee Cake, 111

CAKES
Blackberry Cake, 154
Chocolate Chiffon Cake, 152
Pineapple Bundt Cake, 158

CONDIMENTS
Low-Fat Chocolate Sauce, 162
Southwestern Seasoning Mix, 165

COOKIES
Almond Biscotti, 122
Crisp Sunflower Cookies, 133
Honey-Peanut Butter Cookies, 126
Prune-Pecan Cookies, 124
Valentine Sugar Cookies, 127

DESSERTS
Cherry Bavarian Cream, 147
Cherry Cobbler, 138
Chocolate Date Squares, 158
Easter Nests, 139
Mini Cherry Cheesecakes, 139
Peach Crisp, 217
Peanut Butter Sundaes, 253

MAIN DISHES
Apricot Chicken Stir-Fry, 85
Barbecued Spareribs, 84
Cabbage with Meat Sauce, 89
Chicken and Barley Boiled Dinner, 85
Chicken Parmesan, 93
Cider Beef Stew, 84
Corned Beef and Mixed Vegetables, 281
Country Meat Loaf, 69
Farmhouse Pork and Apple Pie, 83
Favorite Meat Loaf, 77
Grecian Chicken and Potatoes, 82
Ham Loaves, 266
Ham Steak with Lemon, 190
Kielbasa Skillet Stew, 79
Meal in a Mug, 94
Mushroom Beef Skillet, 80
Old-World Stuffed Pork Chops, 89
Pheasant Potpie, 78
Pizza Meat Loaf, 94
Pork Chops Olé, 69
Pork Chow Mein, 73
Pork Tenderloin Diane, 95
Pork with Mustard Sauce, 76
Roast Pork with Apple Topping, 78
Scrambled Egg Casserole, 230
Spaghetti Pie, 72
Sweet-and-Sour Pork, 92

Nutritional Analysis Recipes Index

*Refer to this index when you're looking for a recipe that uses less fat,
sugar or salt and includes Nutritional Analysis and Diabetic Exchanges.
These good-for-you recipes are marked with a ✓ throughout the book.*

The Cook's Quick Reference

From the *Taste of Home* Test Kitchens

Substitutions & Equivalents

Cooking Terms

Guide to Cooking with Popular Herbs

Substitutions & Equivalents

Equivalent Measures

3 teaspoons	=	1 tablespoon	**16 tablespoons**	=	1 cup
4 tablespoons	=	1/4 cup	**2 cups**	=	1 pint
5-1/3 tablespoons	=	1/3 cup	**4 cups**	=	1 quart
8 tablespoons	=	1/2 cup	**4 quarts**	=	1 gallon

Food Equivalents

Grains

Macaroni	1 cup (3-1/2 ounces) uncooked	=	2-1/2 cups cooked
Noodles, Medium	3 cups (4 ounces) uncooked	=	4 cups cooked
Popcorn	1/3 to 1/2 cup unpopped	=	8 cups popped
Rice, Long Grain	1 cup uncooked	=	3 cups cooked
Rice, Quick-Cooking	1 cup uncooked	=	2 cups cooked
Spaghetti	8 ounces uncooked	=	4 cups cooked

Crumbs

Bread	1 slice	=	3/4 cup soft crumbs, 1/4 cup fine dry crumbs
Graham Crackers	7 squares	=	1/2 cup finely crushed
Buttery Round Crackers	12 crackers	=	1/2 cup finely crushed
Saltine Crackers	14 crackers	=	1/2 cup finely crushed

Fruits

Bananas	1 medium	=	1/3 cup mashed
Lemons	1 medium	=	3 tablespoons juice, 2 teaspoons grated peel
Limes	1 medium	=	2 tablespoons juice, 1-1/2 teaspoons grated peel
Oranges	1 medium	=	1/4 to 1/3 cup juice, 4 teaspoons grated peel

Vegetables

Cabbage	1 head	=	5 cups shredded	**Green Pepper**	1 large	=	1 cup chopped
Carrots	1 pound	=	3 cups shredded	**Mushrooms**	1/2 pound	=	3 cups sliced
Celery	1 rib	=	1/2 cup chopped	**Onions**	1 medium	=	1/2 cup chopped
Corn	1 ear fresh	=	2/3 cup kernels	**Potatoes**	3 medium	=	2 cups cubed

Nuts

Almonds	1 pound	=	3 cups chopped	**Pecan Halves**	1 pound	=	4-1/2 cups chopped
Ground Nuts	3-3/4 ounces	=	1 cup	**Walnuts**	1 pound	=	3-3/4 cups chopped

Easy Substitutions

When you need...		Use...
Baking Powder	1 teaspoon	1/2 teaspoon cream of tartar + 1/4 teaspoon baking soda
Buttermilk	1 cup	1 tablespoon lemon juice *or* vinegar + enough milk to measure 1 cup (let stand 5 minutes before using)
Cornstarch	1 tablespoon	2 tablespoons all-purpose flour
Honey	1 cup	1-1/4 cups sugar + 1/4 cup water
Half-and-Half Cream	1 cup	1 tablespoon melted butter + enough whole milk to measure 1 cup
Onion	1 small, chopped (1/3 cup)	1 teaspoon onion powder *or* 1 tablespoon dried minced onion
Tomato Juice	1 cup	1/2 cup tomato sauce + 1/2 cup water
Tomato Sauce	2 cups	3/4 cup tomato paste + 1 cup water
Unsweetened Chocolate	1 square (1 ounce)	3 tablespoons baking cocoa + 1 tablespoon shortening *or* oil
Whole Milk	1 cup	1/2 cup evaporated milk + 1/2 cup water

Cooking Terms

HERE'S a quick reference for some of the cooking terms used in *Taste of Home* recipes:

Baste—To moisten food with melted butter, pan drippings, marinades or other liquid to add more flavor and juiciness.

Beat—A rapid movement to combine ingredients using a fork, spoon, wire whisk or electric mixer.

Blend—To combine ingredients until *just* mixed.

Boil—To heat liquids until bubbles form that cannot be "stirred down". In the case of water, the temperature will reach 212°.

Bone—To remove all meat from the bone before cooking.

Cream—To beat ingredients together to a smooth consistency, usually in the case of butter and sugar for baking.

Dash—A small amount of seasoning, less than 1/8 teaspoon. If using a shaker, a dash would comprise a quick flip of the container.

Dredge—To coat foods with flour or other dry ingredients. Most often done with pot roasts and stew meat before browning.

Fold—To incorporate several ingredients by careful and gentle turning with a spatula. Used generally with beaten egg whites or whipped cream when mixing into the rest of the ingredients to keep the batter light.

Julienne—To cut foods into long thin strips much like matchsticks. Used most often for salads and stir-fry dishes.

Mince—To cut into very fine pieces. Used often for garlic or fresh herbs.

Parboil—To cook partially, usually used in the case of chicken, sausages and vegetables.

Partially set—Describes the consistency of gelatin after it has been chilled for a small amount of time. Mixture should resemble the consistency of egg whites.

Puree—To process foods to a smooth mixture. Can be prepared in an electric blender, food processor, food mill or sieve.

Saute—To fry quickly in a small amount of fat, stirring almost constantly. Most often done with onions, mushrooms and other chopped vegetables.

Score—To cut slits partway through the outer surface of foods. Often used with ham or flank steak.

Stir-Fry—To cook meats and/or vegetables with a constant stirring motion in a small amount of oil in a wok or skillet over high heat.

Guide to Cooking with Popular Herbs

HERB	APPETIZERS SALADS	BREADS/EGGS SAUCES/CHEESE	VEGETABLES PASTA	MEAT POULTRY	FISH SHELLFISH
BASIL	Green, Potato & Tomato Salads, Salad Dressings, Stewed Fruit	Breads, Fondue & Egg Dishes, Dips, Marinades, Sauces	Mushrooms, Tomatoes, Squash, Pasta, Bland Vegetables	Broiled, Roast Meat & Poultry Pies, Stews, Stuffing	Baked, Broiled & Poached Fish, Shellfish
BAY LEAF	Seafood Cocktail, Seafood Salad, Tomato Aspic, Stewed Fruit	Egg Dishes, Gravies, Marinades, Sauces	Dried Bean Dishes, Beets, Carrots, Onions, Potatoes, Rice, Squash	Corned Beef, Tongue Meat & Poultry Stews	Poached Fish, Shellfish, Fish Stews
CHIVES	Mixed Vegetable, Green, Potato & Tomato Salads, Salad Dressings	Egg & Cheese Dishes, Cream Cheese, Cottage Cheese, Gravies, Sauces	Hot Vegetables, Potatoes	Broiled Poultry, Poultry & Meat Pies, Stews, Casseroles	Baked Fish, Fish Casseroles, Fish Stews, Shellfish
DILL	Seafood Cocktail, Green, Potato & Tomato Salads, Salad Dressings	Breads, Egg & Cheese Dishes, Cream Cheese, Fish & Meat Sauces	Beans, Beets, Cabbage, Carrots, Cauliflower, Peas, Squash, Tomatoes	Beef, Veal Roasts, Lamb, Steaks, Chops, Stews, Roast & Creamed Poultry	Baked, Broiled, Poached & Stuffed Fish, Shellfish
GARLIC	All Salads, Salad Dressings	Fondue, Poultry Sauces, Fish & Meat Marinades	Beans, Eggplant, Potatoes, Rice, Tomatoes	Roast Meats, Meat & Poultry Pies, Hamburgers, Casseroles, Stews	Broiled Fish, Shellfish, Fish Stews, Casseroles
MARJORAM	Seafood Cocktail, Green, Poultry & Seafood Salads	Breads, Cheese Spreads, Egg & Cheese Dishes, Gravies, Sauces	Carrots, Eggplant, Peas, Onions, Potatoes, Dried Bean Dishes, Spinach	Roast Meats & Poultry, Meat & Poultry Pies, Stews & Casseroles	Baked, Broiled & Stuffed Fish, Shellfish
MUSTARD	Fresh Green Salads, Prepared Meat, Macaroni & Potato Salads, Salad Dressings	Biscuits, Egg & Cheese Dishes, Sauces	Baked Beans, Cabbage, Eggplant, Squash, Dried Beans, Mushrooms, Pasta	Chops, Steaks, Ham, Pork, Poultry, Cold Meats	Shellfish
OREGANO	Green, Poultry & Seafood Salads	Breads, Egg & Cheese Dishes, Meat, Poultry & Vegetable Sauces	Artichokes, Cabbage, Eggplant, Squash, Dried Beans, Mushrooms, Pasta	Broiled, Roast Meats, Meat & Poultry Pies, Stews, Casseroles	Baked, Broiled & Poached Fish, Shellfish
PARSLEY	Green, Potato, Seafood & Vegetable Salads	Biscuits, Breads, Egg & Cheese Dishes, Gravies, Sauces	Asparagus, Beets, Eggplant, Squash, Dried Beans, Mushrooms, Pasta	Meat Loaf, Meat & Poultry Pies, Stews & Casseroles, Stuffing	Fish Stews, Stuffed Fish
ROSEMARY	Fruit Cocktail, Fruit & Green Salads	Biscuits, Egg Dishes, Herb Butter, Cream Cheese, Marinades, Sauces	Beans, Broccoli, Peas, Cauliflower, Mushrooms, Baked Potatoes, Parsnips	Roast Meat, Poultry & Meat Pies, Stews & Casseroles, Stuffing	Stuffed Fish, Shellfish
SAGE		Breads, Fondue, Egg & Cheese Dishes, Spreads, Gravies, Sauces	Beans, Beets, Onions, Peas, Spinach, Squash, Tomatoes	Roast Meat, Poultry, Meat Loaf, Stews, Stuffing	Baked, Poached & Stuffed Fish
TARRAGON	Seafood Cocktail, Avocado Salads, Salad Dressings	Cheese Spreads, Marinades, Sauces, Egg Dishes	Asparagus, Beans, Beets, Carrots, Mushrooms, Peas, Squash, Spinach	Steaks, Poultry, Roast Meats, Casseroles & Stews	Baked, Broiled & Poached Fish, Shellfish
THYME	Seafood Cocktail, Green, Poultry, Seafood & Vegetable Salads	Biscuits, Breads, Egg & Cheese Dishes, Sauces, Spreads	Beets, Carrots, Mushrooms, Onions, Peas, Eggplant, Spinach, Potatoes	Roast Meat, Poultry & Meat Loaf, Meat & Poultry Pies, Stews & Casseroles	Baked, Broiled & Stuffed Fish, Shellfish, Fish Stews